Animation and Effects with Macromedia® Flash™ MX 2004

Jen deHaan

Animation and Effects with Macromedia® Flash™ MX 2004

Jen deHaan

Published in association with Peachpit Press, a division of Pearson Education.

Macromedia Press
1249 Eighth Street
Berkeley, CA 94710

510/524-2178 800/283-9444
510/524-2221 (fax)

Find us on the World Wide Web at:
www.peachpit.com www.macromedia.com

To report errors, please send a note to errata@peachpit.com

Macromedia Press Editor: Angela C. Kozlowski
Editor: Susan Hobbs
Technical Editor: Nathan Derksen
Production Coordinator: Becky Winter
Copy Editor: Nancy Sixsmith
Index: Joy Dean Lee
Interior Design: Maureen Forys, Happenstance Typo-O-Rama
Cover Design: Mimi Heft

ISBN 0-321-30344-X

9 8 7 6 5 4 3 2 1

Printed and bound in the United States of America

Dedication

This book is dedicated to Statler and Waldorf.

About the Author

For a few years, Jen deHaan has been in transit. In pursuit of the perfect toque, she has moved from Calgary to Vancouver to Toronto to Calgary, and will soon (as of late 2004) find a permanent home in San Francisco. The only thing she'll miss about this life is her Tim Hortons coffee. We doubt that she'll find that toque.

Along the way, Jen has met some interesting characters, faced memorable experiences, put in a lot of miles on a small rickety car, and written a stack of literature on Flash (if you can call it literature—it really isn't). Her first experience working for Macromedia Press (the publisher of this book) was writing the uber-tutorial called *Flash MX 2004 Training from the Source*, which taught her the meaning of long hours and hard work for a good reason/cause. Jen has also written books for Sybex and Wiley (on more than one occasion) and other books for assorted publishers. Some of her favorite writing experiences were for the Macromedia Developer Center (aka DevNet), and helping with a recent Flash documentation update.

Jen is a 'deseloper' (designer/developer), and is an enthusiastic Zack Morris fan. Jen thinks the Domo Kun is extremely cool, and plans to befriend the person who mails her one.

Acknowledgments

THERE WERE MANY people who directly or indirectly helped this poor author along the way. Not sure if anyone mentioned in this section will actually read this, but hey, it's worth a shot. First of all, Craig Goodman gets sincere thanks. Without your good word earlier this year, I definitely wouldn't be sitting here writing this book. I shudder to think what I'd be doing instead. I won't forget that, I'm definitely a fan, and you rock. Also, sincerest thanks go to Lucian Beebe and Kristin Kleiderer. I truly owe you all huge.

Thanks Angela Kozlowski of Peachpit and Susan Hobbs for their excellent and much appreciated direction, development, and editing. They both made the writing process smooth and enjoyable. Many thanks to Nathan Derksen (www.nathanderksen.com) for his technical edits—the book is much better because of his efforts and stepping through each exercise in detail. I also send thanks to Nancy Sixsmith for the copy edits, and Chris Gillespie of Happenstance Type-O-Rama for the sweet layout. Thank you to Carole for handling this book.

Thanks to the IMD team who had to put up with me the most—I learned a lot from you guys during "the process." Thanks to Julee, Shimi, Erick, Jody, Francis, Mary, Jay, Nivesh (engineer/component-boy), Tim, and Sheila. The editors Rosana, Linda, Lisa, Mary(s), Noreen, and Anne deserve huge thanks and kudos for their patience, help, and what (and how) they taught me. All of you are awesome.

And just when you thought I might finish this up, I haul out a few more names. Nate Weiss receives acknowledgment for being the finest piece of geek in my recollection and experience. Not only is he a geek, but also diverse with many talents. I don't want to just thank him; I want to *be* him. Not only that, but Nate is easy on the eyes (I'm not). George Fox—thanks for being so cool. Amy Wong—you're also cool and perhaps the fastest replier *ever*. Sarah—I don't know you, but thanks for putting up with the ever-changing mock bios that don't work with your include files. FlashMX2004.com moderators get daily thanks for their continuing efforts on the forums. Thanks a million, guys and girl.

Peter—thanks for not giving me a black eye while enduring the nagging. If anything's wrong with this book, it's entirely my fault. If I add any more names, I'd just be making them up.

TABLE OF CONTENTS

CHAPTER 4 DRAWING FRAME-BY-FRAME ANIMATION   117

CHAPTER 5 CHARACTER CREATION AND ANIMATION   155

CHAPTER 6 ACTIONSCRIPT FOR EFFECTS   201

INTRODUCTION

OVER THE YEARS, Macromedia Flash developed from a tool used to create lightweight animations for the Web to an authoring environment that is used to create animation, effects, applications, widgets, CD-ROMs, to display video, and more. But although the programmatic side of Flash has received a lot of attention in the past few years (particularly in books and online), the design and animation side has almost been forgotten about in certain places. It's easy to find books and articles about building sites with components, using code, or learning ActionScript. However, a recent (and decent) *step-by-step tutorial* on using tweens or creating a character is difficult to find. And that's why you have this book in your hands.

Using Flash to present content for the web is a wise choice. If you look at how many computers can display Flash in a browser (www.macromedia.com/software/player_census/), you'll notice that you have an excellent chance that all your visitors will be able to see your animations and effects. In fact, Flash is more likely to display your content in all the different browser and OS combinations than other tools used to display effects or animation (such as DHTML or JavaScript). This is significant when you create a website for the masses, and it's why you should consider Flash for menus, galleries, applications, effects and more (which you'll start learning how to do in Chapter 1).

This book shows you how to build animation and effects over the course of 10 hands-on projects, written in a tutorial format. All you need to do is follow the steps—you won't find any guesswork involved or incomplete examples; only room for your own creativity.

Who Is This Book For?

This book is for those of you who want to start designing and animating with Flash. You might be an experienced artist, animator, or graphic designer who is new to Flash. This book lets you take your artistic and creating skills, and then apply them to the Flash authoring tool. You will find these projects open-ended enough that you can use your own ideas and creativity to either modify them during the project or after it's complete.

You don't need to be artistic to take advantage of this book. You might be experienced with Flash, but only with Flash development instead of design. For you, the drawing tools have been used for placeholder graphics, but not much else. You might be familiar with building a class file, but not as familiar with using the Tween class or putting together a design-centric effect with code. Although this book doesn't cover building applications or effects with hundreds or thousands of lines of Action-Script, you will learn how to put together a design and make effects using code. And more importantly, you, the Flash developer, will also be able to draw and animate your own character by the end of this book. And you'll be comfortable using those elusive *motion tweens on the Timeline,* no less.

Maybe you don't have art experience, you don't write code, and you haven't used Flash before. That's OK, too, because you'll quickly discover that you can follow along with the tutorials without that prior experience. This book doesn't assume that you have knowledge of either art or Flash, so you will also feel comfortable following along.

Outline

This book shows you how to animate and create effects, using techniques that range from motion tweens to ActionScript. The book includes 10 different projects, which you complete using hands-on tutorials. You build the projects step-by-step from start to finish (these projects range from little or no ActionScript, to a moderate amount of code). Although it's almost impossible to build many effects with at least some amount of code, the ActionScript you use in this book is fully explained for those who are new to the language.

The following list outlines the topics covered in each project-based chapter.

- **Chapter 1:** Read a simple introduction to publishing your first FLA file (which includes animation and a bit of interactivity).

- **Chapter 2:** Create a panning animation with motion tweens and a motion guide.

- **Chapter 3:** Create a simple interface and animation by using primarily shape tweens.

- **Chapter 4:** Learn how to use frame-by-frame animation to make a pirate dance.

- **Chapter 5:** Create a character using Flash (a robot) and then animate it.

- **Chapter 6:** Learn the fundamentals of ActionScript when you build a simple draggable shape game.

- **Chapter 7:** Learn about scripted animation when you create a text effect and movie clip animation.

- **Chapter 8:** Build a website using motion tweens, ActionScript, and animated masks. You cover working with video, transitions, and movie clip buttons in the process.

- **Chapter 9:** Build an animated menu system using graphics, ActionScript, and the Tween class.

- **Chapter 10:** Build a gallery that dynamically displays a series of JPEG images that load from your server. Images tween when they load into the container SWF file, and they react and respond to mouse rollovers.

Companion Website and CD-ROM

You can find the companion website at www.FLAnimation.com. This website includes the published and finished examples from each chapter, updates, tips, answers to frequently asked questions, and errata/corrections. Additionally, you can find extra examples, tutorials, news, and links to useful articles.

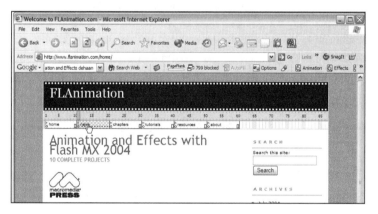

The companion website contains examples, updates, and related information. FLAnimators FLAnimate!

Check the website frequently while you complete your projects for any hints and tips that might make your workflow easier.

This book also includes a CD-ROM with all the completed example files, starter files, and media files that you need to finish projects. Each chapter has its own chapter, organized by number (01, 02, 03 and so on). Inside each chapter folder is a start and complete folder that contains the associated files for a project. The beginning of each chapter includes a list of these required files and where you can find them on the CD-ROM.

You don't need to use all the files on the CD-ROM, but it can be useful to see how the project turns out before you get started. You might want to look at the organization of the FLA file or publish the SWF to check out the finished result. Use the FLA files to copy and paste ActionScript from, if you prefer to do so. Try to type out some of the code from this book instead of pasting it all. Typing ActionScript helps you learn how to use the language.

Standard Elements In the Book

This book uses several conventions in its layout and the way information is organized. You should be familiar with these elements before you start with the tutorials.

New terms are written in *italics*, and defined immediately afterward.

Items that you need to type into Flash (such as instance names or properties) are in **boldface** font. For example, if you change the size of the Stage, you see the dimensions in bold.

Code snippets are written in monospace font. If you see any **bold monospace** font within a code snippet, it means you need to modify the bold section. The rest of the snippet is ActionScript from an earlier step that you do not need to add or modify. Modify or add the bold code, and the rest of the code snippet remains the same.

The following layout style is used throughout this book.

◆ **Note:** Additional related information you should remember for the current or future projects.

◆ **Tip:** Interesting related information that will help your Flash workflow.

◆ **Caution:** Cautions you about potential problems with the software or a particular procedure, or things you might want to avoid doing with Flash.

◆ **Cross References:** Points you to other parts of the book or web site where you can find related information.

◆ **Sidebars:** Interesting tips and information that does not fit within an exercise, but will benefit other projects you work on. For example, a project might use custom buttons to scroll text. A sidebar within that project might detail how to use the ScrollBar component.

Minimum System Requirements

For this book, you can use Macromedia Flash MX 2004, Regular or Professional version. You can even use an earlier version of Flash for many of the projects in this book.

System requirements for Flash MX 2004 are as follows:

Windows
600 MHz Intel Pentium III processor or equivalent
Windows 98 SE (4.10.2222 A), Windows 2000, or Windows XP
128 MB RAM (256 MB recommended)
347 MB available disk space

Macintosh
500 MHz PowerPC G3 processor
Mac OS X 10.2.8 and later, 10.3.4
128 MB RAM (256 MB recommended)
280 MB available disk space

The Flash 7.2 updater

The Flash MX 2004 7.2 updater was released in mid-2004. This important updater release resolves many of the performance issues and bugs that existed in the initial Flash release (September 2003). It's strongly recommended that you download and install this updater. Not only will you notice many improvements in the software, you will be able to work with Flash much more efficiently. The program is much more stable and less prone to crashing. Additionally, the updater addresses and fixes many bugs in ActionScript, components, the authoring environment (performance), and documentation. Although you don't need the updater specifically for this book, it will certainly affect your work with Flash outside of these tutorials.

Installing the Flash MX 2004 7.2 Updater **is strongly recommended**. Download it for free at www.macromedia.com/software/flash/special/7_2updater.

Read the release notes here: http://www.macromedia.com/support/documentation/en/flash/mx2004/releasenotes.html.

FIGURE 1.A

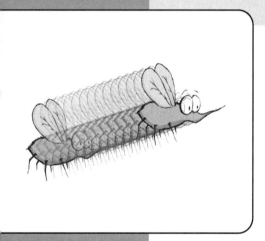

FIGURE 1.B

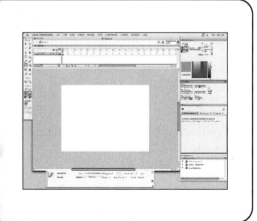

FIGURE 1.C

What you learn

► Related software for animation

► How to navigate the Flash workspace

► How to create and save a file

► How to animate an object

► How to test and publish a file

Lesson Files

Start:

01/start/first.fla

01/start/skeeter.png

Finish:

01/complete/first.fla

01/complete/first.swf

01/complete/first.html

1

Introducing Flash

Macromedia Flash MX 2004 and Macromedia Flash MX Professional 2004 are tools you can use to create engaging and interactive multimedia presentations, websites, or CD-ROMs. Flash excels at vector drawings and animations, but the software can be used for manipulating or displaying bitmap graphics, editing video, and even manipulating sound files.

You can use Flash for different kinds of presentations, from e-commerce applications to streaming video, games, and cartoons. You might create data-rich software applications in Flash or simple animated banners. Flash content is versatile, and it can be accessed on many platforms as well. You can view Flash on Windows, Macintosh, Linux, mobile devices, and phones; and you benefit from a relatively consistent presentation on all platforms. You also benefit because you do not necessarily have to completely redo your content for each platform.

This chapter introduces you to the Flash workspace and the architecture of Flash documents, giving focus to the features you use for creating animation and effects. A short project leads you through the general workflow from start to finish. You will create a new document, add a short animation that you control by using a button, test the document in Flash, and publish the file for the web.

▶ ▶ **FLASH MX VERSUS FLASH MX PROFESSIONAL**

There are two different "editions" of Flash MX: a regular version, and a professional version. Flash MX Professional includes all the features and capabilities of Flash MX, and has additional features built into it. Flash MX Professional includes a new screens-based authoring environment, which helps application developers avoid the Timeline. The professional edition also includes additional components, a Project panel for working in teams, a script editor, and additional ways to integrate data.

For a full comparison, see www.macromedia.com/software/flash/ productinfo/features/comparison/

You do not require Flash MX Professional to complete this book—you can use either edition of Flash MX. In fact, you can use the previous version of Flash MX (released in 2002) for 8 out of the 10 projects. The chapters discuss many of the features new to Flash MX 2004, however it's rare that the latest software is required to make the projects run. This is primarily due to many of the new features involving code and development as opposed to drawing and animation.

INTRODUCING FLASH

To learn the difference between Flash MX 2004 and Flash MX Professional 2004, refer to the Introduction. You can use either edition for the projects in this book.

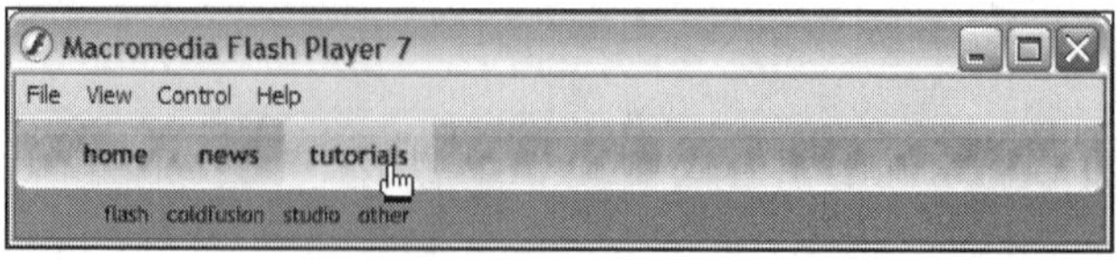

Flash MX 2004 and Flash MX Professional 2004 are different editions of the same program: Flash MX. You can use Flash to create animations, effects, vector graphics, interactive applications, software, presentations, and websites. All the content is built into the Flash authoring environment and saved as its native file format: FLA. You edit the FLA file, which contains all the assets (such as pictures, videos, and sound), and code. Flash *publishes* SWF files, which are small efficient files that display consistently on a variety of platforms using Flash Player (Figure 1.1). A SWF file is a compiled version of the FLA.

FIGURE 1.1

A Flash SWF file playing in the standalone version of Flash Player.

Flash is a well-established medium for presenting multimedia content, such as interactive animations, sound files, effects, and video that combine a variety of elements. You can import text, graphics, video, vector files (including Illustrator and FreeHand documents), PDFs, and audio files (such as WAV and MP3) into an FLA document. You can dynamically load content into a SWF file when it plays online, such as MP3, Flash video, and JPEG files. Flash Player lets you connect to sources of data, too, so you can integrate with a database, XML, or web services. With all these capabilities, you can add rich animation and effects to data-driven applications.

For information on importing file formats into Flash, see the sidebar in the section "Understanding the Flash Architecture" later in this chapter.

Why use Flash for animation and effects?

One advantage of using Flash is the wide audience of people who can see your content. Flash Player is included with most desktop computers when they are purchased. The player is widely available in part because of its small size: It is fast to download and install, which encourages users to download and update Flash Player.

> ▶ ▶ **FLASH PLAYER**

Flash Player is software that you use to play SWF files that Flash generates. Flash Player is a typical "viewer" application like Windows Media Player or Quicktime. SWF files can play in a browser window by using a Flash Player browser plug-in, or in a standalone version of the player.

Flash Player ensures that the Flash content you create can be viewed as consistently as possible, regardless of the platform it plays on. Make sure that you are working with the latest version. Go to http://www. macromedia.com/software/flashplayer/ and click Get Flash Player to check and download the latest player.

Flash MX 2004 has had two updater "patches" since it was initially released to the publish. You should also ensure that you are running the Flash 7.2 updater for the Flash authoring environment, so you're using both the latest version of Flash and the test environment Flash Player version. Visit www.macromedia.com/software/flash/special/7_2updater/ to download the 7.2 updater. To see Flash Player in action, visit www.FLAnimation.com.

Flash for web animation

Flash is a good choice over other forms of web animation for a variety of reasons. Other forms of web animation, such as Dynamic HTML (DHTML), Scalable Vector Graphics (SVG), JavaScript, and animated GIF files are limited when compared to Flash for several reasons.

◆ Some of these formats result in larger file sizes for animations, menus, or interactive content. Flash Player delivers some of the smallest possible file sizes for animation and effects.

◆ When you use non-Flash formats to display effects, you have a smaller audience who can view your work because it's more likely their computers do not have the proper requirements to view the format you're using. For example, some users turn off JavaScript or do not have DHTML-compatible browsers. This is particularly true in large establishments and corporations.

◆ Some of these formats are inconsistently displayed across browsers. For example, it's often difficult and costly to make an animated DHTML or JavaScript menu behave the same way in each browser. You would probably end up creating different versions of the same menu for different browsers. You can avoid these cross-browser problems by using Flash to create animated menus.

◆ Some of these formats have much larger plug-ins. SVG has a sizable browser plug-in that users might have to download and install before they can see your content.

There are at least one-half dozen common web browsers that people use, each of them supporting different features and working in slightly different ways. If you use Flash, you can ensure that your animation works the same way on almost every machine. Flash is more powerful than using DHTML and Cascading Style Sheets (CSS) because it supports dynamic loading of JPEG images, text, XML, streaming video, and other SWF files.

Flash for video

Flash is a superior player for presenting video content. More users can see your content because Flash Player has greater penetration than other media players such as QuickTime and Windows Media Player. Although the compression settings are more limited at the time of writing, often the difference in video quality is usually negligible. You can also avoid creating multiple versions of the video for different players.

Flash uses the ActionScript language to create interactivity for animation as well as for other purposes such as creating web applications, software, and CD-ROM presentations. This scripting language, which is based on ECMAScript standards, is a powerful object-oriented language. There are two versions of ActionScript–ActionScript 1.0 and 2.0, although you can use either version in your documents. You will use ActionScript throughout projects starting in Chapter 6, where you'll learn the differences between the two versions. Despite having the capability to add scripts to your work, you do not need to use ActionScript to create animations or effects. However, you can use more creativity and have many more capabilities when you use some ActionScript in your Flash files. In many cases, such as when you create animated menus, it is impossible to avoid using scripts completely. You learn how to add ActionScript in later projects, and if you haven't used code before, you might be surprised at how easy it is to learn.

Conceptualizing Animation, Effects, and their Tools

Animation is the art of creating a series of differing images that creates the appearance of movement when played in rapid succession over time. In Flash, these images are placed on frames, which play at a rate that you specify. Faster frame rates create animation and effects that appear smoother to the eye. Slower frame rates (lower numbers) create jerkier animation. The kind of animation or effect you create determines how fast you need your frame rate to be.

Many people consider drawing and cartooning (such as character animation, lip syncing, and manipulating drawn objects) to be *animation*. Effects are very similar to animations, and some people might even consider them to be the same thing. *Effects*, in the context of this book, include ways of manipulating color, changing brightness, fading objects, and integrating video in Flash. You might consider these to be *visual effects*. These kinds of effects often involve the same techniques as animation, although they typically produce very different visual results in your SWF files.

There are many different tools that you can use with Flash to create animation and effects. It is easier to produce amazing effects and animation when you combine the power of several different software packages and use a variety of techniques to integrate the technology. For example, you can use Swift 3D (Electric Rain) to create 3D effects and then import the files into Flash to display. Or, you could composite video effects using Adobe After Effects and import a rendered video file into your FLA document where you could add Flash animation to complement the video. Although using external software like Swift and After Effects goes beyond the scope of this book, you will learn how to use Flash to create animation you could combine with other technologies such as these.

Finding software for effects and animation

There is a lot of software available for you to use in conjunction with Flash to create animation and effects. Although you do not have to use anything more than the Flash authoring tool for your effects and animations in the following projects, you might be interested in investigating some of the other tools that you can use to further the capabilities of your SWF files, and enhance your creativity.

Toon Boom Studio: Used for creating amazing 2D animation, Toon Boom is an excellent choice for drawing and creating graphics for Flash. You can even create simple animations using the powerful drawing tools, and then import native files from Toon Boom into Flash using an extension or output directly to a SWF file. Toon Boom also includes lip-sync and 3D camera tools.

Swift 3D: You can use Electric Rain's Swift 3D to create 3D animations quickly and efficiently. You can export directly to a SWF file or import the native file format into Flash by using an extension. You can import raster images, model realistic 3D objects, and animate those objects using this software.

Adobe Photoshop and Macromedia Fireworks: One of the leading graphics and photo-editing software packages, Photoshop provides a vast amount of control over your photos, creates bitmap graphics, and combines images and effects to achieve original and creative results. The native file format, PSD, can import directly into Flash. Macromedia Fireworks is an inexpensive web graphics program that integrates seamlessly with Flash MX 2004, enabling you to switch between the two programs quickly and effortlessly. You can maintain editable objects in Flash when you import a Fireworks PNG file. PNG is perhaps the best image file format to import into Flash. Other popular choices for image creation and editing include Corel Painter and PaintShop Pro.

Adobe After Effects: Adobe After Effects (and other video editing and compositing packages) lets you edit videos and add effects and produce professional-looking content. You can also create text effects and modify content by using a timeline and keyframes, much like Flash. After Effects can output to a SWF file; if you have Flash MX Professional, you can output FLV (Flash Video) files.

Adobe Illustrator: Illustrator is an industry leading vector-graphics program. Illustrator is used to create static vector drawings, from technical illustrations and diagrams to cartoons and greeting cards. Many Flash designers use Illustrator to create vector illustrations that they import into Flash to animate. Flash has a range of import settings for Illustrator's AI files.

Inputting your art

If you are cartooning or animating drawings, you might need to get your drawings from paper into digital format. Many artists and animators use a scanner to input drawings into the computer. They might scan the image into a program such as Photoshop. Then the artist traces the scanned image in Photoshop, Flash, or another image-editing program, typically by using a graphics tablet. Then the artist uses Flash to manipulate and animate the illustrations, as you'll do in this book.

Other artists might draw directly into Flash or image-editing software using a graphics tablet. A *tablet* is an input device that lets you draw directly into the computer and uses a pen as the input device. The pen acts as the mouse pointer. Tablets have varying amounts of pressure sensitivity. If you press down harder on the tablet, the marks you make in Photoshop or Flash appear darker or wider, just as if you were drawing with a pencil. The software that you use must

FLA files are the native file format in Flash because you can edit only FLA files using Flash. SWF files (that you export from Flash) are open format. Therefore, other programs can import and export SWF files, and the files can play in different players.

support pressure sensitivity. For example, Flash supports pressure sensitivity when you use Wacom tablets.

Tablets greatly range in price, depending on quality, size, and features. Many tablets are relatively inexpensive. If you purchase a tablet to draw in Flash, make sure that you purchase one that is compatible with the software. Flash is compatible with Wacom tablets, but if you choose a different brand, you should do research on the compatibility or make sure you can return the product if it doesn't work with Flash.

Some artists feel more comfortable with a pen, or pencil and paper, than a tablet. However, tablets work very well and can create drawings that look incredibly similar to pencil drawings and even paintings. Either way works very well, so it is up to you which method works the best for you personally.

Using and mimicking video

Video is commonly used for effects and content in Flash, particularly with the improved editing support available in Flash and effective compression offered by the FLV (Flash Video) format. The benefit of using Flash to present video footage is that you can integrate animation and effects with video, which is not as easy or even possible in other media players. This can be done quickly and easily in Flash, and allows you to use video footage in projects that wouldn't otherwise support using it, such as SWF banners on a website.

If you don't use video, you can use a series of bitmap images to mimic video content. You might use Photoshop or Fireworks to create a series of images that you import into Flash and add sequentially across frames on the Timeline. You can also use a video editor to output a series of images instead of a video file. This effect is sometimes used for Flash content because transparent video is not yet supported in Flash.

You can edit transparent video in another program (such as Final Cut Pro), and then output to an image format that supports transparency (such as PNG). Then you can import the series of PNG files into Flash for further editing, and you can use what appears like transparent video in Flash.

> ► ► **TRANSPARENT VIDEO**

Transparent video allows you to create a video with transparent regions; for example, a transparent background. A person who edits video might remove the background using blue screen technology (software can be used can easily remove a very color—such as bright blue—from footage), and then overlay the remaining video over different footage, an image, or a Flash animation! When you see a SWF file with video of a person appearing to stand in front of a Flash animation, it's possible that blue screen was used to remove the former background and replace it with the same color as the SWF file's background. However, transparent video was not used for this effect.

An everyday example of blue screening is used in the nightly news when a weather person appears to stand in front of a giant map of your region. He or she typically stands in front of a blue (or green) screen, and the video of the region or weather patterns is added for the television broadcast. This kind of technique is also commonly used for special effects in movies, such as when they use large amounts of computer animation.

Using color and palettes

When you design a website, color is an important consideration for several reasons. A wise combination of colors looks attractive and affects the look and feel of your site. You can use colors to communicate messages to your visitors, enhance quality, and generate interest in your content. However, you need to be careful about which colors you use when you target specific audiences.

Flash contains palettes and swatches that you use to select colors (Figure 1.2). You can use predefined palettes that you select in Flash, or you can create your own and import palettes from other files and programs. You can apply these colors to your drawings or to the background of the SWF file.

FIGURE 1.2

When you click a Color control in the Tools panel, a color pop-up menu opens where you can select a swatch.

You can also specify colors by their hexadecimal, Red Green Blue (RGB) or Hue Saturation Brightness (HSB) values. These color modes represent colors in different ways, and you can switch between them in Flash. RGB uses three numerical values to define a color, and HSB uses a value for the degree of rotation on the color wheel, and uses percentages for saturation and brightness of the color. Hexadecimal color mode uses a base-16 system of representation. It's a combination of six numbers and letters that define the color, which you are probably familiar with if you've ever defined color in an HTML file or set color values in ActionScript. These six numbers and letters (made up of 0-9 and A-F) use sets of two characters for each color channel: red, blue and green. It organizes the sets as RRGGBB, where RR specifies the red value, GG specifies the green value, and BB specifies blue. You can view the RGB color mode equivalents to a specified hexadecimal in the Color Mixer panel (Window > Design Panels > Color Mixer).

This book primarily uses hexadecimal values for defining colors.

You can select colors by clicking them anywhere in Flash or on the desktop with what's called the Eyedropper tool.

USING THE FLASH INTERFACE

The Flash workspace is typically called the *authoring environment*. The authoring environment is made of many panels that surround a Stage (see the following figure) that you use to input information, control, and edit content. The Stage is where you place, load, or add content that your visitors see when you export your Flash files and put them online.

Flash files are based on one or more timelines, which is where most of the assets you use (such as graphics and text) are organized. A timeline is a sequence of frames, much like a roll of film has frames and can display images in sequence. A playhead moves along a Timeline while a file plays in Flash Player, and when the playhead reaches a frame, it is displayed and any code on that frame executes.

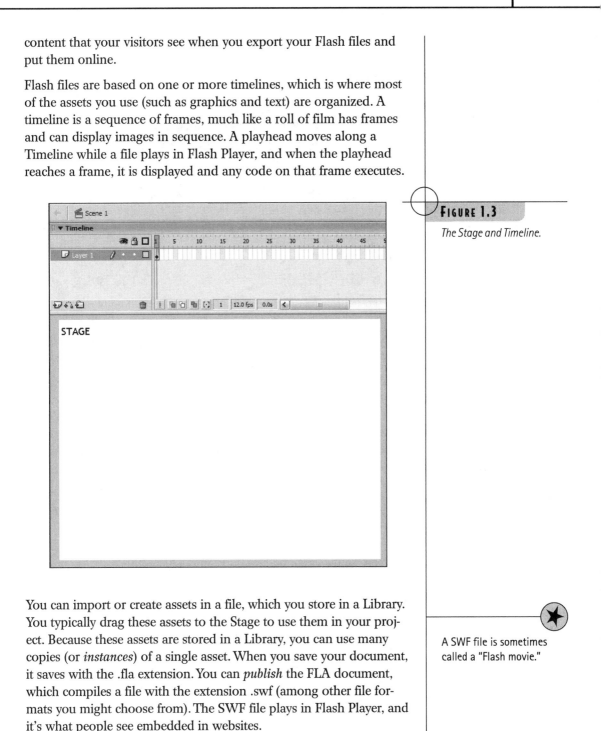

FIGURE 1.3

The Stage and Timeline.

You can import or create assets in a file, which you store in a Library. You typically drag these assets to the Stage to use them in your project. Because these assets are stored in a Library, you can use many copies (or *instances*) of a single asset. When you save your document, it saves with the .fla extension. You can *publish* the FLA document, which compiles a file with the extension .swf (among other file formats you might choose from). The SWF file plays in Flash Player, and it's what people see embedded in websites.

A SWF file is sometimes called a "Flash movie."

The authoring environment contains several different parts that help you control the authoring process, and create amazing effects. Take a look at them now.

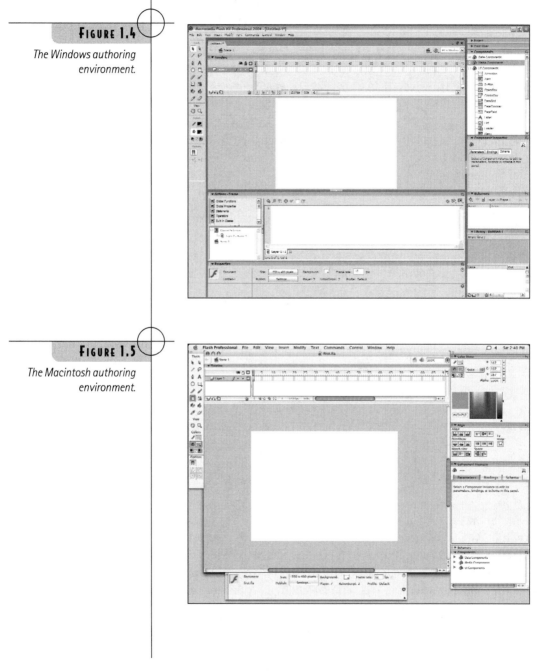

Timeline: SWF files play on a Timeline that contains one or more frames organized in a numbered row. Frames can be empty, contain visual content or code, and initiate changes in the file (called *keyframes*). The Timeline is made of one or more layers that stack vertically, which allows you to layer your graphics over top of each other. Each layer contains a row of frames that contain the content mentioned previously. When you create your animations, a playhead moves across this Timeline, and plays each frame as the playhead reaches it.

Stage: The Stage is below the Timeline. The Stage area is the visible region of the SWF file; it's where you put your animations, buttons, graphics and interactive assets. Your animations, graphics, and effects are visible on the Stage.

Menus: The menus in Flash are much like those in any other program. You can control file functions, run commands, test SWF files, and more. Also look for menus in panels by clicking the button at the upper-right side of the panel. Sometimes you will find many options hidden in these menus as well.

Panels: Panels contain buttons, text fields, menus, and other controls that help you create and edit parts of your file. For example, the Tools panel contains drawing tools. Panels also contain information about your file and things that you select in your file. You can open and close panels by using the Window menu.

Property inspector: The Property inspector is a context-sensitive panel used to display information about whatever you have currently selected. If you do not select an item, you can edit the properties and settings for the overall SWF file. For example, you could edit the dimensions of the Stage or the frame rate of the SWF file.

Document tabs and the Edit Bar: Document tabs and the Edit Bar are next to the Timeline. The Edit Bar helps you navigate through parts of a document, and select elements to work with. Document tabs (Windows only) allow you to select different files to work on.

You can control how fast this playhead moves along the Timeline (the frame rate), which you control in the Property inspector. You set the value for the "fps" which means "frames per second".

Document tabs are available only in Windows. The Edit Bar can be placed above or below the Timeline. To change the location of the Edit Bar, press Shift+Alt and double-click the bar (Command+Shift and double-click on the Mac).

Using panels

Panels are vital for editing your documents and making particular settings. You can open and close panels from the Window menu, and most panels are found in the Design panels, Development panels, and Other panels submenus. When Flash opens, there is a selection of panels open by default. You can save your own custom layout by opening and arranging panels and then selecting Window > Save Panel Layout. Type in a name for your custom layout and click OK. Then you can open your custom panel layout by selecting Window > Panel Sets > *your panel set name*.

Panels are easy to use, and most of them work the same way. You can maximize and minimize panels when you click the title bar. You can click the button on the right side of the title bar to open the Options menu for that panel, which might contain a few (or many) commands that you can select from, as shown in the following figure.

FIGURE 1.6

Examining the functionality of a panel.

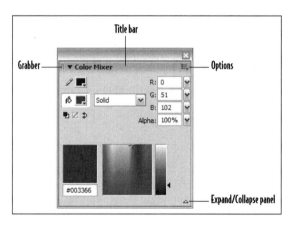

The dots that appear on the left side of the title bar are called the *Grabber*. If you work on a Windows system, you can dock and undock panels from the workspace. When a panel is undocked, it is "floating" and has a button you can use to close and drag the panel. Click and drag the Grabber to dock or undock a panel. When you see an area highlighted, you can release the mouse button to dock the panel in that location.

If you work on a Macintosh system, you can attach panels to a floating column of panels or leave them floating around the Stage. Several panels, such as the Actions and Help panels, are best left floating because of their dimensions. Click and drag the Grabber to dock or undock a panel from the column. When you see a solid black bar, release the mouse button to attach the panel to the column.

Using the Tools panel

You use the Tools panel to draw and edit shapes and lines, select objects, and change the view of the Stage. There are four main sections of the Tools panel: Tools, View, Colors, and Options (Figure 1.7). The Tools section contains tools with which to create and modify graphics. The View section contains tools used to move the Stage around the authoring environment or magnify the Stage. The Colors area allows you to select colors for strokes and fill areas.

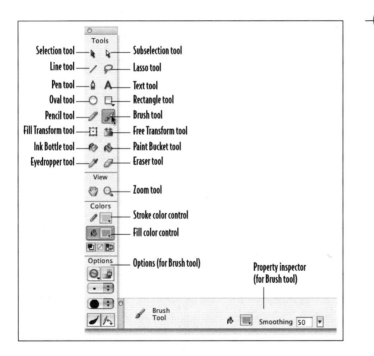

FIGURE 1.7

There are four main areas in the Tools panel and a wide selection of tools you can use to create graphics and animation.

The Options section is context sensitive: it changes depending on what you currently have selected in the panel. The Property inspector also changes depending on the selected tool and displays the available options. So after you select a tool, make sure that you look at the Options area of the Tools panel and the Property inspector to see how you can modify the properties of the tool.

Understanding the Flash Architecture

Understanding how Flash organizes assets and where to put all your content is important before you start to create FLA files. You need to learn where to put your assets, and the kinds of things that they are capable of in Flash.

Sometimes wrapping your head around the structure of a Flash file can take some work. However, if you have ever worked with time-line-based software (such as After Effects or Final Cut Pro), you're a step ahead. Flash is also based on a Timeline that you put your assets on, such as graphics, video, sound, and even code. The following sections describe what you can create in Flash and how you can organize it in a document. The following projects in this book use all these assets and organizational strategies.

▶ ▶ Importing Into Flash

You can import many different kinds of files into Flash. This is particularly useful when you have content built using other software that you want to use in Flash, such as graphics made in Photoshop or video edited in After Effects.

The following file formats can import into Flash: PNG, GIF, JPEG, PICT, BMP, TGA, TIFF, QuickTime image, Silicon Graphics, MacPaint, Photoshop, Illustrator, AutoCAD DXF, FreeHand, SWF, AIFF, MP3, Sound Designer II, Sun AU, WAV sound, QuickTime Movie, Video for Windows, MPEG, Digital Video, Flash Video, and PDF.

On Windows, you can also import EMF and WMF files.

You might be able to import video formats other than those listed previously, depending on the codecs you have installed on your computer. A codec is software that you use to compress and decompress files such as video files. Codecs are explained in more detail in Chapter 8. Not all formats are supported on both Macintosh and Windows. You should have Quick-Time installed, which Flash uses to help import a variety of file formats. Some companies develop tools that let you import additional kinds of files into an FLA file. For example, Electric Rain has developed an extension that enables you to import the native file format of its software Swift3D. This extension enables you to create 3D content and import it directly into Flash without losing the functionality if you were to import a SWF file instead.

Looking at symbols and instances

Symbols are one of the main parts that make up a Flash document. Symbols form a collection of assets that might form the graphics, bitmap images, video, sounds, fonts, components, buttons, and animation. Symbols are stored in the file's Library (Figure 1.8), and they are assets that you can reuse throughout your file numerous times. You can drag symbols onto the Stage, and even between Libraries of different FLA files.

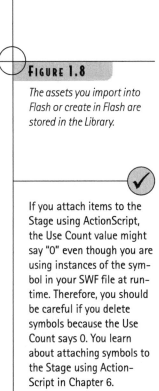

FIGURE 1.8

The assets you import into Flash or create in Flash are stored in the Library.

Select Window > Library to open the Library. An icon and name represent each symbol, and you can tell what kind of asset the symbol is by referring to the Kind column. When you create a new symbol, you can name and choose the type of symbol it will be. The Use Count column lets you know how many instances of a symbol are used throughout your document.

Before you start to organize a file, you need to understand what symbols are and why they are useful in a file. Symbols help you reduce file size in a SWF because you can reuse a symbol numerous times and it's referenced only once in the Library. You can even modify that single symbol that's in the Library instead of creating a new instance of it (which would increase the file size of your SWF file). You can drag *copies* of a symbol in the Library to the Stage—when you do so, it is called an *instance*. You can give some instances a name using the Property inspector, which means that you can control them using

If you attach items to the Stage using ActionScript, the Use Count value might say "0" even though you are using instances of the symbol in your SWF file at runtime. Therefore, you should be careful if you delete symbols because the Use Count says 0. You learn about attaching symbols to the Stage using Action-Script in Chapter 6.

On Windows, the Library of the current FLA file is white, whereas the Library of an FLA that's not currently being edited is entirely grayed-out. On the Mac an inactive Library's text is grayed out instead of the entire background.

You learn how to create a symbol later in this chapter, and you learn how to add and use instance names in Exercise 2.

ActionScript. This is called its *instance name*, which is different from the name you see in the Library, and it must be unique.

For example, you might use ActionScript to change the size, color, or behavior of the instance. All instances, even if they cannot have instance names, can be modified using the Property inspector (Figure 1.9). If you modify an instance using ActionScript or the Property inspector, the modifications change only the instance itself, not the symbol in the Library. If you edit the symbol in symbol-editing mode, all instances that are on the Stage update with your changes. Therefore, you need to be careful when you edit a symbol that you want to change all the instances of it on the Stage as well.

You will find out how to use symbol-editing mode later in this chapter in Exercise 1.

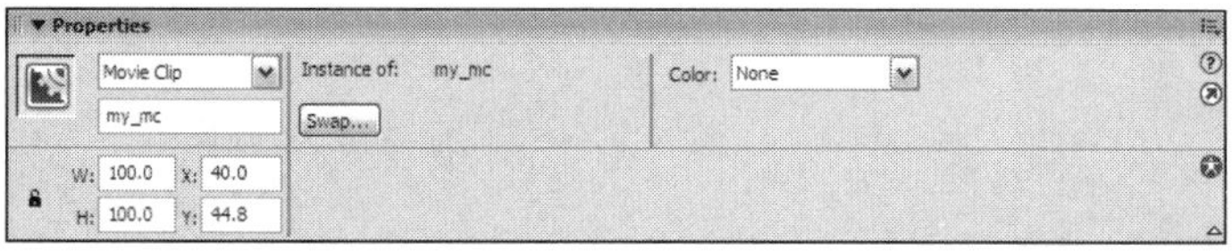

FIGURE 1.9

You can give a name to an instance on the Stage using the Property inspector.

You can even create a symbol using the Library. Click the button in the upper-right corner of the Library panel. The menu that opens is called the Options menu, and you can use it to create a new video symbol or font symbol, and change the settings of selected symbols. You will learn more about this menu in later chapters.

You can create a duplicate of an symbol if you want to make changes to a single instance. You will learn more about this later on in the book.

Understanding symbol functionality

Flash has three primary kinds of symbols that you can create directly in the authoring environment by using tools in Flash: graphics, buttons, and movie clips. You will create some of these symbols later in this chapter, but first you find out what you use each symbol for.

Graphic symbols are useful when you want to add a reusable static image to an FLA file. A graphic symbol might consist of drawings that you made in Flash, simple animations, or images that you import into the file and want to reuse. Graphic symbols do not have an instance name, so you cannot control them by using ActionScript. If you needed to control an image, you would instead make it into a kind of symbol you can control, such as a movie clip.

Buttons are symbols containing four states (frames), each state controlling how the button looks and functions in relation to the mouse pointer. You use buttons to create interactivity, such as hotspots, rollover effects, navigational menus, and clickable elements. Buttons are limited in functionality, but they are beneficial for their simplicity. Despite their limitations, buttons are easy to create and use.

Movie clips can be very simple or very complex symbols. Movie clips have their own timelines, just like the main Timeline you see at the top of the authoring environment. This means that a movie clip can run completely independent from the main Timeline. What does this mean? You can have a movie clip that animates when the rest of your SWF file sits still. Or, you can have several movie clips that all animate separately from each other.

Working with the Timeline and frames

When you add content to the Stage, it is organized somewhere on a Timeline. The playhead moves along the Timeline and shows the current frame or executes a script. You can also move the playhead around the Timeline when you are editing an FLA file, which is called *scrubbing*.

The Timelines in Flash are long successions of frames and keyframes that exist over time. Frames might or might not contain content, and you might or might not include multiple frames in an FLA file. If you include multiple layers in your document, you can stack frames on top of each other, which lets you layer graphics and animations in your files and also helps you separate content. The Flash authoring environment has several different kinds of frames: keyframes, frames, empty frames, and empty keyframes as shown in the following figure.

You can import bitmap images into an FLA file. These images are stored in the Library like symbols, and you can drag instances of the bitmap onto the Stage. You can add several instances of the image without increasing the file size. You do not need to change these imported bitmap images into a symbol unless you require additional functionality that a symbol might provide (such as applying effects, or editing a symbol in one location).

Graphic symbols are ideal if you need to view the symbol's animation while working on the main Timeline because the graphic symbol's Timeline works in sync with the main Timeline. So when you move the playhead on the main Timeline (called *scrubbing*) you can view the graphic symbol's animation.

FIGURE 1.10

There are several different kinds of frames in Flash, which appear differently in the Timeline.

When a frame contains new or changed content or animation, you see a solid, filled dot that signifies a keyframe. A keyframe represents a change in the content from the previous frame on the layer. However, if you animate an object in Flash using motion or shape tweens, you see keyframes only in the frames in which you make settings for that animation. In-between each keyframe are *frames*. You use keyframes to create the beginning, and use end frames for a particular transition or animation. When you apply a tween (animation) in Flash, the software creates the movement by filling in the changes that occur between the two keyframes with a series of frames. If you decide to change one of those frames (say, to add a new position for your tween), it changes into a keyframe.

Frames are used in-between keyframes to fill in parts of an animation. Frames also include content on the Stage that does not change from the previous frame. You can also have empty keyframes and empty frames on the Timeline. However, if you want to add new content to a frame, you must create and select a keyframe.

Most Flash documents include more than one Timeline. Movie clips, buttons, and even graphic symbols include a Timeline (although buttons and graphics have limited timelines). Movie clip timelines are just as robust as the main Timeline above the Stage, which enables you to make a nested SWF file inside your main document.

Button symbols: These symbols include four frames that represent each state of the button: Up, Over, Down, and Hit. You can add graphics to each of these states and add ActionScript to control the button's functionality and appearance.

Graphic symbols: These symbols have a Timeline that you can use to create layered drawings and simple animations. Unlike movie clips with their independent timelines, graphic symbol animations run in sync with the main Timeline. The main Timeline must be as long or longer than the graphic symbol's animation, but you can scrub the main Timeline and view the graphic symbol's animation.

Movie clip symbols: These symbols run independently of the main Timeline. If the main SWF file had only a single frame, you would not need to extend the Timeline of your movie clip. Movie clips, like

You learn how to create frames and keyframes later on in Exercise 2.

buttons, can be manipulated by using ActionScript. You can even place ActionScript inside of a movie clip and put other movie clips inside your movie clip.

You will quickly discover how important it is to use the Edit Bar (Figure 1.11) to navigate though documents that contain nested symbols. The Edit Bar gives you a good idea about what you are editing and where you are within the nested symbols, and allows you to navigate between instances, nested instances, and the main Stage.

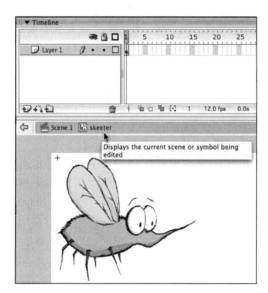

Generally speaking, you shouldn't nest too many symbols within other symbols. Many layers of nested symbols within nested symbols can make a document exceedingly complex and usually create an FLA that is complicated, intensive, and difficult to work with.

Figure 1.11

The Edit Bar shows you when you are in symbol-editing mode. Click the name of an instance to navigate to that instance or click Scene 1 to return to the main Stage.

Navigating layers

Layers on the Timeline are stacked vertically. Each layer can and should be named according to the assets you place on it. You can use layers to separate and group similar assets because this lets you modify a group of elements and find an asset that you are looking for quickly and easily. Using layers also lets you create an effect of depth on the Stage because you can make some graphics appear in front of another, as shown in the following figure.

Layers can be organized
into folders. Layer folders
are typically used to hold
several layers that are
related to each another. For
example, you might have all
your bitmap graphics on
three layers that you put in
a single folder. Folders can
be named, and you can
open and close the folder to
view or hide the layers contained within.

You also add ActionScript to frames on a layer. The ActionScript
should always be on frames in the top layer, and you should name
the layer *actions*. Putting your code on a single frame that doesn't
contain any graphics makes the code easy to find, and helps you
avoid potential conflicts between the code and other assets on the
same layer. It is not advisable to place instances and code on the
same frame, which could potentially cause conflicts in your SWF file.

Setting preferences

Preferences let you control parts of Flash, from editing vector graphics to settings for the code editor. You can control the default settings
for each document you create in Flash.

Select Edit > Preferences (Windows) or Flash/Flash Professional >
Preferences (Macintosh) to open the Preferences dialog box (Figure 1.13). This dialog box contains several tabs that let you control
different settings in Flash all at once. The General tab contains basic
settings that you use to control authoring files. The Editing tab contains settings for drawing, vectors and text. You use the Clipboard
tab to control how your images copy to the clipboard, which primarily affects gradients and Freehand text. The Warnings tab lets you
choose which warnings you see in the software. The ActionScript tab
allows you to make settings for the code editor.

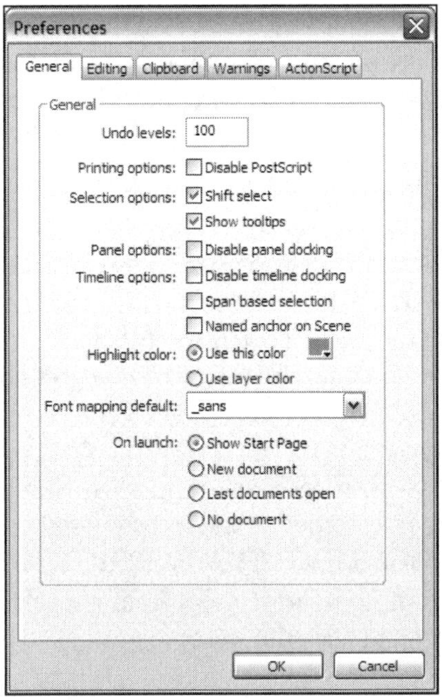

Preferences

General | Editing | Clipboard | Warnings | ActionScript

General

Undo levels: 100

Printing options: ☐ Disable PostScript

Selection options: ☑ Shift select
☑ Show tooltips

Panel options: ☐ Disable panel docking

Timeline options: ☐ Disable timeline docking
☐ Span based selection
☐ Named anchor on Scene

Highlight color: ◉ Use this color
○ Use layer color

Font mapping default: _sans

On launch: ◉ Show Start Page
○ New document
○ Last documents open
○ No document

OK   Cancel

FIGURE 1.13

The Preferences dialog box lets you control and customize the authoring environment.

You should consider the following preferences in this window:

Undo levels: Change the undo levels accordingly. The number of Undo levels sets the number of times you can step back through the edits and commands you make in your project by selecting Edit > Undo. You should choose a low number of undos if possible if system resources are a concern. Flash consumes more memory on the computer if you use a high undo level. Instead of relying on a vast number of "undos", you should periodically save new versions of your FLA documents using File > Save As. Not only does this reduce the size of your FLA file by removing the undo history, but it also lets you save older copies to revert back to if you make a large mistake or corrupt a copy of a file.

Change your drawing settings: There are several ways you can modify how the drawing tools work. The *Connect lines* setting determines how close two line ends have to be before they snap together to make a single line. The *Smooth curves* setting determines how much smoothing applies to a line, which removes jagged edges in hand-drawn lines and can improve performance and file size. The

Recognize lines setting modifies lines that are nearly straight to exactly straight, and *Recognize shapes* modifies shapes that you draw so they are precise renditions of common shapes. *Click accuracy* modifies how close the mouse pointer must be to an object for it to be recognized as clicked and selected.

Customize your Tools panel: To open the Customize Tools Panel dialog box, select File > Customize Tools Panel (Windows) or Flash/Flash Professional > Customize Tools panel (Macintosh). You can rearrange the Tools panel and even add extra tools into the software if you install them as an extension (plug-in) on your computer (Figure 1.14). For example, you might be able to find and install custom shape tools. You can select tools to add or remove from the panel, and even create menus that open when you click a tool's button on the panel. First, select a tool to modify from the far left of the dialog box. Then select a tool to add to its menu in the list of tools in the pane to the left, and finally click the Add button to add your selection. If you want to remove a tool from a menu, click the tool in the list to the right and click the Remove button.

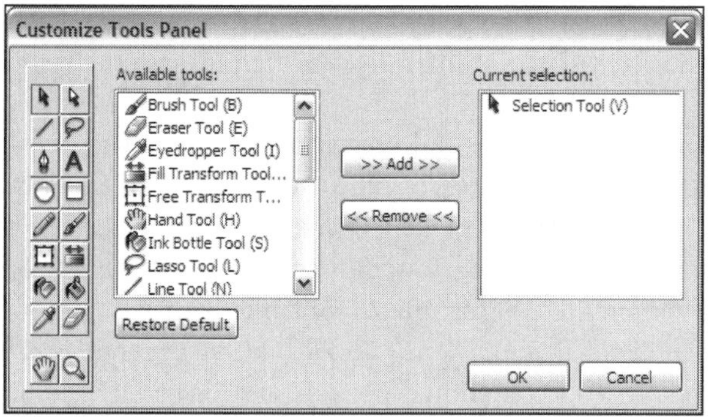

FIGURE 1.14

Customize the Tools panel using the Customize Tools Panel dialog box. You can create menus in the Tools panel and add or remove default or custom tools.

ANIMATING IN FLASH

Flash is a great tool to choose for animation, particularly because it can handle so much more than just animation and effects. These capabilities allow you to create projects that include amazing graphics and creativity, and advanced functionality and features of an application. Most other animation programs do not enable you to do so.

You create a simple animation using tweening in the following project. In Chapter 2, you learn about much more about animating in Flash using different kinds of *tweens*. A tween refers to an automated process in Flash that animates a specified object on the Stage. You make settings of how you want the properties of the object to change, and Flash makes the calculations and movement by filling in the changes that occur.

You can create two different kinds of tweens in Flash: *motion tweens* and *shape tweens*. You can use shape tweens to modify a vector line or shape, such as changing a circle into a square. Motion tweens change properties of an object, such as moving them around the Stage or fading something from a visible to invisible state. Flash can also be used to create traditional frame-by-frame animation, where you draw or put images on each frame to create the appearance of motion "manually." A *frame-by-frame animation* is a traditional way of creating animation. Instead of using Flash to create a tween using automatic calculations, you draw and position each part of the movement by hand in a series of keyframes. This form of animation lets you create complicated effects, particularly when motion and shape tweens don't allow you to create the kind of animation you require. Frame-by-frame animations can be more time-intensive to create and add more file size to your SWF file. However, they are sometimes necessary and can result in unique and amazing animations. You will learn more about these forms of animation in the following chapters.

The Timeline appears differently, depending on what kind of animation you use (Figure 1.15). If the animation is a motion tween, the frames are colored purple and include an arrow. If you add a shape tween, the background is light green. If there isn't any animation in the frames, frames appear as a light grey color.

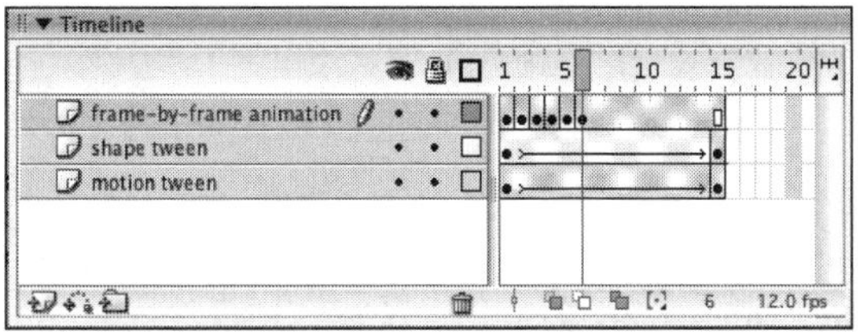

You can also create scripted animation using ActionScript and instances, such as movie clips. You can also draw lines and shapes using ActionScript, and move them around on the Stage. You will discover more about scripted animation in Chapter 7.

FIGURE 1.15

Frames appear differently depending on the content (or lack of content) and kind of tween or animation you add.

PROJECT 1: CREATING YOUR FIRST ANIMATION

There are several kinds of documents you can build using Flash. In this project, you create a simple FLA file that animates an object on the Stage. You save and publish this document, and you can optionally try placing it on the Internet. You find out how to make some basic settings in a file, and create a SWF and HTML file from it.

Before you get started, create a new folder on your hard drive and copy all the files from the CD-ROM into this folder. Create a second folder for all the files you create for this book. You might want to also create subdirectory folders for each project to help organize the content.

Exercise 1: Creating a file and symbol

In the first exercise, you create a brand new Flash document and add two symbols to the file. The first symbol is a movie clip that you create from an image that you import into the FLA. The second symbol is a button that you create from a vector graphic made in Flash. Open Flash, and let's get started.

1. Select File > New and select Flash Document to create a new FLA file, or click Flash Document from the Create New section on the Start Page. The Start page displays whenever you open Flash, although it can be disabled in the Preferences dialog box (Edit > Preferences[Windows] or Flash/Flash Professional > Preferences[Macintosh]).

    You can open existing files from the Start page or by selecting File > Open. The Open dialog box with a standard file chooser opens, which lets you select an FLA document to open. If you want to open a recent file, select File > Open Recent from the main menu and select the name of a file from the submenu.

2. Select File > Save As from the main menu to open the Save As dialog box. Type **first.fla** into the File name or Save As text field. Choose a location on your hard drive for the new file, and click Save.

3. Select File > Import > Import to Stage, and navigate to 01/start/skeeter.png from the book directory on your hard drive. Click Open to import the file (a drawing of a mosquito), which is put directly on the Stage.

For the projects in this book, you should import the images and other assets that you copy to your hard drive. Avoid importing files into Flash directly from the CD-ROM. Sometimes you will encounter unexpected results in Flash if you try to import files directly from a CD-ROM.

You can create new files and open recent files from the Start page. You can also create a new file based on a template. The Start page also allows you to search keywords on www.macromedia.com and displays news about Flash.

The Start Page and New Document dialog box look different in Flash MX 2004 and Flash MX Professional 2004. The Professional edition has several additional file formats you can open and create.

4. Select the PNG file on the Stage by using the Selection tool in the Tools panel. Click the arrow tool to select the tool.

5. Select Modify > Convert to Symbol from the main menu to "convert" the graphic into a symbol (Figure 1.16). The Convert to Symbol dialog box opens, in which you can select a type of symbol to convert the image to. You can also name the symbol, which is the name it's given in the Library.

 You can also import directly into the Library if you do not want the imported item to be placed on the Stage. To do this, choose File > Import > Import to Library.

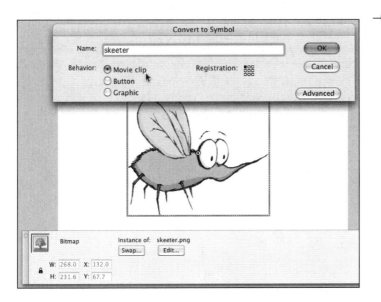

 FIGURE 1.16

The PNG image imports to the Stage, and you convert it into a symbol.

You can convert both drawings on the Stage or items that you import

6. Type **skeeter** into the Name text field. This is the name the symbol displays in the Library. Select the Movie clip radio button as its Behavior. Then click OK to close the dialog box and convert the image into a movie clip.

The skeeter symbol is stored in the Library, and you now have an instance of the movie clip on the Stage. Select Window > Library to open the Library, and you see the symbol called skeeter stored in the panel. You will also see that the Library shows you a movie clip icon next to the symbol's name, and "Movie Clip" displayed in the Kind column. This reminds you what kind of symbol it is.

You can also select an image and press F8 to open the Convert to Symbol dialog box and convert the selection into a symbol.

7. Double-click the skeeter instance to open the movie clip in symbol-editing mode. The PNG is placed inside a movie clip symbol. If you open the movie clip in Flash, you see the PNG placed on a new layer on the Timeline of the movie clip.

When you double-clicked the symbol, the movie clip opened in symbol-editing mode. So you can edit the symbol itself, add to the symbol, delete content from it, and so forth. You can even nest another symbol inside the symbol that's open in this mode. You can tell that you are in symbol-editing mode by looking at the Edit Bar, as discussed earlier in this chapter.

You can also enter symbol-editing mode by double-clicking the symbol in the Library, or right-clicking (Windows) or control-clicking (Macintosh) the instance on the Stage, and selecting Edit or Edit in Place from the contextual menu. If you select Edit, you do not see the Stage area surrounding the symbol. If you select Edit in Place, you continue to see other items and the Stage area (although they are not selectable), which is the same editing mode as double-clicking the instance. This is useful if you need to edit your symbol in relation to other elements on the Stage.

8. Click the Scene 1 button on the Edit Bar to return to the main Stage.

9. Click the Stroke and Fill color controls in the Color section of the Tools panel to select a fill and stroke color for a new shape that you create in the following step.

10. Select the Oval tool from the Tools panel, and click and drag horizontally on the Stage to create an oval shape. Release the mouse button to complete the shape, as shown in Figure 1.17.

11. Select the oval on the Stage using the Selection tool; click and drag around the shape to select it, after which you see a checkered pattern over the shape. You can use the Selection tool to move the shape around on the Stage when it's selected.

12. Select Modify > Convert to Symbol from the main menu to convert the vector graphic into a symbol. Type **playbutton** into the Name text field. This is the name the symbol displays in the Library. Select the Button radio button to convert the selection into a button symbol. Then click OK, and now you have two different kinds of symbols in the Library.

If you press the Shift key while drawing the shape, you can draw a perfect circle.

FIGURE 1.17

Select the Oval tool, and draw an oval on the Stage.

That was easy, and now you have created both a movie clip and button symbol. In the following exercises, you will animate the movie clip, and add some functionality to the button. Save the document (File > Save) before you move on.

Exercise 2: Animating and testing your work

In this exercise, you will animate the movie clip symbol, and add a simple script that stops the Timeline and plays the movie clip when you click the button instance. You will also test the file in the testing environment. You should still be working with the **first.fla** file from Exercise 1.

1. Create a new layer in the Timeline by clicking the Insert Layer button (a small button directly below the layer name *Layer 1*). Double-click Layer 2 in the Timeline and type in a new name for the layer: **movie clip**. Rename Layer 1 to **play button**.

2. Select the skeeter symbol on the Stage, and select Edit > Cut. Select frame 1 of the movie clip layer and select Edit > Paste in Center.

3. Select frame 15 of the movie clip layer; then select Insert > Timeline > Keyframe from the main menu. This adds a new keyframe at frame 15 and gray colored frames between frame 1 and 15.

> **▶ ▶ THE COORDINATE SYSTEM**
>
> Flash's coordinate system starts at the upper-left corner of the Stage, which is 0, 0. Meaning that both the X and Y coordinate are at 0, 0. For example, if you move 10 pixels to the right and 5 pixels down, your X, Y coordinates are 10, 5. You can set these coordinates for an instance in the Property inspector. If you want to move the mosquito instance to 10 pixels from the upper-left corner, you would set both the X and Y coordinates to 10 pixels in the X and Y text fields in the Property inspector.

4. Select frame 15, and use the Selection tool to move the skeeter movie clip to a new location on the Stage.

5. Select frame 1 of the movie clip layer, and select Insert > Timeline > Create Motion Tween. This is the command that adds the motion tween, which changes the background of the frames to a purple color with an arrow across the frames. The skeeter tweens between the position at frame 1 (the center of the Stage) to the location where you moved the clip in step 4.

You can "scrub" the Timeline to see how the movie clip moves. Click and drag the playhead between frames 1 and 15 to see the animation. Also, you can click the Onion Skin button in the Timeline to view multiple frames at once (Figure 1.18). Click and drag the handles that appear where the frames are numbered in the Timeline to toggle how many frames you view at once.

6. Test the SWF file by selecting Control > Test Movie, or by pressing Ctrl+Enter (Windows) or Command+Return (Macintosh). The test environment displays the document in Flash Player, which is how the animation would appear if you publish the FLA. The animation continuously loops, meaning that it plays from the beginning to the end of the animation and returns to the beginning to play again. The playbutton instance appears only on the first frame and then disappears when the playhead moves past frame 1.

Click the Close button to return to the authoring environment. In the following steps, you add a couple of actions to the FLA file that controls the animation using the button instance and ActionScript on the Timeline.

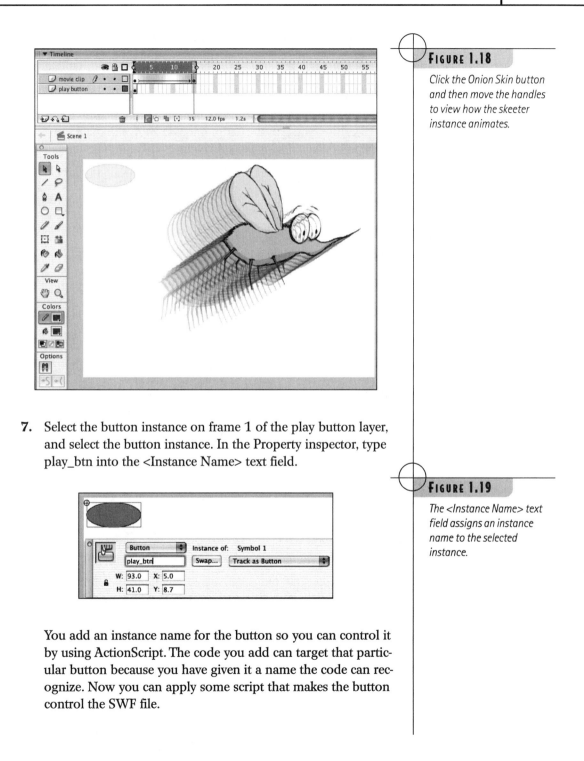

FIGURE 1.18

Click the Onion Skin button and then move the handles to view how the skeeter instance animates.

7. Select the button instance on frame 1 of the play button layer, and select the button instance. In the Property inspector, type play_btn into the <Instance Name> text field.

FIGURE 1.19

The <Instance Name> text field assigns an instance name to the selected instance.

You add an instance name for the button so you can control it by using ActionScript. The code you add can target that particular button because you have given it a name the code can recognize. Now you can apply some script that makes the button control the SWF file.

8. Click the Insert Layer button in the Timeline to insert a new layer. Rename the layer by double-clicking the new layer's name, and type **actions**.

9. Select frame 1 of this layer, and open the Actions panel by choosing Window > Development Panels > Actions. Then type the following into the Script pane, as shown in the following figure:

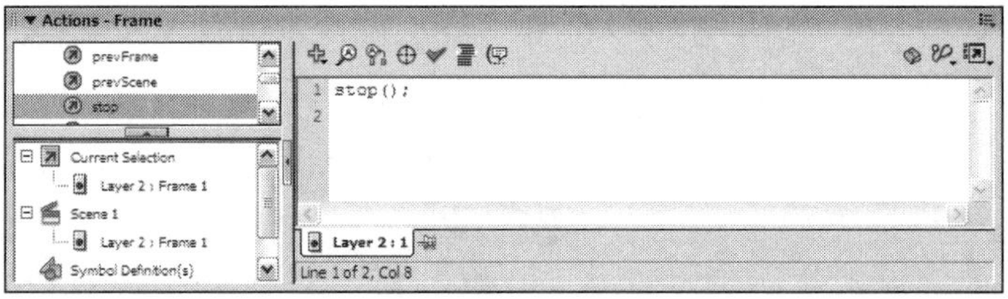

FIGURE 1.20

Type stop(); into the Script pane to stop the main Timeline from looping.

This ActionScript is used to stop the Timeline. This means that instead of looping, the playhead stops on Frame 1. Because it is stopped automatically, you can play the animation using code that you apply to the button.

10. Following the stop(); action you added in step 9, add the following code:

```
1 play_btn.onRelease = function(){
2   play();
3 };
```

You use the code to play the main Timeline. It targets the play_btn instance, and tells the button (play_btn) to play the main Timeline (play();) when the button is clicked. The onRelease refers to the button being clicked and released by the user.

11. Test the animation again by selecting Control > Test Movie. Click the play_btn instance, which plays the main Timeline. The skeeter instance animates, and then returns to frame 1 and stops. It no longer loops because you added the stop(); action on frame 1. This means whenever the playhead reaches

frame 1 in the SWF file, it stops. If you click the `play_btn` instance again, the animation plays again.

Not too bad for a first SWF file! Don't worry about the specifics of the code you just entered because you will learn more about Action-Script and how it works in later projects.

Exercise 3: Frame rate, publishing, and uploading

When working with animations, one of the most important steps is to make sure that you have an appropriate frame rate selected. This step isn't as important if you're building an application in Flash because typically an application has limited movement, and sometimes you work only with a single frame. However, if your SWF file has a lot of motion that needs to appear smooth, it might be necessary to increase your frame rate above the default value of 12 frames per second. You can test what different frame rates look like by checking the document again in the test environment. You can then publish and upload the project to your server, or look at it in a browser window on your hard drive.

1. Click anywhere outside the Stage using the Selection tool and open the Property inspector to change the frame rate of the document. Type **21** into the Frame rate text field to change the SWF file frame rate to 21 fps (frames per second).

    Optionally, you can also modify the background color of the Stage in the Property inspector by clicking the color chip next to Background and selecting a new color swatch. Change the dimensions of the Stage by clicking the Size button and type new values into the width and height text fields in the Document Properties dialog box.

2. Select Control > Test Movie to test your file in Flash Player again. This time, the animation plays a lot faster, almost twice as fast, as it did in Exercise 2.

3. Select File > Save to save changes you have made to the document.

Do not change your frame rate to a number that's too high. If your frame rate is very high, it might be difficult for processors to keep up with the animation. You shouldn't need to go beyond 31 frames per second for your animations.

▶ ▶ THE SAVE VERSUS SAVE AND COMPACT

The Save and Compact option compresses the size of an FLA file by removing unnecessary information from the file that causes file bloat, such as the History (undo steps and so on). In this way it is similar to using File > Save As, which similarly removes this information (with the added capability of renaming your file). You should use Save and Compact as a final step when you're working on a project. As soon as you select File > Save again, your file returns to the large size it was before you chose Save and Compact. Remember that this command deletes all the history in your file, and you cannot access this information again. If you might need to undo steps in your process, do not select this option: select Save instead, which stores undo information in the FLA file. The issue with this option is that even if you delete assets from the Stage and Library, the FLA file saves these changes. Even if you delete items from the FLA file, they are still preserved within the FLA in case you choose to redo these steps. You can also select File > Revert to reload the current Flash document from the last saved version, which helps you avoid closing and reopening the document.

There are other options for saving the file. You could save a new version of the file by choosing File > Save As and typing a new name for the FLA file. This is a good way to save different version of a project, particularly if you might want to revert back to an earlier version. This is only necessary for larger projects.

4. Select File > Publish Settings to open the Publish Settings dialog box shown in Figure 1.21.

This dialog box lets you publish your FLA to various different formats, including a static image, video file, animated GIF, series of bitmap images, or even a "projector" file—which is a Windows or Macintosh executable with Flash Player built in. This lets you distribute your Flash work, perhaps on CD-ROM, to users who might not have Flash Player.

To publish a file while skipping the Publish Settings dialog box, select File > Publish or press Shift+F12.

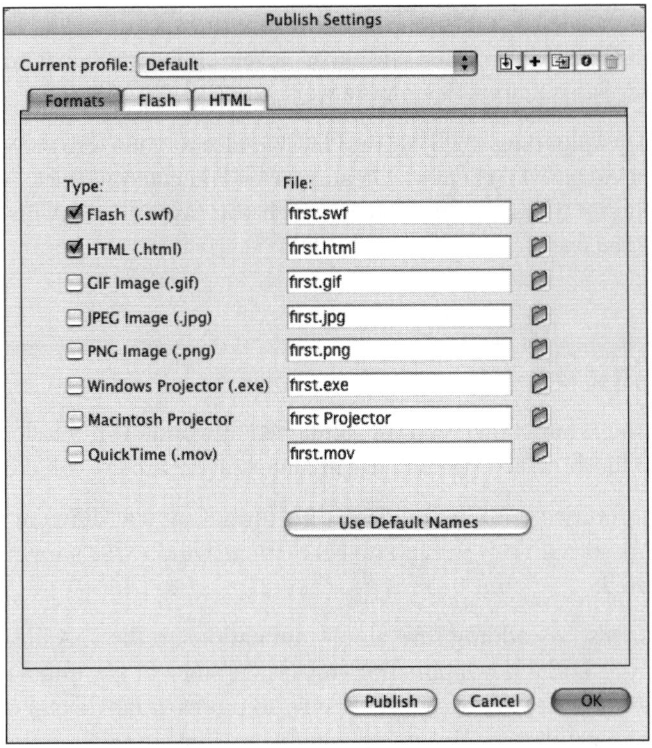

FIGURE 1.21

The Publish settings dialog box allows you to publish to a variety of formats and make specific settings for each format.

5. Make sure Flash and HTML are both selected under the Formats tab, which is the default setting in Flash. This means that a SWF file and HTML file generate in the directory in which you saved the FLA document. Most selections you make in the Formats tab has a corresponding tab that appears in the dialog box, so if you select GIF Image, an additional tab appears.

The settings for this project are not important because of its basic nature. At any rate, explore the options in the Flash and HTML tabs to see which options are available when you publish a SWF file. These options will be covered in later tutorials when they are applicable. Click OK to close the dialog box.

You will discover options for detecting whether your visitors have Flash Player installed in Chapter 15. You also explore the many options for embedding SWF files in a web page.

If you do not have an FTP client, try downloading SmartFTP from www.smartFTP.com. The program is easy to use and is free for educational, personal, and nonprofit use. There are other options available for Windows and Mac at www.download.com.

6. Select File > Publish Preview > HTML to view the SWF file embedded in a browser window. The browser opens in your default web browser, and most closely shows you what your project will look like on the web.

7. Try uploading the SWF and HTML files to your web server using an FTP client or Dreamweaver. You can find these two files in the same directory in which you saved the FLA file in Exercise 1.

Moving On

This project has shown you the fundamental workflow in Flash, from start to finish, which you will use in almost every project you create.

Try outputting your file to different file formats and at different frame rates. You can do this in the Publish Settings window, as shown in Exercise 3.

You can also try adding several new animations to the FLA file. When you add a new animation, repeat the steps of creating a new animated movie clip, except remember to put each movie clip on their own new layers. You might want to try importing your own content into the FLA file, and converting what you import into a movie clip symbol.

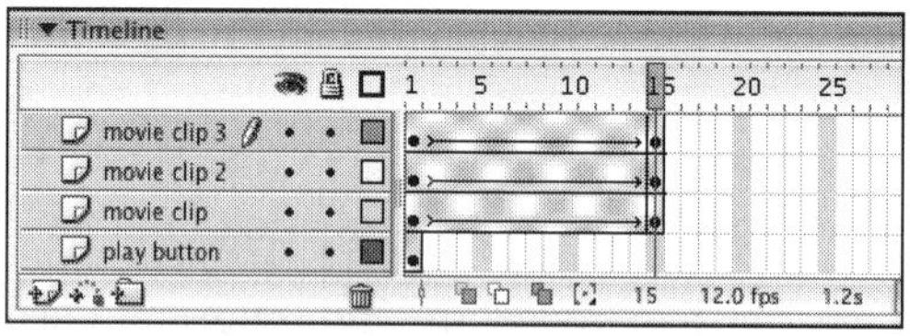

FIGURE 1.22

Add more instances onto new layers that you create on the Timeline.

FIGURE 1.23

Add new animations to the project.

FIGURE 2.A

FIGURE 2.B

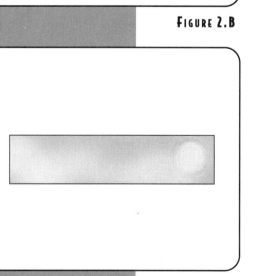

FIGURE 2.C

What you learn

▶ Understanding types of tweens

▶ How tweens work

▶ How to import bitmap graphics

▶ How to create movie clips to tween

▶ How to manipulate the Timeline

▶ How to add motion guides and paths

▶ How to animate object properties

Lesson Files

Start:

02/start/images (folder)

02/start/panning_start.fla

Finish:

02/complete/panning.fla

2

ANIMATING WITH MOTION TWEENS

LEARNING HOW TO do tweening in Flash is the fundamental part of using the software to animate your images and vector graphics. Animation is based on an event called *persistence of vision,* which is when the eye sees an image slightly longer than it actually appears, and another image replaces it. The sequence of images, when shown in rapid succession, creates the appearance of motion.

In this chapter, you animate bitmap drawings that you import into a SWF file. The motion you create mimics the panning movements of a camera. You add motion tweens and change the properties of the tween itself and the instances that move to add a variety of animation types to the document. You also use motion guides to add custom tweens that follow a path instead of a straight line.

Website: www.FLAnimation.com/chapters/02

UNDERSTANDING TWEENS

There are four kinds of animation you can do in Flash: motion tweens, shape tweens, frame-by-frame animation, and scripted animation. Only two of those forms of animation are *tweens*. A tween is the motion that you create between a beginning and an end state. It refers to the "in-between" frames on the Timeline that create the appearance of motion. Essentially, "tween" is short for "in-between".

To create a tween, you add a start and end keyframe on the Timeline for an object, and let Flash create the animation for the frames between those two keyframes. The object's size, color, position, or other properties change between the keyframes, which creates the appearance of motion or animation.

You typically use motion tweens to create movement and effects in Flash. (You learn more about using motion tweens in the following section, "Using motion tweens"). Although shape tweens can be complex to create, they can produce some amazing results. Shape tweens let you "morph" shapes; for example, you can tween a rectangle into a circle, make a line appear to grow, or tween one block of text into another. Like motion tweens, shape tweens enable you to modify an object's location, color, alpha, and size. The main differences between shape and motion tweening is that shape tweening morphs one (raw) shape into another; motion tweens can animate objects (instances) along a path. You use shape tweens to create animation in Chapter 3.

Often, you can use different forms of tweening or animation to accomplish similar results. Despite the fact you usually have a few ways to attain the same results, some forms of animation are better than others for specific tasks.

If you animate an object across the Stage, you could use any form of animation: motion tween, shape tween, frame-by-frame, or scripted animation. If you want to animate along a curved or irregular path, motion tweens are typically the best and easiest solution. All you need to do is draw a path, as shown in this chapter's project, and attach the object to that path.

Other forms of animation should be used depending on the situation. Motion tweens create motion, and shape tweens should be used for morphing objects into other shapes. You should use frame-by-frame animation for complex effects or fine-tuning. Scripted

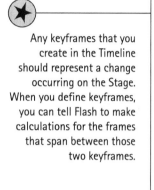

Any keyframes that you create in the Timeline should represent a change occurring on the Stage. When you define keyframes, you can tell Flash to make calculations for the frames that span between those two keyframes.

Frame-by-frame and scripted animations are covered in Chapters 4 and 7, respectively.

For examples of each form of animation, see www.FLAnimation.com/ chapters/02/ani_examples.

animation should be used when you need to reuse animations, create animation that depends on something happening (such as an image loading into the SWF file), or very simple or repetitive tasks.

Using motion tweens

You use motion tweens to move, rotate, modify size, and modify alpha levels of an object on the Stage. You can also use motion tweens to force an object to follow a path you create (which can be useful when you want to make a car drive around a track or a bird fly in a specific path, for example). Motion tweens let you accomplish these kinds of animations without creating a series of complex drawings or adding many tweens to a project. You make changes to a selected instance on the Stage using keyframes, and then add the motion tween to the Timeline.

Before you create a motion tween, you must *group* any vector drawings, or convert the drawing or image into a symbol such as a movie clip or graphic symbol. (As discussed in Chapter 1, symbols are assets in a file that are reused, so they help you reduce file size and improve performance.) You can also group drawings you make on the Stage by choosing the object and then selecting Modify > Group. Group raw data to make them easier to select and use in an FLA file. The objects you group must be on the same layer, or if you create a symbol the objects merge onto the same layer.

You add motion tweens in several different ways. Select the keyframe you want to add the motion tween to, and then do one of the following:

◆ Select Insert > Timeline > Create Motion Tween.

◆ Right-click (Windows) or Control-click (Mac) and select Create Motion Tween from the context menu.

◆ Choose Motion from the Tween pop-up menu in the Property inspector.

It is important to understand that you can have only one motion tweened instance existing on a single layer on the Timeline, and no other graphics should be on that layer. If you attempt to tween multiple instances on the same layer, you encounter unexpected, and unwanted, results. Essentially, your animation won't animate properly, such as motion tweening in the wrong direction and so on.

Remember that grouping data does not add the group to the Library. Therefore, grouping does not help reduce SWF file size. Instead, you should use symbols when possible.

When you separate tweened instances onto their own layers, you might end up with a large number of layers on the Timeline. To help organize the layers, use layer folders. Click the Insert Layer Folder button on the Timeline to create a new folder and then drag all the similar layers on the Timeline into that folder. This procedure lets you expand and collapse folders in the Timeline, which keeps the Timeline more organized and manageable. Using layer folders does not affect the appearance of layers on the Stage.

Project 2: Tweening a Landscape

There are a few different ways to add motion tweens to an FLA document, which you learn how to do in the following exercises. In this project, you add several kinds of motion tweens to an FLA file to animate an environment. Your motion tweens make the scene appear as if you are *panning* across it. At the end of this project, you add a *stop* action to stop the animation from repeatedly looping when the SWF file plays, and you also add a replay button. When you pan a subject, it means that you are horizontally scanning across the displayed image. Traditionally, this term refers to when a video camera moves the lens across a subject in this way. When you pan in Flash, it means you want to treat the Stage in the same way as a camera's viewfinder.

This tutorial shows you how to pan a landscape to create the illusion of a panning environment in Flash. There are several parts of this scene that pan in different ways and at different speeds. Such a scene might have a foreground, middle ground, horizon, and sky or background. In this particular project, you will add grass in the foreground, a bird as a subject, mountains in the horizon, and clouds in the sky (created by the background). You also add a sun in the sky too, as seen in the following figure.

FIGURE 2.1

Optionally add a sun in the sky.

USING VECTOR AND BITMAP GRAPHICS

When you create an animation, you can choose between vector and bitmap graphics, or use a combination of the two. Remember that vector drawings are the graphics you usually create in Flash, and bitmaps are imported images. You should consider whether you need a very small SWF file and optimal performance; or whether you need the detail that a bitmap image yields. Flash is a vector-based program, which means that the vector shapes you might draw in the program are remembered as mathematical calculations. Programs like Photoshop are bitmap-based, and bitmaps typically result in larger files than vector graphics. However, if you need realism or "painterly" effects, sometimes bitmap graphics are necessary.

The following image displays the difference between a bitmap image and a vector graphic. As you can see, vectors are best for line drawings, and bitmaps are best for images that require pixel detail.

You can turn a bitmap graphic into a vector graphic by using the trace bitmap feature in Flash. Select Modify > Bitmap > Trace Bitmap to change the bitmap into vectors, which results in a file that is similar to the original, as seen in the following figure.

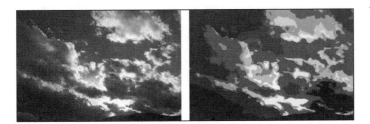

You should avoid animating partially transparent bitmaps over another bitmap in Flash, which is very processor-intensive. Most transparency in Flash is processor-intensive, but you can successfully use it in small amounts in a SWF file without much of a negative impact.

FIGURE 2.2

A vector drawing is on the left, and a bitmap image is to the right. Notice the difference in edges, clarity, and the potential for detail.

FIGURE 2.3

Trace a bitmap image to turn it into vectors.

You can choose varying amounts of accuracy when you trace bitmaps, which is measured in color threshold, corner threshold, curve fit, and minimum area parameters. The smaller the numbers you choose for color threshold and minimum area, the more accurate the image appears when you convert it to vectors. Curve fit lets you choose how smoothly curves draw (*pixels* being the most accurate), and corner threshold lets you choose whether sharp edges are smoothed out (*many corners* being the most accurate). The bitmap that you transform using this procedure is not always a smaller file size after it is changed to vectors, and the resulting image is sometimes rather resource-intensive. Computer processors might have difficulty or be slow making all the calculations that are necessary to draw the vectors in the SWF file. Make sure that the traced bitmap is better than the original in file size or that the output is what you wanted.

You need to start with graphics before any of the animation magic can begin. You might create your graphics directly in Flash, or you might use an external editor such as Fireworks or Photoshop. The projects in this book use both processes for creating graphics, and in this project you will import graphics that were made in an external editor. Portable Network Graphics (PNG) files are the best kind of graphics to import into Flash. These images hold transparency and color information in each pixel, which is retained well by Flash. So you can create images with transparency that you can import into Flash for animation or layout purposes, and your SWF file will be a desirable quality when you publish the file. In the following exercise, you will import a series of PNG graphics into a SWF file to animate. Although you can create vector graphics in Flash, you need to use an external editor to create bitmap graphics for your animations because Flash includes only vector-drawing tools. External editors are useful when you need to create realistic drawings, manipulate photos, or create specialized effects such as drop shadows, embossing, or lighting effects.

Because bitmaps add more file size to a SWF file than vector graphics, they should be used sparingly. Whenever possible, you should use vector graphics.

You can add motion tweens to either vector or bitmap graphics. In Chapter 3, you discover how you can shape only tween raw vector graphics in Flash.

In later projects, particularly Chapter 5, you learn how to use the vector drawing tools in Flash to create graphics for animation. You also learn how to integrate external editors with Flash to do what's called round-trip editing.

▶ ▶ Performance and Vectors

Although it is primarily a cosmetic choice when you choose between using vectors and bitmaps, you might also consider the performance and scalability between the two forms of graphics when choosing to animate them. You should always change any vector drawings that you make directly on the Stage (which is raw data) into symbols before publishing the FLA. Vectors that are raw data have a crosshatch pattern over them when they are selected. Raw data placed on the Stage has to be rendered out (drawn on the Stage using calculations when the SWF file plays) every time the playhead reaches that frame on the Timeline because the information is not stored in the Library. By changing the raw data into a symbol, you can reduce the SWF file size so the information has to be referenced only once in the Library instead of many times individually on the Timeline. It also makes the graphic easier to select on the Stage. However, you can shape only tween raw vector graphics, and certain other elements (such as motion guide paths) must be raw vectors as well.

Exercise 1: Importing graphics

The first step of creating the animation is to import the graphics to animate. These graphics were created for you already: The graphics for this project were drawn by hand in Photoshop using a graphics tablet (this could have just as easily been accomplished using Fireworks). Each graphic was created on separate layers and then exported as PNG files with transparency. Feel free to replace these graphics with your own. You can draw your own graphics, or you might even manipulate several photographs and use them instead.

Your images should be wider than the Stage dimensions of your FLA file. If you use the same dimensions as the file in this exercise, make sure that your images are approximately 550 pixels wide or more.

1. Select File > New; then select Flash Document and click OK to create a new FLA file. Then select File > Save As to save the file, and type **panning.fla** into the File name (Windows) or Save As (Mac) text field. Click OK to save the document.

2. Locate the 02/start/images folder on your hard drive. If you have not transferred the contents from the CD-ROM to your hard drive, copy over the 02 folder first before you import the PNG graphics for this exercise.

3. Select File > Import > Import to Library from the main menu. Select all the PNG files in the 02/start/images folder. To select all of the files simultaneously, hold down the Shift key while you click each file to select the entire directory, or select one file and hold Shift while you press your arrow keys. Click Open (Windows) or Import to Library (Macintosh) to import the files into the FLA document.

All the PNG files are now stored in the Library. Open the Library (Window > Library) to see that all seven PNG files imported successfully.

4. Select the Stage and open the Property inspector (Window > Properties) to change the dimensions and color of the Stage. Click the button next to Size to open the Document Properties dialog box. Change the dimensions of the Stage to 500 (width) by 400 (height). Then click the Background color control, and type **#99CCFF** into the text field at the top of the color pop-up menu, as shown in the following figure. This hexadecimal color specifies a light blue color for the background.

FIGURE 2.4

Specify a background color and dimensions for the Stage using the Document Properties dialog box.

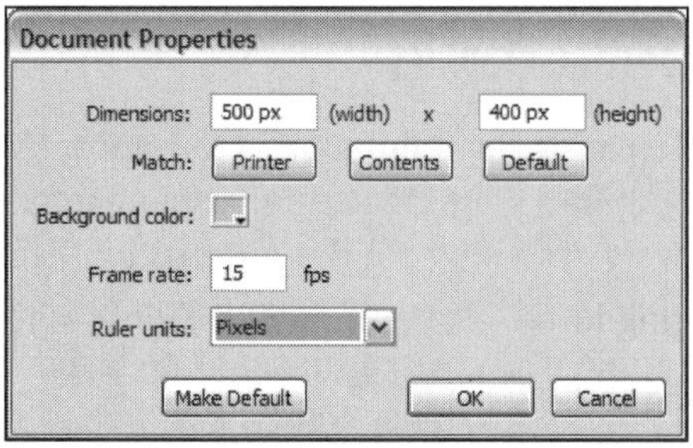

It is always a good practice to rename your layers in a meaningful way. If the name of the layer represents the content placed on that layer, you will have an easier time editing your files. Otherwise, it is difficult to know what is specifically on that layer.

5. Create five new layers (one layer for of the movie clips you will create, and one layer for the tween) so that you have five layers total. Click the Insert Layer button (which is below Layer 1) until you have five layers. The Insert Layer button is a small square with a plus (+) icon on it.

6. Rename each layer to represent the content that will be placed on that layer. Double-click each layer and type in a new name as follows (from top to bottom): **clouds**, **grass**, **sun**, **bird**, and **mountains**, as seen in the following figure:

FIGURE 2.5

Your layers should be named the following (from top to bottom): clouds, grass, sun, bird, mountains.

Remember that each movie clip you intend to tween needs to be on its own layer without any other graphics or movie clips on that layer.

7. Select File > Save to save your changes.

In the next exercise, you will create movie clips that include each of the images you just imported.

Exercise 2: Creating movie clips

This exercise creates movie clips from each of the images that you imported. The three parts of the bird image (body, wing, and leg) are each converted into movie clips, and then the wing and leg are nested inside the body movie clip. You do this so the bird as a whole can be tweened, and then you can tween the wing and leg individually as well.

1. Open the Library in panning.fla, and drag the following PNG files to the following layers:

   ◆ clouds.png to the clouds layer

   ◆ grass.png to the grass layer

   ◆ sun.png to the sun layer

   ◆ bird-body.png to the bird layer

   ◆ mountains.png to the mountains layer

   The order of these layers is important because the layering adds a sense of depth. The mountains must be on the lowest layer because they are farthest in the background. The grass must be on the top layer because it is the closest to the viewer and creates the foreground.

There are two different ways to modify the Timeline by creating or converting frames. You can use the shortcut F-keys on your keyboard (such as F5 and F6). Or, you can use menu commands (such as Insert > Timeline > Keyframe). Because you create so many keyframes and frames when you animate, it is a typical and recommended workflow to use the shortcut F-keys. Using menu commands is not only awkward, but particularly time consuming for an animation workflow. When you're animating (or doing any Flash development), you'll find that you want to work quickly and efficiently. Both menu options and F-key equivalents will be used in Chapter 2. However, each subsequent chapter uses shortcut keys only.

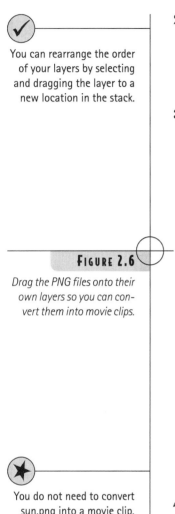

You can rearrange the order of your layers by selecting and dragging the layer to a new location in the stack.

FIGURE 2.6

Drag the PNG files onto their own layers so you can convert them into movie clips.

You do not need to convert sun.png into a movie clip. This image is not animated, and therefore does not need to be converted into a movie clip symbol.

2. Select each PNG image that you added to the Stage, and select Modify > Convert to Symbol (or press F8) to convert them into movie clips. Name each movie clip the same name as the PNG file (remove the .png extension). When you finish, you should have one movie clip on each layer.

3. The following process adds the bird-wing and bird-leg PNG files *inside* the bird-body movie clip. Double-click the bird-body movie clip to open the instance in symbol-editing mode. Create two new layers inside the movie clip by clicking the Insert Layer button, and rename the two layers **bird-wing** and **bird-leg**, respectively. Rename Layer 1 to **bird-body**. Drag the two PNG files to their respective layers.

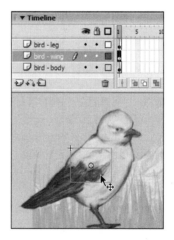

4. Inside the bird-body movie clip, select the bird-wing.png image and then select Modify > Convert to Symbol (or press F8) to convert it into a movie clip into a symbol. Then select the bird-leg.png image and convert it into a movie clip (select Modify > Convert to Symbol). Name each of these movie clips the same name as the PNG image (remove the .png extension).

5. Arrange the wing and leg so they are correctly positioned in relation to the bird's body (as shown in the figure following step 7).

6. Click Scene 1 in the Edit Bar to return to the main Stage from symbol-editing mode. Notice that the bird-body instance now appears with a leg and wing on the Stage.

7. Select the movie clips and drag them so they are arranged properly in a layout. You will tween the clouds, mountains, and grass layers from right to left; and you will tween the bird from left to right. Therefore, you should align the clouds, mountains, and grass to the left side of the Stage; and also place the bird near the bottom left of the Stage. Try to lay out the movie clips similar to the following figure. Save your changes before moving on to the next exercise.

FIGURE 2.7

Align all the movie clips so they form a layout that you can tween.

In the following exercises, you tween each of these movie clips so the scenery appears to be panning and the bird movie clip appears to be animating across the Stage.

CREATING MOTION TWEENS

The animation uses several motion tweens to achieve the effect of movement on the Stage. There are many properties that you can manipulate by using tools, the Timeline, or the Property inspector to create movement.

First of all, the Timeline has several tools that can help you when creating animation. Three buttons next to each layer let you show/ hide, lock/unlock, or show as outlines to change the view of the layer's content.

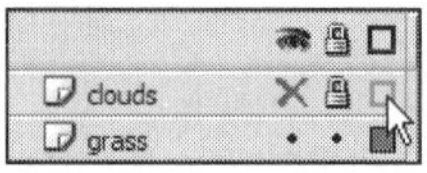

FIGURE 2.8

From left to right, the Show/Hide, Lock/Unlock and Show as outlines buttons in the Timeline.

◆ **Show/Hide:** Toggle the content between a visible and invisible.

◆ **Lock/Unlock:** Lock the layer so no content can be added to the Stage or modified on this particular layer.

◆ **Show as outlines:** Represent all content on the layer as an outline on the Stage. You can toggle between the actual view and the outline when you click this button.

Understanding motion guides

Motion guides let you specify a special path for an instance to animate along. A *motion guide* is a special layer in the Timeline that contains only a path that you want to use for your animation. Then you can specify a layer with an instance that uses the path to control its movement when you motion tween the instance, which then indents under the motion guide layer, as shown in the following figure.

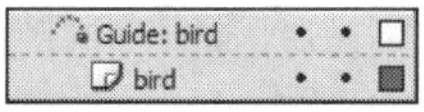

FIGURE 2.9

Guided layers are indented under a motion guide.

One or more layers can use a single motion guide layer to provide the path they animate along. These layers are called *guided layers*. You will create a motion guide in Exercise 4 that controls the motion of the bird-body movie clip.

Exercise 3: Adding tweens

In this exercise, you set up the Timeline for the animation. The animation is 40 frames long, and all the layers span across these frames. You will make changes in the position of the mountains, grass, and clouds movie clips on frame 40, so the animation spans between the two frames. You are still working with panning.fla in this example.

1. Select frame 40 of the clouds layer, and select Insert > Timeline > Keyframe (or press F6) to insert a new keyframe at frame 40 on the Timeline. After you make the selection or press F6, there

is a keyframe at frame 1 on this layer, and at frame 40. Gray-colored frames span between frames 1 and 40.

2. Repeat step 1 for the grass, bird, and mountains layers: select Insert > Timeline > Keyframe (or press F6) to insert a keyframe at frame 40 for each of these layers.

3. Select frame 40 of the sun layer, and select Insert > Timeline > Frame (or press F5) to insert a frame on the Timeline. The sun layer does not need a keyframe at frame 40 because you do not animate this instance. When you finish, all layers span between frames 1 and 40 on the Timeline, as shown in the following figure.

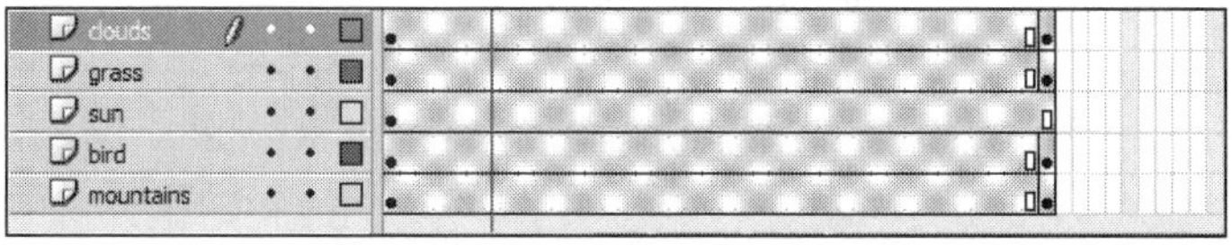

FIGURE 2.10

All frames span between frame 1 and 40.

4. Click the Lock button on the sun layer to lock the layer because you do not need to make any more changes to this layer. You cannot accidentally select or modify this layer when it is locked.

5. Double-click the bird-body movie clip. Repeat step 1 for the bird-wing and bird-leg movie clips: Select frame 40 and select Insert > Timeline > Keyframe (or press F6) to insert a keyframe for each of these layers. Select the bird-body layer and select Insert > Timeline > Frame (or press F5) to insert a frame on the Timeline (this graphic does not need to be animated inside the movie clip), and then lock the layer. Click Scene 1 on the Edit Bar to return to the main Timeline.

6. Select frame 40 of the clouds layer and make sure that the clouds movie clip is also selected. When it's selected, you see an outline appear around the movie clip.

7. After you select the clouds movie clip, move the instance approximately 50 pixels horizontally toward the left and 20 pixels vertically downward. To quickly move the instance, you can press and hold the Shift key while pressing the left-arrow key five times. Then, with the Shift key still pressed, press the down-arrow key two times.

If you have an instance that you want to appear only for a shorter timeframe, you have the frames span only for the duration that you want to see it on the Stage.

You can also use the Property inspector to modify the position of the instance by using X and Y coordinates. To move an instance beyond the left side of the Stage, use negative numbers. If your clouds are positioned at X: 0, Y: 0 coordinates on frame 1, you enter an X coordinate of **–50** and Y coordinate of **20** into the text fields in the Property inspector.

When the clouds animate, you will see them move toward the left and downward in a diagonal fashion.

8. When you finish animating the clouds layer, click the Lock button in the Timeline for the clouds layer.

9. Select frame 40 of the grass layer, and make sure that the instance is selected. This time, move the instance approximately 150 pixels horizontally toward the left. Do not move the grass vertically. To quickly move the instance, you can press and hold the Shift key while pressing the left-arrow key 15 times.

10. When you finish animating the grass layer, click the Lock button in the Timeline for the grass layer.

11. Select frame 40 of the mountains layer, and make sure that the instance is selected. Move the instance approximately 30 pixels horizontally toward the left. Do not move the mountains vertically. Press and hold the Shift key while pressing the left-arrow key three times to move the instance. When you finish, the instances on the Stage should look similar to the following figure.

FIGURE 2.11

When you click a Color control in the Tools panel, a color pop-up menu opens where you can select a swatch.

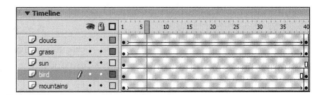

By moving the mountains fewer pixels than the grass, it means they appear to move more slowly. When you move an object in the background at a slower pace, it creates the illusion that it's further away or on the horizon. Because the grass moves quickly in the foreground, it appears to be closer to the viewer. Both of these techniques enhance the sense of realism.

12. Add motion tweens for each instance, like you did in Chapter 1. Select frame 1 of the clouds layer. Right-click (Windows) or Control-click (Macintosh) frame 1, and select Create Motion Tween from the context menu. Repeat these steps for the grass and mountains layers until you have motion tweens on all three frames. You see the frames change color, and an arrow appears between frame 1 and 40 to indicate the tween.

13. Click the playhead above the layers, and drag it between frames 1 and 40. You should see the three instances animate between the two frames. Save your changes (File > Save).

14. Select Control > Test Movie to view the animation in the test environment (Flash Player), which loops continuously. After the playhead reaches frame 40, it returns back to frame 1 because there is no action on frame 40 to stop the animation. You add the stop action and a button to control the animation in a following exercise. Close the SWF file when you finish testing the file.

You added animation for the environment, so it mostly pans horizontally toward the left at varying speeds. The differences in speed mimic how you might actually see items move in the far distance (or close to you if you were actually panning a scene using a video camera).

Exercise 4: Animating clips with motion guides

Although the environment around the bird is moving, you have yet to animate the bird. You need to add a motion guide to create customized movement for the bird tweening across the Stage, and you will also animate the wing and legs of the bird. Because the wing and leg are inside the bird-body movie clip, you can animate the entire character on the main Stage and then animate the movie clips nested inside the bird-body clip so both movie clips can animate simultaneously.

1. Select the bird layer in panning.fla and click the Add Motion Guide button to add a motion guide for the layer. The Add Motion Guide button is directly under the layer names in the Timeline (it has a red dotted curve above two small shapes). The bird layer indents beneath the new guide layer that you created.

2. Select frame 1 of the motion guide layer and then click the Pencil tool in the Tools panel. You will use the Pencil tool to draw the path for the motion guide.

3. In the Options area of the Tools panel, select Smooth from the Pencil mode pop-up menu. This mode helps you draw smooth, curved paths because Flash applies smoothing to the lines that you draw. If you do not want as much smoothing to be applied, choose Ink. Straighten mode straightens the paths that you draw, but isn't desirable for this particular animation.

4. On the Stage, draw a single path on the Stage similar to the one shown in the following figure:

Make sure that you have several curves, and that one of the curves toward the right half of the Stage is larger than the others.

5. Click the Selection tool in the Tools panel. Make sure that the Snap to Objects button is selected in the Tools panel (it looks like a magnet). When you select this button, it lets you snap the movie clip instance to motion guide paths you create.

The Free Transform tool allows you to rotate, skew, and resize a movie clip in addition to moving the snap ring.

6. Select the Free Transform tool in the Tools panel and then click the bird-body movie clip on the Stage. You see a large white circle in the middle of the movie clip, which is the *snap ring*. This ring is what you use to snap the movie clip to the path, and it's the location where the instance attaches to the path. By default the snap ring is in the middle of the movie clip, but you can move it around when you select the instance by using the Free Transform tool.

7. Move the snap ring near the bottom of the bird's feet, as shown in the following figure.

FIGURE 2.13

Move the snap ring so the bird's feet snap to the path you created previously.

8. Select frame 1 of the bird layer and click the Selection tool in the Tools panel. Select the movie clip by clicking the snap ring, and move the instance so the snap ring overlaps the *left end point* of the path you created. The snap ring increases in size to indicate the instance has snapped onto the path. When you see this happen, release the instance at that location.

9. Select frame 40 of the bird layer, and this time move the bird-body instance so the snap ring overlaps the *right end point* of the path you created. When the snap ring increases in size indicating the instance has snapped to the path, release the instance at that location.

10. Select frame 1 of the bird layer, and right-click (Windows) or Control-click (Macintosh) and select Create Motion Tween from the context menu. This creates a motion tween between frames 1 and 40 on the Timeline.

11. Determine what frames to animate the leg and wing in. Click the playhead above the layers, and drag it between frames 1 and 40. You should see the three instances and now the bird animates between the two frames. The bird should move along the path you just created.

    You probably added one large curve for the bird to follow. During this part of the animation, you will animate the leg

If you want to adjust the curve, then make sure that you have the layer containing the motion guide unlocked and then select the Selection tool. Move the tool close to the curve until you see the cursor change so there's a small curved line next to the arrow icon. The line must be unselected in order for the cursor to change. When the cursor changes, you can click and drag the curve to modify its size and shape.

and wing. While scrubbing the Timeline, write down what frame numbers this part of the curve spans across. In the following figure, the curve spans approximately between frames 20 and 30.

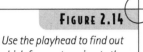

FIGURE 2.14

Use the playhead to find out which frames to animate the wing and legs in (this grass layer is hidden in this figure).

12. Double-click the bird-body movie clip to open the instance in symbol-editing mode and create motion tweens for the bird-wing and bird-leg layers. Select frame 1 of each layer, right-click (Windows) or Control-click (Macintosh), and select Create Motion Tween from the context menu, so each layer has a motion tween spanning between frames 1 and 40.

13. Select the first frame that you wrote down in step 11 in the bird-wing in the bird-wing layer. For example, for the Timeline shown in Figure 2.14, you would select frame 20 on the bird-wing layer. Select Insert > Timeline > Keyframe (or press F6) to insert a keyframe at this frame.

14. After you insert a keyframe for the first frame number you wrote down, select and insert a keyframe for the second keyframe you wrote down. For example, the bird-wing layer for the example shown in Figure 2.14 would have keyframes at frame 1, 20, 27, and 35.

15. Now, select a keyframe approximately between the two locations you determined in step 14 (which should be approximately in the middle of the large curve). After you select a keyframe that sits in-between the two keyframes you wrote down, select Insert > Timeline > Keyframe (or press F6).

This keyframe is about where you want the "change" to occur. The two keyframes you just created have the wing at the same original location. However, you want to change the wing so it animates from the original position to a new position, and then animates back to the original position.

16. Select the keyframe you created in step 15 and click the Free Transform tool in the Tools panel. Move the mouse over one of the four corners until you see the rotation icon, as shown in the following figure.

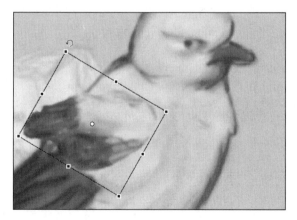

FIGURE 2.15

Rotate and move the wing using the Free Transform tool until it's positioned approximately like this.

Click and drag the movie clip until it's rotated about 30 degrees. Then click the center of the wing to move the wing until it's positioned approximately like the preceding figure. Click and drag the playhead to scrub the Timeline to test your animation.

17. Add keyframes to the bird-leg layer on exactly the same frames as the bird-wing layer. Select the keyframe that's over the "middle" of the curve, and (as you did in step 16) rotate and adjust the leg to animate it by using the Free Transform Tool. Your adjustments might look similar to the one in the following figure.

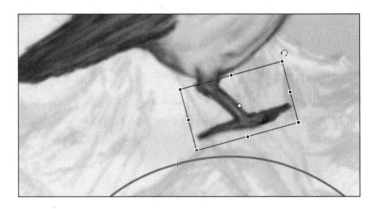

Click and drag the playhead to scrub the Timeline to test your animation.

18. Select Control > Test Movie to view the animation in the test environment (Flash Player), which loops continuously.

19. Close the SWF file to return to the authoring environment. If necessary, make adjustments to your animation by using the Selection or Free Transform tools. When you finish, click Scene 1 to return to the main Stage. Save your changes before moving on.

USING THE PROPERTY INSPECTOR

The Flash Property inspector is a useful, context-sensitive tool. When you select an object on the Stage, a frame, or a tool (in the Tools panel), the Property inspector updates to reflect your selection. Various relevant tools, text fields, buttons, sliders, and controls appear as a result, depending on that selection. You use the Property inspector to modify the properties, location, or instance name of a selected object. In some cases, you can modify properties over time by using keyframes and tweening. You can create the appearance of animation or movement over time using the Property inspector.

For example, you can change the color tint of a movie clip using the Property inspector and make it animate between the two tinted colors using a motion tween. Imagine that you have a movie clip on frame 1 that is orange. If you want the movie clip to tween between orange and another color by frame 10, you need to create a keyframe on frame 10. You select the movie clip located at frame 10 and then select Tint from the Color pop-up menu in the Property inspector, as shown in the following figure.

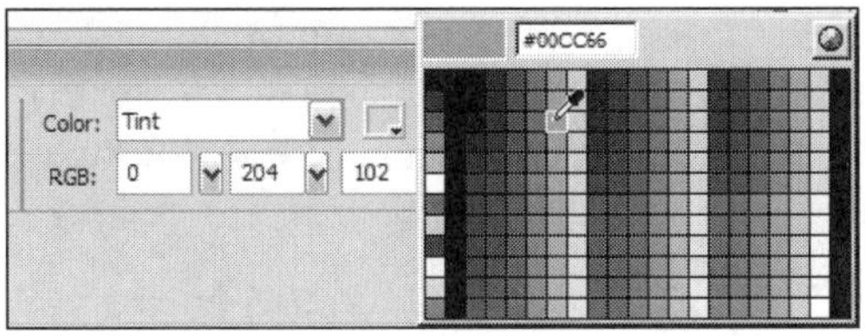

FIGURE 2.17

Selecting an option from the Color pop-up menu.

After you select the Tint option, a number of additional options appear in the Property inspector. You can use these options to select a color to tint the orange movie clip by frame 10. After you select a color for the keyframe at frame 10, you can create a motion tween between the two frames, and the color animates when the SWF file plays. Exercise 5 shows you a variety of ways to create animation by using the Property inspector.

Understanding motion tween properties

When you select a *frame* on the Timeline (not an instance), you can choose to modify properties of the motion tween itself by using the Property inspector. For any motion tween in your Flash document, select a frame and open the Property inspector (Window > Properties). Changing the properties of a tween is different from changing the properties of an instance. Instead of modifying the appearance of the instance itself, you modify the way the motion tween animates (for example, its change in speed and rotation).

First of all, if you are scaling an object in your motion tween, make sure that Scale is selected in the Property inspector.

Another choice in the Property inspector for a motion tween is to *ease in* or *ease out*. Ease in and ease out are ways to soften the movement in your animations in a naturalistic way. As an object moves, it usually accelerates from a resting position or slows down instead of stopping instantly. When you ease-in, you accelerate the object gradually so it speeds up. When you ease-out, you slow an object down until it stops.

The Property inspector also enables you to add rotation to the motion tween so the instance that it is tweening rotates. To do this, choose Auto, CW (clockwise) or CCW (counter-clockwise) from the Rotation pop-up menu. Select None for no rotation or choose Auto to rotate the object one time in the direction that requires the least amount of rotation.

Exercise 5: Adding properties

As discussed, there are many properties you can animate when motion tweening movie clips in a SWF file. In this exercise, you fade the clouds movie clip, add scaling and easing to the bird movie clip, tint the grass movie clip, and modify the brightness of the mountains movie clip.

1. Open the Property inspector (Window > Properties) and then select the instance on the Stage at frame 40.

2. In the Property inspector, select Alpha from the Color pop-up menu. A text field and slider bar appears in the Property inspector, which you use to change the alpha of the instance, which refers to the amount of transparency the object has. Drag the slider to set the alpha level to 0.

3. Click and drag the playhead above the Timeline to scrub between frames 1 and 40, and notice how the clouds gradually fade out as they motion tween across the Stage.

4. Select the bird-body movie clip on the Stage at frame 40, and then select the Free Transform tool in the Tools panel. Mouse over one of the corner handles of the movie clip until you see a double-ended arrow cursor, as shown in the following figure.

FIGURE 2.19

Scale the bird image using the Free Transform tool.

Click and drag the handle toward the center of the instance while you press and hold the Shift key. Make the instance only slightly smaller, which makes the bird appear as if it is moving away into the distance. Make sure that the Scale check box is selected in the Property inspector when you select one of the motion tween frames on the bird layer.

5. Select frame 1 of the bird layer and find the text field next to Ease in the Property inspector. Enter **100** into the text field so the movie clip eases out. The bird animation will slow down gradually at the end of the tween, instead of coming to an abrupt stop.

6. Now select the grass movie clip on frame 1. In the Property inspector, select Tint from the Color pop-up menu. Several color controls appear after you select this option, and you can choose a color to tint the grass. Select a darker green color, and then enter **25** into the Tint Amount text field.

✓ The Snap to Objects button causes the rotation to snap to set degrees. You can make subtle changes if you disable the Snap to Objects button in the Tools panel. Disable the Snap to Objects button if necessary.

FIGURE 2.20

Tint the grass movie clip using the Property inspector.

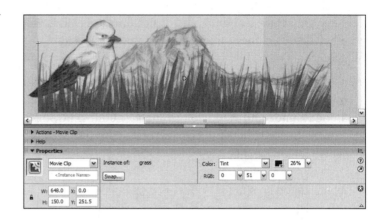

7. Select Control > Test Movie to test the animation in the test environment. You should be able to see the bird movie clip animating across the Stage, decreasing in size, and slowing down toward the end. The ease-out effect will be very subtle. You will also see the grass movie clip tween from a darker to lighter green between frames 1 and 40.

    Now that you have used most of the movie clip tweening properties, you should add a button to the document that controls the overall animation. Save your changes before proceeding to the next exercise.

ADDING BASIC SCRIPTS

In Chapter 1's project you created a button that stopped and played the SWF file. You used ActionScript to add some functionality to that button. ActionScript can be added to a SWF file to add all sorts of functionality, which you will learn about beginning in Chapter 6. In this project, you will add an action that controls the Timeline, instead of allowing the user to specify when the animation starts or stops. To do this, you add the stop action to the Timeline, instead of putting it within the button code. Then, you will create a button, much like in the project in Chapter 1, which plays the animation from frame 1 when the user clicks the button.

Exercise 6: Adding stop and a replay button

First, you add an action directly to the Timeline, and then you will create a button and add ActionScript to the Timeline that controls the button.

1. Select the top layer in the Timeline (which should be a layer called *clouds*), and click the Insert Layer button two times. Double-click the name of the first new layer, and type **button**. Double-click the name of the second layer, and type **actions**.

2. Open the Components panel (Window > Development panels > Components) and find the Button component, which is inside a folder called UI Components. Components are reusable assets (essentially movie clips) that designers and developers use to quickly add functionality to SWF files. You do not use many components during this book because you typically use your own graphics that are created in Flash or imported from other graphics programs.

3. Drag the Button component from the Components panel onto the button layer. Position it in the lower-right corner of the Stage, as shown in Figure 2.21. The button should span across all 40 frames because empty frames were added automatically when you inserted the new layer in step 1.

4. Open the Property inspector (Window > Properties) and select the Parameters tab. There are several options available in a list, which are used to control the appearance and functionality of the component. Select the text Button (next to the *label* heading) and delete it. Type **replay**.

5. Still in the Property inspector, type the following into the <Instance Name> text field: **replay_btn**.

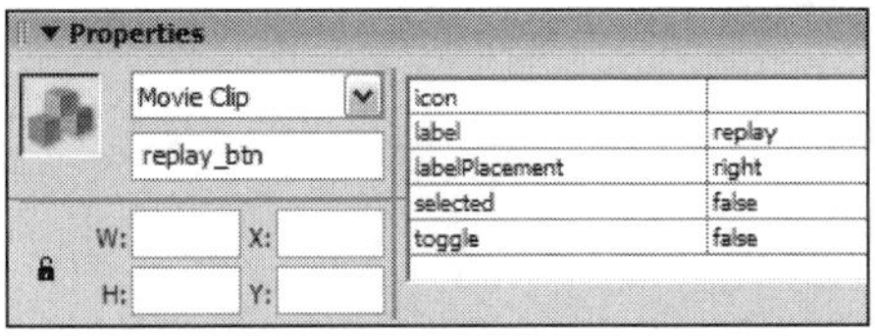

FIGURE 2.21

Using a component to add instant functionality.

6. Select the bird-body movie clip and type the following into the <Instance Name> text field in the Property inspector: **bird_mc**. Because the movie clip has an instance name, you can control it by using ActionScript.

7. Select the keyframe on frame 1 of the actions layer and open the Actions panel (Window > Development panels > Actions). Enter the following ActionScript:

```
replay_btn.onRelease = function(){
  gotoAndPlay(1);
  bird_mc.gotoAndPlay(1);
};
```

This code sends the playhead back to frame 1 and plays the animation again. Essentially, it says the following: "When the user clicks and releases the replay button, go to frame 1 of the main Timeline and play it. Also play the bird_mc movie clip's Timeline from frame 1."

8. Create a keyframe on frame 40 of the actions layer by selecting the frame and then select Insert > Timeline > Keyframe (or press F6). Open the Actions panel again, and enter the following line of code:

```
stop();
```

This ActionScript stops the animation at the end: frame 40. The user must determine whether it is replayed from frame 1 by clicking the button.

9. Double-click the bird-body instance and select the top layer. Click the Insert Layer button on the Timeline to create a new layer. Rename this layer **actions**.

10. Create a keyframe on frame 40 of the actions layer by selecting the frame and then selecting Insert > Timeline > Keyframe (or press F6). Open the Actions panel again, and enter the following line of code:

```
stop();
```

This ActionScript stops the animation inside the bird-body movie clip at frame 40. Therefore, the movie clip also stops at the end of the animation until the user clicks the replay button.

11. Finally, select Control > Test Movie to test the SWF file's animation. Click the replay button after the animation stops at the end. When you do so, the animation plays again and stops at frame 40 until you click the button. If you click the button during the animation, it returns to frame 1 and plays the animation from the start. Save the changes you have made to the document (File > Save).

TESTING AND PUBLISHING

When you have completed the animation and tested the SWF file during the project's progress, you might notice things that you want to change. By now, you should be relatively happy with the animation because you have tested and fixed or modified the tweens to your liking during each exercise. However, you might want the animation to run slightly faster or smoother. To do so, you can increase the frame rate as you did in the first project. Select Modify > Document and change the frame rate to 15. If you change this number so it is too high, your animation plays too quickly. By raising the frame rate and speeding up the animation, you eventually end up with a higher file size: You have to add more content to the SWF file to meet the same length of animation (in seconds).

Another issue you might notice, particularly if you are using Windows, is that the animation extends beyond the borders of the Stage instead of the areas around the edge of the Stage. You need to publish the file to an HTML browser window to see the animation play while appearing "cropped." To view the animation in a browser window, select File > Publish Preview > HTML. This procedure opens a browser window automatically, which displays the animation within the proper boundaries. On Macintosh, the document plays in a sized SWF file when tested, so this step should be unnecessary unless you want to see what the animation looks like in a browser.

FIGURE 2.22

Viewing the animation with its proper dimensions.

MOVING ON

You have now completed a basic panning scene. It's easy to elaborate on this project by adding additional items to the scene to pan. Panning can take on many different looks. You might try zooming into a character, as well. Select the instances you want to zoom into (probably the entire scene), and then scale the instances using the Free Transform tool. Select multiple instances by pressing the Shift key and then clicking each instance using the mouse. Insert a new keyframe, and then scale the instances larger to enlarge them.,using the Free Transform tool. Then insert a motion tween between the two keyframes so the instances appear to zoom in by scaling larger. You will also use this effect in Chapter 5 when you create a character information.

There are many other kinds of motion tweens that you can create. There is simply not enough room in this book to detail all of the different kinds of motion tween that you can create. Try experimenting further with the easing and color properties in the Property inspector. Select an instance and change the properties between two keyframes, and then insert a motion tween. Try tweening brightness, alpha and colors to create interesting transitions between two states. For example, you can make instances appear to "flash" when you make a brightness tween.

FIGURE 3.A

FIGURE 3.B

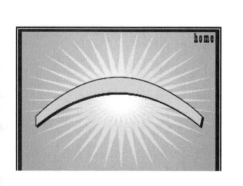

FIGURE 3.C

What You Learn

▶ About creating shape tweens

▶ How to use vector drawing tools

▶ About using color in your graphics

▶ How to edit your graphics

▶ How to align objects on the Stage

▶ How to use guides and the grid

▶ How to animate with shape hints

Lesson Files

Start:

03/start/star.ai

03/start/star.png

Finish:

03/complete/interface.fla

03/complete/interfa*Figure*.

3

CREATING SHAPE TWEENS

MOTION TWEENS AND SHAPE tweens go hand in hand. They help you add movement, animation and graphic effects in your SWF files. However, shape tweens enable you to create effects that are entirely different from those you can create with motion tweens. And shape tweening can be more complex and involved to work with at times, but let you achieve the results you want to see. The outcome can be worth the extra effort though: Many of the bouncy animations, moving lines, and growing shapes are all created using shape tweens.

You create an animated interface in Project 3, which uses several different kinds of tweens to produce a simple website. You create the menu and content for several different pages. Animation forms the basis of the menu and effects for the border and title areas of the site.

Website: www.FLAnimation.com/chapters/03

If you create complex shape tweens, you might need to use shape hints to control the animation. Shape hints are discussed later in this chapter, in the section called "Animating with Shape Hints."

You can apply easing to shape tweens just as you added to the motion tweens in Chapter 2 to create a natural feeling to the motion.

Understanding Shape Tweens

You use shape tweens to morph shapes and lines in Flash MX 2004. As you learned in the last chapter, motion tweens change the location or appearance of an object. Shape tweens can actually modify the shape of the drawing itself, however. The shapes and lines that you morph must be vector drawings in a SWF file that you create using the drawing tools in Flash, or vectors in another program such as Adobe Illustrator or Macromedia FreeHand. You might make your vector drawings by using a mouse, or you might use a graphics tablet. In the following section, "Using the Drawing Tools," you learn about which drawing tools are available in Flash.

To create a shape tween, you draw one shape on the Stage; later on, you draw a second shape on the same layer. Flash calculates and creates the animation between those two points on the Timeline, like a motion tween. Although you can shape tween one or more shapes, tweening a single shape typically yields the best results. If you choose to tween multiple shapes together, they must be on the same layer. To tween text or bitmaps, you must "break apart" the text or image first, so it is represented as raw data. You use this command later in Exercise 9.

In the following sections, you explore the drawing tools in Flash that you need to create the vector drawings you will modify using shape tweens.

Using the Drawing Tools

The drawing tools in Flash let you create a variety of simple to complex vector lines, shapes, and brush strokes. There are many properties available that you can manipulate to construct original and creative designs without leaving Flash. For example, you can skew objects to create depth or use brush modifiers with a graphics tablet that respond to the pressure you apply with a stylus.

As discussed in Chapter 2, vectors are mathematical calculations of curves, lines, color, and position. Vectors are *resolution-independent*, which means that you can scale the vector graphic up or down (larger or smaller) without losing quality. When you scale a bitmap, you typically see jagged edges caused by the scaling. However, vectors remain clear, smooth, and accurate regardless of scale. This is why vector graphics in Flash are a great medium for animation: you can tween shapes larger and smaller, yet retain a high level of quality and small file size. Therefore, vectors are great for the web.

About strokes and fills

When you draw a shape in Flash, it has two parts: a *stroke* and a *fill*. The stroke defines the outline around the fill shape or a line, and the fill is the color (or lack thereof) that is inside a closed or open shape. An example of a closed shape is a circle, whereas an open shape might be a curved line. A shape might only have a stroke *or* a fill.

FIGURE 3.1

A shape can be open or closed, and have a stroke or a fill.

The stroke can be of varying thickness and color, and might also have a style (such as dashes or waves). You can set properties using the Property inspector.

You can use lines to create closed or open shapes. Some tools (such as the Oval, Rectangle, and Paint Bucket) help you create filled shapes. When you create a shape with a fill and stroke, the two elements are not grouped together.

Remember that using line styles consumes a lot of processor power to render the line on the Stage. For this reason, use special line styles sparingly.

When you have multiple drawings on the same layer, you can use a fill to cut away another fill or use a stroke to divide a fill into two separate regions. For example, create a shape with a fill on the Stage and then draw a differently colored stroke across that shape on the same layer. You can select the fill on either side of the stroke and separate it from the shape, as shown in the following figure.

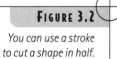

FIGURE 3.2

You can use a stroke to cut a shape in half.

To use a hairline stroke, set the thickness in the Property inspector to hairline. A *hairline stroke* is a very thin line that does not grow in thickness when you scale or zoom it in. Other strokes appear larger if you zoom them in (this includes scaling a shape using animation).

All fills or strokes that touch that have the same color are selected as a single element on the Stage; however, if you draw two shapes that are different colors on the same layer and then move one over top of the other, the fill underneath is lost. You can use this feature to "cut away" parts of a shape. For example, you might have a red and blue circle on a layer, and then overlap the red circle over the blue circle. If you select and move the red circle, you are left with a blue crescent similar to the one in the following figure.

FIGURE 3.3

Overlapping shapes on the same layer results in pieces being cut away and "removed" from another shape.

►► USING THE SELECTION TOOLS

There are several tools in Flash that you can use to make selections. You have used the Selection tool already. You can also use the Lasso tool to draw lines around objects to select them, and the Lasso has modifiers that let you select objects by drawing lines freehand, or by clicking points to make a straight edge shape around objects in "polygon" mode. The Lasso also has a Magic Wand modifier that lets you select a single color or similar adjoining colors from vector drawings or bitmap images that have been broken apart. When you have the Lasso selected, you can set the tolerance properties for the magic wand by clicking the Magic Wand Properties button in the Options area of the Tools panel.

A *gradient* is a gradual transition between colors, and you can create gradients as a fill. Gradients add more file size to your documents than solid colors do, and they also take more computer processing power to render. If you use gradients in your files, you should create them in Flash to reduce the file size.

If you don't want to change the shapes you draw using these techniques, separate your graphics onto their own layers. If you do this, shapes don't join or they separate when they overlap or intersect.

Changing drawing settings

When you set up Flash, you can make specific settings to control how the drawing tools work. These settings can change how the drawing tools make strokes, and how objects snap to each other or guides. Some of these tolerance settings depend on how zoomed in the Stage is or the monitor's resolution. Settings can be turned on or off as well. To access the preferences for drawing tools, select Edit > Preferences (Windows) or Flash/Flash Professional > Preferences (Macintosh). When the Preferences dialog box opens, select the Editing tab to access the drawing settings.

◆ **Connect lines:** Controls three functionalities in Flash. The preference sets how close a line end has to be drawn to another line before they snap together. The setting also controls how vertical or horizontal a line has to be before it's drawn exactly vertical or horizontal when you create it. Finally, the setting controls how close objects must be before they snap to each other when you have Snap to Objects enabled.

◆ **Smooth curves:** Controls the amount of smoothing that is applied to curved lines when you have the Straighten or Smooth modifiers enabled for the Pencil tool. When you set this option to "rough," curves are more accurately rendered to those you draw.

◆ **Recognize lines:** Sets how straight a line has to be drawn before Flash renders it perfectly straight.

◆ **Recognize shapes:** Controls the amount of precision that's necessary before a common shape (circle, rectangle, oval and square) is rendered perfectly when you draw shapes on the Stage using the Brush or Pencil. This setting controls the level of accuracy that is necessary before this happens. If you draw a shape that's similar to a rectangle, Flash changes it into a perfect rectangle.

◆ **Click accuracy:** Sets how close the mouse pointer must be before you select the object.

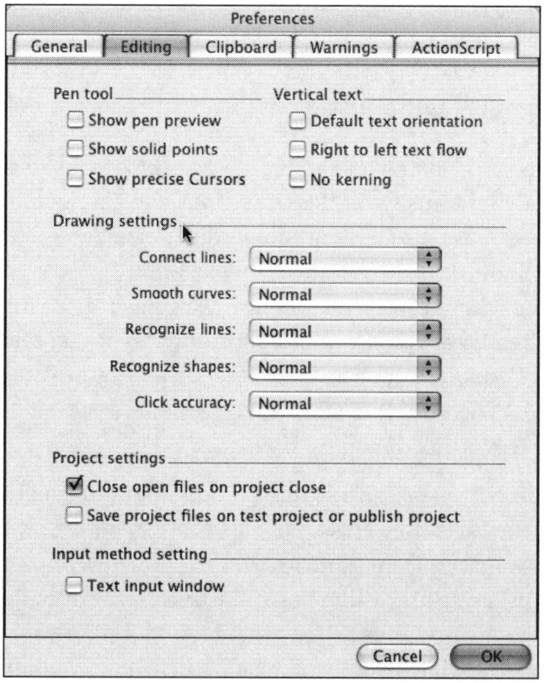

FIGURE 3.4

You can find the drawing preferences under the Editing tab in the Preferences dialog box.

You can also modify the drawings you make by choosing Modify > Shape > Optimize. This will smooth curved segments and also reduce vector points. Doing this helps optimize the SWF file by removing data that lowers file size and improves performance.

Changing drawing modifiers

The options for drawing tools also extend to the Tools panel and Property inspector. After you make settings in the Preferences dialog box, you can set *modifiers* after you select a tool. Modifiers are usually buttons and values that you set each time you draw with a particular tool. You find many of these modifiers in the Options area of the Tools panel.

◆ **Rectangle:** Use the modifier in the Tools panel Options area to toggle rounded edges on and off. When the modifier is turned on, the four corners round to the number of pixels that you specify.

◆ **Pencil:** Select from several different drawing modes in the Options area of the Tools panel. Choose Straighten to draw straight lines and convert approximate shapes to perfect ovals, circles, rectangles, squares and triangles. Select Smooth to draw smooth lines, and choose Ink to draw lines only with minor smoothing applied.

◆ **Brush:** Modifiers let you choose a brush size and shape from two pop-up menus in the Options area of the Tools panel. If you use a graphics tablet that is compatible with Flash (for example, Wacom tablets), you can also apply the pressure and tilt modifiers. The Pressure modifier varies the width of the brush stroke depending on the pressure you apply to the tablet, and the Tilt modifier changes the angle of the brush stroke. The Brush Mode modifier lets you select among several different ways in which the brush fills objects on the canvas. For information on the Lock Fill modifier, see the description for Paint Bucket.

◆ **PolyStar:** If you select this tool, click the Options button in the Property inspector. Select Polygon or Start to choose a shape the tool will create and a number of sides for the shape. For Star Point Size, you can enter a value between 0 and 1 for the star's depth.

FIGURE 3.5

You can select drawing modifiers in the Options area of the Tools panel. These modifiers are for the Brush tool.

◆ **Paint Bucket:** The gap size modifier lets you choose Don't Close Gaps to close gaps manually before you fill the shape. Or, you can select a close option so Flash fills shapes even if they have small gaps in the drawing. Large gaps usually have to be closed or made smaller before the shape can be filled. If you select the Lock Fill modifier, all the objects you paint on the Stage share the same fill. This means if you select this modifier and use a gradient or bitmap fill, the same gradient spans across all of the objects as shown in the following figure.

◆ **Free Transform:** Select the Rotate and Skew or Scale modifiers to modify the object's appearance after you select an object using the Free Transform tool. If you select a raw graphic, you can additionally use the Distort and Envelope modifiers to change the graphic.

Using colors in your graphics

You already chose colors to use in earlier exercises—specifically for the background of your documents. When you select colors, you choose them from a palette, or you enter a hexadecimal value. You also select colors for fills and strokes. There are different kinds of palettes you can use, or you can create your own. There are several different parts of the Flash workspace in which you can select colors to use. You can select different palettes from the Color Mixer panel

(Window > Design panels > Color Mixer), and you can add custom colors to a palette or remove colors using the Color Mixer panel. To add a color to a palette, choose a color in your work or on the desktop by using the Eyedropper tool, and select Add Swatch from the panel's Options menu (the button in the upper right corner of the panel opens this menu).

You can define colors in several different ways, which are called *color modes*. A color mode is a way of defining a color—so you can describe or represent a single color in several different ways, depending on the color mode you use. You can switch between the modes using the Color Mixer panel's Options menu. You can use these color modes in Flash:

◆ **RGB (Red, Green, Blue):** Adds three double-digit numerical values to define a color.

◆ **HSB (Hue, Saturation, Brightness):** Uses a value for the degree of rotation on the color wheel, and percentages for saturation and brightness.

◆ **Hexadecimal:** Uses a base-16 system, which is a combination of six numbers and letters.

You might be familiar with the hexadecimal color mode if you have written HTML because it is the standard color mode used on the Web. It is the color mode you will use in this book as well.

If you select a fill color using the Eyedropper tool, you can apply that new color only to other fills. If you select a stroke color, the selected color can only be applied to other strokes.

▶ ▶ THE EYEDROPPER TOOL

Use the Eyedropper tool to select colors in your document or on the desktop to use in your work—select the tool and then click a color. You can use the Eyedropper to select colors in a palette, on the Stage, or on the desktop; and, you might use it to replace the currently selected color. You can use the Eyedropper to help match colors with one another or quickly pick up a color from a layout you designed in Photoshop or Fireworks. To select colors using the Eyedropper outside of the Flash authoring environment, click a color control square in the Tools panel, but do not release the mouse button when you drag the cursor. Move the Eyedropper anywhere on the desktop. When you find the color you want, release the mouse button, and the Eyedropper selects the color you released the mouse button over.

Editing shapes

You can set and modify the color of the stroke and fill using the color controls in the Tools panel, and several properties of a shape using the Property inspector. For example, you can use the Eyedropper to select a new color and replace a fill. Or, you can use the Ink Bottle tool to apply a new stroke or a new stroke color to a fill on the Stage.

To change the properties of a vector graphic, you need to select it so there is a cross-hatch over the shape. Click the Selection tool in the Tools panel, and then click the fill or stroke to select it. Double-click the shape's fill to select both the fill and stroke. Double-click a stroke to select all sides of a stroke that has multiple sides.

If you select an object and see a bounding box around the selection, you need to double-click the object to edit the symbol directly. You can then move the object around the Stage or change its properties in the Property inspector.

When you want to change the shape of an object, such as bending a line or moving a point, you then need to *deselect* the object and move the cursor near a corner of the shape until a special cursor appears, as shown in the following figures.

FIGURE 3.6

Special cursors mean you can change the dimensions of a shape or the curve of a line or side.

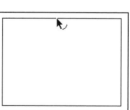

When you see the special cursor, you can click and drag the point or line to change the drawing's shape and dimensions, or change a straight line into a curved one. Move the cursor over an edge (not a corner) to change it into a curved line.

When adding a fill to a shape, you can use the Options area in the Tools panel to make settings about how large the gaps in an open or closed shape can be.

▶ ▶ **GROUPING DRAWINGS**

If you want to change several objects or drawings as a single entity, or move them around the Stage as such, you need to group them. To group objects, you need to select them on the Stage and then select Modify > Group. Grouped objects do not behave like a symbol, so they are not added to the Library. Therefore, if you need to reuse these grouped items in your document you should change them into a graphic or movie clip symbol instead.

Using guides, snapping, and alignment

When you lay out an interface, it is particularly important to be able to align objects to each other or at specific locations on the Stage. One of the most important tools is *snapping*. In Chapter 2, you made sure that snapping was turned on so you could add an object to a motion guide. This meant that the object could easily attach to the path. Flash has several tools available to help you accurately place objects on the Stage, as well as snap them to each other.

First, you should make sure that you enable snapping in the authoring environment. Select one or more options from the View > Snapping submenu or click the Snap to Objects button in the Tools panel. As you can see, there are several options for different kinds of snapping in the authoring environment.

To add guides to the Stage, you need to view rulers (View > Rulers) and then click and drag from the horizontal or vertical rulers. Green lines represent guides on the Stage, and objects can snap to these lines. Guides are useful for tasks such as aligning objects and measuring. You can hide/view, clear, lock/unlock, or edit guides by selecting an option from the View > Guides submenu.

When you enable Snap Alignment (View > Snapping > Snap Align), you see dotted lines on the Stage when you drag an object. The lines appear to show you the object's relation to other objects on the

If you do not want to accidentally move guides on the Stage, make sure that you lock them (View > Guides > Lock Guides).

Stage. You can set the number of pixels where this line appears. If you set the feature to Horizontal Center alignment, the dotted line appears when the objects have their center vertices aligned. Otherwise, the lines appear when the edges are aligned and a specified number of pixels apart. You can make these settings by selecting View > Snapping > Edit Snap Align.

FIGURE 3.7

Dotted lines appear when you use snap alignment. You can use these lines to help you easily align objects to each other.

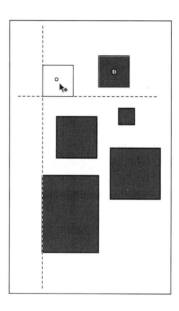

You can align objects with each other using *object snapping*, which lets you snap an object directly to another object's edge. Or, you can snap objects to a guide or the grid. When you have the Snap to Objects modifier selected in the Tools panel, you see a snap ring change to a larger ring when the object will snap to another object. (This occurred in Chapter 2 when you snapped an object to a motion guide.)

Finally, you can use *pixel snapping* to snap objects to actual pixels or lines on the Stage. Objects snap to a pixel grid on the Stage, which is visible if you magnify the Stage by 400% or greater. Select View > Snapping > Snap to Pixels to enable this option.

The Align panel (Window > Design Panels > Align) helps you align, distribute, or resize objects with each other or with the Stage. If you want to align several buttons with each other, select all the buttons you want to align and then click one of the Align buttons in the top row of the Align panel. You can also distribute and space objects in relation to each other by using the many buttons in this panel.

Aligning objects and layout is important when you are creating interfaces and graphics. Practice using these tools in Flash to help you gain the precision that is often necessary when animating and laying out an interface.

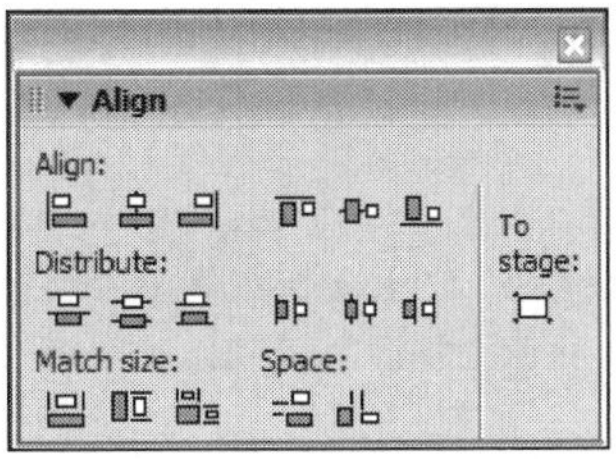

FIGURE 3.8

The Align panel has a large number of buttons that help you align and distribute objects on the Stage.

PROJECT 3: CREATING AN ANIMATED INTERFACE

Now that you have run through the various tools you can use to create and organize an interface, you are ready to create a simple Flash document that is based on animation. This project uses shape tweens and motion tweens to create a simple user interface.

Open the final SWF called interface.swf, or go to www.FLAnimation.com/chapters/03 and take a look at the finished version of the animation you create in this chapter. Several parts of this file use animation: the title area that holds the name of each page, the border, and several buttons at the bottom of the interface.

Remember to save the files for this chapter on the CD-ROM to your hard drive before opening or importing the content into Flash.

Exercise 1: Creating the layout

The layout for this site is relatively simple, but it does take some work to set up. The layout consists of a gradient that you create in Flash and an Illustrator AI vector drawing that you import into the FLA file.

1. Create a new FLA document, and select File > Save As to name the file. Save the new file as **interface.fla** in a new directory on your hard drive. You will use the file that you create for this chapter in a project for another chapter.

   Make sure that Snap to Objects and Snap Align are enabled (a check mark appears next to View > Snapping > Snap to Objects and Snap Align when you enable them).

2. Click the Stage, and select Modify > Document to open the Document Properties dialog box. Change your settings to the following values, and click OK when you finish.

   ◆ Change the width to **300 px**.

   ◆ Change the height to **500 px**.

   ◆ Change the background color to **black**. (Click the color control and select a black swatch from the color pop-up.)

   ◆ Change the frame rate to **15** fps.

3. Rename Layer 1 and create a new layer. Double-click Layer 1 and type **background** to rename the layer. Click the Insert Layer button on the Timeline, and rename the new layer that you create to **star**.

4. Select the Rectangle tool in the Tools panel, and then open the Color Mixer panel (Window > Design Panels > Color Mixer). Select Radial from the Fill Style pop-up menu, and you see a gradient definition bar appear with a default transition between black and white. Click the left pointer (directly below the gradient definition bar: it's black), and then click the color control in the upper-left corner of the panel.

FIGURE 3.9

Selecting colors for a gradient in the Color Mixer panel.

5. Type **#CEE4F4** into the color pop-up menu, and press Enter (Windows) or Return (Macintosh). Back in the Color Mixer panel, click the color pointer to the right (directly below the gradient bar; this one's white) and click the color control again. This time, type the hexadecimal **#6BA8E2** into the color pop-up menu. Now the gradient transitions between darker and lighter shades of blue.

6. Create a rectangle without a stroke. Select frame 1 on the background layer. In the Tools panel, click the pencil icon next to the stroke color control, and then click the No Color button (the button beneath the two color controls that's a white square with a red line through it). Then click and drag the Rectangle tool on the Stage to create a rectangle that's approximately the same size as the Stage (similar to the large rectangle in Figure 3.1).

7. Modify the gradient graphic so the radial gradient appears at the top of the image. Click the Paint Bucket tool in the Tools panel. Then click near the top of the rectangle you just created, as shown in the following figure.

   This moves the radial gradient so the center of the gradient appears near the top of the shape, instead of at the center (the default location).

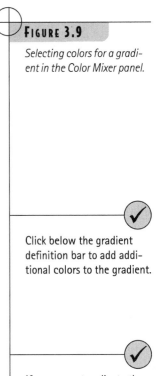

Click below the gradient definition bar to add additional colors to the gradient.

If you cannot replicate the gradient exactly as shown in Figure 3.10 when you click the Stage, then use the Fill Transform tool to modify the location of the gradient. Select the tool in the Tools panel, and then click the gradient on the Stage. Then, click and drag the handle (a square) to resize the gradient.

FIGURE 3.10

Select the Paint Bucket tool and click near the top of the rectangle to move the center of the radial gradient.

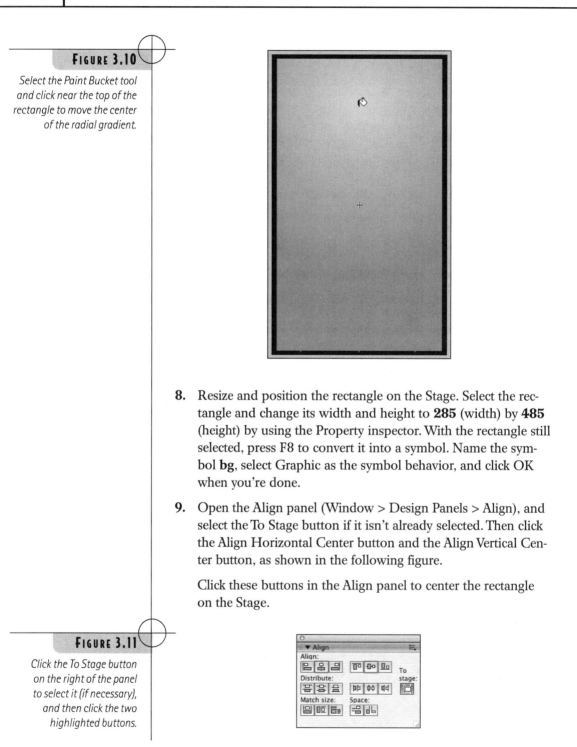

8. Resize and position the rectangle on the Stage. Select the rectangle and change its width and height to **285** (width) by **485** (height) by using the Property inspector. With the rectangle still selected, press F8 to convert it into a symbol. Name the symbol **bg**, select Graphic as the symbol behavior, and click OK when you're done.

9. Open the Align panel (Window > Design Panels > Align), and select the To Stage button if it isn't already selected. Then click the Align Horizontal Center button and the Align Vertical Center button, as shown in the following figure.

   Click these buttons in the Align panel to center the rectangle on the Stage.

FIGURE 3.11

Click the To Stage button on the right of the panel to select it (if necessary), and then click the two highlighted buttons.

10. Import the PNG file called star.ai from the chapter's start files on your hard drive. Select File > Import > Import to Library and choose 03/start/star.ai. This graphic was created by using Illustrator (which uses the extension AI for its native files), but you do not need Illustrator to import the file into Flash.

When you import the AI file, a dialog box appears where you can adjust the settings of how the file imports. Click OK to accept the default options, because the file you are importing does not have multiple frames, layers, or pages.

After you import the image, you see a graphic symbol called star.ai in the Library.

11. Select the star layer. Drag the star.ai symbol onto the Stage and position the image near the top of the interface. Select the Free Transform tool and click the graphic. Scale the graphic by using the handles that appear around the bounding box, so the graphic does not overlap the black borders of the interface. Feel free to make the image slightly narrower, as shown in the following graphic:

Some complex Illustrator drawings or filters might not import well (or at all) as vectors. If this occurs, try exporting the image as a PNG file from Illustrator and importing the raster image. You can also rasterize the image using Flash's import dialog box, but sometimes you don't maintain the quality doing this, and you see better results exporting a PNG from Illustrator. A PNG file has been provided on the CD-ROM if you prefer to use this format.

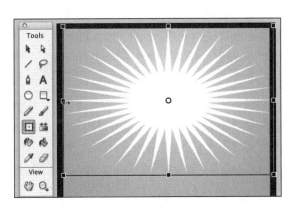

FIGURE 3.12

Modify the shape of the star graphic using the Free Transform tool.

12. Change the transparency of star.ai. Select the graphic instance on the Stage, and open the Property inspector (Window > Properties). Select Alpha from the Color pop-up menu, and then type **30%** into the text field that appears. This means that the star graphic is mostly transparent and can blend in with the radial gradient you created earlier in this exercise.

For a quick tutorial on how to create the star pattern that you import into the FLA, go to the book's website at: www.FLAnimation .com/tutorials. Even though it's in Illustrator, it's surprisingly easy to do.

FIGURE 3.13

Make the star slightly transparent, so you can see the gradient though the star.

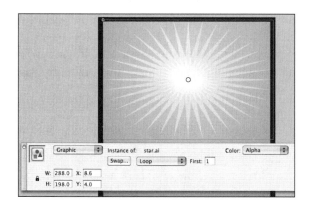

✓ Although it would be possible to animate this star graphic, it would be particularly processor-intensive. The SWF file needs to make many calculations to render out an animated transparent graphic that's placed over a gradient. Creating an effect like this is fine when they are limited in your SWF file, but there are several other animations you create in this particular interface. Therefore, the star graphic will remain stationary for now.

13. Lock the background and star layers when you are finished editing them. Click the Lock button on each layer, which is to the right of the layer's name on the Timeline.

14. Select the topmost layer (star), and create two new layers by clicking the Insert Layer button on the Timeline. Rename the top layer **actions** and the second layer **labels**. Lock both of these layers when you finish renaming them.

Now you have completed setting up the FLA document and have added a background for the interface. The next step is to create some animation that will be used for the menu system. Save your changes (File > Save) before moving on to the following exercise.

▶ ▶ USING GRAPHIC SYMBOLS

When you use bitmap images in a FLA file, you can either drag the bitmap directly on the Stage, or convert it into a Graphic symbol. Remember, if you need to take advantage of the functionality of a symbol (such as changing properties in the Property inspector or swapping the bitmap at a later time). Because you are just using the bitmap once, you do not need to change it to a Graphic symbol because in this case it does not make a difference (although, you can if you choose to). If you plan to reuse the bitmaps in your FLA file or need to change their properties, you should make a habit of converting the bitmaps to a symbol. However, remember that you should never animate a Graphic symbol – only animate Movie clip symbols which offer more flexibility and do not clog up your library with ugly "Tween" references.

Exercise 2: Animating lines

The menu system uses shape tweens to create movement of the lines and uses motion tweens to move and rotate the buttons that contain the text. The first shape tweens in this exercise essentially "grow" and "animate" a line inside a movie clip instance. In this exercise, you create the three movie clips that serve as a basis for the interface's menu.

1. In interface.fla, select the star layer and create a new layer above it. Click Insert Layer button on the Timeline. Rename the new layer **menu**.

2. Select the Line tool in the Tools panel. In the Property inspector (Window > Properties), change the stroke height value to **3**. Make sure that you set stroke's color to black if it's currently another color.

3. Create a line and convert it into a movie clip symbol. Click and drag vertically to create a line near the bottom of the Stage. Make sure that it is quite short (only a few pixels in length), as shown in the following figure. When you finish, select the line you created and press F8 to convert it into a movie clip symbol. Name the symbol `info clip` and make sure that you select Movie Clip as the symbol behavior.

Some Flash installations might experience difficulties with the Property inspector changing context after you select a new tool. Therefore, after you select the Line tool, the Property inspector might not change its appearance so you can set the properties of the line before you create it. You might also experience this when you select the Text tool and Rectangle tool. If so, create the line first (step 3), and then select the line and change its properties. Or, click the Selection tool and then click the Line tool, or click the Stage. Often, the Property inspector will display the tool's properties at this time.

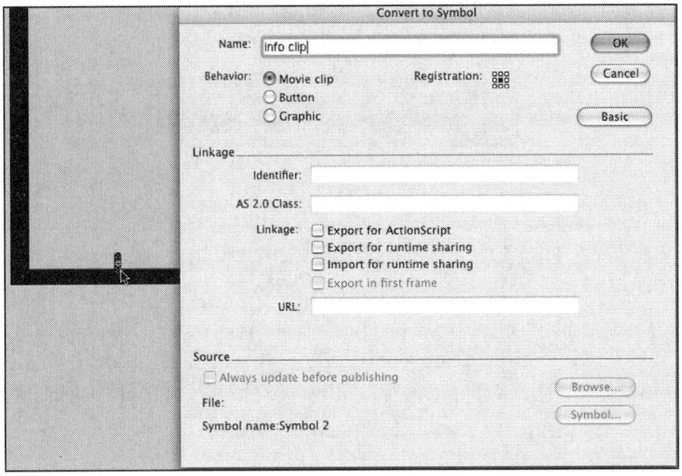

FIGURE 3.14

Create a short vertical line and convert it into a movie clip.

4. Double-click the info clip instance on the Stage using the Selection tool to enter symbol-editing mode. When you are in symbol-editing mode, double-click Layer 1 to rename it **menu tween**.

5. Select frame 6 on the menu tween layer and press F6 to insert a keyframe. Click outside the Stage to make sure that nothing is selected. Using the Selection tool, hover the mouse pointer over the top point of the line until you see the mouse pointer change so it has a backward L-shape next to the pointer. Drag the line vertically so it "grows" in length.

   Again, make sure that the line is not selected. Then hover the mouse cursor over the middle of the line until you see the mouse pointer change so it has a curved line next to it. Drag the line horizontally toward the right so it curves. Your line should look similar to the following figure.

FIGURE 3.15

Curve the line using the selection tool.

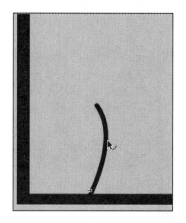

6. Add a shape tween and test the animation. Select any frame between 1 and 6, and open the Property inspector (Window > Properties). Select Shape from the Tween pop-up menu. Click and drag the playhead to test the shape tween: The line should grow from the bottom of the Stage upward and curve while doing so. The animation should match the one you saw in the final animation (www.FLAnimation.com/chapters/03).

▶ ▶ DISTRIBUTIVE AND ANGULAR

When you create a shape tween, there are two options for the "blend" between frames. The default option is Distributive, which is what you should use for this particular animation. Distributive creates shapes during the tween that are smooth and slightly irregular. If your shape does not have any corners or straight lines, Flash reverts to this option anyway. The Angular option creates a shape tween that attempts to maintain corners and straight lines during an animation, so you might select this option if your shape has these attributes. Otherwise, you should use Distributive.

7. Select frame 9 on the menu tween layer, and press F6 to insert another keyframe. Click outside the Stage area to make sure that nothing is selected. Hover the mouse pointer over the middle of the line until you see the pointer change so it has a curved line next to it. Drag the line horizontally to the left so it curves in the opposite direction. Your line should look similar to the following figure.

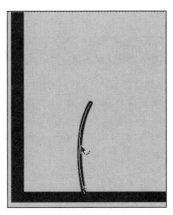

FIGURE 3.16

Curve the line in the opposite direction. The line eventually tweens between these two curved positions after you add a shape tween.

Click any frame between frame 6 and 9 on the menu tween layer and then select Shape from the Tween pop-up menu in the Property inspector. After you add the shape tween, click and drag the playhead to test the tween: the animation should bend the line between left and right.

8. Select frame 12 on the menu tween layer, and press F6 to insert a final keyframe. Click outside the Stage area to make sure that nothing is selected. Hover the mouse pointer over the middle of the line until you see the pointer change so it has a curved line next to it. Drag the line horizontally to the right so it curves similar to the line in step 5.

FIGURE 3.17

The Timeline should appear like this after you finish this animation.

9. Click any frame between frame 9 and 12 on the menu tween layer and then select Shape from the Tween pop-up menu in the Property inspector. After you add the shape tween, click and drag the playhead to test the tween: the animation should bend the line between right and left.

10. Repeat steps 2 through 9 two more times, creating two new movie clips. Call the second movie clip **portfolio clip** and the third movie clip **contact clip**. Create slightly varying animations inside these two clips by changing the length of the line, the direction it bends in, and so forth. Use the finished version of the SWF file (www.FLAnimation.com/chapters/03) as a reference.

▶ ▶ **PROBLEMATIC SHAPE TWEENS**

You need to be careful and specific when creating shape tweens. It's easy to end up with lines that "flip" or rotate instead of "grow," just by reversing steps you take to create the tween. If this occurs when you create the animation, remove all the frames after the first keyframe in the animation by selecting them, right-clicking (Windows) or Control-clicking (Macintosh) them, and selecting Remove Frames from the context menu. Then select the first keyframe and remove the tween by setting the Tween pop-up menu in the Property inspector to None. Create a new final keyframe for the end of the tween and modify the line again to create an animation.

11. When you finish tweening the three lines inside each movie clip, click Scene 1 in the Edit Bar to return to the main Stage. Line the three movie clips up to the lower edge of the background gradient, similar to the final version of the interface (refer to Figure 3.A).

Save your changes before moving on to Exercise 3.

Exercise 3: Animating shapes

You should now have three lines, contained in movie clips, forming the basis of the menu for the interface. There is another shape tween in the interface, used to animate the title area near the top of the Stage. This tween is a rectangle that animates both its size and shape, but many of the techniques you use will be familiar from earlier exercises. Closely follow the figures in the following example to modify the shape of the rectangle you create. Continue using interface.fla for this exercise.

1. Select the menu layer, and click Insert Layer button on the Timeline to create a new layer. Rename this new layer **title**.

2. Create a rectangle on the Stage. Select the Rectangle tool, and then click the fill color control in the Tools panel. Enter **#CBE1F4** in the text field at the top of the color pop-up menu and press Enter (Windows) or Return (Macintosh). Then click the stroke color control, and choose a black swatch from the color pop-up menu. In the Property inspector, type **0.5** into the stroke height text field to create a thin stroke.

3. Create a rectangle and convert it into a movie clip symbol. With the Rectangle tool still selected, click and drag near the top of the Stage to create a rectangle that is approximately 245 px (width) by 50 px (height). After you finish, double-click within the blue fill area of the rectangle so you select both the fill and the stroke. Press F8 to convert the shape into a symbol, and select Movie Clip as the symbol's behavior. Type **title** into the Name text field.

4. Double-click the title symbol to enter symbol-editing mode, and rename Layer 1 to **title tween**.

5. You need to modify the shape on frame 1, which will be the beginning state of the title area and the animation. With the shape not selected, move the mouse cursor over the top stroke of the rectangle until you see the mouse pointer change (it will have a curve next to it). Then drag the stroke upward, so it is curved similar to the top stroke in Figure 3.18. Then hover the cursor so it is over the bottom stroke of the rectangle, and curve the stroke the same way. When you are finished, the rectangle should look similar to the following figure.

FIGURE 3.18

The rectangle's shape has been significantly modified after two simple actions.

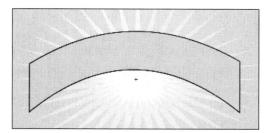

6. Now hover the mouse pointer over the upper-left corner of the rectangle until you see a backward L-shape next to the pointer. Click and drag the corner downward until the left side of the rectangle generally matches Figure 3.19 (approximately 15 pixels in height—select the line and look in the Property inspector to check). Then click and drag the right corner of the rectangle so it is the same length as the left side of the shape. If you drag the line slowly, you will notice that the line "snaps" as soon as it's the same length. The shape should look similar to the following figure after you're finished.

FIGURE 3.19

Click and drag the top corners to create this shape.

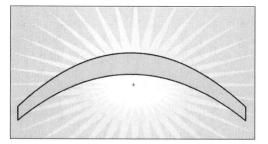

7. Select frame 8 and press F6 to create a new keyframe. At frame 8, click outside the Stage area to ensure that nothing is selected. Hover the mouse pointer over the upper-left corner of the rectangle again, and when the mouse pointer changes, click and drag the corner upward so the side's length generally matches Figure 3.20 (approximately 50 pixels).

   Move the cursor to the upper-right corner, and when the mouse pointer changes, click and drag the corner upward to match the right side. When you finish, the shape should look similar to the following figure.

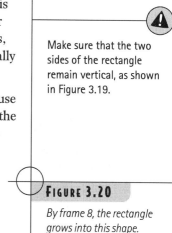

Make sure that the two sides of the rectangle remain vertical, as shown in Figure 3.19.

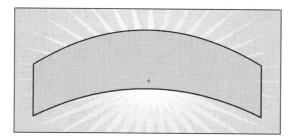

FIGURE 3.20

By frame 8, the rectangle grows into this shape.

8. Select frame 11 and press F6 to create a keyframe. Then select frame 14 and press F6 to create a keyframe. Copying frame 8 in both keyframes means that you can modify frame 11, and then have the animation ultimately animate back to the same shape it was on frame 8.

9. Before you move on, click any frame between frame 1 and 8, and select Shape from the Tween pop-up menu in the Property inspector. Click and drag the playhead between frames 1 and 8 to make sure that the tween resembles the title animation in the finished version of interface.fla.

10. At frame 11, deselect any graphics and move the mouse cursor over the left side of the rectangle until you see the mouse pointer change so it has a curve next to the pointer. Click and drag the side of the rectangle so the left side curves outward (similar to Figure 3.21). Repeat this step for the right side of the rectangle.

11. Make sure that the rectangle is deselected. Still at frame 11, move the mouse over the top stroke of the rectangle, so you see a curve icon next to the mouse pointer. Drag the top of the rectangle upward until the curve is slightly higher. Repeat this step for the bottom side of the rectangle, so the shape looks similar to the one in the following figure.

FIGURE 3.21

Curve the two sides of the rectangle using the Selection tool.

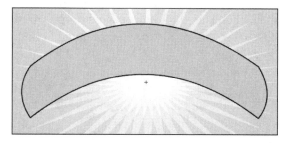

12. Click any frame between frame 8 and 11, and select Shape from the Tween pop-up menu in the Property inspector. Repeat this step for any frame between frames 11 and 14.

When you finish, drag the playhead across the Timeline to check out the animation you created. The shape should grow in size and change its shape over time. Save your changes before you move on to the next exercise.

Exercise 4: Copying and editing animations

You might notice that there is a "shadow" that animates behind the title animation in the finished version of interface.fla. This is an exact replica of the animation created in the previous exercise. However, you don't actually have to repeat all of the steps in that exercise, trying to match the modifications you made to the rectangle. That would be much too time-consuming, and the animation might not be exactly the same. In this exercise, you copy the tween you created in the previous exercise, and change the color of the shape. And we all know how useful copy and paste can be.

1. Make sure that you are still in symbol-editing mode for the `title` movie clip instance. If not, double-click the `title` instance on the Stage to re-enter symbol-editing mode.

2. Select the title tween layer, and click Insert Layer to create a new layer. Rename the new layer **bg**. Then, click and drag the bg layer beneath the title tween layer. You see a black (Windows) or grey (Macintosh) highlight bar when you drag a layer to change its ordering on the Timeline. When that highlight bar is beneath title tween, release the mouse button to move the layer, as shown in the following figure.

FIGURE 3.22

Click and drag the new bg layer to a new position. Release the mouse button when you see a highlight bar similar to this in the location where you want the layer to be.

3. Copy the frames on the title tween layer. Using the Selection tool, click and *without releasing the mouse button*, drag across all the frames on the title tween layer, so they are selected.

When frames are selected, they're highlighted on the layer. Right-click (Windows) or Control-click (Macintosh) and select Copy Frames from the context menu.

4. Now you need to paste the frames that you copied. Select frame 1 of the bg layer. Right-click (Windows) or Control-click (Macintosh) and select Paste Frames from the context menu.

5. You might notice extra frames at the end of the animation. If so, select the extra frames using the Selection tool. After they are highlighted, right-click (Windows) or Control-click (Macintosh) and select Remove Frames from the context menu.

6. Now you need to move the copied frames at each keyframe. First, click the dot under the lock icon in the title tween layer to lock the layer. Then, click the Selection tool in the Tools panel and select frame 1 of the bg layer so the entire contents of the layer are selected. Press the down-arrow key two times, and then press the right-arrow key two times.

Repeat this step for each keyframe, so each rectangle graphic is offset from the title tween layer's graphics (as seen in Figure 3.23).

If you select a frame (click and release), and then drag the frame it moves the position of that frame on the Timeline. If you click and drag across the frames, then you can select frames on the Timeline.

FIGURE 3.23

Change the color of the entire graphic to a solid black.

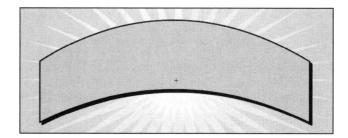

7. The next step is to change the color of each graphic to solid black, which is done in almost the same way as the process in step 6. Click the Selection tool in the Tools panel and select frame 1 of the bg layer so the entire contents of the layer are selected. Click the fill color control in the Tools panel, and select a black color swatch from the color pop-up menu.

   Repeat this step for each keyframe, so all the rectangle graphics are completely black. Click and drag the playhead across all the frames on the Timeline to view the animation.

8. If you were to play this animation, it would loop endlessly on the Stage. Select the topmost layer and click the Insert Layer button on the Timeline. Rename the new layer **actions**. Select frame 14 of this new layer, and press F6 to insert a keyframe. Open the Actions panel (Window > Development Panels > Actions) and type the following code into the Script pane:

   ```
   stop();
   ```

   Now the animation stops at the end of this Timeline, instead of looping endlessly.

9. Click Scene 1 on the Edit Bar to return to the main Stage. Select the title instance and position it near the center of the star graphic, similar to the way it's positioned in the following figure. Remember to save the changes you've made before moving on.

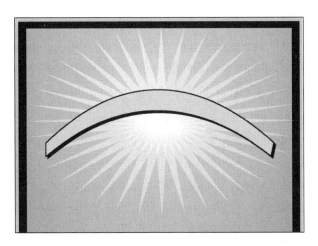

FIGURE 3.24

Position the title movie clip near the top of the Stage, slightly above the center of the star graphic.

ANIMATING WITH SHAPE HINTS

Now that you have created a few shape tweens, you will try creating a shape tween using shape hints. Shape hints help you create and control tweens that might be complex, or not morph correctly otherwise. If you need more control over *how* the shape tween animates, it might be necessary to add shape hints to help Flash predictably animate. You can shape tween fills (including gradients), strokes, and alpha.

Small icons represent shape hints, and the icons contain a letter between A and Z; each of these icons has a corresponding start and end icon. For example, a yellow A icon on frame 1 would match its corresponding green A end icon on frame 5. The shape tween at this point remains at this particular point throughout the animation.

Exercise 5: Adding tweens with shape hints

Sometimes when you animate shape tweens in Flash, you notice that the animation folds awkwardly into itself, rotates, flips, or otherwise looks awful. Flash has a feature called "shape hints" that can help you control how a shape tween displays on the Stage. You can specify where a part of the animation starts, and where it finishes

Always try to keep the shape hints in the same order as their corresponding shape tweens. Also, you should always try to place shape hints in a clockwise or counterclockwise fashion and move sequentially around the shape. The hints should always start at the upper-left corner.

You need to place shape hints on a corner or edge of the shape you're tweening. If you do not do this, the shape hint remains red and Flash ignores it.

between two keyframes. So, if the animation rotates across the Stage, you can instead specify for it to tween directly between two points (instead of making the rotation).

In the interface animation, there is a rectangle that animates around the border of the website. If this shape was tweened without shape hints, it might rotate in a circle before resembling its finished shape. This isn't what anyone would find useful. Therefore, if this happens, you can use shape hints to control how it animates.

1. Select the star layer and click the Insert Layer button. Rename the new layer **border**.

2. Select frame 1 of the border layer, and select the Rectangle tool from the Tools panel. In the Tools panel, click the paint bucket icon next to the fill color control and click the No Color button beneath the color controls (white box with a red line through it). Click the stroke color control and select a white swatch (#FFFFFF).

3. Create, position, and set the dimensions for the rectangle. Click and drag on the Stage to draw a medium rectangle. Draw the rectangle approximately around the border of the Stage, as shown in the following figure.

FIGURE 3.25

Create a white outline within the border of the interface.

4. Using the Selection tool, double-click the rectangle to select all four sides of the shape. You can use the Property inspector to change the rectangle's dimensions or its coordinates. In the Property inspector, type **295** into the width text field, and enter **495** into the height text field. Open the Align panel (Window > Design Panels > Align) and make sure the To Stage button is enabled. Then click the Align Horizontal Center and Align Vertical Center buttons. Refer to the figure of the Align panel in Exercise 1 for the correct buttons to click.

5. Using the Selection tool, double-click the rectangle's stroke to select all four sides. Press F8 to convert the shape into a movie clip. Give the symbol a name of **border**, and set the symbol behavior to Movie Clip.

   Double-click the movie clip to enter symbol-editing mode.

6. Select frame 10 on the **border** Timeline and press F7 to insert a blank keyframe.

7. Select the Rectangle Tool, and then click the Round Rectangle Radius button in the Options section of the Tools panel to launch the Rectangle Settings dialog box. Set the corner radius to **5** points and click OK to apply the settings and close the dialog box.

   Click and drag on the Stage to draw a rectangle that's approximately the same size as the one you created in frame 1.

8. Double-click the rectangle that you just created on frame 10 to select it. In the Property inspector, set the width, height, and coordinates to match the rectangle you drew in step 3. You might have to select the rectangle on frame 1 and write down its dimensions and coordinate location. Make sure that the dimensions **and** the X and Y coordinates are the same on frame 1 and frame 10.

9. Select frame 1 in the Timeline and change the Tween drop-down menu to Shape. Drag the playhead across the frames to scrub the Timeline. The rectangle might rotate counterclockwise into an oval-like shape. This would not work well with the interface, so shape hints are useful. Even if it doesn't rotate (results differ depending on your rectangles), follow steps 10 through 12 to add shape hints so you can learn the process.

10. Select frame 1. of the border layer, and make sure that Snap to Objects is selected in the Tools panel Add a shape hint by selecting Modify > Shape > Add Shape Hint from the main menu. Drag the shape hint that looks like an "a" inside a small red icon, and place it at the middle of the left edge of the rectangle.

FIGURE 3.26

Move the first shape hint to the left side of the rectangle.

To remove a shape hint, right-click (Windows) or Control-click (Macintosh) and choose Remove Hint.

If you want to hide the shape hints from view and still have them active, you can toggle their visibility by selecting View > Show Shape Hints (Ctrl+Alt+H) from the main menu.

11. Select frame 10 on the Timeline and align the shape hint in the same position as you did on frame 1 (in step 10). The icon changes to green, and when you return to frame 1, the first shape hint turns yellow.

12. Repeat steps 10 and 11 two more times, placing shape hints along the top side of the rectangle and then the right side. Remember that you not only need to add shape hints to frame 1, but you also need to align the corresponding shape hints on frame 10.

13. Scrub the Timeline again. Now you should see that the edges remain in place and the rectangle morphs into the rounded rectangle a bit more realistically.

14. If you were to play this animation, it would loop endlessly on the Stage. Select the topmost layer and click the Insert Layer button on the Timeline. Rename the new layer **actions**. Select frame 10 of the new layer, and press F6 to insert a keyframe. Open the Actions panel (Window > Development Panels > Actions) and type the following code into the Script pane:

```
stop();
```

Save your changes before moving on to the next exercise. Try this process with other shapes in a new test FLA file, particularly if your rectangle didn't rotate.

FINISHING THE INTERFACE

Although the interface is almost complete, there are a few elements left that you need to create: the text and some buttons. You use the drawing tools in Flash to create vector graphics for each of these elements, which keeps the overall file size low (a definite plus). Additionally, you use the Free Transform tool to modify the text for the titles so it appears to bend with the rectangle title graphic you created previously.

Exercise 6: Creating movie clip buttons

Although part of each menu movie clip is shape tweened, as you finished in an earlier tutorial, the buttons in the menu are motion tweened instead. Continue using interface.fla for this example, which creates some simple movie clip buttons for the interface. Exercise 8 motion tweens the buttons.

1. Double-click the `info clip` instance on the main Stage. Click the Insert Layer button on the Timeline to create a new layer, and rename the new layer to **button**.

2. Create a black rectangle on the button layer. Select the Rectangle tool and then click the fill color control. Select a black color swatch from the color pop-up menu. Click the pencil icon next to the stroke color control and then click the No Color button (the button beneath the two color controls that is a white square with a red line through it).

You created a rounded rectangle in an earlier exercise, so make sure that the Corner Radius value is set to 0. Click the Round Rectangle Radius button in the Options area of the Tools panel, and type *0* into the Corner Radius text field.

Click and drag on the Stage to create a small rectangle. Select the rectangle using the Selection tool, and then enter new values into the width and height text fields in the Property inspector: **78** (width) by **27** (height).

3. Select the black rectangle and press F8 to convert the drawing into a symbol. Type `info buttonmc` as the symbol's name, and select Movie Clip as the behavior. When you finish, click OK and return to the main Stage. Although you have created a movie clip, you can apply the same behaviors as a button using ActionScript. For example, you can use simple ActionScript so a user can click the movie clip and have something happen in the SWF file. This lets you layer graphics inside the clip, animate parts of the movie clip button, or the clip itself yet have the movie clip function like a button.

4. Double-click the `info buttonmc` instance to enter symbol-editing mode. Double-click and rename Layer 1 to **bg**. Then click the Insert Layer button twice to create two new layers above bg. Rename the first layer **front**, and the second layer **text**. The text layer must be the topmost layer on the Timeline.

Lock the bg layer when you finish creating the layer.

5. Create another rectangle on the front layer. Select the front layer, and then select the Rectangle tool from the Tools panel. Click the fill color control in the Tools panel, and enter the following hexadecimal value into the color pop-up menu: **#C3DCF2**. Then click the stroke color control and select a white swatch from the color pop-up menu. Set the stroke height to **1 px** in the Property inspector.

6. Double-click the new rectangle's fill to select the entire shape. In the Property inspector, change the dimensions of the rectangle to the following: **75** (width) by **24** (height). With the rectangle still selected, position it over the black rectangle on the bg layer as follows.

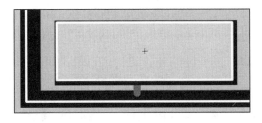

FIGURE 3.27

Create and position a new rectangle for a button.

Lock the front layer after you finish.

7. Add some text for the button. This button directs users to the "information" page of the website. Therefore, you need to add some text that will let them know where the button takes them. So select the Text tool in the Tools panel, and choose a font from the Font pop-up menu in the Property inspector. Click the Text (fill) color control in the Property inspector and select a black swatch from the color pop-up menu. Choose a font size that is large enough to fill most of the button without overlapping the edges, and make sure that you choose Static text in the Text Type pop-up menu.

   Select the text layer on the Timeline, and then click the Stage and type **INFO**. When you finish, choose the Selection tool and move the text field so it is roughly centered within the blue rectangle.

8. When you finish, click Scene 1 in the Edit Bar to return to the main Timeline. Save your changes before you proceed to the following exercise.

Static text means that the text will not change during the course of the SWF file, and is represented on the Stage somewhat like an image. Even if your visitors do not have the particular text on their hard drives, they can still see the font face you chose.

Exercise 7: Duplicating movie clips

You need to add movie clips for each of the menu items on the Stage. However, following all the steps in the previous exercise would be rather tedious and is also unnecessary. Because each movie clip needs to be different (they each contain different text), you cannot use several instances of the same clip. However, you can duplicate the movie clips in the Library and then modify the text that's contained within. It's very quick and easy to do.

1. Duplicate the info buttonmc movie clip symbol two times. Open the Library (Window > Library) and right-click (Windows) or Control-click (Macintosh) the info buttonmc symbol.

Select Duplicate from the context menu. In the Duplicate Symbol dialog box, type **portfolio buttonmc** as the symbol's name and select Movie Clip as the symbol type. Click OK and the symbol duplicates in the Library.

Repeat this step, except name the second duplicated movie clip **contact buttonmc**.

2. Add new text to the portfolio clip. Double-click the `portfolio buttonmc` symbol in the Library, so it opens in symbol-editing mode. Using the Selection tool, double-click the text field on the text layer so you can edit it. Type in **PORTFOLIO**.

3. You might need to modify the size of the bg and front layers inside the `portfolio buttonmc` symbol. If so, unlock both layers, and select both frames. Press Shift while you click each frame to select both of them simultaneously. Then select the Free Transform tool, and click and drag the handle on the left or right side of the bounding box as shown in Figure 3.28. You might need to lock the text layer before you complete this step.

FIGURE 3.28

Resize the rectangle's width so the text fits on the button properly.

4. Add new text to the `contact clip` symbol. Double-click the `contact buttonmc` symbol in the Library, so the symbol opens in symbol-editing mode. Using the Selection tool, double-click the text field on the text layer so you can edit it. Type in **CONTACT**.

5. Now that you have edited the duplicated clips, you need to add them to the movie clips that contain the shape tweened animation. Double-click the `portfolio clip` instance you created in Exercise 6, which is on the Stage. Inside the movie clip, create a new layer and rename it **button**. Drag `portfolio buttonmc` from the Library to the button layer.

Repeat this step for the `contact buttonmc` symbol and `contact clip` instance.

6. When you finish, you'll have three movie clips on the Stage. Each contains a movie clip button similar to what you see in Figure 3.29.

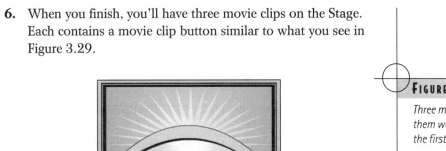

FIGURE 3.29

Three movie clips, and two of them were duplicated from the first.

Save the changes you made to the FLA file. In the following exercise, you position and motion tween the three movie clip buttons, so they appear to sit on top of the shape tweened lines.

Exercise 8: Adding motion tweens

Right now, you might have the buttons scattered within the three movie clips that form the menu navigation. In this exercise, you position and motion tween those three buttons so they animate with the three lines that shape tween.

1. Double-click the `info clip` instance to enter symbol-editing mode. Lock the menu tween layer, so you don't accidentally modify the shape tween.

2. The button should be on the layer above the menu tween layer. Select the button on frame 1 using the Selection tool and position it so the button sits on top of the short line.

3. Select frame 6 on the button layer, and press F6 to insert a keyframe. Select frame 9 and press F6, and then click frame 12 and press F6. All three of these keyframes will have the info buttonmc at the same location, but you will modify its position and rotation at each keyframe.

4. Select frame 6 and then select the button. Move the button to the top of the line again, which should be above the button. You probably want to rotate the button because the line bends. With the button selected, click the Free Transform tool in the Tools panel. Handles will appear around the bounding box of the info buttonmc instance. When you hover the mouse over one of the corners, the pointer changes and a circular arrow appears. When you see this icon, click and drag the pointer to rotate the button so it appears similar to the following figure.

FIGURE 3.30

Rotate the button using the Free Transform tool to match the curve of the line.

5. Select frame 9 and click the button to select it. Move the button clip to the top of the line's current position, and rotate it accordingly by using the Free Transform tool.

   Repeat this step for frame 12. When you finish, the info buttonmc instance should be in a different position and rotation on each keyframe.

6. Right-click (Windows) or Control-click (Macintosh) any frame between 1 and 6, and select Create Motion Tween from the

context menu. Repeat this step for any frame between 6 and 9, and then repeat it for any frame between frames 9 and 12.

Click and drag the playhead across all of the frames to check out your animation. If the animation looks good, move on to the next step. If you feel it needs some modification, select a keyframe and move the button clip using the Selection or Free Transform tools. This modifies the animation accordingly.

7. Select the top layer and click the Insert Layer button on the Timeline. Rename the new layer labels. Select frame 9 of this layer and press F6 to insert a keyframe. Then open the Property inspector and type over into the Frame Label text field, as shown in the following graphic.

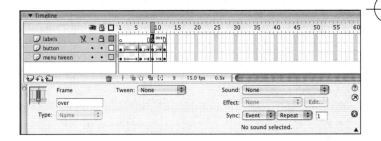

FIGURE 3.31

Type over in the Frame Label text field to create the over label on the Timeline.

In a following exercise, you will add ActionScript that uses this frame label to move the playhead to this location in the animation. If you wanted to change where the playhead moves, all you need to do is click and drag the frame label to a new location on the Timeline.

8. If you were to play this animation, it would loop endlessly on the Stage. Select the labels layer and click the Insert Layer button on the Timeline. Rename the new layer actions. Select frame 12 of this new layer, and press F6 to insert a keyframe. Open the Actions panel (Window > Development Panels > Actions) and type the following code into the Script pane:

```
stop();
```

9. Repeat the previous steps for the *portfolio clip* and *contact clip* instances on the Stage.

▶ ▶ **USING FRAME LABELS**

Frame labels are used for a couple reasons. They can alert you to the contents of a particular frame, or a change in the animation. More importantly, you can reference frame labels in your ActionScript. Perhaps you want the playhead to skip to a specific position on the Timeline. You could reference that location using the frame number. However, if you modify your animation, the location you want to specify in your code might need to change. This could potentially lead to errors if you forget to change the number accordingly. If you reference a frame label in your ActionScript, you can change the location of that frame label when you make modifications to the Timeline or animation and the ActionScript does not need to change. This is much easier than remembering to change a frame number in your code.

Exercise 9: Modifying text

In the final version of this file, you probably notice that there are titles for three different areas of the website: Information, Portfolio, and Contact. You create the text in Flash and then use the Free Transform tool with the envelope modifier to make changes to the text field. Before you can edit text in this way, you must break the text apart by using the Modify > Break Apart command.

You can use the Break Apart command to separate bitmap graphics, instances, or grouped graphics into editable, ungrouped elements. When you break apart a block of text (that has multiple characters), it first converts the text into single character fields. If you reapply the command, it converts the character(s) to raw vector data.

Many elements cannot be modified until they're broken apart. For example, the Distort and Envelope modifiers cannot be used on a symbol or text unless you break it apart. The following exercise shows you how to modify the shape of the text you use in interface.fla.

1. Make sure that you are on the main Stage. If not, click Scene 1 on the Edit Bar to return to the main Stage. Select the title layer, and click Insert Layer button on the Timeline. Rename the new layer text.

2. Select frame 30 on the title layer, and press F5. This spans the frames between frame 1 and 30 on this layer, so these elements are visible when the playhead is at any of these frames. Repeat this step for the border, menu, star and background layers as well.

3. Select frame 10 on the text layer and press F6 to create a keyframe. Then create a new keyframe at frames 15, 20, and 25 as well. Each of these frames displays different titles that create each page.

4. Select frame 10, and then select the Text tool. Make sure that Static is selected in the Text Type pop-up menu in the Property inspector. Choose any bold and large font from the Font pop-up menu, such as Impact. Set the font size to anywhere between 30 and 50 pixels (it depends on your font choice).

   Click the Stage and then type **MY SITE** into the text field.

5. With the new text field selected, select Modify > Break Apart to separate the text into separate characters. Then select Modify > Break Apart again so the text changes into outlines. With the text still selected, click the Free Transform tool in the Tools panel. Then click the Envelope modifier under the Options area in the Tools panel. Handles appear all around the text outlines.

Try to select a font and font size that you think will fit within the borders of the title movie clip animation you created earlier.

FIGURE 3.32

When you select a graphic with the Envelope modifier, many handles appear that enable you to modify the graphic's shape.

6. Click and drag the handle that is at the top, center of the selection upward. When you drag the handle upward, the text bends in that direction, as shown in the following figure.

Then, click and drag the handle at the bottom center of the text field upward. You might want to slightly modify the text further using the handles that lay in between the corners and the two handles you just modified.

FIGURE 3.34

Use the handles that are next to the ones you dragged earlier to fine-tune the modification. Specifically, the handles extending from the four corners were dragged toward the text and vertically upward.

7. Select frame 10 on the text layer again so you select all of the content on the layer. Then press F8 to convert the content into a symbol. Type **mysite-text** as the symbol's name, and select Graphic as the symbol's behavior.

8. Repeat steps 4 through 7 with three new text fields. Select the keyframe at frame 15 and create a text field. Click the Stage and type **INFORMATION**; break apart the text, and then use the Free Transform tool to modify the shape of the text. Then convert the text into a graphic symbol and give it a unique name. Continue to add Graphic symbols for PORTFO-LIO (on frame 20) and CONTACT (on frame 25) on the text layer as well.

9. Add labels for each page you just created. Insert a new keyframe on frame 10 (select it and press F6) and type **mysite** into the Frame Label text field in the Property inspector. Insert

keyframes at frame 15, 20, and 25 on the labels layer. Then insert the following frame labels at these keyframes:

◆ Frame 15: information

◆ Frame 20: portfolio

◆ Frame 25: contact

When you finish, the Timeline should look like the following figure.

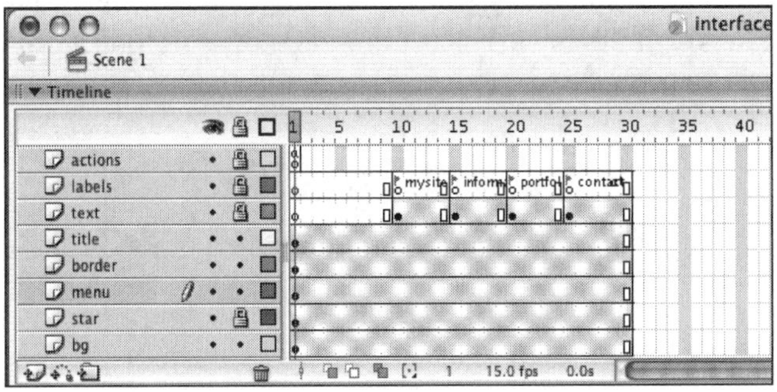

FIGURE 3.35

Pages are added to the Timeline.

10. You need to test the SWF file to see whether the title animation tweens and aligns with the text properly. However, if you test the SWF file at this time, it will loop continuously between each of the pages you just created. Therefore, you need to add some stop actions to the Timeline so the file does not loop.

Select the keyframe at frame 1 of the actions layer. Open the Actions panel and type the following line of code into the Script pane:

```
stop();
```

11. Double-click the title animation and select the final frame where you added the stop action in exercise 4. Add the following ActionScript after the stop action that you find on the last frame of the actions layer:

```
this._parent.gotoAndStop("mysite");
```

This ActionScript executes when the playhead reaches it. This occurs at the *end* of the title animation. When the animation

The following exercises add ActionScript so you can navigate to each page in the website.

finishes playing, the site progresses to the mysite label on the parent Timeline. The parent timeline refers to the main Timeline (which is the parent of this movie clip). Don't worry if this doesn't make sense to you. You will learn more about ActionScript starting in Chapter 8.

12. Select Control > Test Movie to see whether the text and the title animation match up. Move the text for MY SITE accordingly on the Stage until it looks right. When you have the position correct, add a guide to the Stage that matches the top of the MY SITE graphic. Make sure that Rulers are visible (View > Rulers), and then click and drag the mouse pointer from the ruler onto the Stage. Position the guide as follows.

FIGURE 3.36

Click and drag the mouse pointer from a Ruler to add a guide to the Stage.

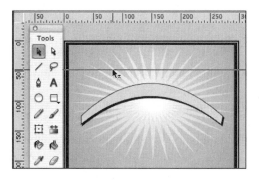

Then line up the INFORMATION, PORTFOLIO, and CONTACT text graphics with the guide you added to the Stage. Save your changes before proceeding to the next exercise.

NAVIGATING PAGES AND PUBLISHING

An important part of any interface is having some kind of navigation or interactivity in the interface. For example, if you have buttons, you need to add some kind of ActionScript so they can work. Because you're working with Flash, there are several ways to accomplish this task. You will add some simple code to the main Timeline at frame 1 that makes the buttons interact with the mouse. Then, you add some code that moves the playhead to a specific frame label when you click the movie clip button.

Exercise 10: Creating interactive buttons

In Exercise 8, you added "over" frame labels within each menu animation. You needed to do this is so the playhead can move to this
frame and play the animation from the specified frame to the end.
Specifically, you will add ActionScript in this exercise so this happens when the mouse rolls over each movie clip.

1. Make sure that you are on the main Stage. Click Scene 1 in the
    Edit Bar to navigate back to the main Stage if necessary.

2. Give each movie clip an instance name, so you can control
    each instance using ActionScript. Select the info clip instance
    and open the Property inspector. Type **info_mc** into the
    <Instance Name> text field.

3. Repeat this step for the other two movie clip instances. Select
    the portfolio clip instance and type **portfolio_mc** into the
    <Instance Name> text field. Then select the contact clip instance
    and type **contact_mc** into the <Instance Name> text field.

FIGURE 3.37

*Give each symbol an
instance name using
the Property inspector.*

4. You can add ActionScript to control these instances, now that
    the instances have instance names. Select frame 1 on the
    actions layer. Open the Actions panel and type the following
    ActionScript into the Script pane, following the stop action
    you added in an earlier exercise:

```
info_mc.onRollOver = function() {
   this.gotoAndPlay("over");
};
portfolio_mc.onRollOver = function() {
   this.gotoAndPlay("over");
};
contact_mc.onRollOver = function() {
   this.gotoAndPlay("over");
};
```

The ActionScript you added previously stops the SWF file on frame 1. Then you tell each button (info_mc, portfolio_mc and contact_mc) to do something when the mouse rolls over the instance (onRollOver). You tell each movie clip to move the playhead to the over frame label and play the movie clip. Therefore, the movie clip plays from the over label, which results in a short tween animation.

5. You created several pages and text headings for each of the different areas for the website. Then, you added some interactivity to the buttons you have for the websites menu. Now you need to make sure that the navigation can happen, so visitors can view each page in the site.

Add the following ActionScript to the Script pane, following the code you added previously in step 3.

```
info_mc.onRelease = function() {
   gotoAndStop("information");
};
portfolio_mc.onRelease = function() {
   gotoAndStop("portfolio");
};
contact_mc.onRelease = function() {
   gotoAndStop("contact");
};
```

This ActionScript tells the playhead on the main Timeline to go to the information, portfolio, or contact frame labels and then stop the playhead. Therefore, you do not need to add stop actions on each of those frames like you do at the end of each animated movie clip.

6. Select Control > Test Movie to test the animation and each button. If your buttons do not work properly, go back to the Actions panel and make sure that there are no problems with your code. If you see the Output panel appear with errors, there is probably a syntax error with the code in the file.

You should also check to see that the text you added for the title section of each page is correctly aligned with the animated rectangle. If not, return to the main Timeline and modify the position of the text in question.

7. You created a great deal of movie clips in this FLA file. When you look in the Library, there is a great number of assets to sort through. A good practice to adopt is to use Library folders, as mentioned in an earlier chapter. Click the New Folder button (that's in the bottom-left corner of the Library) twice to create two new library folders. Double-click the folder's name to rename those folders **movie clips** and **graphics**. Click and drag all the movie clip symbols into the movie clips folder, and likewise for the graphics.

Moving On

This interface obviously isn't a finished product, mostly because you have not added content into the site. You can add content onto each page, just as you added the text for each page title. In Chapter 8, you add a transition to the interface, and load content into each page. The transition makes something happen when the user clicks a button in the menu: The content area animates as it is removed from the interface, and a new content area appears. However, some Action-Script is required to achieve the effect, so it's covered in a Chapter 8.

Of course, this particular interface would greatly benefit from more creative graphics. You might want to change the movie clip buttons in the menu to something more interesting and perhaps animated (such as flowers that grow from the ground, or sign posts).

FIGURE 3.38

Change the graphics a bit or a lot for your own look.

FIGURE 4.A

FIGURE 4.B

FIGURE 4.C

What You Learn

▶ About frame-by-frame animation

▶ How frame-by-frame animation is used in Flash

▶ How to animate a character using only single frames

▶ How to use onion skins

▶ How to edit the center point for rotating instances

▶ How to add sound to a document

▶ About optimizing drawings

Lesson Files

Start:

04/start/pirate_start.fla

04/start/disco.wav

Finish:

04/complete/pirate.fla

04/complete/pirate.swf

4

Drawing Frame-by-Frame Animation

You might think of frame-by-frame animation as doing things the "old-fashioned" way. Creating a frame-by-frame animation is the closest you'll get to a traditional form of animation in Macromedia Flash. In fact, you might have animated this way in an elementary school art class. And you've probably seen this form of animation during the Saturday morning cartoons. Flash lets you animate cartoons and effects by drawing on individual frames, or by dragging instances onto each frame to create the illusion of movement over time.

In this project, you use predrawn graphics that are placed on individual frames to create the movement you see in the final project. You use the Onion Skin feature to help move the instances around, and you edit the center point of instances so you can rotate them appropriately. Even if you were to draw your graphics manually, you might use these same techniques to modify the animation. By the end of the project, you create a dancing pirate on a disco floor with music playing in the background.

Website: www.FLAnimation.com/chapters/04

LEARNING ABOUT TRADITIONAL ANIMATION

There are several principles of traditional animation that were developed many years ago by artists at animation studios such as Disney. These principles helped animators make drawings look lifelike and natural, despite being drawn by hand on a 2D surface. You can apply these principles to the drawings you make to animate in Flash. There are many resources available about traditional animation, and many of the techniques used in traditional animation can help you with frame-by-frame animation.

Let's look at the fundamental process of traditional animation. This process varies greatly depending on the medium used (ranging from ink to 3D), and the people involved. A broad overview of animation might include the following steps:

◆ **Planning.** Think about the scene and how it progresses. Then sketch thumbnails that outline the scene and its contents. Draw thumbnails for each major change in content, such as a sudden movement (Figure 4.1).

FIGURE 4.1

Thumbnails help you determine how an animation progresses over time.

◆ **Revisions.** Take the thumbnails you create and make sure that you solved any problems with the animation. Make any revisions, alterations, or changes at this stage. Don't move on to the animation before you work out the major ideas, including length. If you think you might want to change the story, do it at this point—not while you are animating. Try to foresee any problems you might encounter and deal with them using thumbnails. It's much more difficult to change a finished or full-size animation.

◆ **Animation.** Digitize (scan) your thumbnails if necessary, and make them full size or import them into Flash. Space out each thumbnail on frames across the Timeline, as necessary. Trace the thumbnails using tools, delete the thumbnails, and then animate all the frames in-between each thumbnail. At this point in the process, you deal with the dialog, characterization, spacing, and timing.

There are many principles of animation, such as how items move when animated. This is covered further in Chapter 5.

This process might resemble your existing process if you practice a traditional form of animation with Flash. The most important thing you can do, regardless of your project, is to plan it out before you actually begin to draw. Use a pen and paper, brainstorm, and sketch your ideas. Know what the beginning, middle, and end of your animation will be like. Before you even start Flash to begin working, think about the climax of your story or any special movements your character might make. Frame-by-frame animation has a lot of overhead when you work—mistakes take a longer time to remedy than when you work with motion or shape tweens in Flash.

About frame-by-frame animation

You might have created or seen frame-by-frame animation in grade school or at a science center. An example of this is a flipbook, which causes drawings on each page to animate when you rapidly flip through pages in a book. You see the animation because of the rapid progression of images. Another form you might have seen shows multiple images drawn inside a wheel that's placed horizontally on a table (originally called a zoetrope). When you spin the wheel and look at the images inside, they appear to animate. Both of these forms are largely the same as frame-by-frame animation in Flash, except you draw them on each keyframe on the Timeline instead of drawing images individually on pieces of paper. For more information on zoetropes, search "zoetrope" at http://whatis.techtarget.com which includes a thorough definition and links.

Frame-by-frame animation is a tedious process. So why do it at all? Because this form of animation lets you add details you wouldn't otherwise be able to add.

Frame-by-frame animation is very different from the "automated" tweening you did in earlier projects. This frame-by-frame format is the "manual" way of creating animation. You don't use the tween features in Flash to create the movement for you. Instead, you create the movement yourself, sometimes just as you would if you were drawing on paper. Frame-by-frame animation is not as easy or as quick, but it can help you make awesome, creative, and amazing effects that

In addition to the time involved, frame-by-frame animation typically leads to larger file sizes because you replicate and modify the content in nearly every frame.

If you want to modify the graphics of an instance, you must duplicate the symbol first and make sure that you modify it instead. If you try modifying the instance on the Stage, you end up modifying the graphics of every instance of the symbol, not just the current selection.

FIGURE 4.2

Your Timeline might include both frame-by-frame animations and motion tweens.

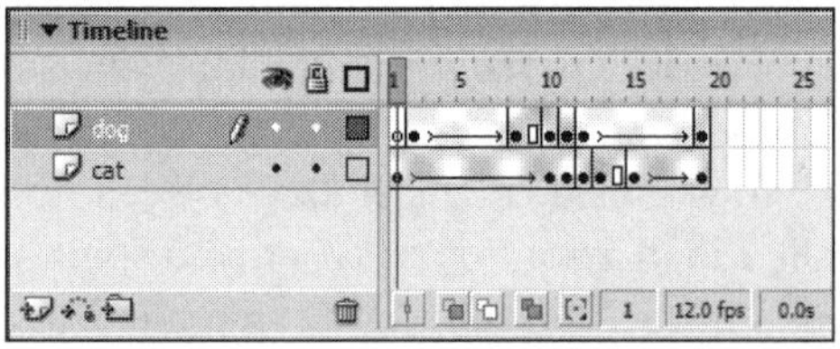

motion tweens don't let you create. Or frame-by-frame animation could help you when you need additional control over your animations. Often, using a combination of motion tweens and frame-by-frame animation helps you create a finished animation. You commonly use this form of animation in conjunction with motion tweens to produce a finished effect. For example, an animator might create a walk cycle and need special control over the arm and leg movements. He might use motion tweens for much of the leg movement, but in a particular spot of the animation (perhaps where the leg and foot meet the ground), he could use frame-by-frame animation to achieve the precise effect required for the animation.

There are several different ways to use frame-by-frame animation in Flash. You might have finished symbols that you either duplicate or modify for a particular frame's content. Or, you might draw on each frame and use the Onion Skin tool to help create the animation. Frame-by-frame animation doesn't mean having a keyframe on every frame. You might use the technique in only a couple of choice spots in an animation that primarily uses motion tweens (Figure 4.2). In this project, you primarily use frame-by-frame animation simply to learn about moving, modifying, and placing graphics to form a slightly crude animation.

So if you have a series of thumbnails that you want to turn into an animation, scan each thumbnail onto your computer and import it into Flash. Place the thumbnails along the Timeline where each should appear in the animation. You would trace each thumbnail, and then fill in the frames between each thumbnail, either by drawing or moving instances around.

You could also create vector artwork in another program such as Illustrator. Create various assets that you import into Flash and modify. Illustrator also has a command that creates several symbol states of a single graphic (such as an arm) that you can import into Flash. You learn more about this process in Chapter 5.

Changing the center point

By editing the center point (or snap ring), you change the location where the instance snaps to other items (such as a path), or the center of rotation. You did this in Chapter 2 when you changed the snap ring, which affects where the instance snaps to the motion path. You can use the Free Transform tool to edit the center point.

Select the Free Transform tool, and try to rotate the instance. Hover the mouse over a corner handle until you see a round arrow, and then click and drag to rotate the instance. Notice *that* the instance rotates around the center point (Figure 4.3 *on the* left). Then click and drag the circle from the center of the instance to a new location. Try to rotate the instance again; this time, it rotates around the new position of the circle (Figure 4.3 *on the* right).

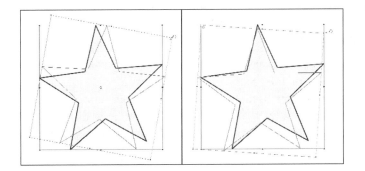

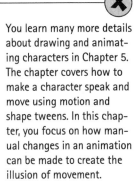

You learn many more details about drawing and animating characters in Chapter 5. The chapter covers how to make a character speak and move using motion and shape tweens. In this chapter, you focus on how manual changes in an animation can be made to create the illusion of movement.

FIGURE 4.3

Change the center point to modify the point that the instance rotates around.

You want to change the center point before you animate any instances that use rotation. This is particularly important when you create motion tweens. If you change the center point after you begin to tween, your earlier tweens change to reflect the instance's new center point, which can ruin your animation. Therefore, change the center point to the point where you want the instance to rotate around right after you add the instance to the Stage.

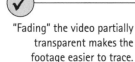

See Chapter 8 for details on how to import video (such as how to specify quality settings and change FPS—which is set as a ratio).

"Fading" the video partially transparent makes the footage easier to trace.

Because drawing every frame uses up a lot of file size, it's a good idea to draw only one image every few frames (or more). You should be conscious of how many details you add to the animation because more details ultimately means a higher file size.

About rotoscoping

Rotoscoping is a fun technique to try. It uses frame-by-frame animation to create the effect of animation, except you use an existing source such as video footage. The basic principle of rotoscoping (in this context) is to create animation by tracing the footage. You can trace the footage in any number of ways by using the drawing tools. For example, you might use the Brush tool to draw around people or animals in the video. Or, you might use the shape tools to copy the basic shapes of buildings panning across the Stage. If you are uncomfortable animating or if want to replicate a specific effect easily, rotoscoping could be the perfect technique for you.

There isn't room in this book to show a project using rotoscoping, but it's very easy to try. Import a video into a new FLA file (File > Import > Import to Stage and select a video on your hard drive). Import the video at a lower FPS rate, such as 15, and a size that fits on the Stage. Import the video using 100% quality because the file size doesn't matter (you delete the video before you export the SWF file).

Place the imported video on Layer 1. Insert a new layer above the video, and place a semitransparent square over the video. This "fades" the video out, so it's easier to trace. Lock these two layers.

On a new (third) layer, you can then animate frame-by-frame by tracing the video. Trace the video in the first frame, and remove any subsequent empty frames. Then select and press F6 in the next frame that you want to trace, and modify the lines, draw new ones, or remove existing lines as necessary (Figure 4.4). You might want to trace every frame of video, or perhaps every second frame—it depends on how smooth you want the animation to be or if you are concerned about the file size. It is almost necessary to have a graphics tablet (such as a Wacom tablet) for tracing video, to speed up the process and improve the look of the result. Drawing by hand can be very time consuming.

Hide the video layer and test the animation for how smooth or accurate it appears. When you finish, delete the video and "fade" layer; you are left with an animation in a movie clip. As great as this technique can be, there is one large drawback. Rotoscoping typically generates very large file sizes. If you rotoscope by tracing each frame by hand, as with any drawing, you want to optimize the lines you create (select a line and select Modify > Shape > Optimize). There is more information on optimizing lines later in this chapter.

After you finish tracing the video, delete the layer from the Timeline and remove the video footage from your Library. You're left with a great lifelike animation.

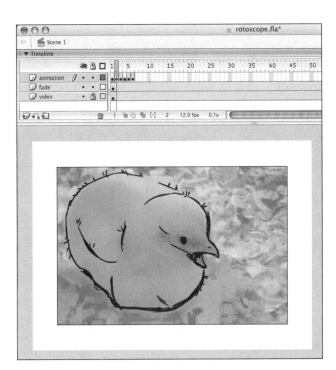

PROJECT 4: ANIMATING BY USING FRAMES

You used the drawing tools in Project 3 to create lines and shapes. In this project, you can continue to use the drawing tools in Flash to create a character to animate, or you can use a character provided on the CD-ROM for this project. This character contains several separate symbols for each part of the character (such as head, feet, and arms), some of which have several variations you can use to animate the character. Within the project, you can read some pointers on using drawing tools for frame-by-frame animation if you make a series of drawings to animate a character.

You might use this exact process if you import blended symbols from Illustrator. When Illustrator blends parts of a character, it creates several symbols that appear to be gradually changing. You then have to import these vector assets into Flash, where you might use motion tweens, shape tweens, or frame-by-frame techniques for animation.

FIGURE 4.5

Contents of the starter file's Library.

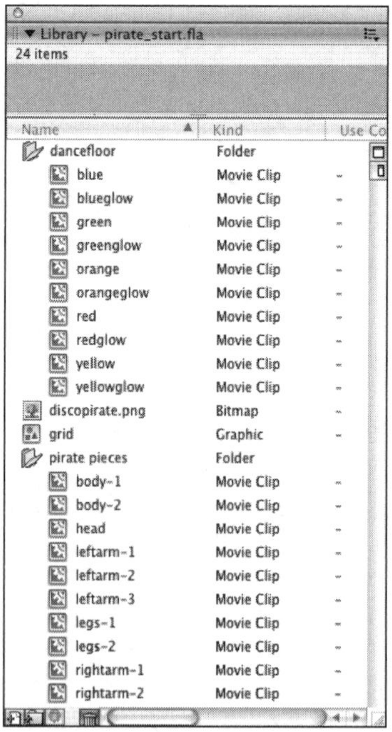

If you have problems opening the FLA file, save a copy to your hard drive first before opening it in Flash.

Exercise 1: Creating or importing a character

There are a couple of ways to animate a character frame-by-frame. You might trace the character from one you've drawn already, and then draw the frames in-between by hand using the Onion Skin feature in Flash. You might draw pieces of a character (such as an arm, leg, and head), and rotate the pieces using the Free Transform tool.

Before you start, view the finished animation online at www.FLAnimation.com/chapters/04.

1. Open this project's starter file called pirate_start.fla from the CD-ROM. You can find the file on the CD-ROM at 04/start/pirate_start.fla. Save a new version of the file as **pirate.fla**. Open the document and review the contents of the Library (Figure 4.5). There is a folder for the character and another for the contents of the room the character dances in.

The pirate has one, two, or three states for each body part that moves in the animation, such as the arms and legs. The symbol names have numbers representing what state the graphic is in. For example, the left arm has three different states, so it has three symbols for each state: `leftarm-1`, `left-arm-2`, and `leftarm-3`.

The size (*550* by *650*), frame rate (*24*), and background color (*#333333*) for this document have already been set for this project.

You should select a frame rate near the beginning of your animation, in case you choose to synch your animation to sound or other elements, where changing frame rate will affect the synchronization negatively. You might need to do some quick tests to select a good frame rate for your animation. Cartoon animations do not necessarily need a high frame rate like some effects you might make. For example, this chapter's project still looks ok (yet a bit more choppy) at a lower frame rate. Cartoon-based animation still looks nice (and can run relatively smoothly) at lower frame rates. Slowing down the frame rate does not reduce the file size of the actual graphics, but it does make the animation "longer," which reduces file size if you need to make a cartoon that lasts for a given length of time. For example, if you set your animation to 31 fps, it might be only five seconds long. However, if you set the same animation to 15 fps, it might be 10 seconds long, but it contains the same content. Therefore, that animation is twice as long but exports at the same file size. If you need to make an animation that's a certain length of time, reducing the file frame rate to make it last longer also reduces the file size of the project.

You can modify the symbols you find in the Library as much as you like. You can still easily follow the exercises in this chapter using your own graphics.

▶ ▶ IMPORTING CHARACTERS

If you create a character in another program, you import the character into Flash by choosing File > Import > Import to Library. Depending on the format that you import, you might see a dialog box with options for importing the character. For example, if you import an AI, Fireworks PNG, or Freehand document, you see a special import dialog box. These dialog boxes let you choose how and where to import the content (for instance, to individual layers or keyframes). You might also require QuickTime for importing some file formats, such as PSD and TIF.

2. Click the Insert Layer button four times. When you finish, there should be five layers total on the Timeline. Rename the five layers as follows (from bottom to top): **right arm**, **legs**, **body**, **left arm**, and **head**. Optionally, you can put move head layer below the body layer depending on the look you prefer.

3. Open the pirate pieces folder in the Library, and drag the following instances onto the Stage:

   ◆ Drag an instance of `rightarm-1` onto the right arm layer.

   ◆ Drag an instance of `legs-1` onto the legs layer.

   ◆ Drag an instance of `body-1` onto the body layer.

   ◆ Drag an instance of `leftarm-1` onto the left arm layer.

   ◆ Drag an instance of `head` onto the head layer.

   These instances make up the pirate character in its beginning state. To create the final animation, as you see in the final version of the file, you will either swap or modify these instances on the Timeline.

4. Click and drag the instances using the Selection tool to arrange them on the Stage according to the following figure.

FIGURE 4.6

Assemble the pirate.

You don't need to be exact. Arrange them approximately near the middle of the Stage, as you see in the figure. When you finish these steps, save the changes you made to pirate.fla.

Exercise 2: Animating the character

Now that you have imported the character, you need to do something with all the assets to create the illusion of movement. This exercise involves creating new keyframes and swapping the instances on the Stage with new ones from the Library.

1. Select frame 17 on each layer and press F5 to extend the frames across the Timeline. To select all those frames on each layer, use the Selection tool to highlight the frames. You can click and drag on the Timeline to select all of the frames vertically (Figure 4.7). Then press F5 after you select them to add a frame at the location.

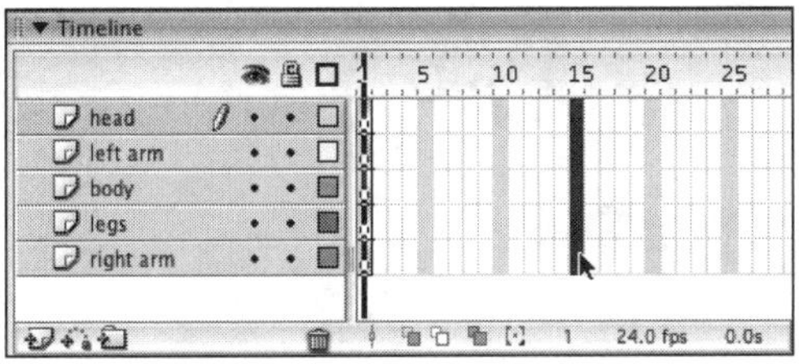

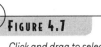

FIGURE 4.7

Click and drag to select frame 17 on each layer and press F5 to insert frames on every layer.

2. You already have a keyframe on frame 1. Insert keyframes at frames 5, 9, and 13 on each layer. Again, select all the frames vertically at the same time by using the Selection tool (Figure 4.8) or the Ctrl (Windows)/ Command (Macintosh) keys and press F6 to insert keyframes at that location. When you finish, all ayers have keyframes at frames 1, 5, 9 and 13, as shown in the following figure.

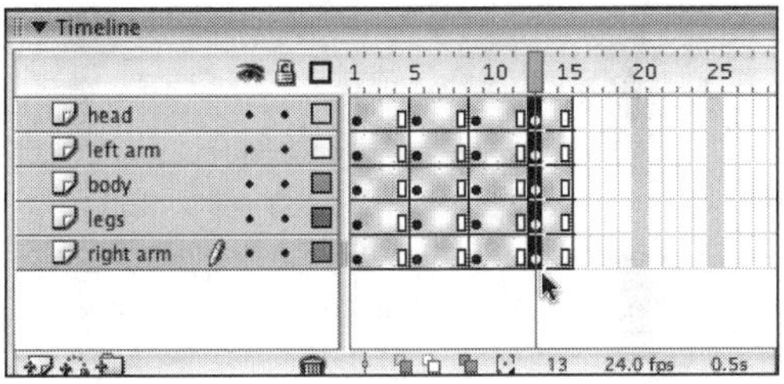

FIGURE 4.8

Keyframes along the Timeline. You will change the graphics at these keyframes.

See "Changing the center point" earlier in this chapter for more information.

The reason you add keyframes at these locations is these frames will contain new graphics that you swap with the instance currently on the Stage. Therefore, the new graphics directly replace the instances on each keyframe.

3. Before you swap instances, you need to edit the center point of your instances. You edited the center point in Chapter 2, when you motion tweened the character along a motion path. You edited the snap ring so the character snapped to the path from a certain location. In this chapter, you rotate each piece in certain ways, but you want to rotate it using a particular part as the center rotation point.

   For this exercise, place the center points according to the diagram shown in Figure 4.9. Select each instance on each keyframe by using the Free Transform tool and drag the center point to a new location.

FIGURE 4.9

Move the center points to these locations after you put the instances on the Stage.

You want the head to hinge at the bottom of the instance, so it appears to move where the neck attaches to the body. The body can remain at the middle because you don't rotate the instances in the animation. The arms hinge where the arm attaches to the body, and the legs attach near the hip. None of the hinging needs to be accurate, nor is it meant to even approach realism, although it works for this basic cartoon animation.

You need to hide the body layer to move the center point on the right arm. Click the eye icon on the Timeline for the body layer to hide it while you adjust the right arm's center point. Show the layer again when you're finished.

4. Select frame 5 on the left arm layer; then click the `leftarm-1` instance on the Stage. Open the Property inspector (Window > Properties) and click the Swap button, as shown in Figure 4.10. The Swap Symbol dialog box opens, in which you can choose a different symbol from the Library to swap the instance with. Select the `leftarm-2` symbol from the list of available items in the Library and click OK.

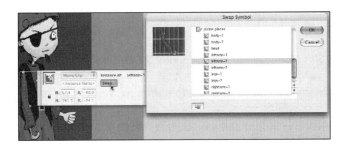

FIGURE 4.10

Click the Swap button to swap instances.

Select frame 9 on the left arm layer and select the `leftarm-1` instance on the Stage. Click Swap in the Property inspector so the Swap Symbol dialog box opens. Choose the `leftarm-3` symbol from the list of available items in the Library and click OK. Select the `leftarm-1` instance on frame 13 on the left arm layer and swap it with the `leftarm-2` symbol in the Library.

5. After you finish all the swapping, click and drag the playhead across the Timeline to test your changes. The arm should appear to move choppily with each symbol swap.

6. After the new instances are on the Stage, make sure to edit the center point of each swapped instance on the left arm layer in case you need to rotate them. Select the Free Transform tool and move the center point (the white circle) of each swapped instance on the Stage from the center to near the top center of the instance, as you did in step 3.

7. Select the `rightarm-1` instance on frame 5 on the right arm layer.

   Open the Property inspector (Window > Properties) and click the Swap button. Select the `rightarm-2` symbol from the list of available items in the Library and click OK to swap the instances.

   Select the `rightarm-1` instance on frame 9 of the right arm layer. Press Backspace or Delete to remove the instance from the Stage. This part of the animation is when the body would hide the arm, so you can remove the instance from the Stage completely.

   Select the `rightarm-1` instance on frame 13 and then click the Swap button in the Property inspector. Select the `rightarm-2` symbol from the list of available items in the Library and click OK.

8. After the new instances are on the Stage, make sure to edit the center point of each swapped instance on the right arm layer in case you need to rotate them. First, hide the body layer by clicking the eye symbol on the Timeline (for the body layer). After you hide the instances on this layer, you can see the entire `rightarm-1` and `rightarm-2` instances.

   Select the Free Transform tool and move the center point (the white circle) of the `rightarm-2` instance on the Stage from the center to near the top center of the instance like you did to `rightarm-1` in step 3.

   After you finish, click the X icon on the Timeline for the body layer to show the layer again.

9. Select the `legs-1` instance on frame 5 on the legs layer. Unlock the legs layer first, if necessary. Open the Property inspector (Window > Properties) and click the Swap button. Select the `legs-2` symbol from the list of available items in the Library and click OK.

You might want to lock the left arm, body, and legs layers so you don't accidentally select instances on them. Remember that you need to unlock those layers again before you edit the keyframes.

You can leave frame 9 as it is. Because there are only two states for the legs, they switch between the legs-1 and legs-2 symbols.

Select the legs-1 instance on frame 13 on the legs layer, and swap it with the legs-2 symbol in the Library. When you finish swapping, click and drag the playhead across the Timeline to test your changes. The arms and legs of the pirate should all appear to be moving.

10. After the new instances are on the Stage, make sure to edit the center point of each swapped instance on the legs layer in case you want to rotate them. Select the Free Transform tool and move the center point (the white circle) of the legs-2 instance on the Stage from the center to near the top-center of the instance, as you did with the legs-1 instance in step 3.

11. Similar to the legs layer, the body only has two states that it swaps between. Select the body-1 instance on frame 5 on the body layer. Unlock the body layer first, if necessary. Open the Property inspector (Window > Properties) and click the Swap button. Select the body-2 symbol from the list of available items in the Library and click OK.

You can leave frame 9 as it is. Because there are only two states for the body, they will switch between the body-1 and body-2 symbols.

Select the body-1 instance on frame 13 on the body layer and swap it with the body-2 symbol in the Library. You don't need to modify the center point for the body layer instances because you do not need to rotate this instance in the animation.

12. There is only a single state for the head animation. Instead of having multiple graphics to represent different parts of an animation, you just rotate the single instance on the keyframes. Before you do any rotations, you need to edit the center point of the instance. Select the head instance on frame 5 using the Free Transform tool. Click the circle and drag it down to the bottom center of the instance to the same location as you did in step 4. Repeat this for frame 13 so the neck appears to rotate while "attached" to the body.

Select the instance on frame 5 with the Free Transform tool again. Move the cursor over the upper-right handle until you see a round arrow (Figure 4.11). Click and drag to rotate the head slightly, as shown in Figure 4.11.

FIGURE 4.11

Rotate the head slightly on frames 5 and 13.

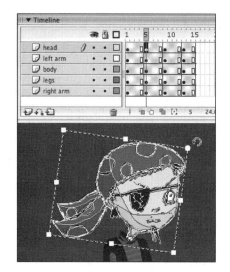

Repeat this step (slightly rotating the head) on frame 13. When you're finished, the head will bob when you move the playhead across the Timeline.

13. Now that you have animated the head, body, legs and arms of this character, select Control > Test Movie to test the movement in your frame-by-frame animation. Make any edits or changes as necessary to fine-tune the movements.

You should expect the animation to look choppy at this point. You make further edits in the next exercise to make the animation look "smoother" by using only frame-by-frame animation techniques. In the following exercise, you rotate some symbols for "in-between" animation using the Onion Skin feature, rotation, and the alpha property to achieve a stylized effect. Save your changes before moving on to the next exercise.

You might want to use the Onion Skin feature to make edits. If so, refer to the following section.

Using Tools to Edit and Test the Animation

If you drew this chapter's pirate animation by hand, the frames you added in the previous exercise would be the major changes in your animation (what you might create thumbnails for). Then, whether you draw the animation or use instances like this project, you need to create the "in-between" frames by modifying existing drawings or creating new ones. For the sake of simplicity, you modify the movie clips you already imported by placing them in-between the major changes in the animation and making changes to their appearance.

Onion skin settings and preferences

The Onion Skin tools, which are very important for frame-by-frame animation, are features that stem from traditional animation. When traditional animators draw, they use transparent layers to draw subtle changes in the animation. For example, if the animator draws a character for frame 1, then she overlays tracing paper and draws a subtle change on frame 2 to create the appearance of motion while using the drawing on frame 1 as a reference because it can be seen through the transparent paper.

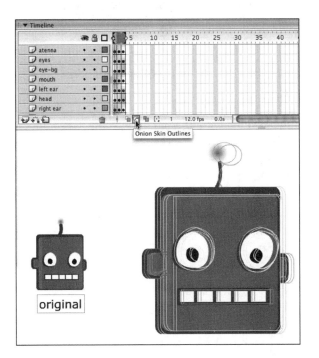

FIGURE 4.12

You create movement by drawing subtle changes from the previous frame. Overlaying tracing paper helps an animator refer to the previous frame. In this figure, Onion Skin with Outlines is active so you can see the outline of previous frames.

Onion skinning lets you work in a similar way. You can draw or place items on the Stage on a particular frame while you see a number of surrounding frames before and after the current frame that are "dimmed" (faded out). With pirate.fla open, select frame 9 and then click the Onion Skin button on the Timeline (Figure 4.13). You see dimmed frames surrounding the currently selected frame.

FIGURE 4.13

Surrounding frames are "dimmed" when you turn on the Onion Skin feature.

Onion Skin   Modify Onion Markers
Onion Skin Outlines   Edit Multiple Frames

original

Make sure that you unlock the layers you want to see as "dimmed" frames. Locked layers won't appear as dimmed when you use the Onion Skin tools.

You can edit only the current frame (where the playhead sits). You cannot edit the onion-skinned (dimmed) frames unless you select the Edit Multiple Frames button.

You can reposition the start and end frames for the onion skin by dragging the markers further away from the playhead, or closer to it. You can also modify the properties of the marker. Click the Modify Onion Markers button (Figure 4.13) and select an option from the pop-up menu. You can choose to display a certain number of dimmed frames around the playhead or all frames (Onion 2, Onion 5, or Onion All), or lock the current position of the onion skin markers (Anchor Onion).

There are two other options for onion skinning. You can enable the Onion Skin Outlines feature or the Edit Multiple Frames feature.

Onion Skin Outlines displays dimmed frames as outlines instead of faded graphics. If you choose the Edit Multiple Frames feature, you can edit the dimmed frames as well as the current frame (unlike the regular Onion Skin feature). This is particularly useful after you create an animation and need to fine-tune your drawings in relation to each other.

▶ ▶ CHANGING FRAME VIEWS

When the Timeline grows in length with your animations, you might want to change the way you view frames. You can change the appearance of the frames in several different ways by selecting the Frame View pop-up menu in the upper-right corner of the Timeline. None of these options actually affect the animation or application you create. You can choose from the following options:

◆ **Tiny to large:** Changes the size of the frames on the Timeline. Larger sizes make the frames wider (horizontally), which is useful when you have a lot of frames in your animation. If you have a lot of frames on the Timeline, choose Tiny or Small.

◆ **Short:** Makes the frames shorter vertically, which is useful when you have a lot of layers.

◆ **Preview:** Lets you see your animation on the Timeline without having to scrub through it.

◆ **Preview in context:** Shows the frame content on the Timeline in correct proportions (or context).

Exercise 3: Testing and editing your animation

The animation might seem a bit clunky if you test it in its current state. You can add frames in-between the existing ones to create smoother animation. If you are working with a drawn cartoon, you might have thumbnails for each keyframe and then draw the transition between the thumbnails using the Onion Skin feature (which you use in this exercise). You will copy and paste existing frames and modify instances on the Timeline, using onion skins for reference.

1. Select the left arm layer and click the Insert Layer button. Rename the layer **left arm - fade**. Then select the right arm layer and click the Insert Layer button. Rename the new layer **right arm - fade**. Then select the legs layer and click the Insert Layer button. Rename the new layer **legs - fade**.

2. Each new layer should extend to frame 17 on the Timeline. Select frame 3 on each of these three layers, and press F6 to insert a keyframe. Then select frame 7 on each of these three layers and press F6 to insert a keyframe. Finally, select frame 11 on all three layers and press F6 to insert a keyframe. Then select frame 15 of the left arm—fade layer and press F6 to insert a keyframe. When you're finished, the Timeline should resemble the following figure.

> If you want to modify the graphics inside one of the instances on the Stage in the FLA, make sure that you duplicate the instance on the Stage first (Modify > Symbol > Duplicate Symbol). If you modify the instance on the Stage, it changes every instance of that symbol on the Stage.

FIGURE 4.14

Add empty keyframes on the Timeline. You will paste frames at these locations.

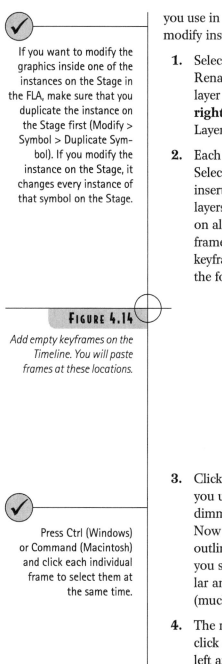

3. Click the Onion Skin button on the Timeline. Make sure that you unlock the layers on the Timeline, so you can see the dimmed frames around the current position of the playhead. Now click the Onion Skin Outlines button, which shows the outline of each frame instead of the dimmed frames. This helps you see the other frames of the animation easier in this particular animation, which uses alpha to create a sense of movement (much like the dimmed Onion Skin frames).

> Press Ctrl (Windows) or Command (Macintosh) and click each individual frame to select them at the same time.

4. The rest of the animation does not need to be exact. Right-click (Windows) or Control-click (Macintosh) frame 1 of the left arm layer, and select Copy Frames from the context menu. Then click frame 3 of the left arm - fade layer and right-click

or Control-click the frame and select Paste Frames from the context menu. This command pastes an exact replica of frame 1 on frame 3.

Click the instance you just pasted with the Free Transform tool. Because the Onion Skin button is active, you can see the position of the two arm states on either side of the current frame. Move the center point of the instance to the upper region of the arm (as you did in the previous example).

Rotate the instance on frame 3 until it is approximately between the two drawn arm states (Figure 4.15). The instance should rotate with the top of the graphic as the center because you changed the center point of the instance.

If you have difficulty selecting the instance on the fade layer, lock the left-arm layer first.

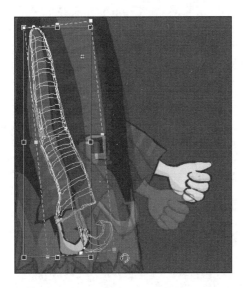

FIGURE 4.15

Rotate the instance in-between the states on frames 1 and 5.

After you finish rotating the instance, make sure that it is still selected and select Alpha from the Color pop-up menu in the Property inspector. Change the Alpha value to approximately 40%, as shown in the following figure.

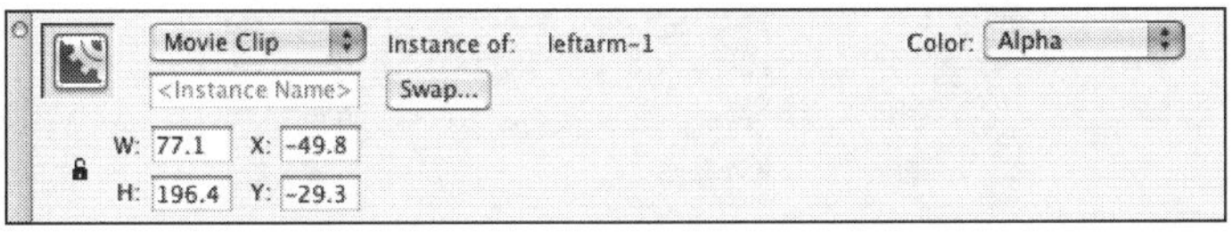

FIGURE 4.16

Change the alpha value to 40%.

If you cannot see the difference between the two surrounding instance positions, extend the onion skin markers. You can move them by clicking a handle and dragging it toward or away from the playhead.

Select frame 5 on the left arm layer and copy the frame. Paste the frame on frame 7 of the left arm - fade layer. Select the Free Transform tool and move the center point of the instance to the upper region of the arm (as you did in the previous example). Then rotate and change the alpha level of the instance. Repeat this step with frame 9 on the left arm layer, and paste it on frame 11 of the left arm - fade layer. With the Onion Skin button selected, you see the dimmed frames around the keyframe that you need to modify. When you finish, all the frames on the left arm - fade layer should be semitransparent and rotated. Then, the keyframe at frame 15 (though 17) should remain empty—this is when the arm doesn't appear in the animation.

5. Right-click (Windows) or Control-click (Macintosh) frame 1 of the right arm layer, and select Copy Frames from the context menu. Then click frame 3 of the right arm - fade layer and right-click or Control-click the frame and select Paste Frames from the context menu.

    Select the Free Transform tool and click the instance you just pasted. Move the center point to the upper-right corner of the instance, as you did in the earlier example. Then rotate the instance between the visible right arm instance and the pirate body, and change the instance's alpha to 40%.

FIGURE 4.17

Rotate the instance in-between the visible right arm and the body after you move the center point.

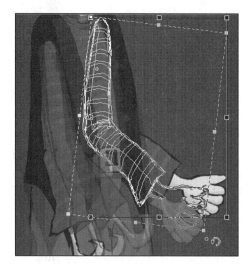

Repeat this step with frame 5 on the right arm layer and paste
it on frame 7 of the right arm - fade layer. Leave the other
frames on the right arm - fade layer empty. When you finish,
all the frames on the right arm - fade layer should be semi-
transparent and rotated.

6. Right-click (Windows) or Control-click (Macintosh) frame 1 of
   the legs layer, and select Copy Frames from the context menu.
   Then click frame 3 of the legs - fade layer, and right-click or
   Control-click the frame and select Paste Frames from the context menu.

   Select the Free Transform tool and click the instance you just
   pasted. Change the center point of the instance, and rotate the
   instance so it appears in relation to the other state of the leg
   graphic, as shown in Figure 4.18. Select the instance and
   change the Alpha value in the Property inspector to 40%.

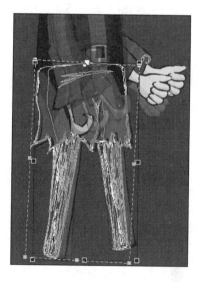

FIGURE 4.18

*Rotate the legs so they
appear in-between the other
two graphics on the Stage.*

Repeat select frame 5 of the legs layer, and copy and paste this
frame onto frame 7 of the legs - fade layer. Rotate and change
the alpha value of the instance to 40%.

Select frame 3 on the legs - fade layer, and right-click (Windows)
or Control-click (Macintosh) the layer. Select Copy Frames from
the context menu; then click frame 11 of the same layer. Right-
click or Control-click again, and select Paste Frames from the

context menu. Because this instance changes between two different states, this "in-between" state can look the same as the earlier position.

Now your Timeline will look similar to the following figure.

FIGURE 4.19

Your Timeline will look similar to this figure when you finish adding the "in-between" graphics.

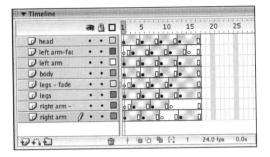

Test the animation and make any modifications as you see fit. When you finish modifying, deselect the Onion Skin button. You might want to add some additional frames or graphics to the Timeline, and you should notice that the animation looks a lot smoother than it did earlier because you had added additional graphics and frames to the animation to fill in areas where there was previously no movement.

You might also notice that the animation loops at the end, and the pirate appears to dance because the graphics change from a beginning position to a finished position and then back toward the beginning position. Therefore, the dancing appears to go back and forth between two positions in a looping fashion. Save your changes before moving on to the next exercise.

Exercise 4: Creating and animating the room

The room contains text and a floor graphic that lights up using motion tweens. The floor contains only five different symbols: one for each color on the dance floor. And each of these symbols contains a nested movie clip to create the motion tween "glow." Each main symbol has many instances on the Stage, which are modified to have a unique shape. The five symbols (containing nested symbols) are already in the start file's Library. Double-click the blue symbol in the dancefloor folder and take a look at the motion tween (Figure 4.20).

You use a motion tween to create the glowing dance floor squares.

The motion tween starts on frame 1 and ends on frame 50. Easing is applied in the Property inspector, so the color has a softer transition as it fades in and out. Double-click the other symbols in the dance-floor folder. Notice that each symbol's motion tween is a different length or starts at a different frame. Thus, the instances creating the dance floor do not tween at the same time: They start and finish the tween at varying times, so the animation is not uniform.

Double-click the grid symbol in the Library. The symbol includes the grid pattern that creates an outline for each color on the dance floor and a gradient that covers the grid pattern to create the appearance of depth. The grid was created in Illustrator using the grid tool, and the gradient was created in Flash using the outer edge of the grid as an outline and filled with a linear gradient of varying alpha levels as shown in the following figure.

A grid pattern and gradient for the dance floor.

▶ ▶ CREATING THE GRADIENT

A gradient fill was added over the grid graphic you added to the Stage. The gradient helps add a feeling of depth and dimension to the floor. To create it, a shape without a fill was drawn that matches the outer edges of the floor's grid pattern. A linear gradient fill that transitions from a transparent black to almost clear was applied to the outline (using the Color Mixer panel). To replicate this gradient effect, select Linear from the Fill style pop-up menu in the Color Mixer panel. Click the left color pointer under the gradient definition bar and select black from the color control near the top of the panel. Then click the Alpha text field and enter 50%. Repeat this step for the right color pointer under the gradient definition bar, except choose 22% for the alpha level. Now the gradient transitions between two transparent black values.

Do not use many gradients in your animations because they take a lot of processor power to render. Detailed calculations must be made for each pixel in the gradient, which can potentially slow down how fast the SWF file plays.

In the following exercise, you add and modify the dancefloor instances. If you double-clicked a symbol to look at its contents, make sure that you click Scene 1 to return to the main Timeline.

1. Select the bottom layer (right arm) and then click Insert Layer to add a new layer near the bottom of the Timeline. Click and drag the new layer underneath right arm so it's the bottom layer. Rename the new layer **floor**.

2. Open the Library (Window > Library) and drag the grid graphic symbol to the floor layer, and position the graphic so it resembles Figure 4.21 or matches the following coordinates: X:-178, Y:565.

3. Select the grid graphic, and press F8 to convert it into a movie clip. Name this symbol **floor**. You nest many movie clip instances inside of this instance in upcoming steps. Double-click the movie clip to edit it in place.

4. Inside the movie clip, lock Layer 1 with the grid graphic on it. Then click Insert Layer to create a new layer. Rename the

new layer **color squares**, and then drag it below the grid layer (Figure 4.22).

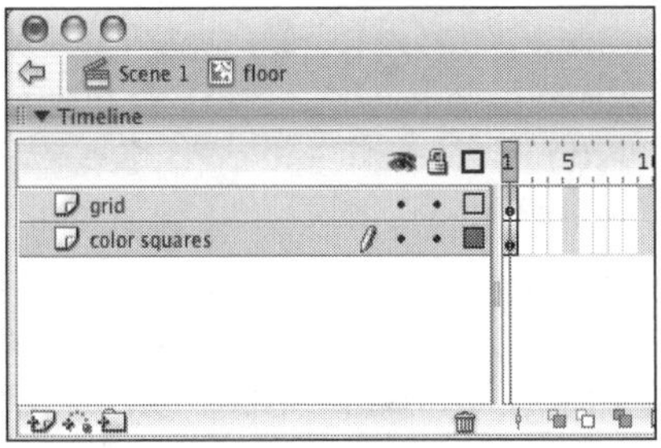

FIGURE 4.22

Drag the new color squares layer beneath the grid.

5. Double-click the dancefloor folder inside the Library to open the folder. Each symbol inside the color squares folder has been prepared for you. Each of the five movie clips has motion tweens that fade in and out at different intervals. These fade the square graphic in and out, starting and ending on different frames. Therefore, when you place all the instances on the Stage they fade at different times.

6. Drag the green symbol instance to the Stage and select the Free Transform tool. Click the instance so handles surround the instance. Move the green instance under one of the grid squares (click and drag the center of the instance to move it). Now use the skew and resize tool to shape the colored square so it matches one of the squares.

Hover over the top of the square until you see the skew icon (Figure 4.23, left). Click and drag to skew the square. You can also use the corner handles to resize the instance (Figure 4.23, right). These two tools are what you use to shape the squares like the floor.

You can also rotate the instance using the Free Transform tool. After you drag the instance to the Stage, rotate the instance so the upper left corners of the instance and the grid match. Then resize and skew the instance so it matches the shape on the grid.

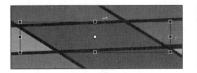 

FIGURE 4.23

Use the skew (left) and resize (right) tools to shape the colored squares like each square of the grid. To access these tools, click an instance by using the Free Transform tool.

7. Place approximately three or four more yellow symbols on the Stage and resize them to match randomly chosen squares on the grid.

8. Repeat steps 6 and 7 for each color, until there is approximately an even number of each instance, and you fill each square on the grid. You need to place, resize, and skew three or four instances of each color on the Stage to fill the floor (Figure 4.21).

9. After you finish adding the colored instances to the Stage, click Scene 1 on the Edit Bar to return to the main Stage. Then select Control > Test Movie to test the SWF file.

►► Blinking Effect

You might notice that many Flash websites use blinking effects. Perhaps a movie clip fades in and blinks rapidly, or a character's eye blinks. This is frequently accomplished by using frame-by-frame animation. If you use frame-by-frame animation, you can take a keyframe with the instance and paste it on a later keyframe; however, you leave the frames between these keyframes empty. So, if you have an eye instance on frame 1, select frame 3 of the same layer and press F6 to copy the keyframe. Then select frame 5 and press F6 again. Select frames 2 and 4, and right-click or Control-click and select Clear Frames. Frame 2 and 4 are now empty, but the instance appears on frames 1, 3, and 5.

When you test the SWF file, the instance appears to blink. How fast the instance blinks depends on the number of frames that separate those instances and also the frame rate. So to slow down or speed up the blinking, either change the frame rate in the Property inspector or insert more frames (or remove frames) between the keyframes. To insert frames, select an empty frame and press F5. To remove frames, select the frame and right-click or Control-click, and select Remove Frames from the context menu.

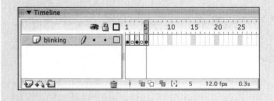

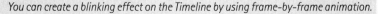
You can create a blinking effect on the Timeline by using frame-by-frame animation.

10. Select the floor layer, and click Insert Layer from the Timeline. Rename the new layer **wall**. Click and drag the wall layer beneath the floor layer so it is the bottom layer on the Timeline.

11. Select the Rectangle tool in the Tools panel. Click the pencil icon next to the stroke color control and click the No Color button. Then select the Fill color control type #222222 in the text field above the palette. Draw a rectangle so the left edge that runs vertically from the upper-right corner of the grid floor, as shown in Figure 4.25. Make sure that the rectangle covers the entire area of the Stage to the right of that upper-right corner of the floor.

FIGURE 4.25

Create a rectangle that covers the right side of the Stage, starting at the upper-right corner of the grid floor.

After you create the wall, select the shape and press F8 to convert it into a graphic symbol. Type in a name for the new symbol (such as **wall**).

12. Find discopirate.png in the Library. This graphic was created in Illustrator, and can optionally be placed on the Stage. Select the topmost layer on the Timeline and click Insert Layer. Rename the new layer text. Then drag an instance of this graphic onto this layer, and position it in the upper-left corner (see the introductory figures at the beginning of this chapter for reference).

Now you have made the finishing touches to the animation. Test the animation again and save your changes before moving on.

ADDING SOUND AND OPTIMIZING

One of the main concerns when you create frame-by-frame animation is the file size of the resulting SWF file. This is particularly true if you draw the character across many frames. Each frame contains new information, which is all data that add to the final SWF file size. When you hand-draw vector graphics, each hand-drawn line contains a certain number of points that require calculations to render (draw out when the SWF plays) curves in the line, which also adds to the file size. Therefore, if you reduce the number of points in the curved lines (or fill shapes) you create, the file size goes down and the animation also requires less power to render each frame.

To optimize lines or fill shapes, you need to select the raw lines on the Stage (not symbols) and then select Modify > Shape > Optimize. The Optimize curves dialog box opens where you can make selections to optimize the shape.

Select an amount of smoothing to apply in the Optimize Curves dialog box. Applying more smoothing (moving the slider toward Maximum) adds a greater amount of optimization to your lines. This changes the lines more; removing more detail and making the new graphic look quite different from the original graphic. If you select Use Multiple Passes, the shape optimizes as much as possible (similar to repeatedly selecting this option). You can also choose whether you want to display the totals message, which provides an overview of how much optimization applies to the graphic.

You can also select Modify > Shape > Smooth or Modify > Shape > Straighten to remove points, depending on how you want the lines to modify.

You can apply Modify > Shape > Optimize again to further optimize the graphic.

FIGURE 4.26

Optimize lines in a curve or in the pirate graphics to reduce file size and improve performance.

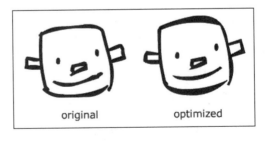

original   optimized

You cannot optimize some simple shapes further; in particular, lines without curves. For example, if you draw a perfect circle, square, or triangle, there are no points that can be reduced. Most optimization needs to occur in complex hand-drawn lines that you create free-hand. The pirate is a good example of lines that can be optimized. This is particularly important in larger animations with more graphics. In Chapter 5 on character animation, you learn how to create an optimized character that is optimal for longer animations on the web.

Sound and video are also assets that add a lot of file size to your SWF files. In the following exercise, you add sound to the animation and optimize it to reduce the file size in the exported SWF file.

Exercise 5: Adding sound

A dancing pirate needs some sound to dance to. In this exercise, you import and add a looping sound to the Timeline, and change the properties of the sound before you export the SWF file.

1. Select all of the frames in the pirate animation. This includes the head, body, left arm, left arm - fade, legs, legs - fade, right arm, and right arm - fade layers. Click and drag over the frames using the Selection tool to select them (Figure 4.27). After you select the frames, right-click (Windows) or Control-click (Macintosh) and select Copy Frames from the context menu.

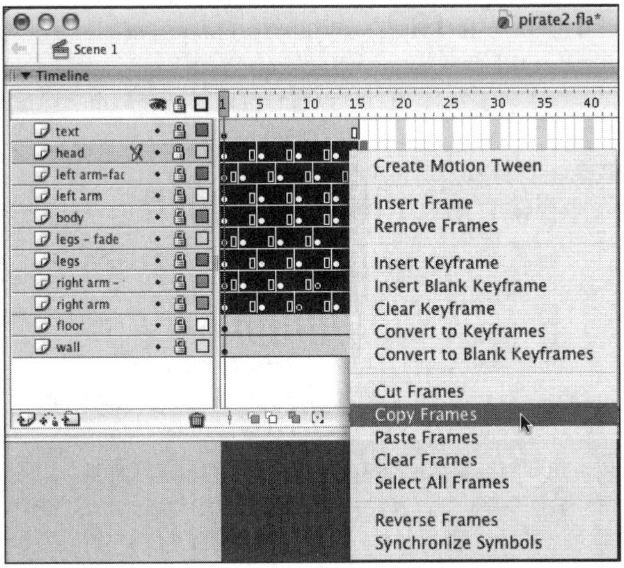

FIGURE 4.27

Select all the pirate animation frames.

2. Select Insert > New Symbol and select Movie Clip. Name the new movie clip **pirate** and click OK to enter symbol-editing mode. Select frame 1 inside the movie clip, right-click (Windows) or Control-click (Macintosh), and select Paste Frames from the context menu. The frames from the main Timeline paste inside the movie clip. Now the entire pirate animation is inside a movie clip symbol.

   After you copy and paste the frames into a new layer, you can delete these layers from the main Timeline. Then you can drag an instance of the pirate symbol onto the main Timeline.

3. Find disco.wav in the Chapter 4 folder on the CD-ROM (04/start/disco.wav). Save the sound file onto your hard drive.

4. Select File > Import > Import to Library. Find disco.wav on your hard drive, and click Open (Windows) or Import to Library (Macintosh). The file imports into your FLA file, and you can find it in the Library.

5. Click Insert Layer to create a new layer, and rename it **sound**.

6. Select frame 1 of the sound layer and open the Property inspector (Window > Properties). Click the Sound pop-up menu and select the name of the sound you just imported (Figure 4.28). Make sure that the Sync menu is set to Start, and that you select Loop from the pop-up menu next to Start. This is particularly important if you have the pirate animation on the main Timeline.

▶ ▶ **SYNCH OPTIONS**

You can select different sync options, such as the Start option you specify in step 6. **Event** syncs the sound to a specific event, such as when you click a button (the event), an event sound plays. The **Start** event is the same as an event, except it doesn't replay the sound if it's already playing. For example, if a playhead reaches a specific frame, it doesn't replay the sound of the playhead as it re-enters that frame. The **Stop** event mutes the specified sound. The **Stream** event synchs the sound to the Timeline, and the Timeline will play to keep up with the stream sound. Stream sounds download from the server each time the sound plays.

FIGURE 4.28

Select and make settings for a looping sound.

7. Find the wav file you imported in Library (Window > Library). Select the sound file, right-click or Control-click the item, and select Properties from the context menu. The Sound Properties dialog box opens, in which you can select export settings for the sound. Select MP3 from the Compression pop-up menu. This means that the file uses the MP3 sound compression settings. Leave the Bit rate at the default value of 48 kbps, which is a lower quality than you find on recorded media, but it is optimal for playback on the Internet. If you want to hear the wav as a stereo sound, deselect the Convert stereo to mono check box. Finally, set Quality to Best. Click Test to listen to the sound file.

Try changing and testing different settings to see what they sound like. If you want to reduce the file size, compress the file further. Select MP3 and choose a lower bit rate in the Sound Properties dialog box.

For more information on sound export settings and optimization see *www.FLAnimation.com /chapters/04/soundexport.*

8. Select Control > Test Movie to see the current status of the project. The music now loops in the background while the pirate movie clip animates.

For information on loading sound using ActionScript, see the following web page: *www.FLAnimation.com /chapters/04/loadsound.*

Exercise 6: Optimizing and publishing

When you test the file, there are several things you can watch for and make better before you finalize and upload the project.

1. Select File > Publish to publish the SWF file. Look at the file size of pirate.swf (which is in the same directory as your FLA by default). Depending on the file size, you might want to optimize the pirate graphics. Your SWF file is probably around 200 KB, which isn't horrible for a frame-by-frame animation with this amount of detail and sound; but you could make it smaller.

Many Flash forums (such as www.flashmx2004.com) have areas devoted to site checks, with other people ready and willing to check your sites for you. Thanks to these forums, it's easier to get by in life without Internet-savvy friends.

If you are syncing sound in your FLA file, then it's unlikely you'll be able to change the frame rate at this point because the animation is tied into the sound. Therefore, if you change the frame rate it will change the synchronization. Because the sound file in this document is a loop and doesn't synch, changing the frame rate does not harm the FLA.

See Chapter 2 for a comparison of vector and bitmap graphics.

2. Open the pirate pieces folder inside the Library (Window > Library) and double click each pirate movie clip symbol. Select the raw graphic drawings inside each symbol (click and drag around the drawings using the Selection tool) and then select Modify > Shape > Optimize. Follow the directions at the beginning of this section for optimizing the raw graphics.

3. Right-click (Windows) or Control-click (Macintosh) discopirate.png in the Library and select Properties from the context menu to open the Bitmap Properties dialog box. Make sure that you select Allow smoothing in the dialog box. Choose JPEG in the Compression pop-up menu. Click the Test button to see how much compression applies to the PNG graphic and the file size of the graphic. Then select Lossless (PNG/GIF) from the Compression menu and click Test again. Determine which compression setting affords the best results, select that option, and then click OK.

4. You can also change the frame rate of the document if you want, if it's possible. In general, high frame rates with frame-by-frame animation can be processor-intensive. To test the frame rate of the SWF file, you should play it on computers with varying amounts processing power. If you know someone with an old computer, ask her to play your animation and see whether it's choppy or erratic when it displays (speeding up and slowing down). If so, you might want to reduce the frame rate so the playback is not as erratic. You can also optimize the graphics further (from step 2) to speed the animation up.

5. Select File > Publish to publish the project. This command generates SWF and HTML file in the directory you saved the FLA file in. You need to upload these two files onto the web to view the page online.

You might want to make the SWF file as large as the browser window the user views it in. Some animators prefer this, but you should make sure the graphics you use are vector-based. If you try resizing bitmap graphics, the images might appear blurry and distorted. Vector graphics are scalable, so they appear nice and smooth when enlarged.

To make the SWF file the same size as the browser window, you need to make some changes to the default settings in Flash. Select File > Publish Settings to open the Publish Settings dialog box. Click the HTML tab, which contains settings about how the code that embeds the SWF file in the HTML page generates. Select Percent from the Dimensions pop-up menu.

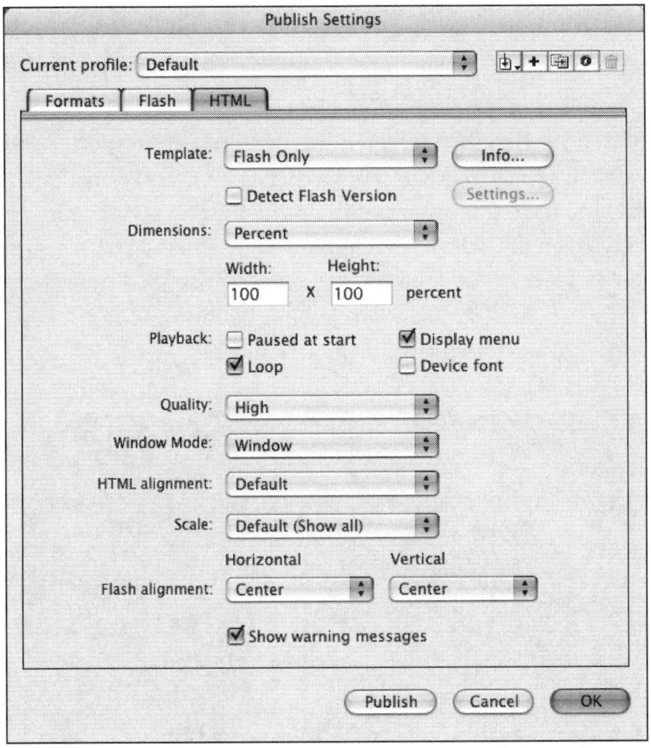

FIGURE 4.29

Change the publish settings to alter how the SWF file embeds in an HTML page.

The SWF file fills the entire browser window regardless of how big or small it is, and changes size if the user changes the size of the window.

Save and publish the document, and double-click the HTML page that Flash generates to view your project in a browser. You just created a file that primarily uses frame-by-frame animation to produce a finished cartoon. As you now know, there are other ways to create a frame-by-frame animation: You can draw each frame or modify instances on the Stage in any way you see fit.

Moving On

Frame-by-frame animation is a lot about experimentation and trial-and-error. There are many different ways to achieve animation by using the frame-by-frame technique. You might want to try freehand drawing for your animation. Draw a character on frame 1, and then press F6 to insert a new keyframe at frame 2. Modify your drawing on frame 2, and then select frame 3 and press F6 (and so on). Use the Onion Skin feature to see the changes between each frame to help you animate along the Timeline.

As for the project you just created, you might want to add details to the background. Create a new layer and then add your frame-by-frame animation to the background. In the following example, music notes have been added on several frames. The Onion Skin feature was used to view earlier frames, which were modified in subsequent frames using earlier frames as a reference. Additional notes are added, and some are removed from keyframes.

FIGURE 4.30

Music notes are added to the background by using frame-by-frame animation.

You might make the eye blink, too. To do this, you need to make the eye its own symbol by copying it from the head symbol and inserting it into a new movie clip symbol. You need to modify the eye on the head symbol so it shows the blink state (Figure 4.31).

FIGURE 4.31

*Modify the head symbol
so it displays the blink
state for the eye.*

Then you need to place the new eye symbol so it overlaps the blink
state on the head symbol. The new eye symbol needs to appear and
disappear on subsequent frames. To create a blinking effect, refer to
the sidebar called "Blinking Effect" in Exercise 4.

FIGURE 5.A

FIGURE 5.B

FIGURE 5.C

What you learn

- ▶ Principles of character creation and animation
- ▶ How to animate a character
- ▶ How to organize a character into assets
- ▶ How to create a character's assets in Illustrator
- ▶ How to create a simple character using shapes
- ▶ How to load a SWF file into a different SWF file

Lesson Files

Start:

05/ bonus/tail.ai   05/start/robot_start.fla

05/ bonus/dialog.fla

Finish:

05/complete/robot_animation.fla

05/complete/robot_animation.swf

05/complete/loader.fla

05/complete/loader.swf

05/complete/loader.html

5

CHARACTER CREATION AND ANIMATION

CHARACTER ANIMATION IS ONE of the traditional uses of Macromedia Flash, and it's also one of the most entertaining aspects of SWF files that you find online. There are many different ways you can create a character in Flash, particularly because there are so many different kinds of characters you can imagine and develop. There are several fundamental aspects of character animation that you will almost always use when you create a project, particularly when you work with Flash.

In this chapter, you build a character using a variety of techniques. First, you create the character in Flash using the drawing tools, mostly the Oval and Rectangle tools. You animate the character using motion tweens and frame-by-frame animation in the second half of the project. This chapter also covers how to make the robot animation into an "intro" animation that users can either watch or skip, and then the site automatically proceeds to your main website. This shows you useful techniques that you adopt in several different situations, whether or not you ever develop an intro.

The purpose of this chapter is to demonstrate how easy it is to create a character in Flash, especially if you do not have a background in drawing or art. You use simple shapes to construct the character, which doesn't involve any "line drawing" or advanced skills. Therefore, even if you are new to the art and animation part of Flash, with or without an art background, you should feel comfortable drawing this character.

Website: www.FLAnimation.com/chapters/05

LEARNING ABOUT CHARACTER ANIMATION

You already learned how to make graphics animate in Flash by using several different techniques: motion tweens, shape tweens, and frame-by-frame animation. However, there are several ways to animate characters or objects to make the movements look accurate, with a heightened realism. These techniques are things to think of before you start creating your tweens or frame-by-frame animations. You can apply one or several of these techniques regardless of which way you choose to create your animations.

One of the most important techniques is to show the effects of the environment on the item (gravity, other objects, and so forth). For example, if a bat hits a ball, the ball flattens slightly when and where the bat connects with the ball.

You might find this technique useful when you animate facial expressions. If you create a character's dialogue by using lip-syncing, you benefit from applying the effects of gravity and stretching to the character's face. You look at lip-sync later in this chapter.

Then, when the ball flies through the air, it appears to be slightly stretched out, as seen in the following figure. This effect is usually exaggerated in character animations. You might also use blurring to achieve the effect of an object's movement, particularly "motion blurs" (a commonly used filter in Photoshop and Fireworks). The more blur that you apply to an object implies a greater rate of speed or motion.

FIGURE 5.1

The ball stretches when it flies through the air.

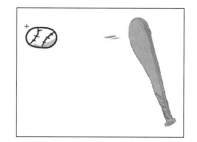

When you create an animation, try to think of the motion you need to display. For example, consider the pirate that you animated in Chapter 4. His head bobbed up and down while he danced. The head bobbing was clearly a secondary motion, compared with the primary motion of dancing that also included swinging arms and moving wooden legs. Considering and paying attention to the primary animation or action in your animation is important, and this motion should overshadow the secondary animations. Animations benefit from having a clear main action (the primary animation).

Similarly, exaggerated actions or features can add quality to your projects. Do not overdo the exaggeration, but use it to tastefully add interest to your caricatures and animations.

When you apply a motion tween to an instance, it moves in a line from the starting point (the first keyframe) to the end (the second keyframe). However, if you apply the movement along an arc (Figure 5.2) by using a motion path (as discussed in Chapter 2), you can achieve more realism than when you animate along a straight line.

At the end of the movement, you might want to apply some residual motion as well. *Residual motion* refers to the small movements that an object makes after it has stopped, while it slows down. Remember that *easing* is another way to achieve more realistic and lifelike motion, which gradually slows down or speeds up an object during the tween. You can apply easing by using the Property inspector (also described in Chapter 2); or for greater creative control, you can manually simulate easing using a series of motion tweens to slow down the character gradually.

The more frames and drawings you have between a start- and endpoint mean that your animation contains more detail and refinements, and can move slower while retaining detail. The fewer drawings you have between two points means that your animation might appear faster and choppier. Choose whatever technique works best for your animation, if applicable.

FIGURE 5.2

An arc is more realistic than a ruler-straight flight path.

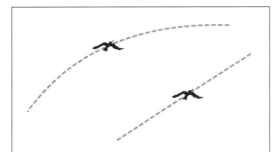

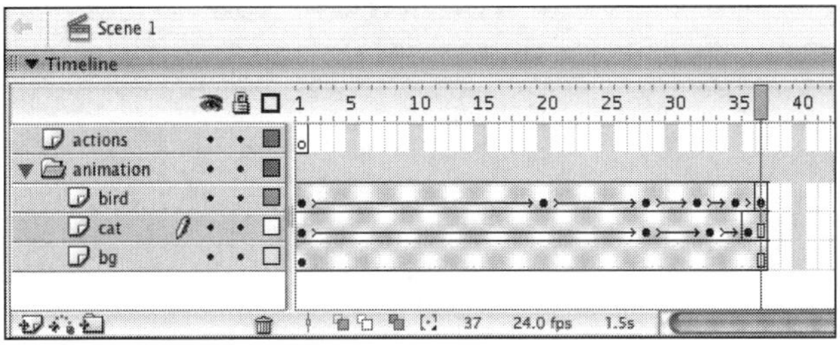

FIGURE 5.3

Each keyframe on this Timeline moves the character a shorter distance, meaning that it appears to slow down gradually.

You apply another important part of character animation *before* a major event occurs—called *anticipation*. Before the event occurs, you might want to animate the character to hint at what is about to happen, so viewers can anticipate what's about to happen. For example, if you animate the bat hitting the ball, you might want to show a character winding up the bat backward before hitting the ball (a forward motion). Or, if your character is about to speak, you might want to show an expression on his or her face that alludes to this change in the action. Using anticipation also helps heighten the realistic nature of your animation.

There are several other aspects that you should consider when you set up your complete animation, which goes beyond the character animation you explore in this project, and it's also beyond the scope of this book. Remember to think about how to form your animation using thumbnail outlines, as outlined in earlier chapters. Think about and plan the timing of your animation in advance. Think about how the frame should look in relation to your character. Will the frame be a close-up of the character or a long shot that shows the scenery around the character? How should you angle the frame and move the character within it? All of these aspects help send your message to the visitor.

Use fewer steps in an Illustrator blend to help reduce file size. The size of your SWF file increases as you add more graphic symbols to the file. Therefore, you should use the smallest possible number of symbols whenever you create a character.

▶ ▶ CHARACTER CREATION IN FLASH

Shortly, you'll discover how to create characters in Flash and learn that you build most of your characters from a great number of instances on the Stage. You need to create a series of symbols—one for each major part of the character (at least the parts you want to animate). Sometimes you'll need several symbols for a single part of the character.

Illustrator can help you create symbols to use in Flash, which is discussed in the following section. Whether you use symbols you create in third-party software or create the entire character in Flash, remember to reuse the assets as much as you can. Use as few symbols as you possibly can to create the effect you want to achieve to reduce the file size of your published SWF file.

Creating graphics for animation in Illustrator

You can use a variety of tools to create graphics to animate in Flash outside of the authoring environment. A popular choice is Adobe Illustrator, which allows you to create vector drawings that you can edit and animate using Flash. Illustrator also lets you "blend" drawings, which creates a series of graphics between two states (for example, an arm or leg bending). You can control how many "steps" exist between the blended shape, each of which you change into a symbol in Illustrator or Flash. These symbols let you create a bunch of poses for your character's arms, legs, tails, and so on—as demonstrated in the following figure.

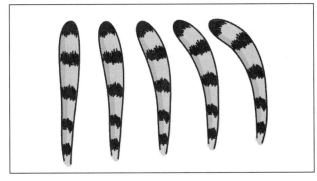

FIGURE 5.4

You can create a series of symbols in Illustrator for each body part in various possible poses without having to draw each possible pose, import them into Flash, and animate them further using tweens.

If you have Illustrator CS, you can follow these steps to create a blended graphic and symbols that you could import into Flash. You won't use these drawings in Project 5, so don't worry if you don't have Illustrator. However, this exercise demonstrates how you can use and benefit from third-party software for the purpose of character animation.

In Illustrator, draw an arm, leg, or tail on the artboard. After you finish, select the entire drawing using the Selection tool. After you select the drawing, drag it into the Brushes palette (Figure 5.5).

You can download a trial copy of Illustrator CS from the Adobe website at www.adobe.com/products/tryadobe/.

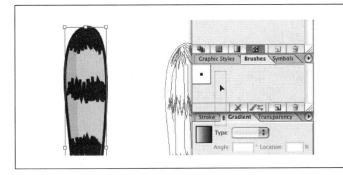

FIGURE 5.5

Draw vectors using Illustrator; then select the entire drawing and drag it onto the Brushes palette.

The New Brush dialog box opens, in which you need to click Art Brush. A second dialog box called Art Brush Options opens; click OK.

Now you create the beginning and end state of your animation. Suppose that you want to have a few different drawings for the tail, from an upright position, and then it bends to the right. You need to create the upright position drawing, and then a drawing of the tail bent completely to the right. Illustrator creates all the drawings in-between those two states—just as a motion tween does in Flash. If you want to use your original drawing as the first state, leave it on the artboard. If not, you need to create a new beginning state and an ending state.

Move your original drawing off the artboard, and make sure it's deselected. Select the Brush tool, and then select the new Brush that you created (Figure 5.6).

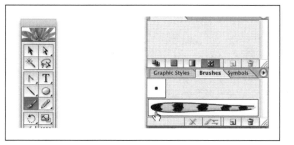

Group your vector drawings before dragging them to the Brushes palette.

FIGURE 5.6

Select the Brush tool in the Tools palette and then choose the Art Brush you created earlier in the Brushes palette.

If you removed the original drawing from the artboard, draw a brushstroke on the artboard to create that shape. To create a straight tail, you need to draw a straight line and the artwork you created earlier appears in the drawing. Create the brushstroke near the left side of the artboard. You might need to experiment a bit first before you get the right look.

Then, on the right side of the artboard, create the finished drawing (representing the final state of the tween). For the tail, draw a curved line to create a curved tail (Figure 5.7).

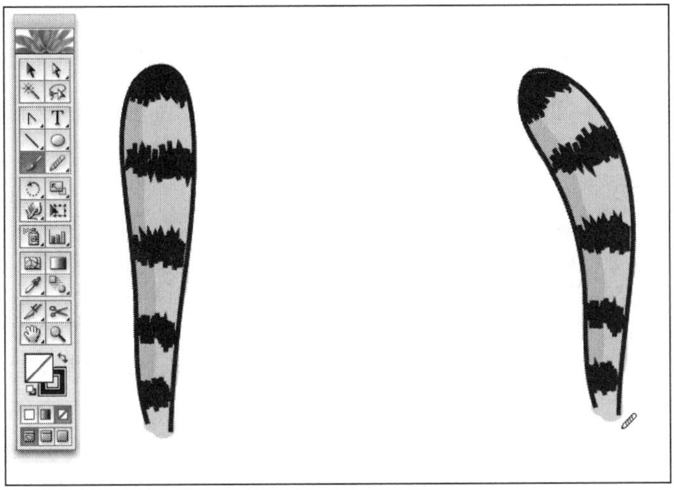

FIGURE 5.7

Draw a curved brushstroke to create a curved tail using an Art Brush.

Select both tails using the Selection tool. Then select Object > Blend > Make from the menu. Several intermediate graphics appear between the two selected objects. Next, select Object > Blend > Blend Options. Another dialog box opens, in which you can choose how many steps Illustrator adds between the two graphics. Select the least number of steps necessary because each new graphic inevitably adds file size to your final SWF.

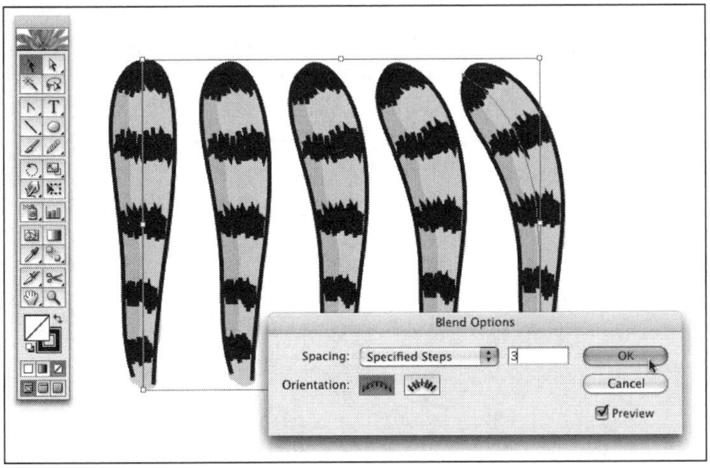

FIGURE 5.8

Select a number of steps to change the number of graphics that generate.

After you finish making the blend, select Object > Blend > Expand to expand the blend into individual objects. Then select Object > Ungroup to separate the grouped graphics.

Create a new file in Flash, and then click a frame on the Timeline and then select File > Import > Import to Stage to import the Illustrator file (.AI) into Flash.

When you import Illustrator files, you have many options available about how to import the file. Convert any pages to keyframes, convert layers to layers, and select the pages you need to import. You can choose whether you want to include invisible layers. Do *not* select Rasterize Everything, or else you'll lose the ability to modify vector graphics (they're turned into bitmap images instead). If you do not need to edit the graphics, and if you discover you lose quality when you import the drawing into Flash, you might want to try importing the file again and select the Rasterize option instead.

Select each drawing and press F8 to convert it into a symbol. You do this the usual way: select the graphics using the Section tool, and press F8 to convert it into a movie clip or graphic symbol. Remember that you can still edit these vectors if you want to shape tween the vectors or modify the graphic's appearance.

Lip-syncing in Flash

Lip-syncing is the process of importing an audio track and animating a character so it appears to speak the dialogue in the audio track. You need to create a series of shapes, called phonemes, for the mouth. The shapes represent a unit of sound—a part of the spoken word. When you combine these shapes together, you can make the character appear to speak along with the dialogue.

With such complicated languages, you might think that making all these shapes is an arduous task. In fact, when you animate in Flash, you can reduce these phonemes to approximately 10 simple shapes because similar sounds can use the same shape instead of slightly different ones.

To get started lip-syncing, create a new FLA document and draw a mouthless face. Leave lots of room around the mouth area, so you can avoid having to animate the nose as well.

You can find a sample Illustrator file (tail.ai) on the CD-ROM.

See Appendix D for online resources related to lip-syncing.

FIGURE 5.9

Draw a mute character.

Import the sound file into Flash (File > Import > Import to Library), create a new layer, and drag the sound from the Library onto the new layer. Press F5 on the Timeline to extend the number of frames the sound spans across. Open the Property inspector and then select the sound on the layer (where you see the waveform). Select Stream from the Sync pop-up menu. Selecting Stream means that you can scrub the Timeline and hear the sound file while you swap mouth shapes. Don't add anything else to this layer—always keep sounds on their own Timeline layer.

FIGURE 5.10

Import the sound and place it on the Timeline. Select Stream from the Sync pop-up menu so you can scrub the Timeline and hear your sound.

It's easiest to create the mouth shapes using the Brush tool, especially if you have access to a graphics tablet. The following figure displays the basic phonemes you can use to animate the mouth of your character.

FIGURE 5.11

Create a series of mouth shapes for animation.

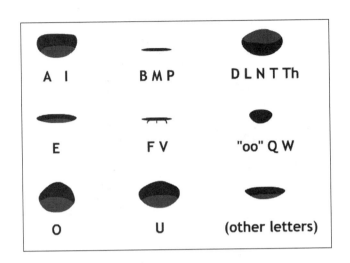

You need to import a sound with spoken dialogue. Many computers come with microphones and software you can use to record your voice (you can use Sound Recorder on Windows or facilitate audio-capture features in iMovie on Macintosh).

You can find a bonus file that includes these mouth shapes and the mouthless face, in the 05/ bonus folder on the CD-ROM. It's called dialog.fla.

Draw your first mouth graphic and convert it into a Graphic symbol. Right-click or Control-click it in the Library; then select Duplicate from the context menu. Modify the duplicated symbol, so you have a frame of reference for each drawing.

Click Insert Layer on the Timeline to add a new layer for the mouth shapes. Create the basic shapes on the Stage (using Figure 5.11 as a guide) and convert them into graphic symbols so you can reuse the assets.

If you don't use one of the mouth symbols, you can always remove it from the Library later on (use the Options menu to choose Select Unused Items). You might create fewer mouth shapes for simpler animations or characters, too. Or, for more variety and realism, you might create more symbols as you animate. Sometimes it helps to have a basic set of mouth drawings ready to start with, ones that you'll definitely use for the animation, and add more while you work on the character.

▶ ▶ CREATING WALK CYCLES

You can create walk cycles in a very similar way to the lip-sync animation. You want to create several different leg drawings for your character (instead of mouth graphics). You want to swap those instances along the Timeline to create the illusion of walking. Copy and paste all the animated frames into a new movie clip, and then you can animate this movie clip across the Stage, so the character appears to walk.

Appendix D has online resources related to creating proper leg positions for walk cycles.

Lip-syncing requires you to add keyframes frequently along a layer. You need to add a new keyframe wherever the dialog has a new sound (typically, each syllable in the dialog). On the layer containing the lip-sync animation, you need to swap instances (select the symbol and then click Swap in the Property inspector), as you did in Chapter 4 for each new sound/syllable of the dialogue. Some longer sounds might need to persist across more frames than short sounds and syllables, which might appear on every frame or every second frame (Figure 5.10).

Use the F5 key to add more frames and F6 to add new keyframes, and scrub the Timeline using the playhead to repeatedly test how the mouth instances sync with the dialogue.

Project 5: Making and Animating a Robot

You begin Project 5 by creating a robot character. You create all the pieces in an optimal way, so you can continue to animate the character using motion tweens or frame-by-frame animation. The animation you create in the second part of this project is simple because you covered the fundamental aspects of these motion tweens in earlier chapters.

Finally, you add this animation to a simple site as an "intro" animation, which begins with a loading progress animation. Your users can skip this animation or choose to watch it before proceeding to your website. By the end of the chapter, you will have a character, animate it, and load it into your site as its own animation.

Exercise 1: Creating the head and face

You need an engaging character to animate. This exercise and a couple of exercises that follow show you how to create a character using the Flash drawing tools. Simple shapes and lines are used in the process, and you can certainly elaborate or simplify the character as you wish. You will quickly discover how easy it is to draw and construct a character that you can animate easily.

Most of the shapes include some form of "shadowing" to create the illusion of depth and dimension to the character. This largely includes selecting and changing the fill color of a shape, or copying

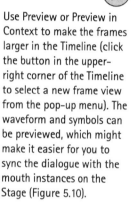

It helps to look in a mirror while you say the words you are animating to select the right mouth shape (or create a new one, if necessary).

Use Preview or Preview in Context to make the frames larger in the Timeline (click the button in the upper-right corner of the Timeline to select a new frame view from the pop-up menu). The waveform and symbols can be previewed, which might make it easier for you to sync the dialogue with the mouth instances on the Stage (Figure 5.10).

There are tools available to make the lip-sync task easier, such as Toon Boom Studio or Crazytalk. You can find links for these programs in Appendix D.

Using simple shapes keeps the file size down in your final SWF file. The extra vector points that you create when drawing with the Pencil or Brush tool add file size and also increase the amount of processing power you use on the user's computer. Sometimes, however, you cannot attain the level of detail or effect you might want by using simple shapes (such as with the pirate character in Chapter 4).

and pasting a basic shape "in place," and resizing it after changing the shape's color.

1. Create a new FLA file, and select Save As. Name the file **robot.fla**, and click Save. Rename Layer 1 **head**. Open the Property inspector, and resize the Stage to 550 px by 700 px. You can leave the background color white.

2. Select the Rectangle tool in the Tools panel and click the Round Rectangle Radius button. In the Rectangle Settings dialog box, enter **12** into the Corner radius text field and click OK. Then open the Property inspector (Window > Properties), and change the fill color of the rectangle to #666666 and the stroke color to No Color (click the pencil next to the stroke color control and then click the No Color button).

3. Draw a rectangle on the Stage that's *approximately* 120 px by 120 px (the actual size you make each symbol at does not matter). When you finish, click within the rectangle to select it, and press F8. Convert the vector into a movie clip symbol, and name it **head**.

4. Double-click the movie clip to enter symbol-editing mode (Figure 5.12). Click the Insert Layer button to create a new layer on the Timeline. Select the rectangle you drew and then press Ctrl+C (Windows) or Command+C (Macintosh) to copy the information to the clipboard. Then select frame 1 on the new layer, and select Edit > Paste in Place. This duplicates the same graphic directly on top of the existing one.

FIGURE 5.12

Create a movie clip from the vector graphic, and then enter symbol-editing mode.

5. The graphic should still be selected on the new layer. If you deselected it, select it again—but you might need to lock the lower layer before to make sure that you select the graphic on the top (new) layer. With the graphic selected, change the fill color to #999999.

6. Select the Free Transform tool in the Tools panel. Select the light gray rectangle on the *top* layer again using the Free Transform tool. Resize the rectangle so it looks approximately like the following figure.

FIGURE 5.13

Resize the light gray rectangle so the dark gray one appears like a drop shadow. Make sure that a dark gray line shows all the way around the head symbol.

Then select the rectangle on the top layer again, and press Ctrl+C (Windows) or Command+C (Macintosh). *Lock the two layers on the Timeline.* Create a new layer, select frame 1, and select Edit > Paste in Place. With the Selection tool, drag a square across the rectangle you just pasted, except for the far right of the shape, where you want some additional shading to appear (refer to Figure 5.B. Delete the selection and then click the leftover shape. Change the color of the leftover shape to a darker gray (#333333).

When you're finished, click Scene 1 in the Edit Bar to return to the main Stage.

7. Click Insert Layer to create a new layer on the Timeline. Rename the new layer **mouth**.

8. Select the Rectangle tool again, and click the Round Rectangle Radius button. In the Rectangle Settings dialog box, enter **5** into the Corner radius text field and click OK. Then open the Property inspector (Window > Properties), and change the fill color of the rectangle to #333333 and the stroke color to No Color (click the pencil next to the stroke color control and then click the No Color button).

9. Draw a rectangle on the Stage that's *approximately* 96 by 24 pixels (the actual size you make each symbol does not matter). When you finish, click within the rectangle to select it, and press F8. Convert the vector into a movie clip symbol, and name it **mouth**.

10. Double-click the mouth movie clip to enter symbol-editing mode (Figure 5.14). Click the Insert Layer button to create a new layer on the Timeline. Select the rectangle you drew and then press Ctrl+C (Windows) or Command+C (Macintosh) to copy the information to the clipboard. Then select frame 1 on the new layer, and select Edit > Paste in Place. This duplicates the same graphic directly on top of the existing one.

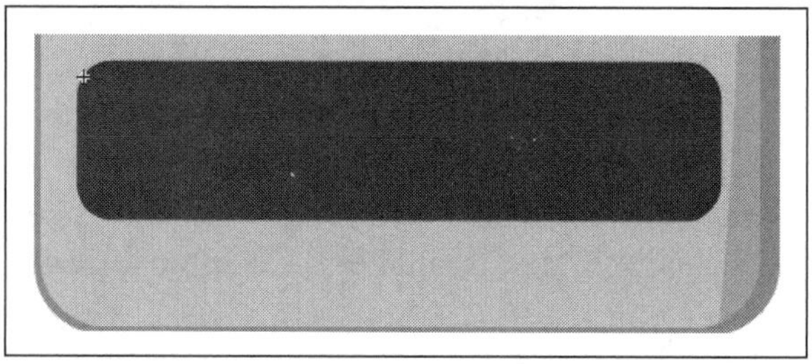

FIGURE 5.14

Create a movie clip from the vector graphic, and then enter symbol-editing mode.

11. The graphic should still be selected on the new layer. If you deselected it, select it again (remember to lock the lower layer if necessary). With the graphic selected, change the fill color to white (#FFFFFF).

12. Select the Free Transform tool in the Tools panel. Select the white rectangle on the *top* layer again using the Free Transform tool. Resize the rectangle so it looks approximately like the following figure.

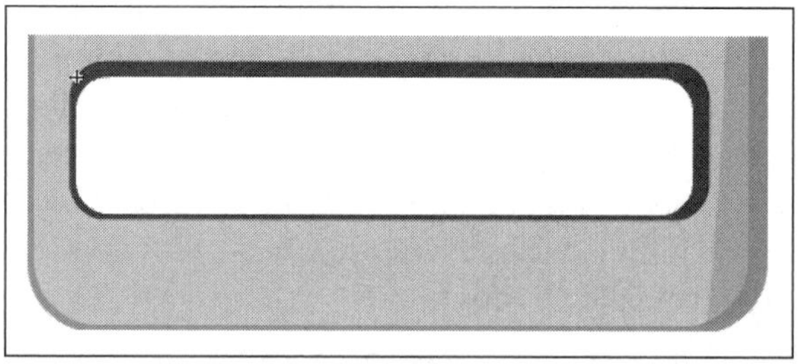

FIGURE 5.15

Create the robot's mouth.

13. Now create a new layer above the layer containing the white rounded rectangle. Select the Line tool, and select a stroke color to #333333. Draw vertical lines across the white rectangle to look like teeth (Figure 5.16).

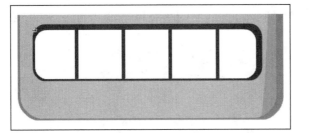

FIGURE 5.16

Create the robot's teeth.

When you finish, click Scene 1 on the Edit Bar to return to the main Stage.

14. Click Insert Layer to create a new layer on the Timeline. Rename the new layer **eye - left**.

15. Select the Oval tool from the Tools panel, and then open the Property inspector. Change the fill color to #333333 and the stroke color to No Color. Select frame 1 of the eye - left layer and draw a circle on the Stage that's approximate 30 px by 30 px. Press the Shift key while you draw the shape to constrain the proportions. You can change the dimensions of the circle in the Property inspector (after you select the graphic).

Select the circle and press F8 to convert it into a symbol. Select the Movie Clip behavior in the dialog box and name the symbol **eye**. Press OK and then double-click the new instance to enter symbol-editing mode.

16. In symbol-editing mode, click Insert Layer to create a new layer above the existing one. Then select the circle you created in step 15 and press Ctrl+C (Windows) or Command+C (Macintosh) to copy the information to the clipboard. Select frame 1 of the new (empty) layer and select Edit > Paste in Place. In the Property inspector, change the color of the instance on the top color to white (#FFFFFF).

17. Lock the top layer inside the eye symbol (the white circle). Then select the Free Transform tool and click the circle on the bottom layer, which is underneath the white circle. Because the white circle graphic is locked, you can click anywhere within the area of the white circle to select the circle beneath it.

Resize the circle using the Free Transform tool until you see a drop-shadow effect similar to the one in the following figure.

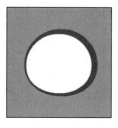

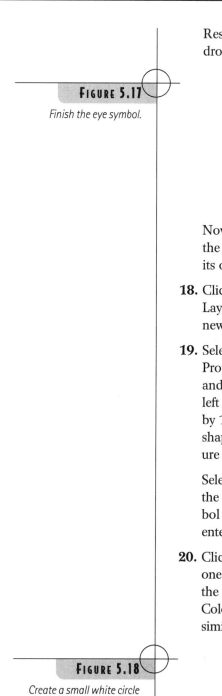

FIGURE 5.17

Finish the eye symbol.

Now you need to create pupils. However, you will animate the pupils separately from the eye, so each pupil needs to be its own symbol on the Timeline.

18. Click Scene 1 to return to the main Timeline and click Insert Layer to create a new layer on the Timeline. Rename the new layer **pupil - left**.

19. Select the Oval tool from the Tools panel and then open the Property inspector. Change the fill color to black (#000000) and the stroke color to No Color. Select frame 1 of the pupil - left layer and draw a small black circle, approximately 10 px by 10 px, on the Stage (press the Shift key while you draw the shape to constrain the proportions) on top of the eye (use Figure 5.B for reference).

Select the circle and press F8 to convert it into a symbol. Select the Movie Clip behavior in the dialog box and name the symbol **pupil**. Click OK. Then double-click the new instance to enter symbol-editing mode.

20. Click the Insert Layer button to create a new layer above the one with the black circle. Select the Oval tool again and change the fill color to white (#FFFFFF) and the stroke color to No Color. Create a small white circle, approximately 3 px by 3 px, similar to the one in the following figure.

FIGURE 5.18

Create a small white circle above the pupil.

21. Click Scene 1 to return to the main Stage. Then click Insert Layer to create a new layer on the Timeline. Rename the new layer **eye - right**. Select the `left eye` instance, and press Ctrl+C (Windows) or Command+C (Macintosh) to copy the instance to the clipboard. Then select the eye - right layer and press Ctrl+V (Windows) or Command+V (Macintosh) to paste the instance on the new layer.

22. Click Insert Layer to create a new layer on the Timeline. Rename the new layer **pupil - right**. Select the `left pupil` instance, and press Ctrl+C (Windows) or Command+C (Macintosh) to copy the instance to the clipboard. Then select the pupil - right layer, and press Ctrl+V (Windows) or Command+V (Macintosh) to paste the instance on the new layer.

Select the `right eye` instance and the `right pupil` instance, and move both of them into proper position (approximately what's displayed in Figure 5.19).

FIGURE 5.19

Position the robot's right eye and right pupil in relation to the left eye and pupil. Save your changes before moving on to the next exercise.

Exercise 2: Creating the antenna and ears

Now the robot has its face, which is made up of separate instances and on separate layers so you can easily animate it. It just needs an antenna and ears to complete the rest of the robots most expressive asset.

1. Click Insert Layer to create a new layer on the Timeline and then rename it **antenna**. Make sure that the layer is at the top of the Timeline.

2. Select the Oval tool and open the Property inspector (Window > Properties) and Color Mixer panel (Window > Design Panels > Color Mixer). Then select Radial from the Fill style pop-up in the Color Mixer panel (Figure 5.20).

FIGURE 5.20

Create a radial gradient that is bright red in the center, fading to fully transparent.

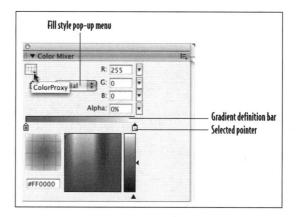

Click the left color pointer under the Gradient Definition bar (Figure 5.20) and then select a red color in the ColorProxy color control (the color square in the upper-left corner of the panel). Then select the right color pointer (under the Gradient Definition bar), and select red again in the ColorProxy color control. Type **0%** in the alpha text field.

Back in the Tools panel, click the pencil icon next to the stroke color control, and click the No Color button.

3. Select frame 1 of the antenna layer; with the Oval tool, draw a small oval or circle approximately 25 px by 25 px on the Stage above the robot's head (use Figure 5.A for reference). When

you finish, select the oval and press F8 to convert it into a symbol. Select Movie Clip as the symbol's behavior, and name it antenna top. Click OK.

4. On frame 1 of the antenna layer, select the Line tool and draw a line between the robot's head and the antenna top (use Figure 5.A for reference). Select the line using the Selection tool and change the stroke color to #333333 using the stroke color control in the Tools panel. Set the stroke height to 3 pixels in the Property inspector.

   After you change the color (and with the line still selected), press F8 to convert the vector into a symbol. Select the Movie Clip behavior and name the symbol **antenna line**. Click OK.

5. Using the Selection tool, select both the antenna top and antenna line instances on the Stage. Then press F8 to combine (or *nest*) the two instances inside a single symbol (Figure 5.21). Name that symbol **antenna** and select the Movie Clip behavior. Click OK. Because both of these symbols nest inside a single movie clip, you can animate them together. Also, it means that you can animate the antenna top instance independently, which you will do later in this project.

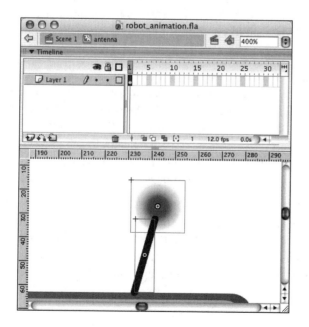

FIGURE 5.21

Nest the antenna top and antenna line inside a single movie clip.

6. Click Insert Layer to create a new layer on the Timeline. Rename the new layer **ear - right**. Click and drag this layer under the antenna layer.

7. Select frame 1 of the ear - right layer and then select the Oval tool. Change the fill color to #333333 and the stroke color to No Color. Draw an elongated oval on the Stage that's similar to the following figure.

   Make sure that the Snap to Objects button in the Tools panel is selected.

FIGURE 5.22

Draw the robot's ear hole.

8. Select the oval on the Stage, and press F8 to convert it into a symbol. Name the symbol **ear** and select the Movie Clip behavior. Click OK. When you return to the main Stage, double-click the oval to enter symbol-editing mode. Rename the layer with the oval on it to **oval**.

9. Click the Insert Layer button to create a new layer, rename the layer **rectangle**, and drag the new layer to the *bottom* of the Timeline (below the layer with the oval). Select the Rectangle tool and change the fill color to #999999 and the stroke color to #333333. Change the stroke height to 1.5 pixels in the stroke height text field. Click the Round Rectangle Radius button to make sure that you have the corner radius set to 0.

   Draw a small rectangle on the Stage that is the same height as the oval. You might want to click at the top of the oval and draw the rectangle toward the left, releasing the mouse button when the bottom of the rectangle reaches the bottom of the oval. When you finish, the shapes should resemble Figure 5.23.

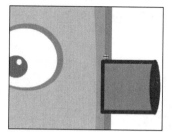

FIGURE 5.23

Using a rectangle to create the ear.

10. Now you need to change the ear shape so it is almost conical. Click the Selection tool and hover the mouse over the upper-left corner of the rectangle until you see a corner point next to the cursor. Click and drag the corner upward. Repeat this step for the lower-left corner of the rectangle, but this time drag the corner downward. Refer to Figure 5.24, if necessary.

FIGURE 5.24

Reshaping the ear.

Then mouse over the left side of the rectangle, away from the edges, until you see a curved shape next to the cursor. Click and drag away to the left until the side bends slightly similar to the bend in Figure 5.24. When you finish, you should have a shape that resembles Figure 5.24.

You might need to move the oval shape slightly to match the edges of the rectangle. Select the shape using the Selection tool and move it using the arrow keys if necessary. You could also resize the shape by selecting it with the Free Transform tool.

11. To add the ear's shading, lock the oval layer. Then select the Selection tool and drag it over the lower half of the ear (Figure 5.25).

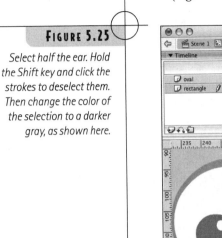

FIGURE 5.25

Select half the ear. Hold the Shift key and click the strokes to deselect them. Then change the color of the selection to a darker gray, as shown here.

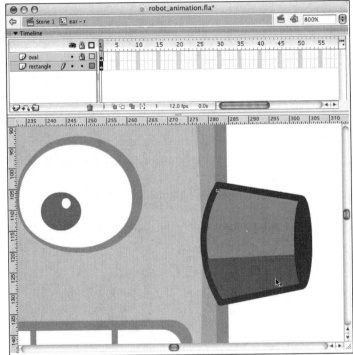

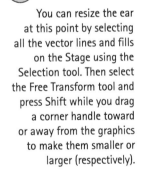

You can resize the ear at this point by selecting all the vector lines and fills on the Stage using the Selection tool. Then select the Free Transform tool and press Shift while you drag a corner handle toward or away from the graphics to make them smaller or larger (respectively).

You can use this technique for shading most of the character.

Doing this selects both the fill and stroke of the rectangle, so you need to deselect the strokes now. Hold the Shift key and click each of the strokes until you have only the lower area of the fill selected. Now, select a darker gray (#666666) from the fill color control on the Tools panel.

12. Click Scene 1 on the Edit Bar to return to the main Stage. Create a new layer and rename it **ear - left**. Drag the new layer to the bottom of the Timeline. The left ear needs to appear behind the head.

Right-click or Control-click the ear symbol in the Library, and then select Duplicate from the context menu. Name the duplicated symbol **ear - left** and drag it to onto the ear - left layer.

Double-click the ear - left instance to enter symbol-editing mode. Delete the oval graphic, select the remaining graphics, and select Modify > Transform > Flip Horizontal. Modify the ear so it resembles Figure 5.26 when you bend the strokes on the left side of the rectangle. Then position it in relation to the head (use Figure 5.B for reference).

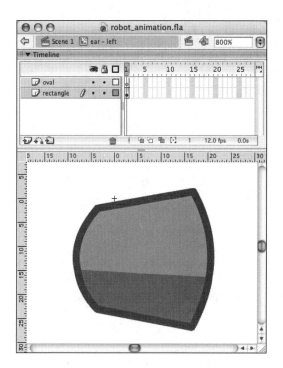

FIGURE 5.26

Modify the ear using the Selection tool to bend the line and fills accordingly. Delete the oval and bend the strokes and fills to replicate this look.

13. When you finish creating all these graphics, you have a lot of layers on the Timeline, and haven't even started creating the robot's body. You should organize all the related instances inside a single folder. Click Insert Layer Folder on the Timeline to create a new layer folder, and rename this layer **head pieces**. Press the Ctrl (Windows) or Command (Macintosh) key and click the antenna, ear - left, ear - right, eye - left, eye - right, pupil - left, pupil - right, mouth, and head layers. After you select all the layers, drag the layers into the head pieces folder.

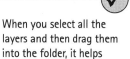

When you select all the layers and then drag them into the folder, it helps you maintain the same layer-stacking order, which is particularly important when you work with characters that depend on specific layer ordering.

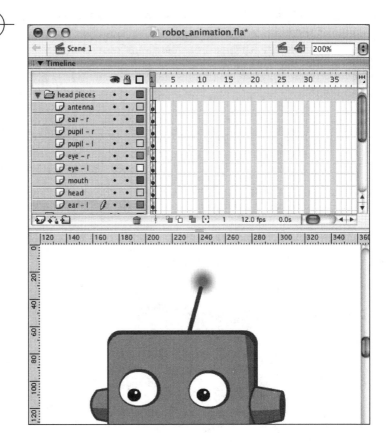

Exercise 3: Creating the robot body

The robot's body is almost exactly the same as its head. Therefore, you can copy the graphics from the head to create the different parts of its body. You can reduce file size when you reuse graphics and instances, and also save some of the time it takes to create the character.

It's possible to copy the head instance on the Stage, and paste it onto a new layer and resize the instance; however, in this exercise you add new assets to the head and modify it a bit. Therefore, the graphics are copied into a new body symbol.

1. Double-click the head instance on the Stage so it opens in symbol-editing mode. Press the Ctrl (Windows) or Command (Macintosh) key while you click each frame on the symbol's

Timeline. Then right-click (Windows) or Control-click (Macintosh) and select Copy Frames from the context menu.

2. Select Insert > New Symbol. Select the Movie Clip behavior and name the new symbol **body**. Click OK to enter symbol-editing mode.

3. Select frame 1 of the symbol's Timeline, right-click (Windows) or Control-click (Macintosh), and select Paste Frames from the context menu.

4. Now you need to resize the graphics in relation to the head. Click Scene 1 on the Edit Bar to return to the main Timeline. Open the Library (Window > Library) and drag an instance of the body symbol onto body layer. The body layer should be outside of and below the head pieces folder. Double-click the instance to edit the symbol in place.

5. Inside the body symbol, use the Free Transform tool to select all the vector graphics. Then use the handles to resize the body in relation to the head. You can use Figure 5.A and 5.28 for reference, or you can create your own original graphics.

6. Now you can add any embellishments to the body by adding new layers and either repurposing the existing graphics on new layers or adding new ones altogether. See Figure 5.28 for a finished and fancier version.

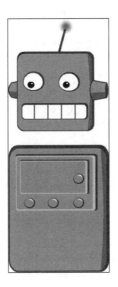

FIGURE 5.28

Resize the head graphics to create the body of the robot.

▶ ▶ CREATING THE ROBOT'S BUTTON

In the finished file on the CD-ROM, robot.fla, you find that a button graphic symbol (see the following figure) was created. This uses the same techniques as the eye symbol, except it uses shades of gray instead. Then, a crescent "glint" was added using the Oval tool. A white circle (with no stroke) was drawn on the Stage. Then, a second circle (with no stroke) was drawn on the same layer, except a different fill color was chosen. This circle was moved to overlap the original white circle. Then, the circle was deleted from the Stage, which also removes the white circle underneath. A white crescent is left over, as shown in the figure that follows.

Create two circles or ovals with different fill colors. Move one circle over the other, and any area that is not overlapped remains when you delete the circle on top.

Exercise 4: Creating the extremities

The rest of the robot should seem fairly straightforward, now that you're a pro at creating the head and body. You can create whatever pieces you want, but you need to make sure that you create each piece as its own instance, on its own layer, and intuitively organized on the Timeline. All this is so you can easily animate the character after you create it.

You can shade the arms (similar to the way you shaded the right ear). Select the entire region of the arm, and then press the Shift key and click strokes or fills to deselect the areas until you have only the region you want to shade selected. Then, change the fill color using the Tools panel.

1. Insert a new layer on the Timeline beneath the head pieces folder, and rename it **neck**. On this layer, create a neck that attaches the robot's head to its body. Refer to Figure 5.B for guidance.

2. Create an upper-left and upper-right arm (the area from the shoulder to the elbow) and create a lower-left and lower-right arm (from the elbow to the wrist). The left arm layers should

be on layers below the body layer, and the right arm should be on layers that are above the body layer.

You can recycle the same graphics or instances for the upper and the lower arms, but make sure that each one is on its own layer.

3. Create an elbow that joins the upper-right arm and the lower-right arm. The elbow layer should be above the upper-arm layer, but below the lower-arm layer. Use the following figure for reference.

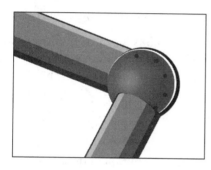

Copy the elbow instance and paste it onto a new layer for the left arm. Select Modify > Transform > Flip Horizontal to flip the elbow instance on the Stage.

4. Create legs that are similar in structure to the arms. There should be instances on their own layers for the upper region of both legs and the lower region of both legs. You can make the knee similar to how you did for the elbow (you could use the same instance, if you want), or you could make a knee above the upper and lower legs, as in the finished version of the robot FLA file on the CD-ROM (shown in Figure 5.30).

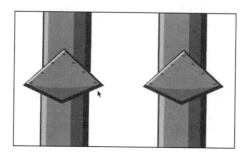

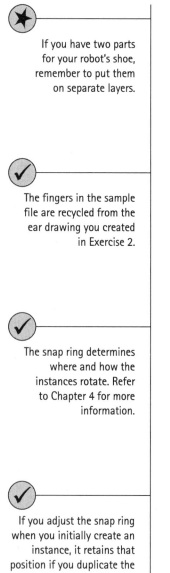

If you have two parts for your robot's shoe, remember to put them on separate layers.

The fingers in the sample file are recycled from the ear drawing you created in Exercise 2.

The snap ring determines where and how the instances rotate. Refer to Chapter 4 for more information.

If you adjust the snap ring when you initially create an instance, it retains that position if you duplicate the instance later on.

In the example file, the leg graphics were recycled from the arm graphics. The leg layers should be beneath the body layer.

5. Create two feet or shoes for the robot character (refer to Figure 5.A). For more flexibility in your animation, you might choose to create a toe region for the foot. This means you can rotate the main part of the shoe separate from the toe. If so, create the vector graphic of the shoe, and then select the toe region using the Selection tool and press F8 to convert just that area into its own symbol. Then select the rest of the shoe region and press F8 to create a symbol for that region.

The feet layers should be above the leg layers.

6. Finally, create two hands for the robot. These layers should be above the arm layers. Optionally, you could create "hips" for the character (also found in the final robot.fla file), which should be above the legs and body layers on the Timeline.

7. Position the snap ring of each instance like you did in Chapter 4, similar to Figure 5.31.

Select the Free Transform tool in the Tools panel, which you can use to reposition the snap ring. Click and instance, and then click and drag the white circle from the center of the instance to a new location (where you want the center of the rotation to exist). For example, if you want the neck of the character to rotate from the base of its neck, you need to move the snap ring from the center of the neck to the bottom of it.

Refer to the following figure for suggested snap ring locations of each instance.

8. Similar to the end of Exercise 2, you should organize your assets into folders. Organize the layers for the right arm and right hand into a folder called **arm - right**. Then organize the layers for the left arm and left hand into a folder called **arm - left**. Remember to press the Ctrl (Windows) or Command (Macintosh) key while you click each layer you want to move into a particular folder, and then drag the layers into the folder. This way, they remain in the same order when you drag them into the folder.

FIGURE 5.31

Use the Free Transform tool to reposition the snap ring for each instance.

Exercise 5: Animating the character

Now you have a complete character that's created for animation and ready to animate. Each of the instances that make up the robot resides on its own layer. This means you can properly animate the character because you cannot animate several instances on the same layer. You probably organized the related assets of the character into Layer folders, so the Timeline is easier to navigate and manage.

1. Select File > Save to save the changes you made to the file so far. Then select File > Save As to save a new copy of the file. Name the new FLA file **robot_animation.fla**, and save the file. Therefore, if you make any mistakes or want to start again, you have the robot.fla file to save a brand new document from.

2. Select Modify > Document and set new dimensions for the Stage. Change the width to 550 px (width) and the height to 450 px (height) and click OK. The former dimensions were appropriate for building the robot character, but you might want to change the dimensions of the Stage for your actual website or cartoon.

Before you start animating, choose a beginning pose for the character, which might resemble the sample FLA file so you can easily follow along with this exercise. You will animate the head and arms in this exercise, so the position those assets are particularly important. Refer to the FLA or Figure 5.A for guidance.

3. Double-click the antenna instance to open the movie clip instance. Use the Selection tool to select both instances, and then select Modify > Timeline > Distribute to Layers. This puts each instance on its own layer, which is appropriate when you want to animate them. Drag the antenna line instance to the bottom layer if necessary, and delete the empty Layer 1.

Select frame 10 of the new layer containing the antenna top instance and press F6 to insert a keyframe. Then select frame 20 of the same layer and press F6 again. Select frame 20 of the antenna line instance and press F5 to insert frames on the layer. Therefore, while the antenna top instance animates, you also see the line instance on all of those frames.

Select the keyframe on frame 10 again, and select the Free Transform tool. Click the antenna top instance on this frame, and then use the handles to resize the instance slightly larger than its original size (Figure 5.32).

Right-click (Windows) or Control-click (Macintosh) any frame between frame 1 and 10, and select Create Motion tween from the context menu. Repeat this step by right-clicking or Control-clicking any frame between frame 10 and 20 on the Timeline to create a motion tween. Now the antenna instance animates continually while it is on the Stage.

Click the Scene 1 button in the Edit Bar to return to the main Stage.

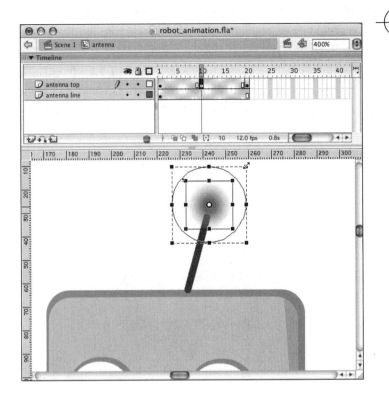

FIGURE 5.32

Resize the antenna top *instance for a motion tween.*

4. Select frame 35 of every layer on the Timeline. You can select each frame by selecting frame 35 of the top layer; then press the Shift key and select frame 35 on the bottom layer. Press F5 to insert frames on each layer.

5. Animate the character's pupils. In Figure 5.33, the pupils were toward the left side of the eye. Press Ctrl (Windows) or Command (Macintosh) and click frame 4 of the pupil - left and pupil - right layers. Then press F6 to insert a keyframe on both layers.

   Select each pupil on frame 4 and use the arrow keys to move it to the center of the eye. Select frame 2 on both layers (press Ctrl or Command to select both layers simultaneously), and then select Insert > Timeline > Create Motion Tween.

   Scrub the playhead to view the pupil animation.

6. Now select frame 4 of both the eye - left and eye - right layers. Press F6 to insert a keyframe. Then insert a keyframe on frame 7 of those two layers, and again at frame 10.

   Select one of the eyes on frame 7 using the Free Transform tool. Resize the eye so it is *larger* than its original size. Repeat this step for the other eye on frame 7, as shown in Figure 5.33.

FIGURE 5.33

Resize both eyes so they are larger.

   Select frame 6 on both the eye - left and eye - right layers, and select Insert > Timeline > Create Motion Tween. Then select frame 8 on both the eye - left and eye - right layers, and select Insert > Timeline > Create Motion Tween. When you finish, scrub the Timeline to view the animation. The eyes should both grow and shrink again following the pupil movement.

7. Select all the instances above the neck, noting which layers they are on (they should all be within the head pieces folder). On each of these particular layers, insert a keyframe on frame 10 and another keyframe at frame 14 (select each layer simultaneously and press F6).

   With all the instances still selected on frame 14, click the Free Transform tool. Then hover the cursor over the upper-right handle, and drag the cursor to rotate the head slightly to the right (Figure 5.34).

FIGURE 5.34

*Rotate the head
to animate it.*

8. When you finish rotating the head, select the Selection tool in the Tools panel. Select frame 13 on each layer and choose Insert > Timeline > Create Motion Tween to insert a motion tween for the head.

9. Select frame 15 of the top layer on the Timeline, and press Shift while you click frame 15 on the bottom layer on the Timeline to select frame 15 on every single layer. Press F6 to insert a keyframe, and then repeat this step for frame 20. While every instance on frame 20 is still selected, click the Free Transform tool.

   Now everything is selected with the Free Transform tool. Press the Shift key while you drag the corner handle outward to resize the robot so it's larger. Resize the robot by dragging a bottom corner handle until it approximately matches the following figure.

   Select frame 19 on every layer, and then right-click (Windows) or Control-click (Macintosh) and select Create Motion Tween from the context menu.

   Scrub the Timeline, and now you will find that the robot "zooms in" towards the viewer.

While each frame is selected for the motion tween, you can apply easing in the Property inspector.

FIGURE 5.35

Resize the robot for his closeup.

10. Find the right arm and hand layers, which you hopefully put in their own folders in Exercise 4. Select frame 22 for the upper - and lower-right arm instances, right elbow, and right hand layers. Press F6 to insert a keyframe on all four layers. Select frame 28 for each of these four layers and press F6 to insert another keyframe.

   Select the Free Transform tool, and click the upper-right arm instance on frame 28. Rotate the upper arm upward, so it is approximately horizontal. Then select the `right elbow` instance and both move and rotate the instance so it sits at the end of the upper arm.

11. Select the `lower right arm` instance using the Free Transform tool. Rotate and move the lower arm so it joins the elbow and bends slightly toward the head, as shown on the right in the following figure.

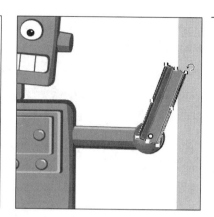

FIGURE 5.36

Rotate and move the upper right arm (left), and then the elbow and lower arm (right).

Rotate and move the right hand so it joins the end of the lower arm on frame 28.

Select frame 27 on each layer, and then right-click (Windows) or Control-click (Macintosh) and select Create Motion Tween from the context menu.

12. If you scrub the Timeline using the playhead, you will probably see that the hand does not move properly with the other instances. It might move erratically during the tween. Or, perhaps even one of the other instances does not tween properly. If this is the case, you need to add additional keyframes between frames 22 and 28 to tween the hand instance.

   Select frame 24 of the layer containing the right hand, and press F6 to insert a new keyframe. Move the hand instance so it joins the end of the lower arm. Continue adding as many keyframes as you need so the right arm tweens correctly between frames 22 and 28 (refer to the animation in www.FLAnimation.com/chapters/05 if necessary).

13. Select frame 35 of the lower arm and hand layers only, and then press F6 to insert a keyframe on these two layers.

   Select the Free Transform tool, and rotate the lower arm towards the robot's head (as shown in Figure 5.37).

   Then select the hand with the Free Transform tool, and rotate and move the hand so it attaches to the end of the lower arm again, in the "thumbs-up" position (also seen in Figure 5.B and 5.C).

FIGURE 5.37

*Rotate and move the hand
and lower arm into the
thumbs-up pose.*

Select frame 34 on each of these layers, and then right-click
(Windows) or control-click (Macintosh) and select Create
Motion Tween from the context menu.

14. When you scrub the Timeline, you'll notice that the hand
moves erratically between frames 28 and 35. Insert a few
keyframes between frames 28 and 35 on the right hand layer
(just as in step 12) and move the hand at each keyframe so it
attaches to the end of the lower arm appropriately. Scrub the
playhead continually to see whether the hand animates (similar to the completed SWF example).

Select Control > Test Movie to test the animation (instead of
merely scrubbing the Timeline!), and make any changes as
necessary.

Now you're finished animating the character, and ready to use it as an intro animation. Optionally, you could select all the frames on the Timeline, copy them, and insert them into a movie clip. Then, you could animate the movie clip on its own Timeline and animate the movie clip instance on the main Timeline as well.

To do this, select all the frames on the Timeline using the Selection tool (click and drag over the frames to select them). Right-click (Windows) or Control-click (Macintosh) the frames and select Copy Frames. Insert a new movie clip symbol, select frame 1 of Layer 1, and then right-click/Control-click and select Paste Frames from the context menu. This inserts the entire character with all its layers inside the movie clip. Now you can animate inside the movie clip or animate the movie clip itself.

> If you create a movie clip for the robot, you don't need all the layers on the main Timeline. You can make modifications and additions inside the movie clip symbol.

Exercise 6: Completing the SWF and loading the animation

The animation is almost complete. You just need to prepare the robot_animation.fla file for the web, and load it into another SWF file that contains a loading animation. In this exercise, you finish and publish robot_animation.fla and then prepare a new SWF file that loads the intro animation.

1. In robot_animation.fla (on the main Timeline or on the robot movie clip's Timeline, if you created one), select the top item in the Timeline (probably the head pieces layer folder), and click Insert Layer to create a new layer. Rename the layer **actions**.

2. Select the last frame of the animation on the actions layer (frame 35) and press F6 to insert a keyframe. Then open the Actions panel (Window > Development Panels > Actions) and type the following ActionScript into the Script pane.

    ```
    stop();
    getURL("home.html", "_self");
    ```

    This ActionScript uses a relative URL to target a new web page at the end of the animation, which loads into the current page (which is "self"). Change the URL to target a different web page (you can also use an absolute URL—an address that starts with "http://"—if you need to target a different web domain).

These dimensions (550 px by 450 px) match the robot_animation.swf. You load the SWF file into this rectangle.

3. Press F12 to test the entire animation, and make sure that it stops at the end. Save the changes you made to robot_animation.fla. Then Select File > Publish to export a SWF file with the animation.

4. In Flash, select File > New to create a new document. Select File > Save As to name the file **loader.fla**. Save the FLA file in the same directory as robot_animation.fla.

   Select Modify > Document to change the document's properties. Change the dimensions to 580 px (width) by 480 px (height), and change the background color to black (#000000).

5. Select the Rectangle tool, and in the Tools panel change the rectangle fill color to white and the stroke color to No Color. Draw a rectangle on the Stage. Then select the rectangle (using the Selection tool) and change its dimensions in the Property inspector. Change the width to 550 px and the height to 450 px.

6. Select the rectangle again and press F8 to convert it into a symbol. Select the Movie Clip behavior and name the clip **loaderClip**. Make sure that the registration point is in the upper-left corner of the movie clip, which means the small black square of the registration grid is selected, as shown in Figure 5.38.

   Click OK to create the symbol.

7. Center the movie clip on the Stage. Open the Align panel (Window > Design Panels > Align) and make sure the To Stage button is selected. This means that objects you select to align or distribute will be arranged in relation to the Stage instead of each other.

   Select the loaderClip instance, click the Align Horizontal Center button, and then click the Align Vertical Center button in the Align panel.

8. Select the loaderClip instance again and open the Property inspector. In the Instance Name text field, type **loader_mc** to assign an instance name for the object. At the end of this exercise, you will add very simple ActionScript to load robot_animation.swf into this movie clip.

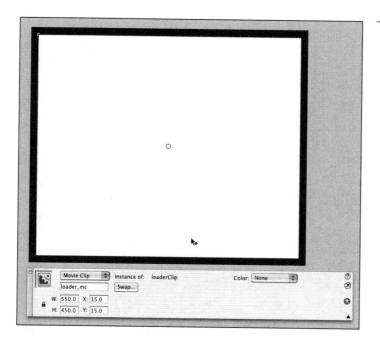

FIGURE 5.38

Create a white strokeless rectangle and change its dimensions in the Property inspector; then convert the shape into a symbol.

9. Click Insert Layer to create a new layer on the Timeline. Select the Rectangle tool, and change the rectangle fill color to red in the Tools panel, and change the stroke color to No Color. Draw a rectangle on the Stage. Then select the rectangle (using the Selection tool), and change its dimensions in the Property inspector. Change the width to 550 px and the height to 450 px.

   Center the shape on the Stage. Open the Align panel (Window > Design Panels > Align) and make sure the To Stage button on the panel is selected. Select the rectangle, click the Align Horizontal Center button, and then click the Align Vertical Center button in the Align panel.

10. Right-click (Windows) or Control-click (Macintosh) the new layer on the layer's name (where you would double-click to rename the layer) and select Mask from the context menu. This masks the movie clip that loads the animation into it.

Therefore, you hide any areas outside the actual dimensions of the robot_animation.swf when the animation loads into this loader file. This is important because the robot character extends beyond the boundaries of the Stage during the animation.

FIGURE 5.39

Create a mask on the Timeline. You mask the indented layer(s) (in this case, Layer 1). The "filled" areas of a mask layer (the part with the rectangle on it) are the areas that display the contents of the masked layer.

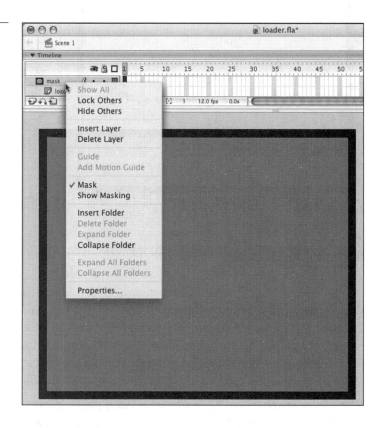

Typically, you should add a progress bar/preloader to any sort of content that loads into a SWF from an external file. Because the content that loads into loader_mc is a very small and simple animation (only about 3 KB!) you don't need to add a progress bar. You will use progress bars throughout future examples.

Even though the SWF file loads into a movie clip, the getURL() action that you added earlier will still open the new web page at the end of the animation.

11. Click Insert Layer to create a new layer on the Timeline, and rename the new layer **actions**. Open the Actions panel and add the following ActionScript in the Script pane:

```
loader_mc.loadMovie("robot_animation.swf");
```

This code loads the contents of the robot_animation.swf movie into the loader_mc movie clip on the Stage. After the content finishes loading, the contents automatically play back in the SWF file.

▶ ▶ **THE HISTORY OF INTROS**

Intro animations, an animation used to introduce a web site or introduce certain content, used to be much more common on the Internet. In fact, Flash introductions used to be the most recognizable use of Flash. However, anything this popular runs the risk of becoming a "trend," and then the next best thing comes along (or sometimes "overkill" is a risk if too many people use the style or feature). Flash intros are less common on the web these days; and, your clients might still request an intro. At any rate, it's a good idea to know how to create an intro and handle it well on a website.

It's possible to have introductory animations that are positive and unique experiences for your users. There are other ways to add creative animations to your site in the "spirit" of an introduction. For example, you might have a menu bar at the top of your website, which includes a background with a series of buttons. Behind the button area, on the menu's background, you might have a subtle animation play when the user first sees the web page. Or, you might have a "skyscraper" (tall and wide) banner-style SWF file on your page somewhere that plays an animation when the page loads, and then stops to show some kind of advertisement. There are several ways to be creative with animation on your page, aside from cartoons and in addition to the usual effects you might see in menus or transitions.

Exercise 7: Skipping the animation

Because we made this animation into a site introduction, you need to give your visitors an option to skip the introduction (or "intro"). You are probably familiar with intro animations, which are the first thing that you see upon entering a website. See the preceding sidebar for a short history of intro animations.

1. Publish both of your Flash files, which include loader.fla and robot_animation.fla. You need the SWF files from both of these documents for your web page. Make sure that you also publish an HTML page with loader.fla. HTML should publish by

default, but to make sure it does, you can check your publish settings. Select File > Publish Settings, and a dialog box opens. Make sure that the HTML check box is selected so the file generates. You will use and modify the generated HTML page for your website.

2. Open the folder on your hard drive that contains the published files. Rename loader.html to **index.html**, and move this document into a new folder with loader.swf and robot_animation.swf.

3. Open index.html in NotePad, TextEdit or an HTML editor such as Dreamweaver. Modify the existing code so that it matches the following snippet (modifications appear in boldface):

```
<!DOCTYPE html PUBLIC "-//W3C//DTD XHTML 1.0
Transitional//EN"
"http://www.w3.org/TR/xhtml1/DTD/xhtml1-
transitional.dtd">
<html xmlns="http://www.w3.org/1999/xhtml" xml:lang="en"
lang="en">
<head>
<meta http-equiv="Content-Type" content="text/html;
charset=iso-8859-1" />
<title>my robot</title>
</head>
<body bgcolor="#000000">
<!—url's used in the movie—>
<!—text used in the movie—>
<object classid="clsid:d27cdb6e-ae6d-11cf-96b8-
444553540000"
codebase="http://fpdownload.macromedia.com/pub/shockwave
/cabs/flash/swflash.cab#version=7,0,0,0" width="580"
height="480" id="loader" align="middle">
<param name="allowScriptAccess" value="sameDomain" />
<param name="movie" value="loader.swf" />
<param name="quality" value="high" />
<param name="bgcolor" value="#000000" />
<embed src="loader.swf" quality="high" bgcolor="#000000"
width="580" height="480" name="loader" align="middle"
allowScriptAccess="sameDomain" type="application/x-
shockwave-flash"
pluginspage="http://www.macromedia.com/go/getflashplayer
" />
</object>
<p><a href="home.html">Skip intro</a></p>
</body>
</html>
```

The only new line of code that you need to add is the single line of code in boldface near the bottom of the code. This line of code creates a basic hyperlink that redirects the browser to the home.html document (which doesn't yet exist). The only other change you make is to the title of the page, within the <title> tags.

The preceding code displays the HTML that automatically generates by Flash (in addition to that one additional line) and is all the code you need to embed a SWF movie within an HTML page. In fact, the code that actually embeds SWF files is the <object> and <embed> tags. You might wonder why there are two tags that embed SWF files and why many of the values are repeated twice. Both sets of tags are needed due to cross-browser issues between Microsoft's Internet Explorer and Mozilla-based web browsers (such as Netscape Navigator or Mozilla Firebird). Therefore, it is very important to remember to change both sets of tags so that all browsers will display the same content properly.

4. The only thing that remains before you test the final version in a browser is to construct the home.html page. Create a new HTML document using your favorite HTML editor. Type in code similar to the following:

```
<!DOCTYPE HTML PUBLIC "-//W3C//DTD HTML 4.01
Transitional//EN">

<html>
<head>
  <title>Home</title>
</head>

<body>

<h1>Welcome to the home page.</h1>

</body>
</html>
```

Although you could use something a bit more formatted and functional before uploading files to your web server, the previous code is sufficient for testing and at least prevents any error messages when Flash tries to redirect your page to the home.html document.

Save the HTML file and close your HTML editor.

5. Double-click index.html in the folder in which you saved all the files. This opens your default browser and displays the animation.

If you watch the three-second robot animation, you will notice that the SWF file redirects to the home.html page when the robot finishes its thumbs-up motion. You can click the Back button in your browser and quickly press the "Skip intro" button below the Flash animation to skip the remainder of the animation and go directly to the home page if you choose and can click that quickly.

▶ ▶ BEWARE OF POP-UP BLOCKERS

Be careful if you decide to use any pop-up windows in any of your websites. If you plan to use a pop-up for an intro or website, make sure that you let the user click a button to spawn the new browser window, or at least include a button they can use to do so. With so many pop-up blockers installed on computers (such as the Google toolbar and the Windows XP Service Pack 2 update), you cannot guarantee that the window will automatically open on all computers. It's difficult to predict how the browser and pop-up blockers are configured or which blockers are even installed for that matter. Even if you do include a button, make sure that you check it with pop-up blockers and Service Pack 2 installed (on Windows).

Moving On

Even if you don't have a background in drawing, hopefully you now understand how easy it is to create a character using Flash. The shape tools and some creativity or imagination can get you started with character animation regardless of your experience in art and drawing.

One of the best ways to experiment with this project is to create a wildly different character, your own creation, and animate it in a different way. Perhaps you want to create a character in Illustrator, and use the blend feature to create a series of symbols that you can use to animate the character. Or you might continue creating a character only using shape tools such as the Rectangle, Oval, and Line tools in Flash. Either way, you now have the basic skills to animate your own characters using Flash and put them online.

The advantage of loading an animation into a loader SWF file is that you will find it easy to manipulate what the animation "player" looks like. Try adding creative content to the loader.fla document. Try adding a square with a mostly transparent gradient over the loaderClip instance. This way, it looks like your animation plays in a screen.

You might try modifying the graphics around the "frame" to enhance the animation as well. Usually it's easier and more efficient to edit the loader SWF instead of the actual animation.

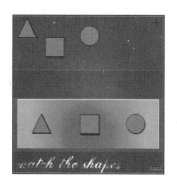

FIGURE 6.A

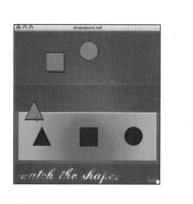

FIGURE 6.B

FIGURE 6.C

What you learn

► How scripts are used for animation

► How to use tools for writing code

► Where to put your ActionScript

► How to manipulate Movie Clips with code

► How to create basic animation with code

► About events and handling events

► About adding basic interactivity

► How to create a custom mouse pointer

Lesson Files

Start:

06/start/shapes.fla

Finish:

06/complete/shapegame.fla

06/complete/shapegame.swf

6

ActionScript for Effects

Before moving on with the rest of the book, you need to cover some of the fundamental aspects of ActionScript. If you are a designer, the thought of coding might be daunting. Or, if you're starting out with Flash, you might think the same thing. Luckily, it's not as complicated or as difficult as you might think. Without some code, it's very hard to create increasingly complex effects using Flash. This chapter begins to show you how easy it is to start moving instances around the Stage in an interactive way by using code.

This chapter walks you through the fundamentals of ActionScript; then you practice writing the code using those fundamentals by building a simple matching game.

Website: www.FLAnimation.com/chapters/06

Using Tools to Create Code

If you're familiar with JavaScript, learning Action-Script might be a minor transition. Both Action-Script and JavaScript are based on the same core specification: ECMA (which stands for European Computer Manufacturers Association).

You have built interactive and animated SWF files in earlier projects. You already know how to make a creative and engaging user experience using Flash, even ones that include a bit of interactivity. However, the kind of interactivity you used didn't involve much complexity because you have used only a limited amount of code. The animation you used so far, such as changing images or moving things around the Stage, didn't involve any ActionScript, either. That begins to change in this chapter, and the good news is that it lets you create more complexity in your files that you cannot achieve without using code.

Scripting is useful when you need to build complex and interactive SWF files, and it's essential if you plan to build applications in Flash. You can use ActionScript to make your sites a bit more dynamic, such as creating an animated menu based on data from an external file, or a menu that loads data or images from the server. Or, you might just use ActionScript to make comments in your files so that you remember what steps you took while tweening animations or include your own copyright information.

You discover different ways to add code to a document in the next section called "Using the Actions panel". You find out how the tools work in Flash for adding, editing, and formatting ActionScript. Then you start to learn ActionScript and afterward jump into a tutorial that demonstrates how the concepts work.

Using the Actions panel

You already added ActionScript to several of the projects you created in this book. It's necessary to add very simple scripts to move or stop the playhead on the Timeline. In the next chapters, you start to add much more ActionScript to your projects. Before you jump into using longer pieces of code and learning how to write ActionScript, you need to know where and how to edit the code.

You can add ActionScript to your documents by typing code into the Actions panel (Window > Development Panels > Actions). The Actions panel lets you write and edit code that you place on the Timeline or directly on an instance, such as a movie clip, button, or component instance.

The Actions panel has many invaluable tools for helping developers write robust ActionScript code (Figure 6.1). Some of the main tools include the following:

◆ Search and replace capabilities

◆ Syntax checker

◆ Error reporting

◆ Code formatting

◆ Code hinting

◆ Code completion

◆ Syntax coloring

◆ Code debugger

◆ Find help

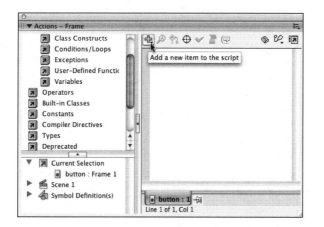

FIGURE 6.1

The Actions panel contains a few main sections: Actions toolbox, Script navigator, Script pane, and a toolbar containing several buttons.

The ability to *search* your ActionScript (Find button) allows you to easily find a snippet of code for a particular instance. For example, if you have a movie clip on the Stage called parrot_mc, you can find all code related to that instance when you click the Find button in the Actions panel and enter **parrot_mc** in the Find dialog box. When you click the Find Next button, you can step through each occurrence of parrot_mc in your code and make edits as necessary in the Actions panel. The Replace button lets you search for a string of text, and replace it directly with a different string of text that you specify in the dialog box.

▶ ▶ Looking at ActionScript 1.0 and 2.0

It's likely that you've heard about ActionScript 2.0, so you might wonder how version 2.0 compares with versions in earlier versions of Flash. You will see code examples of both versions of ActionScript when you search online, so you should be aware of differences between the versions so you can choose what version of the language to use. ActionScript 2.0 is the latest version of ActionScript available in Flash MX 2004. However, it's not a requirement of Flash MX 2004 to use ActionScript 2.0—you can use any version of ActionScript you want with the software. You can use ActionScript 2.0 for Flash Player 6 or Flash Player 7 files, however some features of ActionScript 2.0 only work with Flash Player 7.

There are a few differences between the languages. For example, you can use strict data typing in ActionScript 2.0, but not ActionScript 1.0. This process improves the error-checking process, so it's a good practice to code using strict typing. You learn about strict data typing in Chapter 7 Another improvement in ActionScript 2.0 is improved support for writing object-oriented code. This helps build better applications by allowing you to intelligently organize code into classes, so it is mostly important for developers. You find out more about classes later in this chapter, but you won't use custom classes (classes you write yourself) in this book. You use only classes that are built into Flash.

It's not necessary to use ActionScript 2.0's class-based coding, and it's sometimes overkill and just makes more work necessary in simple applications (or animation/graphics-based files). However, you will use some aspects of ActionScript 2.0 in this book. When you use any part of ActionScript 2.0, you need to publish your SWF files with ActionScript 2.0 selected as the version you are using. You need to select this setting in the Flash tab of the Publish Settings dialog box (File > Publish Settings) to correctly compile (publish) your SWF file.

The *syntax checking* feature (using the Check Syntax button) runs through your ActionScript and checks that the code doesn't throw any errors when you publish it. You only need to click the Check Syntax button in the Actions panel to see whether your code has any syntax errors. Doing this can save you a lot of time because it lets you check that your syntax is valid before you publish the file. Otherwise, Flash might generate various error messages if there are problems with the ActionScript.

One of the best features of Flash's ActionScript is its robust error reporting. You click the Check Syntax button in the Actions panel to check if your code has any syntax errors, and if any errors are found, Flash displays the Output panel. The Output panel displays information or a message about the code that contains errors, and it displays useful debugging information in the Output panel, such as the type of error, frame, and line numbers.

Another great feature in the Actions panel is the *code formatter* (using the Auto Format button). When you click the Auto Format button, all the ActionScript in a Script pane is formatted (such as applying indenting and spacing) based on options you specify in your preferences. You can specify how the code formats by selecting Auto Format Options from the Actions panel options menu (Figure 6.2). The Auto Format Options dialog box opens, which allows you to modify five formatting options and also view how each option affects code by looking at a preview pane, as shown in the following figure.

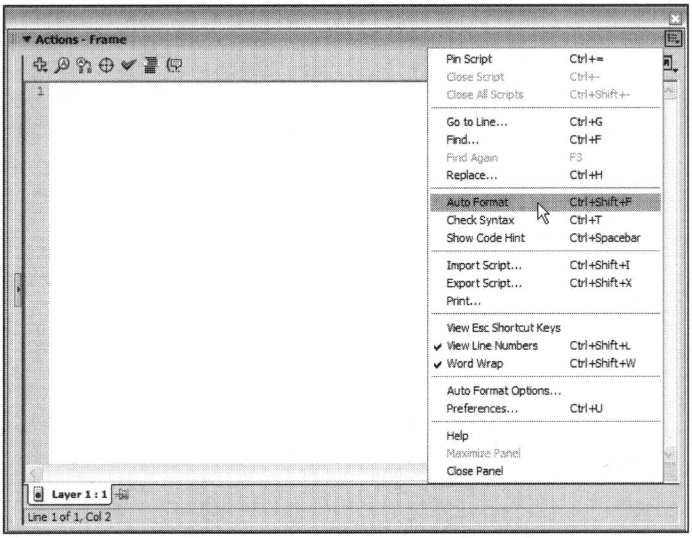

FIGURE 6.2

Select Auto Format Options from the Actions panel options menu, which opens a dialog box in which you can select and preview formatting options.

▶ ▶ **USING THE OUTPUT PANEL**

Sometimes the Output panel opens and displays information about the ActionScript you have written or how the SWF file is working. The Output panel mainly does two things:

1. It alerts you to any problems with your code.

2. It returns values or display information.

Information can be the result of actions in your code that you specifically write, so messages or values display in the panel. You can write these messages using a trace statement. You use the trace statement to send results or values to the Output panel, usually to troubleshoot problems or see what values return to the SWF. You learn much more about the trace statement later in this chapter.

Code hinting and *code completion* help speed up development time, and they help you avoid typing mistakes. Code hints (Figure 6.3) can also help you learn ActionScript and teach you how to format code. Code hints help show you where brackets go, or what you can enter as parameters.

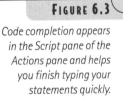

FIGURE 6.3

Code completion appears in the Script pane of the Actions pane and helps you finish typing your statements quickly.

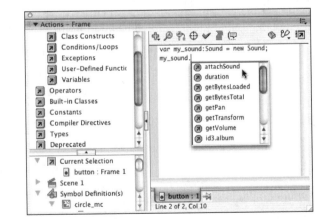

Code completion (Figure 6.4) lets you choose methods and properties for an instance from a pop-up menu. When you type an instance name and press the period key (.), Flash displays the pop-up menu containing methods and properties in the Actions panel. In addition to speeding up the coding process, this feature helps you remember what methods and properties are available.

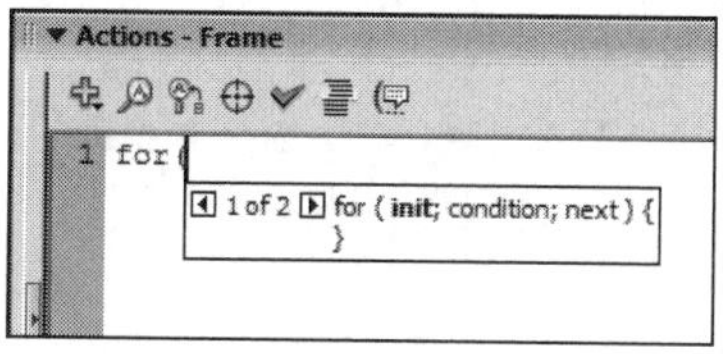

FIGURE 6.4

Code hints, which appear in the Script pane, help you remember proper syntax.

You probably noticed how certain parts of your code have different colors in the Actions panel. ActionScript uses syntax (the structure and ordering of a language's elements), and parts of that syntax display in a specified color. *Syntax coloring* is helpful for beginners and advanced users alike. Colored code lets you quickly see whether your code contains typos by specially coloring different sections of code because incorrect syntax doesn't correctly use coloring. A color helps you understand what that part of the code does (specifically, *keywords*, *comments* and *strings*). To customize the current color scheme, select Edit > Preferences from the main menu. When the Preferences dialog box opens, click the ActionScript tab. This tab lets you control tab size (for indenting), the number of seconds before code hints appear, the font used in the Actions panel, syntax coloring, and a few other options. To change the background color in the Actions panel, click the palette swatch next to the Background label and use the color pop-up window to select a new color. Setting the foreground color sets the text color for instance names. Likewise, you can also set the color for other parts of the ActionScript language.

To take advantage of code completion, you have to give your instance names special predefined suffixes, or explicitly define a variable's data type (Number, String, Date, and so on). You learn how to do this later in the chapter and will practice it regularly when you code.

Highlight a color-coded word in your code (it is part of the ActionScript language). If you click the Reference button (in the upper-right corner of the Actions panel) when it's highlighted, the Help panel displays the ActionScript Language Reference entry for the action. This helps you use the particular action, examine an example for the code, or fix a problem in your code.

Organizing code in an FLA file

There are three main ways to organize the ActionScript that you write for a project:

◆ **On the Timeline:** Select a frame on the Timeline and type **ActionScript** into the Script pane of the Actions panel. A small "a" appears in the frame you added the script to (Figure 6.5).

◆ **Attached directly to objects:** Select an object on the Stage (such as a movie clip or a component) and then type **Action-**

Script into the Script pane. The code you write is applied to that object, unless specified otherwise.

◆ **Placed in external ActionScript files (or classes):** Type code into a code editor, such as the Script window in Flash MX Professional (or a text editor such as Notepad). The external code imports into the SWF file using a statement in the FLA file.

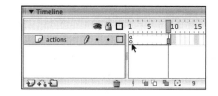

FIGURE 6.5

A frame with code attached to it appears to have an a symbol in the frame.

The preferred and officially (Macromedia) recommended way to write ActionScript is to place as much code as possible either in an external file or on the main Timeline. You should always avoid placing code directly onto instances because it quickly leads to a lot of duplicated code. It also makes the code snippets that you need to fix or edit difficult to find in an FLA file. Placing code all over a FLA file is sometimes referred to as "spaghetti code."

When you write code, it is best to group similar code together. For example, if you have large blocks of code that you use to create and modify similar items (such as movie clips) it makes sense to keep the code that does this together in one location. For example, if you have ActionScript that builds a menu system (or adds functionality to it), try and organize the code for the menu together in one place.

Organizing code logically helps serve many different purposes. First and foremost, it's easier to read, understand, and modify organized code. Disorganized code is often spread throughout a file, perhaps on many frames, put inside movie clips, or attached onto movie clips. When code is put in different locations, it's difficult to find, modify, and figure out. It's difficult to figure out how the Action-Script interacts when it's put in so many places. When the code is placed in one place, you can easily read the ActionScript and figure out how all the pieces work together.

Another way to organize your code is to write it in external Action-Script (.AS) files. There are two different types of external files that

Syntax elements are defined later in this chapter, starting with the section "Coding concepts."

Using external code files lets you incorporate code libraries into several SWF files. This means you can save time by using the same code in several files. You do not use this way of organizing a project in this book, which sometimes involves a more complex way of programming.

In this book, you add all your code to the Timeline in an FLA file.

you often encounter while working with ActionScript. The first one is commonly referred to as an *include* file, where Flash includes the code from the external file in your Flash application when you publish it. You can write this include file in the Actions panel and paste it into Notepad or TextEdit, write it in the Script window in Flash MX Professional (Figure 6.6), or any number of third-party programs (such as PrimalScript or sciTE|Flash).

The second kind of external file you'll encounter is called a *class* file. Class files are similar to include files, except that they require a bit more programming knowledge because they are slightly more structured than the code you might write directly in an FLA file. Class files revolve around only a single core topic. An example of this is Macromedia's built-in Math class.

The Math class has several functions (or *methods*) that relate to math concepts, such as square roots, sines, cosines, and random numbers; and other methods that let you round numbers to their next highest or lowest integer value. Classes are an advanced topic and are often in what is commonly referred to as *Object-Oriented Programming*, or *OOP* for short. You'll work with several built-in classes in this and following chapters.

Another advantage to organized code is that it is easier to reuse in future files. If you can easily find a specific block of code within a file, you can often simply copy and paste the code into a new file instead of writing all the code from scratch. Maximizing code reuse allows you to build applications much faster because you don't constantly rewrite existing ActionScript.

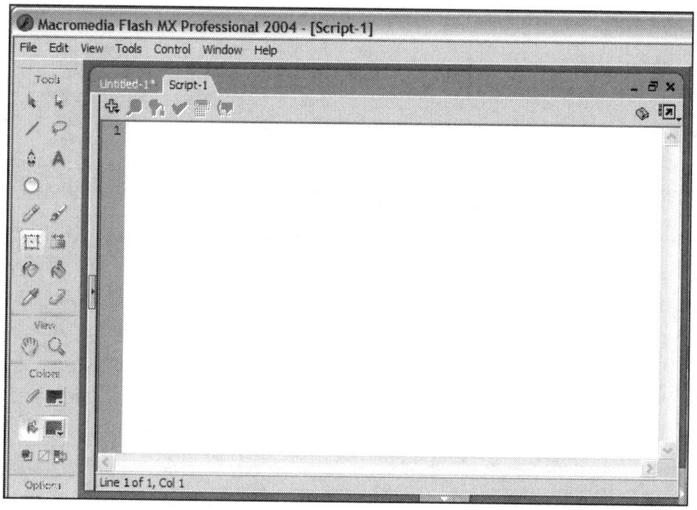

FIGURE 6.6

You can write files that are only ActionScript in the Script window.

A "built-in" class is one that is written by Macromedia and included with the Flash software. That means you can use the methods and properties of these existing classes to make your FLA files work.

Now that you understand how to organize your code, it's time to define the syntax elements of ActionScript and general coding concepts.

Coding Concepts

There are many different parts of the ActionScript language, some of which you have explored and even written so far. There are particularly important parts of the language to learn the fundamentals of, regardless of whether you continue on to create business applications for the boardroom or fantastic graphic effects for a bleeding edge website. However, there are particular parts of the language that are well-suited to animation. You cover the basics of Action-Script syntax here, and in the following chapters you'll continue to piece together more pieces of the puzzle. Syntax forms the rules and guidelines for a particular way of writing your code.

Using data and declaring variables

A *data type* is a type of information, such as a Number (such as 601), a String (such as "pelican"), or a Boolean (either true or false). A *variable* is a container that holds a particular value of any data type. You create variables in Flash, which is called *declaring a variable*. When you declare a variable, you give it a name (for example, myPelican or redCar). When you need to reuse a particular value in your code, such as the score of the Pong game you're creating, variables can be useful. You assign a value to the variable, so you can use it over and over, even if it changes. For example, your Pong score will constantly change when users score points, so the variable for that score can update (change) with it.

> ▶ ▶ **NAMING VARIABLES**
>
> There are several considerations to make when you name a variable. Variables can contain only letters, numbers and underscores. The name can be anything you want, except that it cannot share a name with another variable. So, you cannot have two variables called **myVar**. Variables are case sensitive, so you could use **myvar** and **myVar** as two variable names, except that this is confusing and should be avoided. You should also try to avoid special characters.

Pay special attention to the terminology used in these sections. You encounter them a lot in this and following chapters, so it'll make your life much easier to note down or highlight some of the names and terms used in this chapter.

Variables are also useful when you have long and complex names or paths in your ActionScript. Perhaps you have a long path to a movie clip you need to target. You can save that target as a variable, so you only have to type that instead.

Variables cannot be a keyword; or share the name of an object, method, or property in ActionScript. You want to avoid any part of the ActionScript language, in fact. For example, if you use a keyword as a variable, the variable is treated like the keyword instead, which then breaks your code. For a list of words to avoid, see "Avoiding reserved words" in the Using ActionScript book of Flash documentation (Help > Help). Search "reserved words" in the Help panel to find this section. When you declare a new variable, you use the var keyword. You use the var keyword to declare (create) the variable.

You follow the keyword with the name of the variable (what you use to identify it), which can almost be anything (see the sidebar titled "Naming Variables"). You then use the assignment operator (=) to assign a value to the variable and follow this with the value itself.

Therefore:

```
var myLuck = false;
```

The variable myLuck contains the Boolean value of false.

Later on in the application, the value can be set to true if luck changes. Or, if you use the variable myLuck several times in your code, and later on you want all of those values to be true, all you have to do is change the line above and all the values are updated everywhere you might use it.

For example, perhaps you want to have a series of movie clips that are quite transparent. You might set the transparency in your code, which is set by using a Number value:

```
var myAlpha = 50;
```

You have set 30 movie clips to myAlpha. Later on, you might change the design of your site and decide that much transparency detracts from the design. All you need to do is change the single myAlpha value from 50 (its initial value) to **20**, and every single clip updates. Imagine if you set each clip to the number **50** instead of myAlpha. You would have a lot of updating to do in your code.

Keywords have only a single purpose in a Flash file. Keywords exist in Flash to behave a particular way or to do certain things. For example, you saw that the var keyword was used to declare a variable.

A Boolean is a true or false value. You might use a Boolean to turn something on or off in a SWF file—such as visibility or whether the user can click a button. String values are denoted by quotation marks around the value. Number and Boolean values do not have quotation marks around the value to differentiate them, as seen in the previous code.

Objects, methods and properties are defined in the section called "Understanding Objects" (later in this chapter).

Using dot notation

ActionScript uses *dot notation*, sometimes called *dot syntax*, to address (or target) objects in your SWF files. For example, you need to target a movie clip instance before you can apply an action to it. Dot notation helps you create a path to the instance you need to target.

If you want something to work in your SWF file, you need to target that instance and then tell it to do something, such as by giving it an action or changing its properties. You usually need to define where that instance is in the SWF file (for example, what Timeline it's on or what instance it is nested within) by creating the target path.

Remember that you have given many of your instances an instance name, and then you added code to the FLA file using that instance name. By doing this, you target that particular instance and then tell it to do something (such as move the playhead or open a web page.) The instance name is the name that you type into the Property inspector after you select the instance on the Stage.

An FLA document has a particular hierarchy. You might have instances on the main Stage, or you can have instances that nest inside a movie clip. Or, you might even have instances that nest within a couple of movie clips. If each of these movie clips has an instance name, you can code a target path to one of the nested clips. For example, you might have a target path that's separated by a series of dots, as follows:

```
myClip_mc.myClip2_mc.myClip3_mc.gotoAndPlay(5);
```

This code targets the myClip_mc instance, which sits on the main Stage. Then the ActionScript targets the myClip2_mc instance, which is inside the myClip_mc instance. Finally, you add the action that you want to occur: The gotoAndPlay() method plays the myClip3_mc instance, which sits inside of myClip2_mc.

Remember that each movie clip instance has its own Timeline, which you can not only target with code, but also place graphics, code, or other instances on. So you would use this code if you want to target myClip3_mc and have it go to frame 5 in the movie clip and play that frame onward. Notice that the clip that's manipulated comes right before the action. You'll notice this trend in upcoming sections.

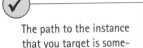
The path to the instance that you target is sometimes called the *target path*.

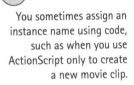
You sometimes assign an instance name using code, such as when you use ActionScript only to create a new movie clip.

For more information on how dot notation and properties work, see "How ActionScript manipulates instances" later in this chapter.

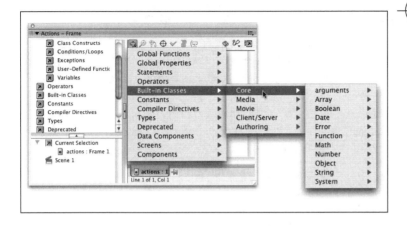

FIGURE 6.7

Use the Add button in the Actions panel to help you add code to the FLA document.

It might seem pretty confusing, and it certainly can be. You should try to keep your FLA documents as simple as you can, but there will be times that you encounter complex nested instances that you need to target by using code similar to the snippet just outlined.

▶ ▶ ADDING SCRIPTS USING THE ADD BUTTON AND TOOLBOX

You can use the Actions toolbox to help you add code to your FLA file if you're new to writing ActionScript or are unsure of ActionScript syntax. The Actions toolbox is located to the left of the Actions panel. The Actions toolbox contains all the actions you can use that are built into Flash. The toolbox contains many "books" that you can click and move throughout to find actions, methods, and properties. When you double-click a method in the Actions toolbox, for example, it adds to the Script pane wherever the cursor is located. You can also use the Add (+) button to add new scripts to your code (Figure 6.7). This useful feature lets you add pieces of code to the Script pane when you select an action from the menu. In some cases, after you add the action, the cursor in the Actions panel is specifically placed where you need to type, and a tooltip appears. The tooltip provides a guide on how you should go about finishing off the script.

You might think that because the myClip3_mc has a Timeline, why not just place the code on that Timeline instead of typing out this long target? You can! However, you might remember that it is a lot easier to keep all your code in one place. Therefore, you can put all your code on the main Timeline together, which is much easier to edit than trying to open up a few clips and dig around for ActionScript.

▶ ▶ **COMMENTING CODE**

When you add code to your Flash documents, the most important thing to remember is to add enough comments to your code. Comments can be any text that you want to write, such as what the code is doing, or any helpful hints you want to add. Comments help you remember what exactly the code is doing if you have to modify the code in the future. Comments also make it easier for other people to understand the code when they modify your FLA files.

Place // in front of a line of code to add a comment, and then type anything you want (the comments) onto that line. Or, if you want to add a large comment, you can type /* at the beginning of the first comment line, and then add another */ at the end of the comment. The comment will be a different color than the rest of your code in the Actions panel (comments are gray by default).

Also try to give your variables descriptive names, which can help with the readability of your ActionScript. If your variables describe what they contain, then other people can better understand what they're used for. Don't make your variable names too long (this helps your performance), but make sure they still describe that they're used for in the SWF file.

ANIMATING WITH CODE

Scripted animation is the technique of animating items on the Stage or from the Library at runtime using ActionScript. You do this instead of, or in addition to, using motion or shape tweens that you add to the Timeline. In many cases, using scripting for your animation has benefits, such as better performance in the SWF file or a lower file size. In some cases, scripted animation might be the only way to achieve a particular effect. For example, if you want to use a custom mouse pointer, you need to use ActionScript to animate the pointer around the Stage. Or, if you base an animation on some kind of user interaction (such as a mouse click), you should use ActionScript. Other forms of user interaction include waiting for a click to occur, and then writing code that executes only when the click occurs. Or, you can take items from the Library, attach them to the Stage, duplicate that movie clip 100 times, and then animate every instance—only using code. Additionally, you can make something happen (maybe play a sound or launch a web page) when the user presses a key or when the mouse moves within 10 pixels of the movie clip instance.

You can animate instances on the Stage using code by learning a few different techniques. Perhaps the most common technique for animating code is to use what's called an onEnterFrame event handler, which is an action that's called each time a frame plays, which is typically multiple times per second, depending on your frame rate.

When you use onEnterFrame, you can make instances smoothly animate across the Stage. Because the code within an onEnterFrame calls continually until the event handler is deleted (using ActionScript), the code continues to run until you want it to stop. The event handler simulates the playhead moving across the Timeline, which executes the code that you might have on the frames when the playhead reaches it. Therefore, you can repeatedly execute a piece of code at the current framerate without having to put code along a Timeline—you put the code inside this event handler instead. Remember that the frequency that the onEnterFrame event handler is called is tied to the frame rate you set the Flash document to. The higher frame rate you set, the code calls more often, which results in smoother animations. However, a high frame rate also requires more processing power on the user's computer.

Events and event handlers are defined later in this chapter, in the section called "Understanding Events and Interactivity."

Another way to animate objects is to use a function in Flash called setInterval(). The setInterval() function calls a function or method at a specified interval. For example, you could write your own function that moves a movie clip five pixels to the right. Then you call the setInterval() function and tell it to call your custom function every 100 milliseconds (1/10th of a second). When you want to clear the interval and stop the movie clip from moving, you call the clearInterval() function, which stops the function from constantly being called.

onEnterFrame can be very resource intensive if you're trying to do simple things. Both onEnterFrame and setInterval need to be cleared or deleted after you are finished using them for this reason. If you only need to call/execute code less frequently, you should use setInterval because you can specify how often the code executes (thus saving resources).

▶ ▶ BENEFITS OF ANIMATING WITH CODE

Using ActionScript to animate objects on the Stage has many benefits over traditional animation methods. One of the greatest advantages is that you can easily reuse code throughout your FLA, and even in different projects. Your code is a lot more maintainable, because changing code in one place might affect several different instances. For example, if you have a dynamically created menu in your SWF file that animates using Flash, you might need to write the code to animate menu items only one time and make each submenu use the same code. Building a file this way lets you modify code in one place and have the changes apply throughout your document. If you animate objects using shape or motion tweens manually and then need to change the way the animation behaves, you might need to change any number of symbols that use a similar effect. If you animate objects using ActionScript, you can make a change to the code in one place, and have that change reflect throughout your document automatically.

Another benefit is that using code can cut down on mistakes or inconsistencies in your animation. If you need to set up keyframes and motion tweens that fade menus in and out, you can make sure that each animation is identical. Having to manually add tweens, keyframes and animations usually increases the chance of small mistakes in the animation—such as misaligned symbols, neglecting to hit test text (add a clickable area for a text button using the Hit frame inside a Button symbol), or adding keyframes on the wrong frame. Using scripted animation ultimately leads to a simpler and more consistent end result. However, remember that not all kinds of effects can be accomplished by using code: Sometimes you need to draw or shape tween graphics to achieve the result you require.

How ActionScript manipulates instances

You have a lot of control over movie clips, buttons, or components that you want to manipulate when you use code. You can change the X and Y coordinates of an instance, set the number of degrees rotation, set the level or transparency (alpha), width, height, or even horizontal and vertical scaling. To manipulate these objects, though, you first need to assign an instance name to objects on the Stage.

Without an instance name, Flash has a harder time targeting specific instances on the Stage. After you give an object an instance name, you can set its properties by prefixing the desired property with the object's instance name and a dot (refer to "Using dot notation" for more information).

For example, if you have a circle on the Stage with the instance name circle_mc and you want to set the level of transparency to 50% you can use the following ActionScript code on the main Timeline:

```
circle_mc._alpha = 50;
```

In this example, circle_mc is referred to as the *target path* as it tells Flash how to find the target instance. If circle_mc was nested within a different movie clip called container_mc, you need to use the following code to properly target the movie clip:

```
container_mc.circle_mc._alpha = 50;
```

In this case, the target path would be container_mc.circle_mc.

Animating a ball with code

If you plan to add instances dynamically to the Stage using Action-Script or want to target an instance using ActionScript and change its properties, you need to make sure that the instance you want to target on the Stage has an *instance name*. Remember: This means you select the instance and type a name into the <Instance Name> text field in the Property inspector.

Moving an instance on the Stage using ActionScript is almost as easy as setting an X and Y coordinate in the Actions panel. To move a movie clip with the instance name ball_mc, you need to set an X and Y coordinate (the location on the Stage), as shown in the following code snippet:

```
ball_mc._x = 15;
ball_mc._y = 20;
```

This snippet moves ball_mc to an X coordinate of 15 and Y coordinate of 20, respectively. If you want to move the instance to a position that's relative to its *current* position, you need to *increment* (increase) or *decrement* (decrease) the coordinates. For example, if you want to move the ball_mc instance 15 pixels along the X-axis, use the following code:

```
ball_mc._x = ball_mc._x + 15;
```

You can move instances around the Stage by modifying the _x and _y properties of that instance instead of using the Property inspector. You use this kind of code in Exercise 1.

If you want to use simpler syntax, Flash has what it calls the *addition assignment operator,* which combines addition and variable assignment in one simple step using +. (You learn more about operators later in this chapter.) For now, you can rewrite the previous code by using the addition assignment operator, as shown in the following code:

```
ball_mc += 15;
```

Both of the previous code snippets perform the same task: Each snippet increments ball_mc's position on the X-axis by 15 pixels. If you want to move the ball to the left instead, use either of the following snippets:

```
ball_mc._x = ball_mc._x—15;
```
or
```
ball_mc._x -= 15;
```

Each of the previous two lines of code do exactly the same thing; however, the second snippet is commonly used because it is easier to read after you're familiar with ActionScript.

If you want to animate ball_mc on the Stage, you need to use one of several techniques to constantly call a snippet of code. You could use one of the following techniques, which describe different scenarios you might replicate to animate with ActionScript.

Add two frames to a new layer. One of the frames modifies the position of ball_mc, and the other frame is empty. This causes the SWF file to loop between those two frames. Because the SWF file loops, each time the playhead goes to the first frame in the Timeline, code on that frame executes. Therefore, ball_mc moves on the Stage.

Create an event handler for the onEnterFrame event that calls once per each frame per second your SWF file is set to. So, if your SWF file is set to play at 30 frames per second, the onEnterFrame event handler also gets called 30 times each second.

Create an "interval" that repeatedly executes a specified function. For example, you could create an interval using the setInterval() function, and it might call a function that decreases the _alpha property (transparency level) of a movie clip every 100 ms (1/10 of a second). The setInterval() function doesn't call the code exactly at the interval, so you must be very careful if you try to build applications with very precise timing requirements. You can clear an interval that you create with setInterval() by calling the clearInterval() function

You might notice that many lines end with a semi-colon, which is used in Flash to end a statement of some sort. It's a little bit like the end of a sentence being finished using a period. Not all lines in Flash are ended by using a semi-colon. If in doubt, use the Auto Format button in the Actions panel toolbar, which adds missing semi-colons to your Action-Script and properly indents your code as well.

and passing the interval's ID as a *parameter*. A parameter is a place-holder that you use to pass a value into a function. You can then use that value within the function to influence the result.

You use these animation techniques in some of the exercises in Projects 6 and 7.

A simple interactive script

You've already seen bits and pieces of ActionScript code throughout this book. A particularly useful piece of ActionScript is the trace statement, which displays values in the Output panel when a SWF file plays *within the Flash authoring environment*. Using the trace statement lets you see when certain events happen, or you can use it to display values or debug code (discover and pinpoint problems with problematic or complicated code). You see an example of the trace statement in the following code:

```
ball_mc.onRelease = function() {
   trace("ball_mc clicked");
};
```

If you test the SWF file (Control > Test Movie), you can tell when (or even if) a user clicks ball_mc because *ball_mc clicked* displays in the Output panel (Figure 6.8).

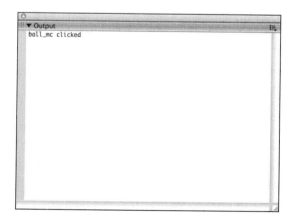

FIGURE 6.8

Information displays in the Output panel. This helps you see whether the SWF file works properly when you test it in Flash.

If you click ball_mc and nothing displays in the Output panel, it might mean that you didn't enter an instance name for the instance on the Stage, or perhaps there's a typo in your code or the instance name. Therefore, a trace statement helps you see whether a function

You cannot use the `trace` statement with SWF files that you embed on HTML pages. The `trace` statement sends information only to the Output panel, which lives in the Flash authoring (and test) environment. If you need to test values or display data with an embedded SWF file, you need to display text in a text field. You learn how to do this in Project 7.

works, and it can also help you display values or data that return from a server. For example, suppose that you have the following code on the Timeline:

```
var x = 15;
trace(x)
```

When you test the SWF file this time, the Output panel immediately opens and displays *15*. As you can probably tell, the `trace` statement is very useful when you write ActionScript.

So now that you know about certain parts of the ActionScript language and have a bit of terminology under your belt, it's time to start building this chapter's project. In this project, you will use some ActionScript you learned earlier, as well as new pieces of syntax. Additionally, you will learn new parts of the language and what they do, such as functions and events.

Project 6: Creating Interactive Animation

In this chapter's project, you build a basic game in which users can match various shapes by dragging them into their respective holes. Even though building the game is fairly complex, building it demonstrates a handful of very useful techniques. The techniques you learn include creating draggable movie clips, a custom mouse pointer, timers, and even collision detection (detection when two instances on the Stage intersect). To view the final project, go to www.FLAnimation.com/chapters/06.

Exercise 1: Setting up the project

In this exercise, you create the shapes using Flash's drawing tools. These shapes are the movie clips that you drag around the Stage in the final project. You also add ActionScript to retrieve the X and Y coordinates of each of the shapes that you create.

1. Create a new FLA file. Choose File > Save As and save the document on your hard drive as **shapegame.fla**.

2. Rename Layer 1 on the Timeline as **shapes**. Draw three shapes on the Stage: a circle, a square, and a triangle by using the Oval (circle), Rectangle (square), and PolyStar tools from the Tools panel (Figure 6.9).

The easiest way to create a triangle (or any multisided nonrectangular shape) is to click the Rectangle tool in the Tools panel and select the PolyStar tool from the pop-up menu. Click the Options button in the Property inspector to open the Tool Settings dialog box, and specify how many sides you want the polygon to have.

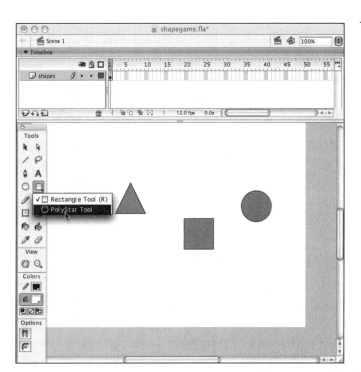

FIGURE 6.9

Draw three shapes on the Stage. Each shape should be about the same size.

✓ *Press the Shift key while you drag each shape tool to create a perfect circle and a square with equal sides.*

3. Optionally, add some depth to each shape by using the drawing tools. You might use the Line or Brush tools and the Paint Bucket to draw and fill each shape. Or, you can duplicate the existing shape and paste the shape on a lower layer and give the new shape a darker color than the original. When you finish, your shapes might look similar to the following figure.

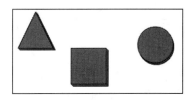

FIGURE 6.10

Add some depth to your shapes by using the drawing tools.

FIGURE 6.11

*Select the entire drawing
using the Lasso tool.*

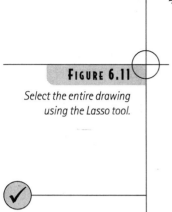

If you want to use some existing shapes for this project, open the following FLA file from the CD-ROM: 06/start/shapes.fla. This file also contains a background that you might want to add to your file (on a new layer at the bottom of the Time-line). If you add this background or your own, create a new layer on the Timeline, and click and drag it so it is the bottommost layer. Lock it after you have added the graphics. You can copy and paste any graphics from this file, or rename the file itself and save it on your hard drive. There is a symbol in the Library that you will use toward the end of this chapter for a mouse pointer graphic.

4. Select one of the shapes on the Stage using the Selection or Lasso tool. Click and drag around one shape using either tool to select all of the drawing, as shown in the following figure.

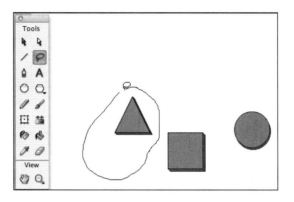

After making the selection, press F8 to convert the drawing into a symbol. Name the shape and select Movie Clip as its behavior. Repeat this step for all three shapes.

5. Select each movie clip instance on the Stage, and give them instance names (select the movie clip and assign an Instance name in the Property inspector). Name your symbols as follows:

circle movie clip: **circle_mc**

square movie clip: **square_mc**

triangle movie clip: **triangle_mc**

6. Click Insert Layer on the Timeline to create a new layer, and rename the layer **actions**. Select frame 1 of the *actions* layer, and type the following code into the Script pane:

```
var circleInitX:Number = circle_mc._x;
var circleInitY:Number = circle_mc._y;
var squareInitX:Number = square_mc._x;
var squareInitY:Number = square_mc._y;
var triangleInitX:Number = triangle_mc._x;
var triangleInitY:Number = triangle_mc._y;
```

This code declares a bunch of variables. It is responsible for saving the current X and Y coordinates for the three shapes into variables (such as circleInitX). Flash stores the current X coordinate of `circle_mc` into a numeric variable named `circleInitX`. In an upcoming exercise, you use these values to reset the position of the shapes after they've been moved around the Stage.

7. Save (File > Save) the changes you made to shapegame.fla.

So far, you have created three drawings and converted each of them into a movie clip symbol. Then, you wrote ActionScript that takes the current coordinates of those instances and saves them in a variable. In the following exercises, you use new objects in the Action-Script language to add elements of interactivity to the project.

Understanding Objects

Flash bases its framework on a model involving classes, instances, and objects. In this section, you take a look at what these things are and how they affect you when you create your documents. A *class* is a collection of methods and properties that you use to describe an *object*. For example, you might have a Soda class. This particular class might have some *methods* and *properties* that help describe the Soda class. A property might be `isDiet`, `packageType`, or `hasCaffeine`. Methods of this class might be `doDrink()`, `setFlavor()`, `getVolume()`, or `getBrand()`. The class is like a blueprint that describes soda, and you might have several different kinds of carbonated beverages described by this single class.

Nearly everything you create or use in Flash can be considered an object. Movie clips have their own sets of default methods and properties, and so do buttons. Not every object in Flash is "visible" (you place visible items on the Stage). For example, Flash has a Date class, which is useful when you need to create or display dates, but you create it using code—not by putting something on the Stage. Concepts will be defined using this class shortly.

To use these methods and properties in a SWF file, you have to create an instance (which is essentially a copy) of the class in an instance that's on the Stage. Except you create this instance using code instead of adding or converting items on the Stage.

Built-in classes are complex data types that you use to make Flash do certain things. The classes have "predefined" methods and properties,

You have used the _mc suffix several times already in this chapter: but why? Using suffixes helps you remember what type of instance each item on the Stage is when you read, edit, or debug your Action-Script. This also makes sure that you can take advantage of code hinting and completion (discussed previously in this chapter).

You cannot create classes directly in the Actions panel. Classes must be created as external files (such as in the Script window) that you save. The files compile into the SWF file when you publish the file. You won't create any classes for this book, but you do use what are called "built-in classes" that are included right in Action-Script itself.

The strict data typing (:Date) shown in this code snippet is outlined in Chapter 7.

which are already written so you can use them to do particular things in your SWF files (such as change a color or return the current time) without creating your own. Examples of built-in classes include the Math, Button, and Date classes. You have used the MovieClip class a few times already, such as when you used the `gotoAndPlay()` method. The MovieClip class also has properties that you can change in an instance, such as `_visible`, `_width`, and the `_x` and `_y` coordinates.

When you create an instance of a class using ActionScript, you use the class' constructor function. To create a new instance using ActionScript, you might write some code like this:

```
var myDate:Date = new Date();
```

In this code, you construct a new instance of the Date class and store an instance in a variable called `myDate`. You use the instance of the Date class to return specific parts of the date (such as year, month, minutes, or seconds). Or you could create two date instances to find the difference in seconds between two dates that you specify.

Just like the Soda class described previously, a built-in class in Flash (or a custom class that you write yourself) contains methods and properties. Methods are functions that associate with the objects class (such as the Date class above) and you use them to do something with the object. A method is just like a function might work in your SWF file. For example, the Color class has a `setRGB()` built-in method. The method *sets* the hexadecimal color value for a specified instance.

Properties are built into the class, too. Properties are similar to variables or data that you use to define an instance, such as the dimensions or transparency of the instance. For example, a property in the MovieClip class is `_visible`, which sets the visibility of an instance. The property can be set to `true` (visible) or `false` (invisible).

An easy way to see what methods and properties belong to classes is to use the Actions toolbox in the Actions panel (Figure 6.12). For example, to view the methods and properties of the MovieClip class you can navigate through several folders. Find the MovieClip class by expanding Built-in Classes > Movie > MovieClip in the Actions toolbox.

FIGURE 6.12

Explore the Actions toolbox to discover what actions are available.

The MovieClip class contains four subfolders: Methods, Properties, Drawing Methods, and Events.

Resizing and fading movie clips

A common technique in Flash is to modify the size of instances on the Stage. This technique can be useful for scaling instances using code or for building progress bars that let you display the loading progress of a SWF file. There are several properties you can use to resize an instance on the Stage, such as the _width and _height properties in the MovieClip and Button classes. These properties let you set the number of pixels that a particular instance is, either vertically or horizontally. Two other properties that can be useful for resizing objects are the _xscale and _yscale properties. Similar to the _width and _height properties, the _xscale and _yscale resize a particular instance, although they let you easily change the dimensions based on the *current* width and height. The default values for _xscale and _yscale are 100; thus, the current scale for each property is 100% wide and 100% high. Create a movie clip on the Stage in any FLA

file, and give the movie clip an instance name of **ball_mc**. Set the
_xscale property to 200 to double the width of an instance, as
shown in the following code:

```
ball_mc._xscale = 200;\
```

If you test your SWF file now, you see that ball_mc is twice as wide
as it was originally. Set the _xscale property back to 100 to reset the
instance back to its original size.

A particularly useful capability of Flash is that you can change the
amount of an instance's *transparency*. You set the _alpha property to
modify the transparency level. By default, instances are at 100% visible (_alpha is 100). If you want to change an instance so it's 50%
transparent, set the _alpha property to 50 as shown in the following
code:

```
ball_mc._alpha = 50;
```

There are a few important things you need to know about using
_alpha and how performance can be compromised in your SWF
files when you use it.

◆ **It can be processor-intensive to have several transparent
 instances on your Stage.** If you have complex animations
 with lots of objects on the Stage, slower computers might
 slow down and cause your animations to play back jerkily
 and slowly.

◆ **If you set an instance to an _alpha level of 0, it's still on
 the Stage and active.** So, if you have a clickable movie clip
 and you set its _alpha property to 0, the user cannot see the
 instance in your SWF file, except the instance can react to
 events and could be clickable. If you have instances on the
 Stage that you no longer need, you should always try unloading them from your SWF file by using ActionScript, or set
 the _visible property to false to hide the instance on the
 Stage (similar to setting _alpha to 0). Setting visibility to false
 causes that instance to stop handling events (so it is unclickable).

Despite these concerns, you will find that changing alpha levels can
create interesting effects that you either want or need to use in a
SWF file. Remember to test your SWF files before you put them
online, and (if possible) test the file on a variety of computers
(for example, on older Windows computers, a newer computer, a

Macintosh computer, and so on). If the performance is unacceptable, try reducing the number of transparent objects in your file.

Exercise 2: Changing color using code

There are two main ways to change color in a SWF file: setRGB() and setTransform() methods. In this exercise, you create new instances and use setRGB() to change the color of several instances on the Stage.

1. Click Insert Layer on the Timeline to create a new layer, and rename the layer **board**. Click and drag the layer below the *shapes* layer.

2. Open the Library (Window > Library). Select the circle symbol and drag an instance of it to the *board* layer on the Stage. Repeat this step to add a second instance of the other two shapes. You have six shapes on the Stage when you finish: two instances of each shape you created in Exercise 1.

3. Open the Property inspector (Window > Properties). Give each of the three new shapes an instance name: **circleHole_mc**, **squareHole_mc**, and **triangleHole_mc**.

4. Select frame 1 of the *actions* layer. Type in the following code into the Script pane, following the ActionScript you added in Exercise 1:

```
var circleHole_color:Color = new Color(circleHole_mc);
circleHole_color.setRGB(0x000000);
var squareHole_color:Color = new Color(squareHole_mc);
squareHole_color.setRGB(0x000000);
var triangleHole_color:Color = new
Color(triangleHole_mc);
triangleHole_color.setRGB(0x000000);
```

This code creates three Color instances in ActionScript (such as circleHole_color) and applies an RGB color value to a specific instance. Each line in this example is a *Color constructor* and it takes a single *parameter* (such as circleHole_mc in line 1), which is an instance name to apply the color value to. The setRGB() method also takes a single parameter (0x000000), which is the color that you want to apply. A *parameter* is a value (in this case, a color) that's passed into your code that affects it in some way.

5. Then add the following code after the ActionScript you added in step 4:

```
triangleHole_mc.gotoAndStop("on");
squareHole_mc.gotoAndStop("on");
circleHole_mc.gotoAndStop("on");
```

This ActionScript will move the playhead of three shapes to the on playhead as soon as the SWF file plays. You need this code if your shapes have depth added to them. You do not want to see this part of the instance on the Stage for the holes the shapes are placed in. You will add this frame label and content for the "on" frames later in the project.

6. Select the Rectangle tool and create a square on the *board* layer (press Shift to constrain the proportions). Select the rectangle and press F8 to convert it into a graphic symbol. Arrange the `circleHole_mc`, `squareHole_mc`, and `triangleHole_mc` instances on the layer (similar to the layout in the final project file).

7. Create a folder in the Library (click the New Folder button at the bottom of the panel to create a folder). Name the folder **graphics**. Move any existing and future graphics into this folder; such as the rectangle you created in step 6. Optionally, you can also create a folder for your movie clip symbols as well.

Save the changes you made to the file. In the next exercise, you begin to add some interactivity to the document, so the user can move some of the instances around the Stage when you play it in Flash Player.

UNDERSTANDING EVENTS AND INTERACTIVITY

When creating animations and effects in your FLA files, you might want to make parts of your SWF files interactive. This might be as simple as letting a user click buttons on the Stage to navigate to different parts a website, or perhaps you're building a complex game in which users can move characters around and interact with an environment. It might also be draggable scrollbars or menus. However intricate your SWF files become, it is important that you understand how to capture user events, such as button clicks, mouse movements, and key presses. Interactivity typically improves the *user experience*—the reaction visitors have to your sites.

An *event*, which is an action that occurs while an SWF file is playing back, is triggered by things happening when the SWF file places. Events could be keyboard input, a sound file finishes playing, external files finish loading, or when you click a button. Events alert you when something happens when the SWF file plays, so you can make something else happen as a result. For example, an event occurs when a movie clip or external file loads, a user clicks a button or moves the mouse, or a playhead reaches a frame. Then, you can use *event handlers* and *listeners* to help manage those events. So, when a user clicks a button, you can make the playhead go to a new frame; or you can create a progress bar that increases in size as a file loads.

Events are the cornerstone of ActionScript; they allow you to detect when things happen in a SWF file. By understanding events and knowing how to handle them, you're on your way to adding interactive elements to your projects.

A few common event handlers in the MovieClip class are commonly used for interactive animation: onRollOver, onRollOut, onRelease, and onEnterFrame.

Exercise 3: Interacting with other objects

Interactivity involving the mouse is quite common. Simple interactivity is adding clickable elements, but it is a bit more interesting when you add draggable elements to the Stage. This exercise adds Action-Script to your file that allows the user to drag shapes around the Stage and try and fit them into the corresponding holes.

1. Select frame 1 of the *actions* layer. Open the Actions panel (Window > Development Panels > Actions). Type the following code into the Script pane, following the ActionScript you added in earlier exercises:

```
circle_mc.onPress = function() {
  circle_mc.startDrag();
};
circle_mc.onRelease = function() {
  circle_mc.stopDrag();
};
```

You create two anonymous functions for circle_mc that executes code when you press the mouse button over the instance and release the mouse button. When you press and hold the mouse button, you can start dragging the instance around the Stage. The instance stops dragging when you release the mouse button.

▶ ▶ Anonymous and Named Functions

A function consists of statements that you write to perform a certain task in your SWF file. You have already used anonymous functions (also sometimes called inline functions) such as the function in step 1. An anonymous function is a function that does not have a name. And a named function is a function with a name. Both kinds of functions do the same thing as each other; however, because anonymous functions do not have names, you cannot call this kind of function throughout your project. So, an anonymous (nameless) function is

```
myInstance.onRelease = function(){
  //do something...
  //trace("clicked");
};
```

And the equivalent named function that you could call throughout your code using its name is

```
function myFunction(){
 trace("clicked");
};
myInstance.onRelease = myFunction;
```

Then you could call the function elsewhere in your ActionScript using the previous format or this one:

```
myFunction();
```

2. Select Control > Test Movie to test the file. Because of the code you added in step 1, you can click the circle movie clip on the Stage and, while holding the mouse button down, drag the symbol (Figure 6.13). Release the mouse button to stop the movie clip from moving.

Figure 6.13

Drag the circle around the Stage using the mouse. The cursor changes to a hand when it's over the circle.

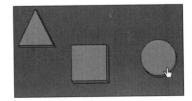

3. Adding interaction is relatively easy because Flash has the capability to detect collisions between objects. This means that an event occurs when one instance intersects another, so you can cause something to happen after this event. Modify the previous code for `circle_mc`'s `onRelease` event handler. Add the following boldface code:

```
circle_mc.onRelease = function() {
  circle_mc.stopDrag();
  if (circle_mc.hitTest(circleHole_mc)) {
   trace("hit");
  }
};
```

Now if you click `circle_mc`, you stop dragging the instance and see whether `circle_mc` intersects with a different instance: `circleHole_mc`. If the two instances intersect, *hit* displays in the Output panel because of the `trace` statement.

4. Select Control > Test Movie to retest the SWF file in the Flash environment. Now the Output panel displays *hit* when you drag the `circle_mc` movie clip instance on top of the `circle-Hole_mc` instance and release the mouse button, as seen in Figure 6.14.

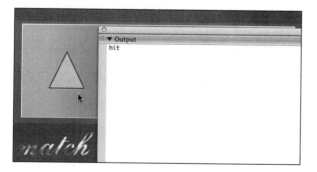

FIGURE 6.14

Hit displays in the Output panel when the two instances intersect.

5. Because text that displays in the Output panel isn't very useful after you upload the file to the Internet, you need to remove the `trace` statement from the previous snippet. Remember, you cannot use `trace` statements to return information outside of the test environment. So, now that you have tested the SWF using `trace`, *delete* the following line of code:

```
trace("hit");
```

Then, replace the line you just deleted with the following two lines of code:

```
circle_mc._x = circleHole_mc._x;
circle_mc._y = circleHole_mc._y;
```

These two lines of code set the X and Y coordinates of `circle_mc` to the X and Y coordinates of the `circleHole_mc`. This code places the `circle_mc` instance directly above the `circleHole_mc` instance, and gives the illusion that the shape is in the hole. You can also set any other properties or even call functions in this part of the code. For example, if you want to modify the shape's transparency, you can set the `_alpha` property of the instance in this part of the code.

6. Repeat steps 1–4 for both the `square_mc` and `triangle_mc` instances. In each of these steps, you need to replace the `circle_mc` and `circleHole_mc` instance names in your Action-Script with those of the other shapes.

7. Select Insert > New Symbol, name the symbol **reset**, select Button as the symbol's behavior, and click OK. Select the Text tool and type **reset** near the center of the Stage, and any other graphics you might want to add.

Select the Hit frame on the Timeline and press F6. Use the Rectangle tool to draw a square over the text you added, as shown in the following figure.

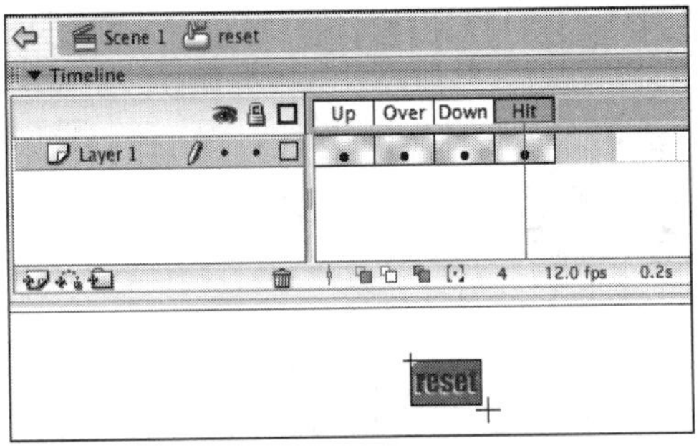

FIGURE 6.15

Add a hit area for the button, so users can easily click the text. Without a hit area, users would have to click exactly within the lines of "reset", which would be difficult and frustrating to do.

Click Scene 1 to return to the main Timeline, and then drag an instance of the button you just created from the Library to the Stage. Open the Property inspector, and give it an instance name of reset_btn.

You use this button to reset the position of the shapes to their original position. This lets users restart a game after they successfully place the shapes or run out of time.

You can select the graphics you create for the button when they're on the Up frame, and convert them into a graphic symbol.

▶ ▶ USING CONDITIONALS

The ActionScript you just added in step 3 is called a conditional statement. A conditional performs a particular action depending on whether a condition exists. For example, if something is true, do this action. You might have code that says if the value of the variable myNumber is 5, then go and play frame 2.

```
if (myNumber==5){
  gotoAndPlay(2);
}
```

This statement checks if a condition (myNumber = 5) is true or false. If it's true, the next statement executes (gotoAndPlay). If the condition is false, ActionScript skips to the next statement outside the block of code. Additionally, you could add an else or else if statement.

```
if (myNumber==5) {
  gotoAndPlay("pageone");
} else if (myNumber=10) {
  gotoAndPlay("pagetwo");
} else {
  gotoAndStop("end");
}
```

In this code, if the first condition is false, ActionScript skips to the else if statement. If myNumber evaluates to true, then the playhead moves to "pageone". If the condition myNumber=10 evaluates to false, the else statement catches it and sends the playhead to "pagetwo". Therefore, any value of myNumber other than 5 or 10 sends the playhead to "end".

There are other kinds of conditional statements that you can use in your code, which you will encounter later in this book.

8. Select frame 1 of the *actions* layer, and type the following code into the script pane, following the code you already have there:

```
reset_btn.onRelease = function() {
  triangle_mc._x = triangleInitX;
  triangle_mc._y = triangleInitY;
  square_mc._x = squareInitX;
  square_mc._y = squareInitY;
  circle_mc._x = circleInitX;
  circle_mc._y = circleInitY;
}
```

Now you can click the reset_btn button and have each shape return to its original position on the Stage when you test the SWF file. If your code in step 3 modifies the transparency or any other properties, you would also want to reset those properties here. Otherwise, if the user tries the game again, the shapes might be too transparent to see easily.

9. Using the hitTest() method again as you did in step 3, you can write a function that checks to see if each piece is successfully released over the hole. Add the following code to frame 1 of the *actions* layer:

```
function checkShapes() {
  if (circle_mc.hitTest(circleHole_mc) &&
square_mc.hitTest(squareHole_mc) &&
triangle_mc.hitTest(triangleHole_mc)) {
    trace("success");
  }
}
```

This named function (see sidebar titled "Anonymous and Named Functions") checks to see if each of the three shapes is currently hitting the corresponding "hole" movie clip in line 2. The && operator is called the *logical AND* operator, and you use it to evaluate both the expressions on each side of the operator to see whether they are true or false.

If each of the expressions is true, the statements within the if statement executes the code that's inside it (*within its code-block*). In this case, if each expression in the if statement is true, the value *success* displays in the Output panel.

You use an operator to specify how to compare, modify, or combine values of an expression. An operator performs these operations on elements that are called *operands*. So in the example in step 9, the logical AND (&&) operator evaluates the expressions on both sides of the operators. Other operators include = (assignment operator that evaluates equality between two expressions) and + (addition operator that concatenates strings or adds numeric values).

10. Add the `checkShapes()` function call to each of the three main shape movie clips on the Stage. Modify the existing code so that it looks like the following:

```
circle_mc.onRelease = function() {
  circle_mc.stopDrag();
  if (circle_mc.hitTest(circleHole_mc)) {
    circle_mc._x = circleHole_mc._x;
circle_mc._y = circleHole_mc._y;
checkShapes();
  }
};
```

Now when you drag a shape over the proper hole, this Action-Script aligns the shape directly over the hole by making sure that the X and Y coordinates match using the assignment operator (=). Flash then checks to see if each of the three shapes is successfully positioned by calling the `checkShapes()` function. If all three shapes are in place, a success message displays in the Output panel.

11. Repeat step 10 for both the `square_mc` and `triangle_mc` instances. Remember to replace all the `circle_mc` and `circleHole_mc` instance names with the instance names of the other two shapes.

12. Select Insert > New Symbol to create a new movie clip in the Library. Name the symbol `success`, and set the symbol's behavior to Movie Clip. Before you click OK, click the Advanced button on the dialog box to display a few more options. In the Linkage section, select the Export for ActionScript checkbox next to the Linkage, and `success_mc` automatically enters into the Identifier field. This lets you dynamically add a copy of the movie clip from the Library to the Stage.

13. Click OK in the Create New Symbol dialog box to enter symbol-editing mode for the `success` movie clip. Draw a medium-sized rectangle on the Stage and using the Text tool that doesn't overlap the shape holes on the Stage, and add a message that appears after all three pieces are placed in their proper holes. You can make the symbol look like anything you want, such as that shown in the Figure 6.16.

If you need to size the symbol in relation to the shapes or holes on the Stage, click Scene 1 on the Edit Bar, and drag the symbol from the Library to the Stage. Double-click the instance to enter symbol-editing mode again, and you can see the items on the Stage while you edit. When you finish, return to the Stage and delete the instance.

FIGURE 6.16

Create a message that the user sees when he successfully matches a shape to its respective hole.

14. Return to the main Timeline. Now you need to *modify* the checkShapes function you wrote in step 9, so instead of displaying text in the Output panel, the success movie clip displays instead. Select frame 1 of the *actions* layer to replace the trace statement in the checkShapes function with the boldface code, so it matches the following:

```
function checkShapes() {
  if (circle_mc.hitTest(circleHole_mc) &&
square_mc.hitTest(squareHole_mc) &&
triangle_mc.hitTest(triangleHole_mc)) {
    attachMovie("success_mc", "mySuccess_mc", 1);
  }
}
```

Instead of using a trace statement to display the success message, now you "attach" the movie clip from the Library onto the Stage when the SWF plays. You can test the SWF file now (Control > Test Movie) and see that after all three shapes position over their matching holes, the success symbol from the library attaches into the SWF file in the upper-left corner using its Linkage ID (success_mc). The attachMovie() method takes three, or sometimes four, parameters. The first parameter is the Linkage identifier (the one that you specified earlier in step 12). The second parameter is the instance name that you assign the symbol when it attaches to the Stage. You need to specify an instance name if you want to move the movie clip on the Stage or be able to get or set any of its properties. The third parameter is the target *depth* of the movie clip.

15. You can use one of two methods if you want to move the mySuccess_mc instance and position it on the Stage after you attach it.

You have already seen the first method. You set the _x and _y coordinates for the instance after you attach the clip to the Stage. This involves setting mySuccess_mc._x and mySuccess_mc._y after you call the attachMovie() method.

The second method of positioning the movie clip is to pass the optional fourth parameter in the attachMovie() method and pass an object containing _x and _y coordinates.

To position the mySuccess_mc instance using the second method, to learn a new way of manipulating movie clips, *modify* the checkShapes() function again to match the following code:

```
function checkShapes() {
  if (circle_mc.hitTest(circleHole_mc) &&
square_mc.hitTest(squareHole_mc) &&
triangle_mc.hitTest(triangleHole_mc)) {
    var initObj:Object = new Object();
initObj._x = 104;
initObj._y = 50;
    attachMovie("success_mc", "mySuccess_mc", 1,
initObj);
  }
}
```

The previous code defines a new Object named initObj and defines two properties (_x and _y). Then you pass this new object to the attachMovie() method by adding it as a parameter: initObj.

Now the mySuccess_mc instance positions at X:104, Y:50 on the Stage. Whichever method you choose is up to you; it's purely a matter of personal preference.

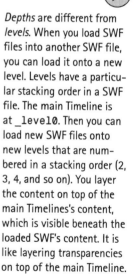

The attachMovie() method has an optional fourth parameter after depth. It is an object that can be used to pass default properties to the movie clip being attached. For example, you could set the _x and _y properties, or set the movie clip's _alpha property so it appears slightly transparent. You use this fourth parameter later in this exercise.

Depths are different from *levels*. When you load SWF files into another SWF file, you can load it onto a new level. Levels have a particular stacking order in a SWF file. The main Timeline is at _level0. Then you can load new SWF files onto new levels that are numbered in a stacking order (2, 3, 4, and so on). You layer the content on top of the main Timelines's content, which is visible beneath the loaded SWF's content. It is like layering transparencies on top of the main Timeline.

▶ ▶ LEARNING ABOUT DEPTH

Depth is important in Flash because it dictates which objects appear on top of other objects. The objects can be on the same layer on the Timeline, and yet still appear stacked on top of each other. Therefore, two objects cannot exist on the same depth.

The one place where depth is extremely important is when you have an instance at depth 1 of your SWF file and you load a second clip into the same depth. Flash then removes the first instance at that depth and replaces it with the second instance that attaches to that depth. Although this might be the behavior that you want because it is an easy way to add and remove a clip from the Stage, in other cases you might want to add multiple instances at different depths. If you want to add several different instances dynamically, you need to keep track of the depths that you use—or you can use the MovieClip class' `getNextHighestDepth()` method to determine the next available depth for a Timeline or movie clip. You use this method in place of setting a numerical depth value.

16. The final step is to find a way to remove the `mySuccess_mc` movie clip when the user clicks the reset button. If you don't remove the movie clip, users probably couldn't see the shapes on the Stage or drag them around using the mouse. *Modify* the `onRelease` handler for the `reset_btn` instance to add the following line of code:

```
reset_btn.onRelease = function() {
  triangle_mc._x = triangleInitX;
  triangle_mc._y = triangleInitY;
  square_mc._x = squareInitX;
  square_mc._y = squareInitY;
  circle_mc._x = circleInitX;
  circle_mc._y = circleInitY;
  mySuccess_mc.removeMovieClip();
}
```

Now when you test your SWF file (Control > Test Movie), the success message should appear only after you correctly position all three shapes, as you can see in Figure 6.16.

The success message disappears after the user clicks `reset_btn`. If you cannot see `reset_btn` because the success movie clip is in the way, you might need to realign the `reset_btn` instance on the Stage, or modify the X and Y coordinates of the success movie clip, which is within the code in step 15.

Replacing the Mouse Pointer

To make the interface more usable, you might want to change the mouse pointer (or *cursor*) when a user moves the pointer over a draggable instance. This helps users easily recognize the items that can or cannot be moved around on the Stage.

When you create a custom pointer, you might want to use that pointer for the entire duration of the SWF file. If so, you'll use code like the following:

```
Mouse.hide();
customPointer_mc.onMouseMove = function() {
  customPointer_mc._x = _xmouse;
  customPointer_mc._y = _ymouse;
  updateAfterEvent();
};
```

This ActionScript takes a movie clip on the Stage with the instance name `customPointer_mc` and uses that movie clip as a custom mouse pointer. First, you hide the default system pointer (an arrow) using `Mouse.hide()` and then you define a `onMouseMove` event handler, which calls every time you move the mouse around the Stage.

In the next exercise you will add ActionScript that's similar to the previous snippet to change the mouse pointer when it hovers over and drags the three movie clip shapes in the SWF file.

Exercise 4: Creating your own mouse pointer

When you add custom mouse pointers in certain areas, you can greatly increase the usability of your SWF files. By default, Flash changes the pointer for buttons (or movie clips, which behave like buttons) to a hand icon to indicate that the particular instance is clickable. Without the hand icon, the user might never know what they can or cannot click. Nothing can frustrate users more than a SWF file that they have no idea how to navigate.

Review the ActionScript in the finished version of the FLA when you complete this exercise. The FLA is found on the CD-ROM at 06/complete/shapegame.fla, and you can find the Action-Script on frame 1 of the actions layer.

In this exercise, you add code to modify the mouse pointer when it moves over draggable instances on the Stage. This notifies users that they can drag certain movie clips.

1. You need to add or create a custom pointer in the Library. Select Insert > New Symbol to create a new symbol. Name it **pointer**, and select Movie Clip as the symbol's behavior. Click OK to enter symbol-editing mode, in which you can draw a graphic for the mouse pointer. Make sure that it's somewhat small (5 to 20 pixels in height and width), similar to the following figure.

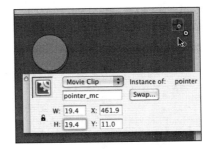

FIGURE 6.17

Your custom pointer should be between 5 and 20 pixels in width and height.

Optionally, you can import graphics from shapes.fla. Open the file 06/start/shapes.fla from the CD-ROM and find the graphic inside the mouse pointer folder in the Library. Select the graphic, and copy and paste it into the pointer movie clip in your current project. After you finish, you should have a graphic similar to Figure 6.18 for the pointer symbol.

2. Drag an instance of the pointer symbol from the Library to the Stage. Open the Property inspector, and give the custom pointer an instance name of **pointer_mc**.

3. You use two custom functions that show the pointer when it's over an instance, and hide the pointer when it isn't. It makes more sense to create this code as its own function instead of putting it within an event handler. This is because you don't want to duplicate the same code multiple times unless absolutely necessary. When you use a function, you can call that same function many times.

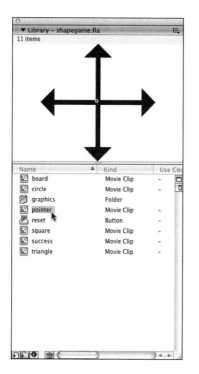

FIGURE 6.18

Create a custom pointer in the Library.

Select frame 1 of the *actions* layer, and type the following code into the Script pane, after the other ActionScript on this frame:

```
function showPointer() {
  Mouse.hide();
  pointer_mc._visible = true;
  pointer_mc.onMouseMove = function() {
   pointer_mc._x = _xmouse;
   pointer_mc._y = _ymouse;
   updateAfterEvent();
  };
}
function hidePointer() {
  pointer_mc._visible = false;
  Mouse.show();
  delete pointer_mc.onMouseMove;
}
```

The first function `showPointer()` starts on line 1. The function begins by hiding the default pointer using the `Mouse.hide()` method.

If you use a custom pointer in Flash, the default pointer is only hidden within the SWF file. After the mouse leaves the boundaries of the Stage, your operating system's default pointer will be visible again.

Line 3 sets the visibility of the custom pointer to `true`, meaning that the pointer is visible within the SWF file. Lines 4–8 define an event handler for the `onMouseMove` event of the `pointer_mc` movie clip. Whenever the mouse moves, whether it is over the `pointer_mc` instance or not, the event handler executes the block of code. The block of code sets the `_x` and `_y` properties of the `pointer_mc` movie clip to the current coordinates of the mouse pointer (denoted by the `_xmouse` and `_ymouse` properties).

The second function, `hidePointer()`, begins by hiding the `pointer_mc` movie clip and showing the default system pointer. The last line of code within the function (line 13) deletes the `onMouseMove` event handler, which you create with the `showPointer()` function. It is always a good idea to delete event handlers when you no longer need them. This helps you save system resources on the user's computer while maintaining as high frame rates as possible. High frame rates help your SWF file play fast and smooth.

4. Now that you wrote functions to hide and show the custom mouse pointer, you need to find a way to call these two functions. To do this, you use the `onRollOver` and `onRollOut` event handlers in the MovieClip class. The `onRollOver` event handler calls when the user's mouse pointer rolls over an instance, similar to the `onMouseOver` event in JavaScript. The other event handler, `onRollOut`, executes when the mouse rolls outside the boundary of an instance. In this case, you add the event handler for each of the three shapes on the Stage.

Add the following code to frame 1 of the main timeline:

```
circle_mc.onRollOver = showPointer;
circle_mc.onRollOut = hidePointer;
```

Unlike the event handlers you used earlier, this code doesn't define its event handlers with an inline function. Instead, it uses the functions you defined in step 3. Because of this, you assign the function name *as* the event handler. It is important to make sure that you don't add parentheses after the function name, or else you'll experience unexpected results.

5. Repeat step 4 by duplicating the code snippet in step 4 for both the square_mc and triangle_mc instances. Add the following ActionScript after the code you added in step 4.

```
square_mc.onRollOver = showPointer;
square_mc.onRollOut = hidePointer;
triangle_mc.onRollOver = showPointer;
triangle_mc.onRollOut = hidePointer;
```

6. Make sure that the custom pointer instance on the Stage is not visible by default. To accomplish this, you need to set the _visibility property for the pointer to false by default, as shown in the following code:

```
pointer_mc._visible = false;
```

In this exercise, you added functions to your code that change the default mouse pointer to a custom one when the pointer hovers over each shape. This increases the usability of the project. In the next exercise, you modify the mouse pointer to have multiple *states*, which means it will look different depending on how the user interacts with the shapes. Save (File > Save) the changes you made to the document.

Exercise 5: Creating multiple movie clip states

If you want to make the game a bit more interactive, you can create multiple "states" for each of the shapes in your SWF file. For example, you could show different images for an object on the Stage when the mouse pointer hovers or drags over them, or after you drop a shape in a hole.

1. Double-click circle_mc on the Stage or in the Library to open the instance in symbol-editing mode.

2. Double-click Layer 1 on the Timeline in symbol editing mode. Rename the layer **shape** and then click Insert Layer two times. Rename the two new layers **actions** and **labels**.

3. Select frame 6 in the *actions* layer and press F6 to create a keyframe. Then select frame 6 on the *labels* layer's Timeline and press F6 to create another keyframe.

4. Select frame 10 of the *actions* layer and the *labels* layer. Press the Ctrl (Windows) or Command key and click each frame to select them at the same time. Then press the F5 to extend the frames on each layer to frame 10.

5. Add the following ActionScript to both frames 1 *and* 6 in the actions layer (as you can see in Figure 6.19).

    ```
    stop();
    ```

6. Select frame 1 of the *labels* layer. Open the Property inspector and type **off** into the Frame text field to add a label for this keyframe. This frame contains the graphic for the pointer when you drag it around the Stage.

Then, select frame 6 of the *labels* layer and assign the frame label **on**. This frame contains the pointer graphic when you placed over the hole and successfully hit tests. When you're finished, the Timeline should look similar to the following figure.

FIGURE 6.19

Add frame labels to the Time-line. This figure shows the symbol's background layer.

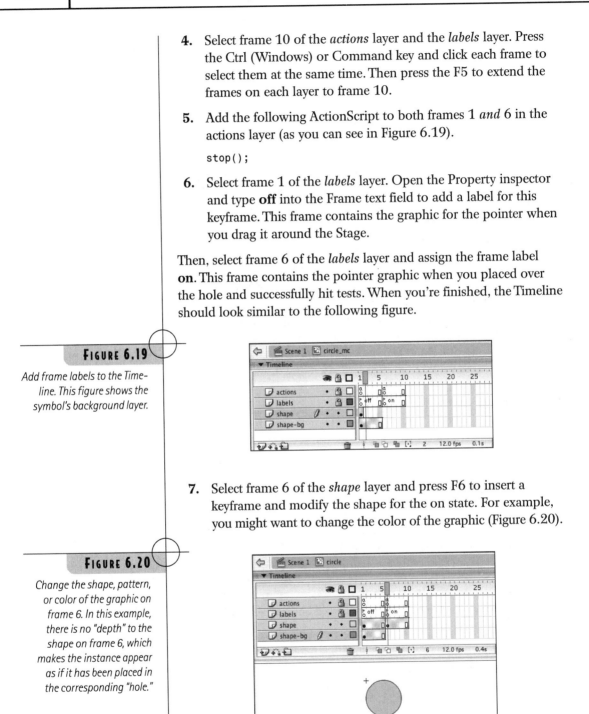

7. Select frame 6 of the *shape* layer and press F6 to insert a keyframe and modify the shape for the on state. For example, you might want to change the color of the graphic (Figure 6.20).

FIGURE 6.20

Change the shape, pattern, or color of the graphic on frame 6. In this example, there is no "depth" to the shape on frame 6, which makes the instance appear as if it has been placed in the corresponding "hole."

8. Click Scene 1 on the Edit Bar to exit symbol-editing mode and return to the main Timeline.

9. Select frame 1 of the *actions* layer and add the following bold-face line of ActionScript to the existing code:

```
circle_mc.onRelease = function() {
  circle_mc.stopDrag();
  if (circle_mc.hitTest(circleHole_mc)) {
   circle_mc._x = circleHole_mc._x;
circle_mc._y = circleHole_mc._y;
checkShapes();
circle_mc.gotoAndStop("on");
  }
};
```

10. Repeat step 9, adding the equivalent ActionScript for the `square_mc` and `triangle_mc` movie clip instances as well. Remember to check the final FLA file (06/complete /shapegame.FLA) for guidance if necessary.

11. Because the movie clip states change when they collide with their matching "hole" movie clips, you need to reset the play-head to the default states when the user clicks the reset button. To return the shapes back to their original states, you need to modify the `onRelease` event handler for the `reset_btn` Button instance to what's shown in the following code. The new ActionScript is in boldface.

```
reset_btn.onRelease = function() {
  circle_mc._x = circleInitX;
  circle_mc._y = circleInitY;
  square_mc._x = squareInitX;
  square_mc._y = squareInitY;
  triangle_mc._x = triangleInitX;
  triangle_mc._y = triangleInitY;
  circle_mc.gotoAndStop("off");
  square_mc.gotoAndStop("off");
triangle_mc.gotoAndStop("off");
  }
```

You add the three new lines of code (the lines in boldface), which you use to reset the playhead back to the `off` frame label when the user completes the game. This makes each shape return to its original position, and appearance. Now you have added all of the code necessary to make this file work, and all that remains is to see that it functions correctly when running in Flash Player.

Test the SWF file in either the Flash environment (Control > Test Movie) or an external browser (F12). When you test the SWF file, you can drag the three shapes around the Stage. You drag a shape over a corresponding hole and release the mouse button; the shape changes to its second state.

When all the shapes are in the proper holes, you then see your movie clip message display on the Stage. When you click the reset_btn Button instance, it returns each of the shapes to its original coordinates and its original state.

Make sure that you save the changes that you made to the file if you are happy with the results.

Moving On

You might use this technique for many different functions, beyond simple games such as this. For example, you might use these functions for image galleries or navigation. For example, you might have a bunch of draggable thumbnail images. The user can click and drag the file to a certain area, after which something happens. A web page or file might open, a movie might play, or a full-size image might display.

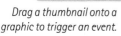

FIGURE 6.21

Drag a thumbnail onto a graphic to trigger an event.

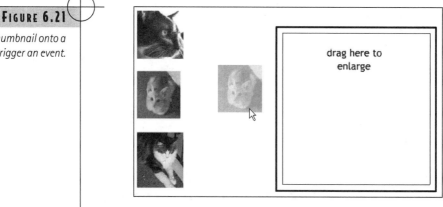

In this example, when the user drags the thumbnail over to a specified symbol, that thumbnail displays a full image.

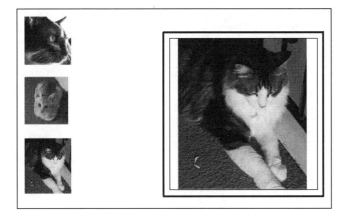

FIGURE 6.22

A full-size image appears after the user drops the draggable movie clip.

FIGURE 7.A

FIGURE 7.B

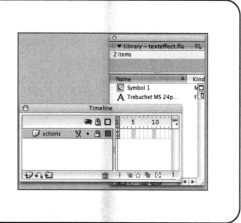

FIGURE 7.C

What you learn

▶ How to use strict data types

▶ About looping

▶ How to add randomness to a project

▶ How to create and format text using ActionScript

▶ About creating text effects using code

▶ How to use the Tween class

▶ About setting intervals and creating duration

Lesson Files

Start:

None

Finish:

07/complete/texteffect.fla

07/complete/texteffect.swf

7

SCRIPTED ANIMATION BASICS

ONE OF THE BENEFITS of learning ActionScript is that it can almost be repetitive. You use certain structures and language elements over and over when you write code, such as functions, keywords, conditions and loops. You used some of these elements in Chapter 6, but there are a few more fundamentals to cover in this chapter's project that are useful to animations and effects.

This project creates a text effect over randomly animating movie clips. This time, the entire project is created without adding a single element to the Stage. All your assets are created using code or attached from the Library. However, don't let that scare you! Luckily, everything is complete in fewer than 50 lines of code. You learn about some different methods and properties found in a few built-in ActionScript classes. You will also use a special Tween class to animate movie clips to create a randomly moving background effect. By the end of this project, you will be comfortable adding and manipulating movie clips and text around the Stage without actually adding anything to it in the authoring environment.

Website: www.FLAnimation.com/chapters/07

Structuring ActionScript

ActionScript has a particular syntax, which you learned a lot about in the fundamental language concepts covered in Chapter 6. For example, you use dot notation, brackets, parentheses, methods, and properties to construct statements and make things happen in your projects. There are some additional concepts to cover in this chapter while you build a fully scripted animation that includes random movement and animated text.

In Chapter 6, you created and used variables and data to make your project work, and found out that the data you used had a type (such as Number or String). ActionScript lets you define the data type when you declare variables, using a colon and then the data type. This means that you specify what *type* of data the variable can contain; specifically, which helps reduce errors in your code. For example, if you create a variable to hold numerical values, you would write the following:

```
var myNumber:Number;
```

Then, whenever you assign values to the variable it must be a Number data type such as:

```
myNumber = 6;
```

However, if you write the following:

```
myNumber = "dog";
```

you then see an error in the Output panel after you publish the file (Figure 7.1), notifying you of the type mismatch error in your code. Strict data typing also helps ensure that you use methods and properties only for the object's type.

You must use the var keyword to strict data type a variable. For this reason, you cannot strict data type global variables.

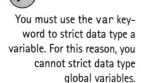

Notice how you don't have to declare the data type when you use the variable again. You need to specify the data type only when you declare the variable.

Figure 7.1

When you mismatch data types, you see an error in the Output panel.

```
▼ Output
**Error** Scene=Scene 1, layer=Layer 1, frame=1:Line 2: Type mismatch in
assignment statement: found String where Number is required.
        myNumber = "dog";

Total ActionScript Errors: 1     Reported Errors: 1
```

Another advantage of strict data typing is that it enables code completion in the Actions panel. For example, if you type:

```
var myXML = new XML();
```

this code creates a new instance of the XML class, but does not use strict data typing. You wouldn't see the code completion menu when you type myXML followed by a dot (.) later in your code. However, when you use strict data typing such as the following code, you see a code completion menu after typing a dot (.).

```
var myXML:XML = new XML();
myXML.
```

You see a menu with all the methods and properties for the XML class listed. Because of the advantages outlined in this section, you use strict data typing for this chapter's project, and in future projects in this book.

About loops

In Chapter 6, you used conditionals in your project to see whether instances intersected; if that condition were true, you executed code. In this project, you use loops to add many objects to the Stage if a condition is true. Loops are similar to conditionals because they execute a statement when it evaluates to true. However, loops execute repeatedly while the condition you specify evaluates to true. There are several different kinds of loops, but they generally follow these criteria.

The ++ (increment) operator adds the value of 1 to the expression and returns the result. The – (decrement) operator does the same thing, except reduces the value by one.

You use for loops in this chapter's project. A for loop has the following structure:

```
for (initialization; condition; update){
  //statements
}
```

The loop starts with the initialization statement (an initial value), which it executes one time. It then executes statements in the body while the condition is true. After each pass (or iteration) through the loop, the update statement executes. So, the following code displays numbers 10 through 59 in the Output panel:

```
for (var i = 10; i<60; i++) {
  trace(i);
}
```

The loop starts with an initial value of 10, and then while i (the variable) is less than 60, it increments the value by 1 and updates the variable. The loop ends when the value of i reaches 60 (or greater).

Loops are useful for a variety of purposes, particularly repetitive actions. For example, if you want to draw or add a bunch of graphics to the Stage, you might use a loop to do so.

Creating a random number generator

To make animations look a bit more interesting and less scripted, you can use Flash's Math.random() method to help generate random numbers. You use the Math.random() method to return a "pseudo" random number (it's not *truly* random, but close enough for many animations). Therefore, instead of having each rectangle move the exact same amount of space, you can have it slide a random number of pixels vertically as well as have it move either randomly up or down. The first step is to create a custom function, which generates a random number between a specified minimum and maximum number.

The randRange() function can be seen in the following code example, and you'll use it later in this chapter's project:

```
function randRange(min:Number, max:Number):Number {
  var randNum:Number = Math.round(Math.abs(max-
min)*Math.random())+Math.min(min, max);
  return randNum;
}
```

The previous function takes two Numeric parameters (min and max) and returns a random integer between the two numbers. Although the code looks a bit daunting, it is fairly basic math.

Applying basic mathematical principles, the code starts by calculating the inner brackets and working outward. The first step is to find the difference between the min and max parameters. For example, if you call the function with a min value of 3 and a max value of 7, the difference is 4. You then multiply the difference that returns by a random floating-point number (a number that can have a fractional part, such as 3 or 1/2) between 0 and 1. The result of the multiplication is rounded to an integer value using the Math.round() method. Finally, the random integer is added to the smallest parameter value. The smallest parameter value is determined by using the Math class' Math.min() method.

PROJECT 7: ANIMATING TEXT AND MOVIE CLIPS

In this project, you animate text and movie clips on the Stage using ActionScript. Not only that; you also add and position the movie clips on the Stage using code. You create text fields with Action-Script, and the fields animate across the Stage. This project shows you how to attach, duplicate, position, and animate movie clips randomly with code to create an interesting background effect. It also shows you how to dynamically create, position, and animate text on the Stage, which is easily updatable and customizable for your own projects. You also embed a custom font to ensure that the text appears the way you expect it to, no matter who views the SWF file.

Creating and formatting dynamic text fields

You created text fields on the Stage using the Text tool in earlier chapters. In this chapter, you create them by using ActionScript instead. You might wonder why you use ActionScript to do this instead of adding them to the Stage. Using tools to create and add objects might seem much easier. There are a few reasons why you might want to create text fields using ActionScript instead of tools.

First, view the project at www.FLAnimation.com/chapters/07 to see the finished text and movie clip effects. Multiple lines of text animate across the Stage. It's quite likely you will want to modify that text, add more strings of text to the animation, and so on. If you manually create and/or animate fields using the Text tool, modifying the project would be time-consuming and picky. Because you create text fields using ActionScript instead, adding and modifying text is extremely quick and easy. All you need to do is add a few more lines of text in the Actions panel to add to the existing project. You have to modify text only in the Actions panel to change the existing text or the text fields' appearance.

An important issue when working with dynamic (or input) text fields is to *embed* the fonts you use. Embedding text means the font's information is stored in the SWF file. When you work with dynamic and input fields, the end user must have the font you choose on her own computer, unless you embed the font in the SWF file. SWF files use system fonts, replacing any nonexistent font with a close equivalent on the users' system, unless you embed the font in your SWF file. You find out how to embed characters in Flash in this project.

To create a text field using ActionScript, you use the `createTextField()` method. This method creates a new (and empty) dynamic text field instance in the movie clip you specify. You can target the current Timeline using `this.createTextField()`; it targets whatever Timeline the code is on, such as the main Timeline (_root) or a movie clip the code is inside. So, to create a dynamic text field you can use the following code:

```
this.createTextField("my_txt", this.getNextHighestDepth(),
100, 100, 300, 100);
my_txt.text = "This is text in my new text field.";
```

This ActionScript creates a new text field instance with the instance name `my_txt`. You create instance on the next available depth (`this.getNextHighestDepth()`) and position it at the X, Y coordinates of 100, 100. The text field's width is 300 pixels and its height is 100 pixels (Figure 7.2).

You can then insert your text into the `my_txt` instance using Action-Script as well. The `my_txt.text` property specifies text for the text field.

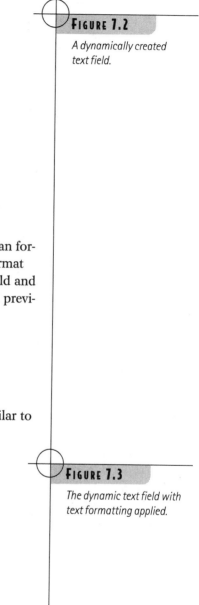

FIGURE 7.2

A dynamically created text field.

You aren't stuck using plain text in the text field though. You can format the text further using ActionScript as well with the TextFormat class. This class lets you apply different fonts, styles such as bold and italic, and change the text color. To format the text you created previously, you can add the following ActionScript:

```
var my_fmt:TextFormat = new TextFormat();
my_fmt.color = 0xFF0000;
my_fmt.bold = true;
my_fmt.italic = true;
my_txt.setTextFormat(my_fmt);
```

Select Control > Test Movie to view the results that will be similar to the following figure.

FIGURE 7.3

The dynamic text field with text formatting applied.

You create a new instance of the TextFormat class called my_fmt. You then set the color, bold, italic properties of my_fmt. Then you apply the my_fmt formatting to the my_txt instance you created earlier. The text you added is now red, bold, and italic; and all of this without adding a single item to the Stage!

Exercise 1: Dynamically create text fields with embedded fonts

Using dynamic fonts with dynamically created text fields is a bit more complex than regular dynamic text fields. Because the text fields are dynamically created, you can't define the font's properties as easily and you need to resort to a bit of additional ActionScript. The extra effort might be worth it, depending on the scope and structure of the animation or effect you're creating.

To embed a font in Flash, you need to add a font symbol to your Library and export the font with your SWF file. But first, start a new project and save it on your hard drive.

1. Create a new document in Flash, and select File > Save As. Save the new document as **texteffect.fla** on your hard drive. Leave the document at the default dimensions (550 by 400 pixels).

2. Open the Library (Window > Library) and add a new font to your document. To add a new font, select New Font from the Options menu, as shown in the following figure.

FIGURE 7.4

Select New Font from the Library's Options menu.

3. In the Font Symbol Properties dialog box (Figure 7.5), select the font that you want to embed, such as Trebuchet MS, from the font menu. Then click the Bold check box. Set the font size to **24** points. Before closing the dialog box, give the font a descriptive name by typing **Trebuchet MS 24pt Bold** in the name text field. This name displays in the Library panel and will serve only as a symbol name for your reference.

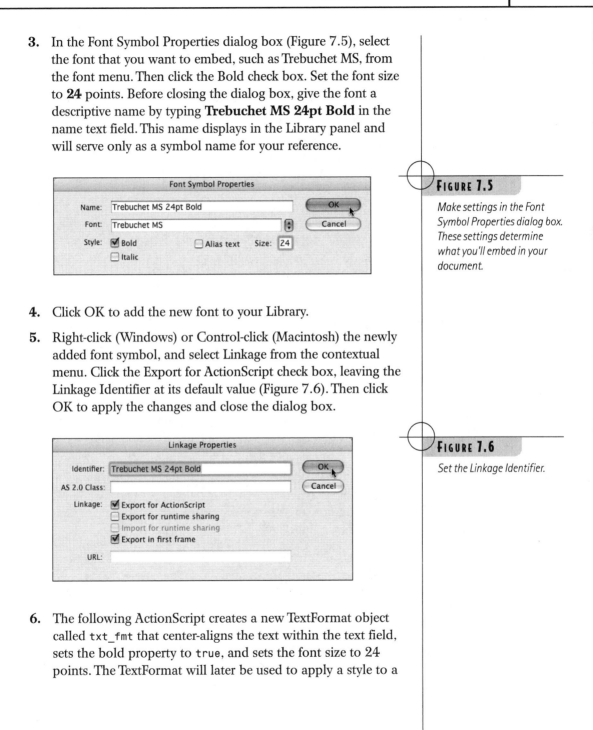

FIGURE 7.5

Make settings in the Font Symbol Properties dialog box. These settings determine what you'll embed in your document.

4. Click OK to add the new font to your Library.

5. Right-click (Windows) or Control-click (Macintosh) the newly added font symbol, and select Linkage from the contextual menu. Click the Export for ActionScript check box, leaving the Linkage Identifier at its default value (Figure 7.6). Then click OK to apply the changes and close the dialog box.

FIGURE 7.6

Set the Linkage Identifier.

6. The following ActionScript creates a new TextFormat object called `txt_fmt` that center-aligns the text within the text field, sets the bold property to `true`, and sets the font size to 24 points. The TextFormat will later be used to apply a style to a

dynamically created text field instance on the Stage. To attach
this TextFormat to a TextField, you will need to call the
TextField's `setNewTextFormat()` method.

Click the Insert Layer button on the Timeline to create a new
layer. Rename the layer **actions** and then type the following
ActionScript into the Script pane:

```
var txt_fmt:TextFormat = new TextFormat();
txt_fmt.align = "center";
txt_fmt.bold = true;
txt_fmt.font = "Trebuchet MS 24pt Bold";
txt_fmt.size = 24;
```

The font property of the TextFormat uses the embedded font,
which lets you modify the `_alpha` of a text field and change the
`_rotation`, similar to the previous exercise. If you don't embed
the font, you find that changing the `_alpha` value has no effect,
and changing the `_rotation` property causes the text field to
disappear altogether.

7. You can create a text field using the MovieClip class' `create-`
`TextField()` method after you add a font to your Library and
set up a TextFormat object. This method takes six parameters:
`instance name`, `target depth`, `X coordinate`, `Y coordinate`,
`width` and `height`. This example creates a dynamic text field in
the next-highest unused depth (`this.getNextHighestDepth()`),
assigns an instance name of `my_txt`, positions the instance at
an X and Y coordinate of 0,0 and sets the width and height to
100 and 20, respectively.

```
this.createTextField("my_txt",
this.getNextHighestDepth(), 0, 0, 100, 20);
```

8. Next, the text format is bound to the text field instance using
the `setNewTextFormat()` method. The `setNewTextFormat()`
method takes a single parameter, which is the TextFormat
object you defined in step 1. Add the following line of
ActionScript:

```
my_txt.setNewTextFormat(txt_fmt);
```

9. After you call the `setNewTextFormat()` method, you can set the `_alpha`, `_rotation` and `text` properties for the text field instance. For the code to work properly, you also must set the `embedFonts` property to `true`. Add the following ActionScript after the code on frame 1 of the actions layer.

```
my_txt._alpha = 20;
my_txt.autoSize = true;
my_txt.border = true;
my_txt.embedFonts = true;
my_txt.text = "lorum ipsum";
```

▶ ▶ Embedding Text in Text Fields

You can still embed fonts if you create dynamic or input text fields on the Stage using the Text tool. Select the text tool from the Tools panel and place a text field on the Stage. In the font pop-up menu, there is a font with the same name as the symbol name you created and made settings for in steps 2 through 5 (it should also have an asterisk (*) next to the font name). Set the font size to 24 points and set the text field to use bold so that the properties match those defined in the embedded font. Finally, give the text field an instance name of **my_txt.** Open the Actions panel and add the following code to frame 1 on a layer:

```
my_txt.embedFonts = true;
my_txt._rotation = 15;
my_txt._alpha = 50;
```

If you don't follow these steps to embed the font within your Flash document, you find that setting the `_alpha` property has no effect on your text. And as soon as you set the `_rotation` property, your text disappears. Currently, Flash doesn't support rotated or alpha dynamic or input text fields unless you embed the font it uses. Remember, you must use the font you created and set Linkage for in the previous steps or this code won't work properly.

Double-click the **my_txt** dynamic text field instance on the Stage and enter some placeholder text, such as "All work no play". Select Control > Test Movie to test your file in the test environment, and you will see your text rotate 15 degrees clockwise at 50% alpha.

10. Test your Flash document (Control > Test Movie). There should now be a text field in the upper-left corner of the SWF with some fairly transparent sample text, as seen in the following figure.

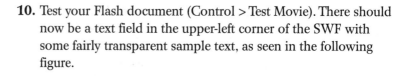

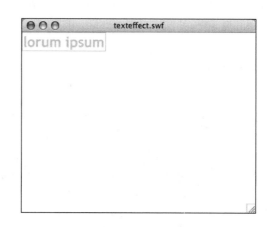

FIGURE 7.7

Formatting is applied to a dynamic text field.

★ You'll remove this text field and create the animating ones later in this project.

Now that you have created and formatted a text field, start adding movie clips to the Stage and animating them. The next couple of exercises show you how.

ANIMATING SHAPES USING THE BUILT-IN TWEEN CLASSES

Although you can animate objects and shapes quite easily using onEnterFrame or setInterval(), you can leverage Flash's built-in tweening equations to easily create professional and fun animations and effects. For example, by adding one line of code, you can make the text field created in the previous exercise animate across the Stage. Add the following line of code to the bottom of the Actions panel:

```
new mx.transitions.Tween(my_txt, "_x",
  mx.transitions.easing.Regular.easeInOut, 0, 550, 3, true);
```

The Tween class' constructor method takes seven parameters: an instance to animate, the property to modify, the easing method you want to use, a beginning and end value for the specified property, the number of seconds or frames that the tween will last, and whether seconds or frames will be used.

The previous snippet causes the text field created in the earlier exercises to animate left to right across the Stage for three seconds until it finally stops just off to the right of the Stage. If you view the animation in the authoring environment, it might be helpful to draw a rectangle around the perimeter of the Stage so you can see where the borders of the Stage are.

The Tween class is useful for your projects because you can easily add movement with many different forms of easing. You need to add only a small amount of code, and you can fully control the advanced effect. The Tween class does all the hard work for you!

Exercise 2: Attaching and duplicating movie clips

The background behind the text effect consists of many rectangles that move randomly on the Stage. First, you need to create a rectangle to use. Many instances of this single rectangle are attached from the Library. Each instance has the dimensions and color modified using ActionScript, and then they animate in a random fashion. In this exercise, you create the rectangle and attach it to the Stage. In the following exercise, you add movement for each rectangle using the Tween class.

1. Select the Rectangle Tool from the Tools panel, and make sure that there is no stroke color (select the Stroke color control and click the No Color button). Draw a medium-sized rectangle on the Stage with any fill color.

2. After you draw the rectangle on the Stage, double-click it again to select the shape and resize the shape's dimensions to 550 pixels wide by 60 pixels high.

3. With the shape still selected, press F8 to convert it to a movie clip symbol. In the Symbol Properties window, enter a symbol name of `rectangle_mc` and make sure that you select the movie clip behavior.

4. If the Symbol Properties dialog box is in Basic mode, click the Advanced button in the lower-right corner of the dialog box.

5. In the Linkage section, check the Export for ActionScript check-box and type an identifier value of `rectangle_id`.

FIGURE 7.8

Making changes in the Symbol Properties dialog box.

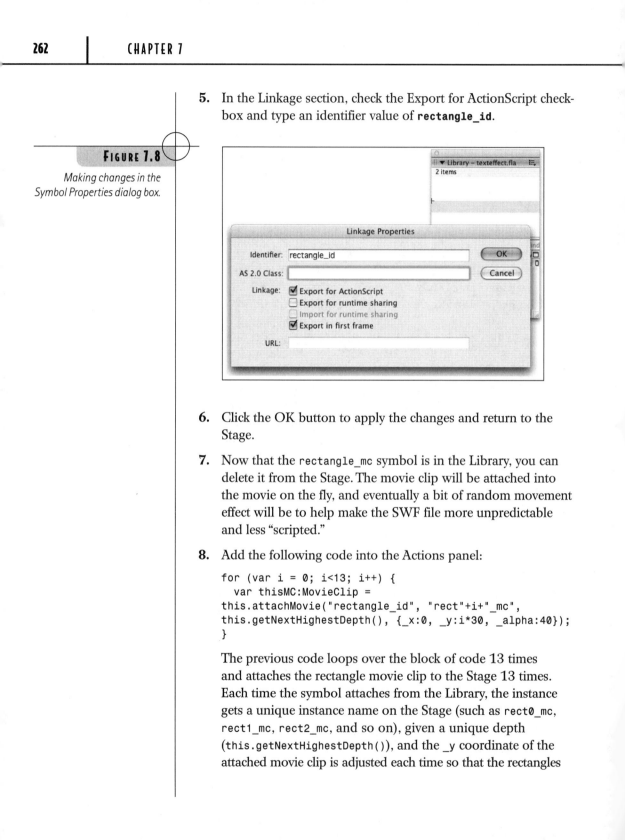

6. Click the OK button to apply the changes and return to the Stage.

7. Now that the `rectangle_mc` symbol is in the Library, you can delete it from the Stage. The movie clip will be attached into the movie on the fly, and eventually a bit of random movement effect will be to help make the SWF file more unpredictable and less "scripted."

8. Add the following code into the Actions panel:

```
for (var i = 0; i<13; i++) {
  var thisMC:MovieClip =
this.attachMovie("rectangle_id", "rect"+i+"_mc",
this.getNextHighestDepth(), {_x:0, _y:i*30, _alpha:40});
}
```

The previous code loops over the block of code 13 times and attaches the rectangle movie clip to the Stage 13 times. Each time the symbol attaches from the Library, the instance gets a unique instance name on the Stage (such as `rect0_mc`, `rect1_mc`, `rect2_mc`, and so on), given a unique depth (`this.getNextHighestDepth()`), and the _y coordinate of the attached movie clip is adjusted each time so that the rectangles slightly overlap. If you were to test the code at this point, you'd see that the rectangles are all the same color and blend together almost giving the appearance of one single rectangle, although the first and last rectangles are slightly more transparent.

9. When you create an array of different colors, you can assign each attached rectangle instance a random color thanks to the `randRange()` function (added in the following ActionScript).

Add the following ActionScript at the beginning of the existing ActionScript on frame 1 of the actions layer:

```
var color_array:Array = new Array(0xBDDBD7, 0x9AC9C2,
0x78B6AD, 0x5CA79D);
function randRange(min:Number, max:Number):Number {
  var randNum:Number = Math.round(Math.abs(max-
min)*Math.random())+Math.min(min, max);
  return randNum;
}
```

This code creates an array with four different predefined colors, and then adds the `randRange()` function, described at the beginning of this project.

For information on the `randRange()` function seen following and returning random numbers using code, see the section called "Creating a random number generator" at the beginning of this chapter.

Choose different hexadecimal values to customize the color of your project.

▶▶ USING ARRAYS

An *array* is a sequential group of values. Each item in an array consists of two parts: an index and a value. Arrays in ActionScript are zero-based, so the first index in an array is always 0. For example, consider the 12 months of the year. The first month is January, the second month is February, and so on. In ActionScript terms, the first item in the month array would have an array index of 0 and a value of January. The second month would have an array index of 1 and a corresponding value of February. If you were creating an array of month names in ActionScript, the code would be the following:

```
var month_array:Array = new Array("January", "February",
"March");
trace(month_array[0]); // output: January
```

When you refer to specific items within the array, you use square brackets ([]) to denote which index you want to set or retrieve.

Now you can combine this array with the randRange() function to assign random colors to the rectangles as they attach to the Stage, as seen in step 10.

10. Modify the ActionScript from step 8, so it matches the following snippet. You can do this by adding the bold face font to your code.

```
for (var i = 0; i<13; i++) {
  var thisMC:MovieClip =
this.attachMovie("rectangle_id", "rect"+i+"_mc",
this.getNextHighestDepth(), {_x:0, _y:i*30, _alpha:40});
  var randomIndex:Number = randRange(0,
color_array.length-1);
  var mc_color:Color = new Color(thisMC);
  mc_color.setRGB(color_array[randomIndex]);
}
```

The second line of code attaches the rectangle_mc symbol from the Library and assigns it an instance name of rect0_mc through rect12_mc. As each symbol is added to the Stage, the code also creates an alias named thisMC to the current movie clip. This way, you can target the proper movie clip without having to use a combination of square brackets and complex paths. The third line of code creates a numeric variable named randomIndex that calls the randRange() function. The randRange() function returns a random number between 0 and the number of items in the color_array , which allows you to retrieve a random color from the array. A new color object named mc_color is created and is passed a reference to the newly attached rectangle movie clip. Using the setRGB() method of the Color class, you can set the color for each newly attached instance of the rectangle_mc. Remember that each rectangle instance is set to an _alpha value of 40, so the colors will be rather transparent. This lets you see each rectangle overlap slightly (Figure 7.9).

11. If you test the Flash document at this point you will see a series of horizontal lines covering the Stage. Each rectangle has its alpha set to 40%, so it is somewhat transparent. Each time you reload the SWF file, the colors should be in different positions and slightly different colors.

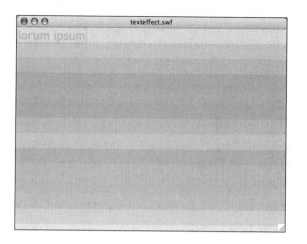

FIGURE 7.9

The semi-transparent rectangles cover the Stage.

There is really no end to how far you can take this example and which modifications you can take. From randomizing amounts of _alpha or how many colors you define, each time you view the document it can look almost completely different.

Exercise 3: Adding random movement

Because the rectangle symbol in the Library is 60 pixels and the value of _y increments (adds) only 30 pixels each time, a new instance of rectangle_mc attaches to the Stage. The design looks fairly square and predictable. By adding one line of code, it's possible to change the _height of each row to a random integer to give the animation a slightly "random" look to it. You use the randRange() function (using the random method of the Math class) that you wrote earlier in this project.

See the section called "Creating a random number generator" near the beginning of this chapter for information on the randRange() function and adding random movement in Flash. You added this function to the project in Exercise 2.

1. Add the following boldface line of ActionScript to the bottom of the for loop on frame 1 of the actions layer.

```
for (var i = 0; i<13; i++) {
  var thisMC:MovieClip =
this.attachMovie("rectangle_id", "rect"+i+"_mc",
this.getNextHighestDepth(), {_x:0, _y:i*30, _alpha:40});
  var randomIndex:Number = randRange(0,
color_array.length-1);
  var mc_color:Color = new Color(thisMC);
  mc_color.setRGB(color_array[randomIndex]);
  thisMC._height = randRange(35, 45);
}
```

Every time a user views the SWF file or refreshes the page the file is on, the height of each rectangle sets to a random integer between 35 and 45 pixels. In this code, you pass these parameters into the `randRange()` function.

2. Publish the Flash document: Each rectangle overlaps anywhere from 0 to 10 pixels, and the rectangles look like they are randomly positioned.

Now that the rectangle's position appears random, it is time to animate the shapes very slightly to give each shape some movement.

3. Add the following bold face code within the for loop (lines X to X, after the call to `mc_color.setRGB()`):

```
for (var i = 0; i<13; i++) {
  var thisMC:MovieClip =
this.attachMovie("rectangle_id", "rect"+i+"_mc",
this.getNextHighestDepth(), {_x:0, _y:i*30, _alpha:40});
  var randomIndex:Number = randRange(0,
color_array.length-1);
  var mc_color:Color = new Color(thisMC);
  mc_color.setRGB(color_array[randomIndex]);
  thisMC._height = randRange(35, 45);
  var rectTween:Object = new
mx.transitions.Tween(thisMC, "_y",
mx.transitions.easing.Regular.easeInOut, thisMC._y,
thisMC._y+randRange(-5, 5), randRange(1, 3), true);
  rectTween.onMotionFinished = function() {
    this.yoyo();
  };
}
```

Instead of using a series of `onEnterFrame` event handlers or working with a large number of `setInterval()` calls, the animation is completed this time by using the easing classes in Flash MX 2004.

Instead of animating some embedded text as in previous examples, this code animates each rectangle instance in a random direction over a random period of time. In this example, you set the animation to start at the current Y coordinate of the rectangle, and animate anywhere from -5 to 5 pixels from its current Y coordinate. If the `randRange()` function returns a negative integer, the rectangle animates upward. However, if the randRange() function returns a positive integer, the rectangle animates downward. You use the randRange() function again in the next parameter, which is the number of seconds that the animation should last. Not only is each rectangle a random color, height, and range of movement, but they also animate at different speeds. In this example, the rectangle instance animates anywhere from 1–3 seconds.

You need to use the Tween class again, but it's unlike the previous time you saw and used the Tween classes. This time you're creating a reference to the actual tween object. By storing a reference to the tween, you can add an event handler that detects when the animation is finished. The animation wouldn't be very exciting if each rectangle moved a few pixels and then stopped, so in this example an event handler is added that will wait for the onMotionFinished event to trigger and then call the Tween class' yoyo method, which tells Flash to reverse the animation back to the properties starting position. For example, imagine that you had a rectangle at a Y coordinate of 30 pixels. This particular rectangle instance will move 3 pixels down to a Y coordinate of 33 pixels. After the rectangle has finished moving, the onMotionFinished event handler triggers, and the animation reverses and returns to its original position. After the rectangle has tweened back to its original position, the onMotionFinished event handler triggers again, sending it back to its previous Y coordinate of 33 pixels. This endless loop causes the rectangles to continually tween for as long as the SWF file plays.

4. Preview the animation in the Flash authoring environment (Control > Test Movie) a few times. If you think that the animation is moving too quickly or too slowly you can modify the values being passed to the randRange() function and increase or decrease the number of seconds accordingly. If you find that the rectangles are moving too much or too little for your liking, just change the values of -5 and 5 in the previous snippet.

The best part of this animation is that it is so easy to configure and modify to make it fit the style that you want.

Calling Code at Specific Intervals

Now that you have a subtle animated background, it's time to add text to the SWF file. You should already have an embedded font in your Library from a previous exercise in this chapter. This example shows you how to create text fields on the fly, trigger scripts at timed intervals, and use a new method in the Tween class: continueTo(), which allows you to continue animating an object. By using the setInterval() function, you can make Flash suspend code execution until an internal timer reaches a certain number of milliseconds (thousandths of a second).

If you set an interval of 2000 milliseconds, Flash calls a specific function after roughly two seconds. It bears mentioning that it won't call the function at exactly 2000 milliseconds, but usually it calls it within a range of 2050–2100 milliseconds—so close enough to 2000 milliseconds that it usually can't be noticed. If you want to see how accurate the setInterval() function calls your function, you can try the following code snippet *in a new Flash document*:

```
setInterval(checkTimer, 2000);
function checkTimer():Void {
   trace("cT: "+getTimer()+" ms");
}
```

This code uses the setInterval() function to call the user-defined checkTimer() function every 2000 milliseconds (2 seconds). Next, you define the checkTimer() function and use it to trace the value of the getTimer() function, which returns the number of milliseconds that have passed because the SWF file starts playing. If you test this script in the Flash environment you'll see that a new string is displays in the Output panel roughly every two seconds.

The setInterval() function takes at least two parameters: the name of a function to call, and an interval at which the function will be called. If you supply more additional parameters, pass to the specified function as arguments. For example, consider the following code:

```
setInterval(checkTimer, 2000, "lorum ipsum");
function checkTimer(my_str:String):Void {
   trace(my_str);
}
```

The third parameter in the `setInterval()` function, the string `"lorum ipsum"` passes to the `checkTimer()` function as the argument `my_str` where it is traced and displayed in the Output panel roughly every 2 seconds.

Exercise 4: Clearing and setting intervals

Before you can begin animating a few sample strings, you need to add a few variables to the top of the Actions panel. You should already have an array of colors that you used earlier to change the color of the rectangles as they were added to the Stage, as well as a TextFormat object that sets the font face to the font embedded in your library.

1. Add the two following lines of code to the Actions panel below the definition of the TextFormat object:

    ```
    var root_mc:MovieClip = this;
    var interval_array:Array = new Array();
    ```

    The first variable, `root_mc`, stores a reference to the main Timeline of the movie clip. This is sometimes necessary when you're working with complex scripts and need to refer to the main Timeline, and you can't use the `this` keyword because it might not always refer to the Timeline. Although it is true that you could instead use `_root` to refer to the main Timeline, it wouldn't always work properly if this SWF file were loaded into another movie at runtime. (Macromedia's best practices guide also discourages the use of `_root` if possible.)

    The second variable, `interval_array`, will be used to hold a numeric ID returned by the `setInterval()` function. This ID will be used later to clear the intervals created using `setInterval()`. You may have noticed that calling `setInterval()` not only calls a function after a set number of milliseconds, but it continues to call that function until the interval is cleared using the `clearInterval()` function and passing an interval ID.

    Now that you understand how intervals work, you add some to the project to call new text fields and animate them across the Stage at specified intervals. This lets you add an element of timing to the file by using ActionScript, so users can view and read the text before it disappears off the Stage.

2. Select frame 1 of the actions layer. Enter the following code snippet at the bottom of the code already in the Actions panel:

```
animateText("string one");
animateText("string two");
animateText("string three");

function animateText(my_str:String,
interval_index:Number):Void {
  trace(my_str);
}
```

3. Select Control > Test Movie to review the Flash document in the authoring environment. You should see each of the three strings (string one, string two, and string three) display immediately in the Output panel (Figure 7.10).

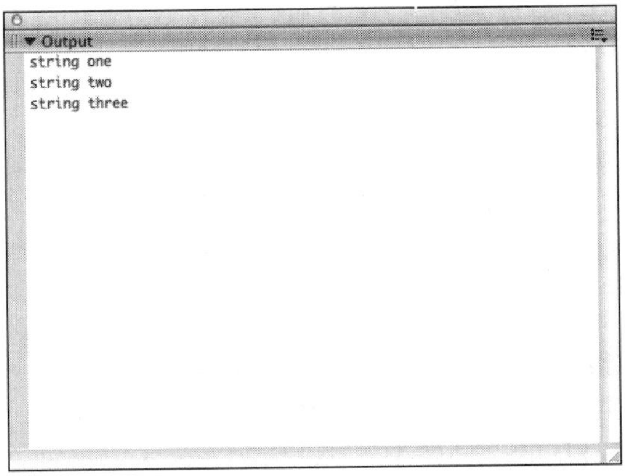

FIGURE 7.10

Three strings immediately appear in the Output panel.

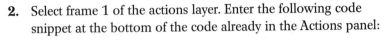

```
▼ Output
  string one
  string two
  string three
```

4. Delete the first three lines of code from the previous snippet in step 1. Replace those three lines with the following code. You still need the animateText() *function* (line 4 and 5 in step 1) so do not delete it.

```
interval_array[0] = setInterval(animateText, 1000,
"string one", 0);
interval_array[1] = setInterval(animateText, 2500,
"string two", 1);
interval_array[2] = setInterval(animateText, 4000,
"string three", 2);
```

5. Preview the Flash document in the authoring environment again and you should see the strings being displayed at different intervals (1 second, 2.5 seconds, and 4 seconds).

Because you're now using the `setInterval()` function, `animateText`, you call the code every 1000 milliseconds and display the string `"string one"` in the Output panel. If you want to have the text displayed only once and then stop tracing the value, clear the interval by using the `clearInterval()` function and pass an interval ID. When you call the `setInterval()` function, the interval ID for that interval is returned by Flash, in the previous code that value is saved into the `interval_array` array.

The `setInterval()` function passes two arguments to the `animateText()` function: a string and a numeric value that corresponds to the array index containing the current interval ID. You'll notice in the first line of code that you're assigning the interval ID to position 0 in the array and passing 0 as a parameter to the `setInterval()` function. This way you know the array index that contains the current interval ID.

6. Modify the `animateText()` function so that the interval clears immediately and is called only one time. Because the second argument, `interval_index`, contains the array index of the interval ID, you need to add one line at the very top of the function, as shown in the following code in boldface:

```
function animateText(my_str:String,
interval_index:Number):Void {
  clearInterval(interval_array[interval_index]);
  trace(my_str);
}
```

7. Preview your code again in the Flash environment and you should see Flash trace the appropriate string after 1000, 2500, and 4000 milliseconds respectively.

Exercise 5: Creating dynamic text fields

Now that your intervals are set and cleared correctly, you can create dynamic text fields and add them to the Stage. Text fields can be created using the MovieClip class' `createTextField()` method, discussed near the beginning of this chapter. The `createTextField()` method takes six arguments: an instance name for the newly created text field, a depth to assign the text field to, X and Y coordinates, and width and height values.

1. Remove the `trace` statement from the `animateText()` function (`trace(my_str);`) and replace it with the following code:

```
function animateText(my_str:String,
interval_index:Number):Void {
  clearInterval(interval_array[interval_index]);
var instance_str:String =
"string"+interval_index+"_txt";
root_mc.createTextField(instance_str,
root_mc.getNextHighestDepth(), 0, 0, 100, 20);
}
```

The first new line of code creates a string named `instance_str`, which contains the instance name for the new text field. Similar to code for attaching the rectangles in a previous exercise, the text fields will be assigned names such as `string0_txt` and `string2_txt`. This lets you target specific text instances on the Stage.

The second line of code creates a new text field to the `root_mc` scope (`root_mc` is a movie clip that was created in a previous exercise and points to the main timeline of the Flash document). You assign the text field the instance name contained in the string `instance_str`, and the next-highest available depth in the main timeline. The final four parameters are X and Y coordinates, width, and height. These values are temporary and you modify them later on in the script.

2. Next, create an alias to the current text field that will point to the newly created text field, which makes it easier to reference the text field and its properties. Add the following line of code to the `animateText()` function:

```
var my_txt:TextField = root_mc[instance_str];
```

Now you can refer to the new text field by using `my_txt` instead of having to resort to the rather inelegant `root_mc[intstance_str]`.

3. In an earlier example, you created an instance of the TextFormat class named `txt_fmt` that uses an embedded font. Call the TextField class' `setNewTextFormat()` method to apply the text format to the newly created text field by adding the following code to the `animateText()` function:

```
my_txt.setNewTextFormat(txt_fmt);
```

Now any new text assigned to the `my_txt` text field use the defined font and styles.

4. Add the following five lines of code to the bottom of the `animateText()` function:

```
my_txt._alpha = 20;
my_txt._y = (Stage.height-my_txt._height)/2;
my_txt.autoSize = true;
my_txt.embedFonts = true;
my_txt.text = my_str;
```

This code sets the `_alpha` of the text field to 20%. Depending on which colors you selected, this might be too little alpha so make adjustments as necessary. Next, the text field centers vertically by setting the `_y` position of the text field to the height of the Stage minus the height of the text field divided by 2. If your Stage happened to be 400 pixels high, and your text field was 100 pixels high, the code would set the `_y` property of the text field to 150 pixels because (400–100)/2 equals 150. This would leave a 150-pixel margin at both the top and bottom of the text field.

You set the text field's `autoSize` property to `true` to resize the text field to fit the text. If the text field is too big, it will become smaller so it just fits the text; conversely, if there is too much text to fit in the text field, it will stretch so that all the text is visible instead of being cut off.

The final line of code sets the text in the text field to the value in the my_str variable, which is the first argument in the animateText() function. This value is passed through the setInterval() function in the previous exercise.

5. Delete the following lines of ActionScript:

```
this.createTextField("my_txt",
this.getNextHighestDepth(), 0, 0, 100, 20);
my_txt.setNewTextFormat(txt_fmt);
my_txt._alpha = 20;
my_txt.autoSize = true;
my_txt.border = true;
my_txt.embedFonts = true;
my_txt.text = "lorum ipsum";
```

Now that you have created alternative text fields, you no longer need this testing code.

6. Preview the code in your default web browser by pressing F12, as seen in the following figure.

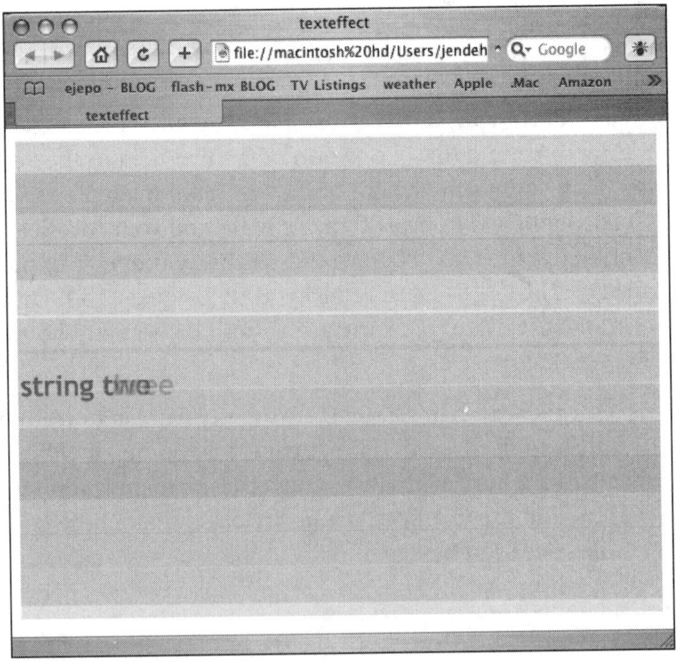

FIGURE 7.11

Press F12 to review your hard work in a browser window. The text strings at the left side of the Stage are expected at this point.

At this point, the background rectangles should continuously animate; and at each interval, the three strings appear along the middle-left border of the Stage. The next exercise demonstrates how you can use the Tween class to animate each text field across the Stage so the text doesn't overlap and become unreadable.

Exercise 6: Animating dynamic text fields

Now that your document adds three dynamic text fields, it is time to add some tweening and animation so they easily glide across the Stage. Using the Tween class lets you not only animate instances with a single line of code, it also lets you choose easing methods so the text field will decrease and increase its speed as it moves across the Stage.

1. Add the following lines of boldface code, which are being added to the bottom of the animateText() function:

```
function animateText(my_str:String,
interval_index:Number):Void {
clearInterval(interval_array[interval_index]);
var instance_str:String =
"string"+interval_index+"_txt";
root_mc.createTextField(instance_str,
root_mc.getNextHighestDepth(), 0, 0, 100, 20);
var my_txt:TextField = root_mc[instance_str];
my_txt.setNewTextFormat(txt_fmt);
my_txt._alpha = 20;
my_txt._y = (Stage.height-my_txt._height)/2;
my_txt.autoSize = true;
my_txt.embedFonts = true;
my_txt.text = my_str;
var first_tween:Object = new
mx.transitions.Tween(my_txt, "_x",
mx.transitions.easing.Regular.easeIn, -my_txt._width,
((Stage.width-my_txt._width)/2)-10, 10, false);
}
```

This block of code animates the my_txt text field and changes the _x property to slide the text field from left to right over 10 frames. The initial value for the _x property will be set to −my_txt._width which causes the text field to appear just off the left side of the Stage, so it slides in from off the screen. Similar to the code that centered the text field vertically in the previous exercise, the text field stops moving just off-center of the horizontal center of the Stage.

2. If you test the document right now, you'll notice that each text field animates from left to right and stops around the middle of the Stage (Figure 7.12). You'll add a couple more tweening effects, which will cause the final animation to tween quickly to the middle of the Stage, slowly move 20 pixels from left to right, and then tween off the right edge of the Stage.

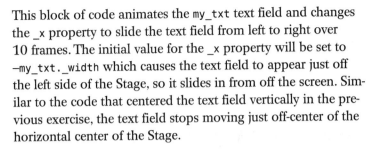

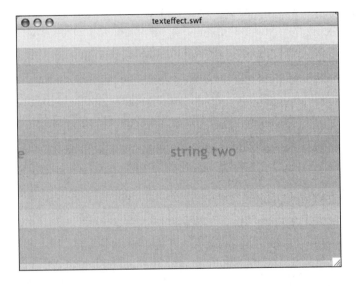

The text stops near the middle of the Stage, and then continues to the right.

3. Add the following lines of boldface code, which are being added to the bottom of the `animateText()` function:

```
function animateText(my_str:String,
interval_index:Number):Void {
clearInterval(interval_array[interval_index]);
var instance_str:String =
"string"+interval_index+"_txt";
root_mc.createTextField(instance_str,
root_mc.getNextHighestDepth(), 0, 0, 100, 20);
var my_txt:TextField = root_mc[instance_str];
my_txt.setNewTextFormat(txt_fmt);
my_txt._alpha = 20;
my_txt._y = (Stage.height-my_txt._height)/2;
my_txt.autoSize = true;
my_txt.embedFonts = true;
my_txt.text = my_str;
var first_tween:Object = new
mx.transitions.Tween(my_txt, "_x",
mx.transitions.easing.Regular.easeIn, -my_txt._width,
((Stage.width-my_txt._width)/2)-10, 10, false);
first_tween.onMotionFinished = function() {
    var second_tween:Object = new
mx.transitions.Tween(my_txt, "_x",
mx.transitions.easing.None.easeInOut, my_txt._x,
my_txt._x+20, 24, false);
};
}
```

This code creates the second tween for each of the three text fields. Again the _x property of the my_txt text field is modified. This time, the text field moves only two pixels from its current position and takes 24 frames, so the animation is much slower. Test the document again in an external browser to see the second animation.

4. Return to Flash and increase the frame rate from the default frame rate of 12 fps to 24 fps. This causes the animation to be a bit smoother and also tween much quicker because doubling the frame rate causes the animations to take half as much time to tween. At 24 fps, each animation should be finished tweening before the next text field appears on the Stage.

5. Add the following boldface code within the `first_tween` `.onMotionFinished` event handler function you added in step 3:

```
first_tween.onMotionFinished = function() {
   var second_tween:Object = new
mx.transitions.Tween(my_txt, "_x",
mx.transitions.easing.None.easeInOut, my_txt._x,
my_txt._x+20, 24, false);
second_tween.onMotionFinished = function() {
second_tween.continueTo(Stage.width, 10);
   delete first_tween.onMotionFinished;
   delete second_tween.onMotionFinished;
};
};
```

This code waits for the second motion tween to finish and then uses the `continueTo()` method to tween each text field off the Stage by moving to the Stage width. Because the registration point for each text field is located in the upper-left corner, setting the _x coordinate to the width of the Stage causes the instance to sit just off the right of the Stage so it's no longer displayed. The last couple lines of code within the event handler delete the `onMotionFinished` event handlers for both the `first_tween` and `second_tween` objects. The text fields are off of the Stage and no longer visible, so you don't need the event handlers now.

6. Test the final animation in your default web browser. If you find the animations move too quickly or too slowly, you can either modify the frame rate or increase the number of frames that the tweens take. If you find that some text fields are long and overlap while tweening, you can increase the intervals in the `setInterval()` function and give them an extra few hundred milliseconds.

Make sure that you save the changes you made to the file.

MOVING ON

There are many things that you can do with this application, from changing the background color to modifying the text so that it says exactly what you want it to say. This is easy to do: simply change the hex values you use in the ActionScript (the array), and you can completely change the look of the animation. Try changing the settings of your text—such as font face, size and style. The animation could also benefit from additional effects layered over the top of the background.

FIGURE 8.A

FIGURE 8.B

FIGURE 8.C

What you learn

► Creating and using masks
► About transitions
► FLV and embedded video, importing video
► Basic video editing with the video import wizard
► Video compression essentials
► Creating movie clip buttons
► Creating button controls for FLV
► Using the ScrollBar component

Lesson Files

Start:

08/bonus/mask.fla
08/bonus/scrollbar.fla
08/start/video1.flv
08/start/video2.flv
08/start/lorem.txt

08/complete/home.fla
08/complete/home.swf
08/complete/about.fla
08/complete/about.swf
08/complete/video1.fla
08/complete/video1.swf
08/complete/video2.fla
08/complete/video2.swf

Finish:

08/complete/site.fla
08/complete/site.swf
08/complete/site.html

8

Masks, Transitions, and Video

When you work on web pages, often you will require media such as audio and video elements. Macromedia Flash is an excellent container for presenting audio and video, partially because so many visitors already have Flash Player installed. You don't need to worry as much about whether a player, such as QuickTime, is already installed on their computer. And in many cases, large percentages of visitors don't have the proper player installed. In the rare cases that Flash Player isn't installed, it is much easier and quicker to do than QuickTime or RealPlayer (which, at the time of writing, even required completely new installs every few months). Additionally, you can fully customize the audio or video controls to match your website and seamlessly meld the media content with all your other site content.

In this project, you build a "mini" website that has movie clip buttons and animated mask transitions to move between pages that load video content at runtime. The site shows you how to animate buttons and present video content, and also how to create a system of animated effects that display each time you go to a new page. The site shows you how to create several fundamental effects, from which you can build on and use your imagination (and the knowledge gained from earlier projects) to take much further.

Website: www.FLAnimation.com/chapters/08

About Masking

In this chapter, you add several different kinds of effects to a simple website built entirely in Flash. You use several techniques to achieve these effects, one of which is by using masks.

Masks are commonly used in Flash for a variety of creative effects. A mask is similar to a window placed over content, that reveals and hides different parts of the "masked" layers below it. You can see through a mask to the layer (or layers) beneath the mask - essentially, you *cover up what you want to see*. Anything solid on a mask layer is like the window, and the background area of the mask layer is the part that hides the content beneath (Figure 8.1).

FIGURE 8.1

The mask (solid part) is much like a window that you create to see through to the contents of the masked layer beneath.

A mask layer can contain only a single movie clip instance, graphic instance, or text field. If you use vector shapes and a movie clip, the vector shapes mask but the movie clip does not. If you must mask using multiple shapes, contain them inside a single instance, nest instances, or use vector fills instead.

A mask can be any of the following objects:

◆ filled vector shape

◆ text

◆ movie clip instance

◆ graphic instance

Masks can be animated or static; therefore, you can have the mask tween over another layer below to create special effects. You can tween a mask over tweening layers. You can even have two masks tweening over several layers. There are so many creative possibilities when you work with masks.

Creating masks

Masks are simple to create. To create a simple mask, follow these steps using a new FLA file. Import an image into the Library (File > Import > Import to Library), and drag the image from the Library onto the Stage.

Click Insert Layer on the Timeline to create a new layer. Make sure that the layer is above the layer with the image. On the new layer, select the Oval tool and draw a shape over a portion of the image.

When you finish, right-click (Windows) or Control-click (Macintosh) the layer name of the top layer (contains the circle). Select Mask from the context menu. After you select this option, both layers lock and the bottom layer indents, as shown in the following figure. The layers must be locked for the mask to appear as it will in the final SWF file while in the authoring environment.

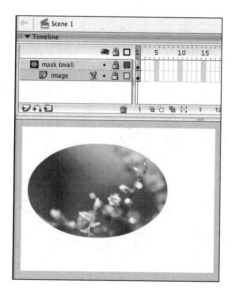

FIGURE 8.2

The oval mask lets you see through to the masked layer beneath that contains the image. Notice how the Timeline changes after you apply the mask.

You can mask multiple layers by dragging more layers beneath the mask layer. If you change your mind and don't want the layer masked, just drag it outside of the indented layers or select Modify > Timeline > Layer Properties and then choose Normal. You can apply animation to the mask layers as well, such as motion or shape tweens.

You can also create interesting effects with animated masks. In a new FLA file, import two images that are the same size as the Stage (or resize the Stage to match the two images). Put image 1 on Layer 1 and image 2 on Layer 2. Then, center both images on the Stage so they overlap.

Insert a third layer. On this layer, create a movie clip that will be the mask for the top image. Right-click or Control-click the layer name and select Mask from the context menu. Inside the movie clip mask, create an animation on the Timeline. In this example, motion tweens and shape tweens combine to create the mask (Figure 8.3).

FIGURE 8.3

Animate the mask movie clip. This animation uses motion and shape tweens, and a motion guide.

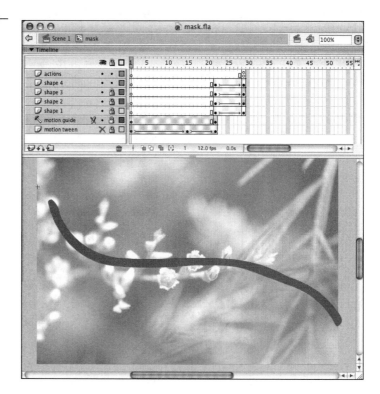

Put a stop action (`stop();`) on the final frame of the mask's tween (as shown in Figure 8.3), and make sure that the end of the tween animates so the entire Stage fills with a shape (meaning that the entire masked image is revealed).

Click Scene 1 in the Edit Bar to return to the main Timeline. Lock the mask and masked layer, which displays the beginning of the mask animation on the Stage (Figure 8.4).

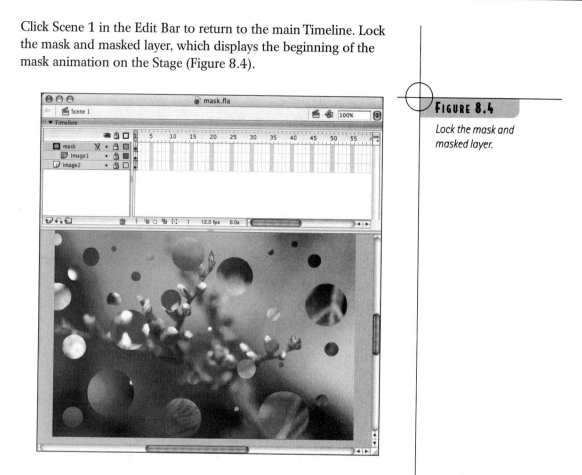

FIGURE 8.4

Lock the mask and masked layer.

Select Control > Test Movie to play the SWF file. You see the animated mask effect, which reveals the second image. If you incorporate a similar animation into a gallery, you can use this kind of effect as a transition between two images.

This example, called mask.fla, is on the CD-ROM within the 08/bonus folder.

Setting a mask using code

You can also set a mask using ActionScript. You can select a movie clip instance and set it as a mask for other objects on the Stage. The movie clip can still animate or interact with the user (such as have draggable properties, and so forth). Another advantage of using code to set a mask is you can toggle the mask on and off at runtime.

See Chapter 6 for information on how to make a movie clip draggable.

Create a new FLA document, and add a movie clip to the Stage that contains some content. Select the instance and give it an instance name **myclip_mc** using the Property inspector; then create a second movie clip (with content) to mask myclip_mc. Select the second movie clip and enter the instance name **mask_mc** in the Property inspector.

Click Insert Layer to create a new layer on the Timeline. Select frame 1 of the Timeline, open the Actions panel, and then type the following ActionScript into the Script pane:

```
myClip_mc.setMask(mask_mc);
```

You can also remove a mask from myClip_mc at runtime. Create a button symbol, and drag an instance of it to the Stage. Select the instance, and give it the instance name **my_btn** in the Property inspector.

Select frame 1 of the Timeline. Open the Actions panel again, and type the following ActionScript:

```
my_btn.onRelease = function() {
  mask_mc._visible = false;
  myClip_mc.setMask(null);
};
```

The first line of the button code (mask_mc._visible = false;) makes the mask movie clip invisible so it doesn't show over the top of the movie clip when you remove the mask. Then you remove the mask for myClip_mc by passing null to the setMask() method.

Limitations of masking

There are several limitations involved with using masks in your FLA files.

◆ If you need to mask device fonts, you must convert the text field into a movie clip and mask using a movie clip mask. If you use non-rectangular shapes to mask the text, the mask assumes the dimensions of the bounding box instead of the shape. Your visitors must have Flash Player 6 r40 or greater to see masked device fonts.

◆ You cannot mask a masking layer.

◆ Masks do not work inside buttons.

◆ Masks applied using the `setMask()` method can only mask movie clips.

◆ You cannot use alpha or semi-transparent fills with masks. Masks are always solid.

◆ You cannot mask using strokes, only fill shapes.

In this chapter's project, you use an animated mask to create a transition effect.

▶ ▶ MASKED LOADING ANIMATIONS

Sometimes animated masks are used to make shapes appear to "grow" in a SWF file or make it look like an image is "filling up" or appearing— particularly for loading effects. To do this, animate a mask over the shape using a motion tween that makes the box larger in size to gradually cover the shape on the lower layer. Sometimes you might overlap two images (as in the previous example) and hide one while you make a second one appear, as shown in the following figure.

A loading animation overlaps two images stacked above each other, and animates a mask to make the second "filled" image appear while the file loads.

▶ ▶ USING TRANSITIONS FOR EFFECTS

Transitions are one of the great benefits of using Flash to create a website. Transitions refer to an animation or effect that occurs when a visitor clicks on a new page in a Flash document. You can create transitions that simulate movement between two pages of content on a Flash website using motion and shape tweens or even frame-by-frame animation. There are many kinds of transition that you can add to a FLA file, too. A transition might be a simple effect that plays, or it might make the current page disappear and a new page appear.

Transitions can be complex—much more so than the one you use in this chapter's project. For the sake of simplicity and page count, the transition in this project remains simple. However, you can apply the following principles and setup to your own transitions and make the animation that plays between the two pages much more elaborate. You might even apply the principles to make an animation play when a page "closes" and a different animation play to "open" the target page.

✦ This chapter details the essentials of setting up a transition. Check www.flash-mx.com for further examples and tutorials on creating transition effects.

VIDEO IN FLASH

The site that you build in this chapter displays video content. There are different ways you can display video in Flash: you can load an external FLV (Flash Video) file at runtime or you can embed video content right inside your SWF file. Loading video at runtime means that you can avoid lengthy load times and separate most of your content from the "container" website—a good way of creating web applications and very easy to update over time. Your visitors can also control how much they download from your website, which is useful when the visitor has a slow or limited internet connection.

✦ For this chapter's project, you'll load external FLV files at runtime; however, both ways of using video are explained for your benefit.

Flash lets you import a video file (such as a MOV or an AVI file), and then place that video right on the Timeline. Alternatively, you can dynamically load a FLV file at runtime, similar to loading an external SWF, JPEG, or MP3 file. Flash supports progressive FLV download or streaming FLV video; however, you must use the Flash

Communication Server to stream video (which is a separate product and goes beyond the scope of this book).

♦ **Progressive video:** Progressively downloads from the server until the file completely loads. Any video that you display *without* using the Flash Communication server downloads progressively, whether it's embedded in the SWF file or loaded at runtime. All SWF files progressively download as well, so if you embed a video it progressively downloads (using the SWF file) as well. External FLV files cache on the users' hard drive, audio and video remains in sync, and the frame rate runs independently from the SWF file. As soon as part of the video loads, it starts to play.

♦ **Streaming video:** Your visitor opens a persistent connection to a server, which downloads a small portion of the video that the user views until the connection is closed. They do not have to load the entire video, and only a small part of it exists on the visitor's hard drive at any given time. Video streams the video from the server, but does not cache the file locally. It is more efficient than progressively downloading the file because this method requires fewer computer resources and memory.

You can create FLV files in the Flash authoring environment or by using the FLV Exporter that comes with Flash Professional (or a number of third-party programs).

Editing embedded video

If you do not use FLV video, you can import and embed video in a SWF file. Using FLV with external files is beneficial because you can encode the video with better tools, it's easier to update your documents with new footage, and the video starts to play after only a portion of it loads into the SWF. However, importing and embedding video can be useful for several different reasons, including the following:

♦ Creating interactive sections of a video, such as hotspot links.

♦ Adding Flash animations on a layer above the video to add interesting effects.

♦ Nest the video content inside a movie clip, and modify the movie clip using code or the Property inspector, thus affecting the video as well.

Flash is an excellent player to display your videos in. It is, by far, the most widely installed player by your visitors that can play video files, so you don't need to worry as much about whether they can view your content or not.

You don't need to use the Flash authoring environment to create SWF files to display FLV files. You can use the Flash Video extension for Dreamweaver, which is an extension that generates a SWF file with a video controller to display the FLV file. You can find more information on this extension at www.macromedia.com/devnet/mx/flash/video.html.

If you do not need to take advantage of any these benefits, you should load FLV video at runtime, which is a much better way of encoding and presenting video to your visitors.

▶ ▶ FLASH FOR VIDEO

This chapter uses video in a SWF file. However, what if you plan to export a SWF file to use in a video? Using Flash in video content can produce amazing results, because you can make your animations appear to float above or interact with video footage. This effect is sometimes used in television advertisements and even music videos.

There are difficulties exporting nested movie clips from Flash within video format (.MOV), because the nested content does not work properly. If you plan to export your work for use in video, use Graphic symbols instead of nested movie clips.

If you want, or need, to use nested movie clips you can adopt the following workflow: export your FLA file in SWF format. Then import the SWF file into Director. From Director, export your content in the MOV format. Then your nested clips should work correctly. This solution and the previous solution (using Graphic symbols) are both workarounds, so investigate changes and improvements in the workflow in future releases of Flash.

Another way to use Flash content in a video is to export it as usual to the SWF format (set to Flash Player 5), and then import it into a video editing program such as After Effects. From After Effects, you can export the content (including the SWF file) to video format.

You can edit video in Flash or in external editors before you import it into Flash. The kind of editing that Flash provides is quite basic, so its usefulness is limited based on what you require. You can create clips from a file and compress a video before you import it. You can also crop the size of the video frame, color-correct the footage and then sew the clips together.

If these features are not enough for editing the video footage, you might want to find or invest in an external editor. There is a wide range of software that varies in price and feature sets. An inexpensive solution is Windows Movie Maker (free but available only for

Windows XP), which actually has a great number of features built into the software. Apple's iMovie 3 for Macintosh computers is excellent and inexpensive video editing software with many built-in capabilities. This software is provided free with some Macintosh computers. QuickTime Pro also offers basic video editing, is very inexpensive, and is available for Macintosh and Windows. Advanced video-editing suites (Adobe Premiere, Apple Final Cut Pro) can be costly, but they offer amazing features that can enhance and control your footage professionally.

Compressing video

You use *compression* to reduce the size of your video file. You accomplish this using complex mathematical equations that remove information from the content that's not necessary for hearing or viewing the video. That means the video, sound, or file you work with will be quicker to download; however, you always lose some quality in the process. All video compresses differently because it depends on the content of the video itself, and the compressor you use. Each frame has a varying number of pixels, and the number of pixels versus the amount of solid flat color sometimes determines how small the file will be. Solid flat areas of color typically compress to a smaller file size than areas of detail with many colors. Some compressors will compress your video to be optimal for the computer's CPU but result in higher file size. Other compressors will lower the file size yet make a lot of demand on the CPU.

There is software you can use (other than Flash) to compress video files. You can use professional solutions such as Discreet Cleaner (Macintosh) or Discreet Cleaner XL (Windows), or Apple Compressor (Macintosh). Inexpensive solutions also exist, such as Quick-Time Pro and Sorenson Squeeze, which can also output FLV video. Some programs can also export using the SWF file format, which is an alternative to importing a video format into your FLA file. Some video-editing programs can also export a compressed video (or SWF) file, although they vary greatly in the quality of output and the control you have over the file that exports.

The most important thing to remember about compression is to always avoid recompressing sounds and video after they have already been compressed. Recompressing material leads to quality loss.

Flash Player uses the Sorenson Spark codec, which is a codec specifically designed for importing video into a document. The codec is built into the video import feature.

Codecs, which stands for compressor/decompressor, are small pieces of software that you use to compress and then decompress files. The video file compresses so you can place it online, and then the file is decompressed by that codec when your visitor views it. Sorenson Video 3, Cinepak, QDesign Music 2, Mpeg4, and DivX are all examples of codecs. If you compress a file using a particular codec, both you and the person watching the video need the codec installed to decompress the video again. Sometimes, codecs are already installed into players such as QuickTime, Windows Media, and Flash Player, but other codecs need to be installed separately by the end user.

▶ ▶ ABOUT FILE SIZE

Even if you are adding great content into a SWF file, you should make sure that you don't get carried away with either video or sound content. Sound, video, and even Flash components can add a lot of bulky file size to a SWF file. You have to make sure that you budge the media that you add to a SWF file and question whether the file is worth the overhead. Video doesn't only add file size, it also adds processor power (your users need to have available RAM to view your video). Video or sound might be the best way of communicating a message, but you should consider alternatives and the bandwidth you have available. Even if you have a very effective codec, video content can still be large because of the amount of data contained in each frame.

There are ways to reduce the file size of your videos if you discover that the file size turns out large. The quickest and easiest way of doing this is to make the frame size (dimensions) of the video smaller. Perhaps your 320 x 240 video can be presented at 160 x 120 instead. Or, you can try lowering the quality of the video compression. Sometimes, you might find that the video quality appears to decrease only slightly, whereas the file size drops significantly. Different codecs produce different qualities of video. Try the FLV Exporter software with Flash Professional, and compare it to Sorenson Squeeze or Wildform Flix. All three produce different results with different videos.

Importing video

You will dynamically load videos for Project 8, but you could also import video content directly into Flash. This section tells you how to import a video file into an FLA document.

Flash lets you import the video after editing it and making compression settings. When you import a video, you can benefit from a number of guidelines. Remember the following guidelines when you import a video file:

♦ **Test your settings.** If file size is a concern, it is beneficial to test different compression settings for your video. All video compresses differently, depending on factors such as color, effects, and movement. If your video looks great when you import it the first time, try changing the settings and compressing the video more (such as lowering the quality or adding fewer video keyframes). The video might still look great, but publishes at a lower file size. Remember not to recompress the compressed video; import the raw (or high quality) video when you try new settings.

♦ **Trim your video.** Blank areas at the beginning and end of the footage add file size that your visitors need to download, but do not necessarily add to the video. Trim these areas when you import the video to remove unnecessary parts of the video.

♦ **Limit movement (such as fading and noise).** You might use effects in your video such as fading in and out or *cross-fades* (when two clips fade into each other). The footage might also contain *noise*, which refers to the speckles that appear over each frame (such as when the footage is dimly lit). Movement might include a tree blowing in the wind, but always involves a lot of pixels moving around the frame. All these factors increase the file size of the video, so you should reduce the amount of noise (sometimes by improving the color levels) using an external editor, avoiding fades, or by editing the video to use the least amount of movement as possible. Footage with a lot of movement is more difficult to compress. You usually need more keyframes to maintain the same quality level, resulting in a higher file size.

Two raw video clips that are exactly the same dimensions, frame rate, and length could be very different in file size.

When you work with FLV files, its timeline is different from the Flash Timeline. If you work with normal video that you import directly into Flash, you cannot add code or keyframes within the video itself when it plays through a video object. However, you can insert the video into a movie clip and add ActionScript to the movie clip's Timeline. You can also add video cue points. Consult Flash documentation for more information.

◆ **Avoid compressing video multiple times.** Every time you recompress a video, you add artifacting to the video, which reduces quality. Artifacting means that you see blocks and pixelation in the video, which looks bad. Because the original footage is already compressed, it probably already contains "residue" of this blockiness, which throws off the second round of compression. Always try to compress video that has the least amount of compression already applied to it.

◆ **Edit for your audience.** If you know that most of your audience will have broadband (fast) connections, larger videos is not as much of a problem as it will be for those on slow connections. If your audience will have slow and fast connections, you should make sure that your videos are small so your visitors don't have to wait a long time to view your footage. Or, provide a couple different videos for your users to choose from.

To import video, you need to follow these steps:

1. Create a new FLA file, set up the document properties you require, and then select File > Import > Import to Library. Find a video file on your hard drive to import, select the file, and click Open (Windows) or Import to Library (Macintosh). This procedure starts the Video Import Wizard.

2. If you import a MOV file, select the radio button to embed the video file in the Flash document and click Next. Select the "Edit the video first" radio button option, and click Next again. Editing the video lets you create smaller video clips from a large video, which is useful for reducing the size of the video.

   After you choose to edit the video, you are taken to a page in which you can create video clips from your single video file. You can then perform basic editing on the file without needing an external editor.

3. In the Editing (Customize) window of the Video Import Wizard, move the in and out points below the scrubber bar to where you want your video clip to begin and end. You can use the playhead (the triangle above the scrubber bar) to move through the video and choose locations. Click the Create Clip button after you are finished. You can rename the video clip at this point.

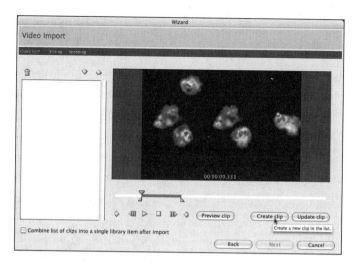

FIGURE 8.5

Choose to edit your video first and then make some video clips.

You can create numerous video clips and have the option of combining them into a single video or leaving them as separate videos. Click the "Combine list of clips into a single library item after import" check box if you want to combine the clips you create. Click the Next button to enter the encoding part of the Video Import Wizard. Here, you enter settings used to compress the video footage.

1. Select Create New Profile from the Compression profile pop-up menu. Selecting this option lets you choose specific settings for bandwidth, quality, video keyframes, and synchronization. Because you are creating a new profile, you can change settings without overwriting the default settings in Flash. You can set the compression level for your video based on bandwidth or quality (Figure 8.6).

    If you select bandwidth, each frame varies in quality based on the setting you make. You can select a setting between 0 and 750, which specifies the download speed in kilobits per second. Lower settings are good for phone modem connections, and 750 is good for extremely fast business-quality connections. Click the Bandwidth radio button and select a setting, such as 256 (a faster connection, such as DSL). Make sure that the setting you make is appropriate for a majority of your visitors.

Even if you have some control over how your video is edited and compressed, and no matter how the good the software you use is, you cannot make bad video footage into great video. Sometimes you can use software to make the video much better through creative editing and compression—sometimes even by using some of the video import features. However, if you work with poor footage to start with, it's unlikely you can make it great using editing features. It's much better to invest the time and effort in taking great footage to work with.

Or, you can click the Quality radio button and select a quality setting for your footage, such as 95 for a very high-quality video. Quality sets all the frames to a specified quality, which can range between 0 and 100. Most of the time, you'll need a setting around 80 or greater for an acceptable quality. You can scrub the video and see how it will encode if you make these settings.

FIGURE 8.6

Choose compression settings for your video.

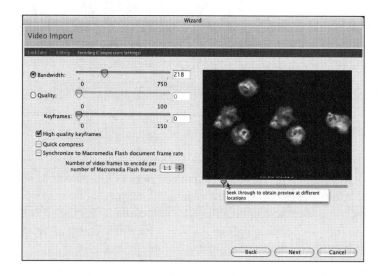

2. Now select a keyframe interval for the video. Video keyframes are different from keyframes in Flash. Each keyframe is a frame that is drawn with great accuracy when the video compresses. Then, the encoder renders each video frame in-between these keyframes by estimating where the pixel changes occur (thus reducing the file size of the video). Therefore, the more keyframes you add make the video appear more accurate to the original, but increase the file size in the end. For example, if you choose 30 as a keyframe interval, the encoder creates one keyframe every 30 frames of video. This is less accurate than selecting an interval of 15, which produces a more accurate and larger file.

3. Set the number of video frames to encode per number of frames in Flash. A setting of 1:1 means that for every Flash frame one frame is encoded, which imports the video at the same frame rate as the current Flash file. If your FLA is set to 12 fps, the

video imports at 12 fps. If you choose one video frame for every two Flash frames, the video imports at half of its original frame rate. This is a way to quickly decrease the file size, but it can result in a rather choppy playback if you greatly decrease the frame rate.

You can choose to deselect the Synchronize check box, so the video does not synchronize to the Flash document's frame rate and can run independently of the SWF frame rate. By deselecting Synchronize, you *avoid* Flash "dropping" frames when the video plays back. *Dropping* frames means some frames on the Timeline might skip (not play) at runtime. If you choose to synchronize the video to the Flash Timeline, the video might drop frames to keep up with whatever's happening in the SWF file, but might play faster in the end.

Quick compress mode speeds up your compression time, but might result in a lesser quality output. Usually, after you've gone to the effort of making your own settings, you won't want to take a gamble with the quality. If you select the High quality keyframes option, you will output a file that's larger (but of better quality). This option is available only if you chose to compress with a Bandwidth setting.

4. Click Next to name the current settings as an encoding profile. Click Next again after you type in a name.

5. Click the Advanced Settings pop-up menu and select Create new profile. A new window opens (Figure 8.7), in which you can set the dimensions, hue, saturation, gamma, brightness, and contrast of the video. All of these options can dramatically change or even improve the overall feeling and quality of your video project.

   ◆ **Hue**: Changes the color value of the footage. You can add colorful effects or correction using this slider, ranging between -180 and 180 degrees.

   ◆ **Saturation**: Changes the amount of grey in the video, compared to the amount of color. You can remove or add color (hue) to the video. De-saturating the video means that you remove the color. Drag the slider downward to remove all the color from the footage.

You should always encode a video at a frame rate that is a fraction of the original frame rate. Therefore, if you are encoding a video set to 30 fps, you could encode at 15 fps. Following this guideline usually produces better results.

If a SWF file drops a frame with ActionScript on it, that code doesn't execute, which can cause problems and errors with the file.

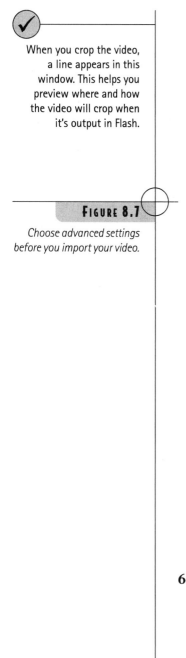

FIGURE 8.7

Choose advanced settings before you import your video.

◆ **Gamma**: Controls the lightness of each frame. Change the values between -0.1 and 1.8. This setting can be useful to correct gamma for different operating systems that do not typically have gamma control built in.

◆ **Brightness**: Changes the brightness of a video's color by adding more black or white to the frames.

◆ **Contrast**: Changes the amount of contrast between the dark and light values in each frame. Create less contrast by dragging the slider downward.

You can also select how to import the video. You can import the video to the current Timeline, into a movie clip, or into a graphic symbol. You can also control the audio track, as integrated with the video (audio imports as part of the video) or separate from the video.

6. Click Next and type a new name for this profile into the Name text field. Click Next to return to the Encoding window and click Finish to start importing your video. After it finishes importing, you can find your footage inside the Library as "embedded video", as shown in the following figure.

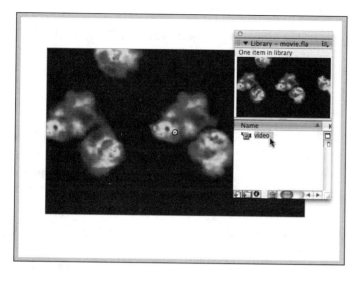

FIGURE 8.8

The video imports into the Library as embedded video. Now you can drag it onto the Stage and use the footage. Nest it inside a movie clip for extended capabilities.

Remember to save your FLA file. You will create a new project in the following section, which uses another method for displaying video content in your site. You will load videos at runtime, instead of importing them directly into the SWF file.

PROJECT 8: CREATING A SITE WITH EFFECTS

This project's website is slightly ambitious for the number of techniques that are used, but they are not difficult. You also get a bit of a break on the ActionScript for this chapter: not much code is used, and what you do add is very simple. Regardless, you probably feel comfortable with the basics after the last couple of chapters!

You'll begin by setting up a website interface that includes animation when the SWF file first loads and when the navigation buttons first appear. You'll add several movie clip buttons that contain animation to the Stage. Then you'll add a transition that appears when your visitors navigate through the website, which includes an animated mask. Finally, you'll add scrollable text and videos as content for the site. You use ActionScript to control the buttons and transitions. You also use ActionScript to load FLV video and formatted text at runtime.

Exercise 1: Setting up the file

You first need to set up the website. This FLA file serves as a "container" file for the main content of the website. Despite this, it also contains the buttons, transitions, and other animations in the site.

1. Create a new Flash document and change the background color to #9CBC7C. Resize the Stage to 600 px wide by 300 px high and set the frame rate to 24 frames per second.

2. Save the new Flash document as **site.fla**.3. In the Timeline panel, rename Layer 1 to **bg tween**. You'll use this layer to animate a semitransparent background that appears behind the other assets on the Stage.

3. Create two new layers in the Timeline and name them **actions** and **labels**. Rearrange the layers so that the actions layer is the topmost layer, followed by the labels layer and finally the bg tween layer at the bottom of the layer stack (Figure 8.9).

4. Create two new layer folders named **content** and **buttons** (Figure 8.9) Drag both of these layers above the bg tween layer.

5. Create five new layers within the buttons folder, as shown in Figure 8.9. Name the new layers (from top to bottom): **home**, **video 1**, **video 2**, **about**, and **button bg**.

FIGURE 8.9

Create five new layers on the Timeline.

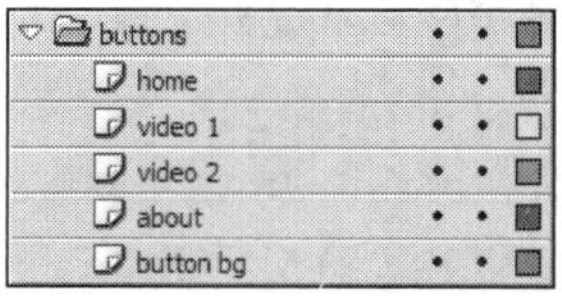

6. Create seven new layers within the content folder and name them (from top to bottom): **content mask**, **home**, **video 1**, **video 2**, **about**, **page label**, and **content bg**.

7. Save the Flash document before you continue. You have now created all the layers you need to be ready for adding some new content.

Exercise 2: Creating the background animation

There are several animations in this example that build the "interface." They are almost entirely decorative instead of functional, but they enhance the overall look and feel of this website. Follow these steps to create a couple of tweens that fill in the background area of the site.

1. Select the Rectangle tool and set the stroke color to No Color. Set the fill color to #B6DB91. Draw a rectangle on the first frame of the bg tween layer and use the Property inspector to resize the rectangle to 400 pixels wide by 250 pixels high.

2. Select the rectangle on the Stage and use the Align panel (Window > Align) to center the shape on the Stage. Make sure that the To Stage button is selected, and click the Align horizontal center button and the Align vertical center button to align the shape (Figure 8.10).

FIGURE 8.10

Center the rectangle on the Stage at frame 1.

3. Select frame 10 on the bg tween layer and press F6 to insert a new keyframe. Select the rectangle on frame 10 and change the width to 586 pixels wide and center the shape on the Stage using the Align panel (Figure 8.11).

4. Select a frame on the bg tween layer between frames 1 and 9 and select Shape tween from the Tween pop-up menu in the Property inspector, as shown in the following figure.

FIGURE 8.11

Resize the rectangle on the Stage and insert a shape tween.

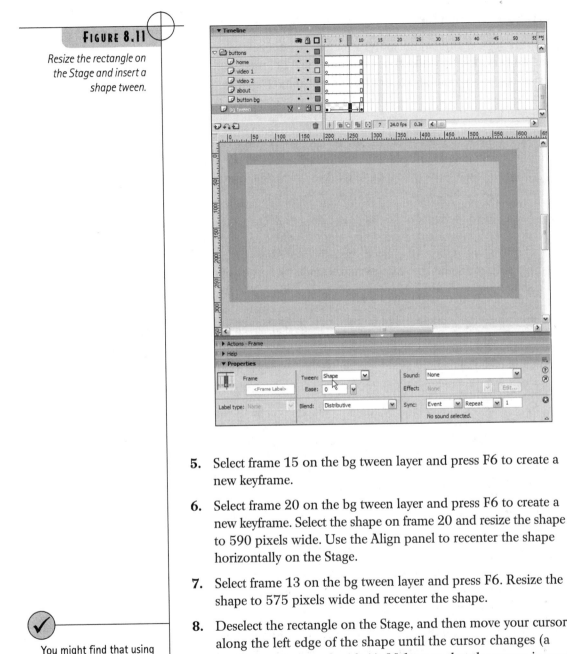

5. Select frame 15 on the bg tween layer and press F6 to create a new keyframe.

6. Select frame 20 on the bg tween layer and press F6 to create a new keyframe. Select the shape on frame 20 and resize the shape to 590 pixels wide. Use the Align panel to recenter the shape horizontally on the Stage.

7. Select frame 13 on the bg tween layer and press F6. Resize the shape to 575 pixels wide and recenter the shape.

8. Deselect the rectangle on the Stage, and then move your cursor along the left edge of the shape until the cursor changes (a small curve appears beside it). Make sure that the cursor is near the vertical center of the shape, and click and drag your mouse toward the center of the shape by approximately 8 pixels as shown in Figure 8.12.

You might find that using the onion skin feature helps for this step and the following step.

Repeat this step on the right side of the rectangle and drag your cursor to the center of the shape by the same number of pixels.

FIGURE 8.12

Bend the left and right side of the rectangle.

9. Select frame 17 of the bg tween layer and press F6 to create another keyframe. You don't need to resize or align the shape this time, but you will need to modify the shape similar to step 8. Move your cursor along the left edge of the rectangle and drag the left edge toward the center of the Stage by about 4 pixels. Repeat this step on the right side of the rectangle and drag your cursor toward the center of the shape by the same number of pixels. When you're finished, the rectangle might resemble Figure 8.13.

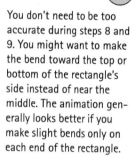

You don't need to be too accurate during steps 8 and 9. You might want to make the bend toward the top or bottom of the rectangle's side instead of near the middle. The animation generally looks better if you make slight bends only on each end of the rectangle.

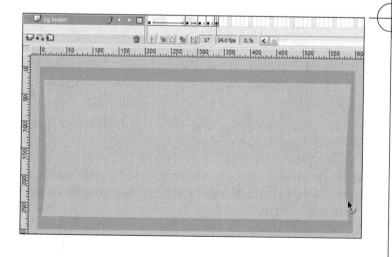

FIGURE 8.13

Bend the left and right side of the rectangle.

See the finished effect on the website at www.FLAnimation.com/chapters/08.

You can use the same principles to grow a stroke using shape tweens (such as when you see lines "grow" in Flash effects and animations).

10. Select a frame between 10 and 13 and insert a shape tween using the Tween pop-up menu in the Property inspector. Likewise, create a shape tween between frames 13 and 15, 15 and 17, and 17 and 20.

11. Select Control > Test Movie to test the background animation in the authoring environment. The rectangle should look like it is stretching and bouncing with a slight elastic effect.

Exercise 3: Creating a background animation for the buttons

When the SWF file first loads in this animation, a box grows from left to right, and then drops vertically behind where the buttons animate in the SWF. This animation provides a backdrop for the buttons, but it's purely decorative. Despite being a decoration, it's a commonly used effect, which you'll learn how to create in this exercise.

1. Select the Rectangle tool, set the stroke color to No Color and set the fill color to a light green (#DDEDCB).

2. Draw a small rectangle on the Stage and resize it to 3 pixels wide by 3 pixels high.

3. With the shape selected on the Stage, press F8 to convert it to a symbol. Select the Movie clip behavior radio button and enter a symbol name of **left_animation**. Click OK.

4. Right-click (Windows) or Control-click (Macintosh) the `left_animation` movie clip in the Library, and then select Edit from the context menu.

5. In the Timeline, rename Layer 1 to **animation**, and create a new layer called **actions**. Drag the actions layer above the animation layer. Then, select frame 10 and press F6 to insert a keyframe.

6. Select frame 10 of the actions layer, and open the Actions panel. Type the following code into the Script pane.

    ```
    stop();
    ```

7. Select frame 5 of the animation layer and press F6 to create a new keyframe. Select the shape on frame 5 and set its width to

194 pixels using the Property inspector. Now the small box changes into a long rectangle. When you apply a shape tween, the small box appears to grow towards the right.

8. Open the Property inspector. Select a frame between frames 1 and 4 of the animation layer and use the Tween pop-up menu in the Property inspector to insert a shape tween.

9. Select frame 10 of the animation layer and press F6. Resize the shape to approximately 196 pixels wide by 68 pixels high (see the finished SWF for guidance).

10. Use the Tween pop-up menu in the Property inspector to insert a shape tween between frames 5 and 10, and then scrub the Timeline to preview the animation. The box should appear to grow in size.

11. Insert a new keyframe at frame 7 of the animation layer and then resize the rectangle to 60 pixels high.

12. Make sure the rectangle is deselected. Move your mouse along the lower edge of the rectangle shape in frame 7 until your cursor changes to an arrow with a small curve beside it. Click the middle of the bottom edge of the shape, drag your cursor slightly upward, and release the mouse. This creates a slight random curve and sense of movement to the rectangle so that your animation doesn't look too "square" (Figure 8.14). If you want to make your shape a bit more irregular, you could even move the mouse cursor to the lower-left corner of the rectangle until your cursor changes again to an arrow with a corner angle icon beside it. Drag the left corner upward by a couple of pixels and then retest your animation.

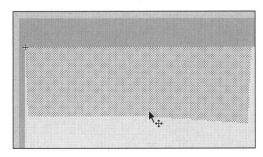

FIGURE 8.14

Trading off margin for padding keeps the links from unexpectedly reflowing.

13. After you're happy with the animation, click Scene 1 on the Edit Bar to return to the main Stage.

14. Select frame 20 on the button bg layer (it should be within the buttons layer folder) and press F6 to insert a new key-frame. Drag a copy of the left animation movie clip symbol from the Library onto the Stage and position it in the upper-left corner of the light green rectangle on the Stage, as shown in Figure 8.15.

15. Lock the button bg layer and save your document before proceeding to the next exercise.

FIGURE 8.15

Position the movie clip on the Stage.

ADDING MOVIE CLIP BUTTONS

There are several different ways to create a button in Flash. You could use a button symbol, a button component, a movie clip with an `onPress` or `onRelease` event handler defined; or you can even create movie clip based buttons with different button states (such as `up`, `over` and `down`). A movie clip button is a movie clip that you apply button functionality and characteristics to, using ActionScript and frame labels. Flash has a built-in functionality to understand when you want a movie clip to act as a button. All you need to do is apply an `onRelease` handler to a movie clip, and it's treated like a clickable button.

When you add the frame labels to a movie clip, Flash knows to move the playhead to each label, depending on where the cursor is. For example, if the cursor hovers over the movie button, Flash knows to move the playhead to the _over frame (if you have one on the Timeline). However, Flash does this only after you add ActionScript for that movie clip (such as an `onRelease` handler).

Creating movie clips with button states is a bit more involved than using a button symbol, but allows you to create intricate buttons with animations, sounds, or whatever you might add to a movie clip. You create movie clip buttons in the following exercises.

▶ ▶ ADDING SOUNDS TO BUTTONS

There are different ways you can add sound to a SWF file. You can make the sound an event sound or a streaming sound. If you add an event sound, the entire sound must load before it plays, and the sound plays independent from the Timeline. A streaming sound only downloads a portion of the sound before it starts to play (great for long sound files), and it plays in sync with the Timeline. The Timeline will drop frames to keep up with the streaming sound, so they're not appropriate if you have ActionScript on the Timeline. Also, even if you play a streamed sound file more than one time, it will redownload the file from the server every subsequent time it plays. Event sounds are appropriate when you want to manipulate the sound using ActionScript, and are best for short sounds, loops, or button sounds.

To add a sound to the movie clip buttons (or any button), drag a sound from the Library and drop it on a new layer inside the button movie clip or onto a frame on a Button symbol's Timeline. Use the Property inspector to set the sound to Event. The entire sound plays during its associated button event. If you place a sound in the Over frame, the sound plays when the user moves the mouse cursor over the button.

Exercise 4: Creating movie clip buttons

You begin by adding an "intro" animation for the movie clip button that spans a small number of frames. You then create a couple of different animations for the over and down states of the button. Because the built-in functionality knows to go to specific frame labels for these states, you need to only add the labels to the movie clip Timeline instead of adding a bunch of code to tell the playhead where to go when specific events occur.

1. Select Insert > New Symbol to create a new symbol, and select the movie clip behavior. Type in a symbol name of **button_ animation** and click OK. The new movie clip opens in symbol-editing mode.

2. Inside the new movie clip, rename Layer 1 to **button intro** and add four more layers (from top to bottom): **actions**, **labels**, **text** and **flash**.

3. Select the Rectangle tool and set the stroke color to No Stroke using the Tools panel. Set the fill color to #F3F8EB and change the alpha level to 20% using the Color Mixer panel (Window > Design Panels > Color Mixer).

4. Select frame 1 of the button intro layer. Click and drag on the Stage to create a rectangle approximately 195 pixels wide by 14 pixels high. You can resize the rectangle to 195 pixels wide by 14 pixels high by using the Property inspector (Figure 8.16).

5. Select frame 6 of the button intro layer and press F6 to insert a new keyframe.

6. Select the rectangle, and change the fill color from 20% to 50% in frame 6.

7. Return to frame 1, and select the shape again. Resize the shape to 40 pixels (width).

Performance might be a concern if you use this effect more extensively or if you're tweening these buttons over a bitmap background. If this is the case, you could change this animation to a color or tint tween instead.

FIGURE 8.16

Resize the shape on the Stage.

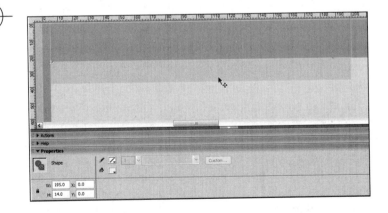

8. Make sure that the shape is deselected. Position your mouse cursor near the right edge of the shape on frame 1 and wait for the cursor to change into an arrow with a curved line beside it. You might need to zoom in to do this. Click and drag the mouse slightly to the left so the right edge pinches in slightly (Figure 8.17).

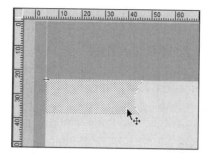

FIGURE 8.17

Change the shape so you can shape tween the button's background.

9. Select a frame between frames 1 and 5 and set the Tween menu to Shape in the Property inspector. Drag the playhead with your mouse to preview the animation on the Timeline. The shape should grow and fade in gradually. Lock the button intro layer when you are done so you don't accidentally move the animation or add any new symbols.

10. Create a new dynamic text field in the text layer. Set the font to Trebuchet MS (or any sans-serif font). The text field should be approximately 185 pixels wide and set the X coordinate to 5 pixels so that the text field centers within the movie clip.

Make sure that the text field's text type is set to Dynamic Text. You use this button for each of the four navigation buttons, so you need to set the text on the button dynamically. Give the text field an instance name of **label_txt**.

Set the font size to 10 points, turn bold formatting on, set the font color to #57733C, set the alignment on the text field to align center and finally make sure selectable and Render text as HTML are turned off. Set the line type pop-up menu to single line. You can see all these settings in Figure 8.18.

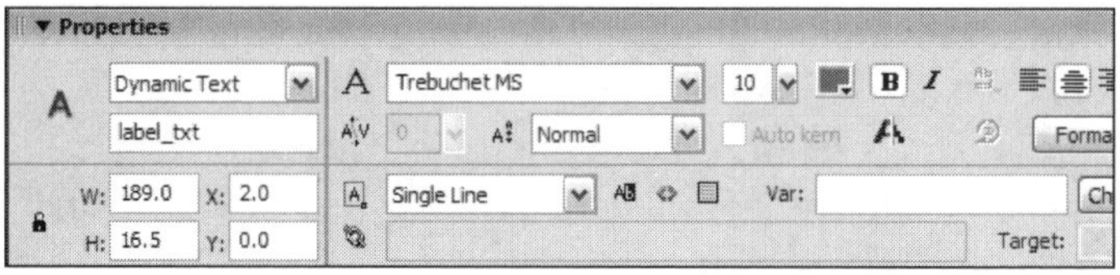

FIGURE 8.18

Make settings in the Property inspector for the text field that will label each button with dynamic text.

Select only the font outline groups that you use within your text fields. Embedding too many outlines increases the size of your SWF files, which means it takes more time for your visitors to load them.

Remember that Flash has special functionality built in for movie clip buttons. If you put specific frame labels inside a movie clip and then write code for the movie clip, it knows to move the playhead to these frame labels at run-time when a user interacts with the button.

11. Because you shape and motion tween these buttons, you'll also need to embed the fonts for this text field. Click the Character button in the Property inspector, and Flash displays the Character Options dialog box. This dialog box allows you to select which characters the font outlines embed. For this example, click the Select Ranges radio button and select the Uppercase, Lowercase, Numerals, and Punctuation ranges. Click OK to apply the changes and close the dialog box. Lock the text layer to prevent moving the text field accidentally.

12. Select frame 6 of the labels layer and press F6 to add a key-frame. Add the frame label **_up** in the Property inspector. When Flash displays the button, this frame is the default state shown when the mouse is not hovering over, or clicked, within the movie clip button. If you use a regular button symbol instead, this frame is the same as the Up frame.

13. Insert a keyframe on frame 6 of the actions layer and add the following ActionScript:

```
stop();
```

This code causes the movie to stop the playhead of the movie clip, instead of continuing to play the remainder of the frames in the instance.

14. Insert keyframes on frame 12 of the actions, labels, and flash layers. Select frame 12 of the labels layer and add a frame label of **_over** in the Property inspector. Then add the following ActionScript to frame 12 of the actions layer:

```
gotoAndPlay("nextFrame");
```

You need to tell Flash to proceed to the next frame when using movie clip buttons because, by default, each of the button states don't move the playhead automatically. This is due to the built-in functionality of movie clip buttons mentioned previously.

15. Unlock the button intro layer and click frame 6. Select the shape on frame 6 and then click frame 12 of the flash layer. Select Edit > Copy to copy the shape. Then select Edit > Paste in Place to paste the rectangle in the same position as the shape that's in frame 6. Select the shape on frame 12 and press F8 to convert it to a movie clip symbol. Enter a symbol name of **button_bg** and click OK.

16. Insert a keyframe on frame 17 of the actions layer and add the following ActionScript code:

```
stop();
```

Insert a keyframe on frame 17 of the flash layer and change the movie clip's alpha level to 30% using the Color pop-up menu in the Property inspector. Click a frame between frame 12 and frame 16 on the flash layer, and select Motion from the Tween pop-up menu in the Property inspector.

17. Insert a keyframe on frame 19 of the actions layer and add the following ActionScript:

```
gotoAndPlay("nextFrame");
```

Create a keyframe on frame 19 of the labels layer and add a frame label of **_down**. Finally, select frame 19 of the flash layer and press F6 to create a keyframe.

18. Create a keyframe on frame 24 of the actions and flash layers. Select frame 24 of the actions layer and add the following ActionScript:

```
stop();
```

19. Select the movie clip instance on frame 24 of the flash layer and set the color drop-down to Tint. Set the tint color to #336633 and set the tint amount to 25%. Select a frame between frame 19 and 24 on the flash layer and create a motion tween using the Property inspector. See Figure 8.19 for the Timeline and how the tint changes the button's appearance.

FIGURE 8.19

The Timeline of a movie clip button.

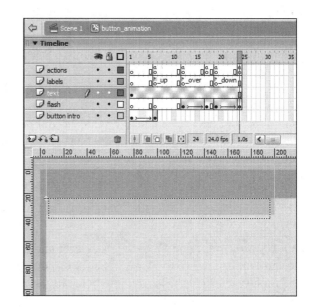

Test the animation by scrubbing the playhead with your mouse and tweak the animation as needed. Save your changes to the FLA after you're finished testing the animation.

▶ ▶ CREATING ADDITIONAL BUTTON STATES

The advantage of using movie clip buttons is that you can add additional states to these buttons. Perhaps you want the button to change color (permanently) after the visitor has viewed a web page—maybe called the visited state at the _visited frame label. You can do this by adding another frame label to the movie clip button, and writing your own ActionScript to determines what happens when the visitor rolls off the button (onRollOut). When the onRollOut event occurs, you can write code to move the playhead to the _visited frame and play the animation that changes the color of the button.

Even though you assign a frame label of _visited in the movie clip, it's important to understand that this label has no special meaning or automatic behavior. You set the frame label to any name you want, and write code to move the playhead there when an event occurs. The underscore can be added to remain consistent with the other (built-in) frame labels.

Exercise 5: Adding the buttons to the Stage

Now that you created the movie clip buttons, you need to add them to the interface. Instead of all the buttons appearing at once, you'll add them along the Timeline shortly after each other, so they appear to tween in succession. This adds a bit of visual interest to your website.

1. If you are still inside a movie clip, click Scene 1 in the Edit Bar to return to the main Timeline. Select frame 27 of the home layer within the buttons layer folder. Press F6 to create a new keyframe, and then drag a copy of the button_animation symbol from the Library onto the Stage.

2. Give the movie clip an instance name of **homeBtn_mc** and position the movie clip in the upper-left corner of the green rectangle that forms the background tween on the bg tween layer (Figure 8.20).

3. Create a keyframe on frame 27 of the actions layer and add the following ActionScript:

```
homeBtn_mc.label_txt.text = "home";
```

This code targets the dynamic text field nested within the but-ton_animation symbol and sets the text field's text property to the string home. Because you use a dynamic text field for the buttons, you can reuse the same symbol for each of the four button instances that you place on the Stage.

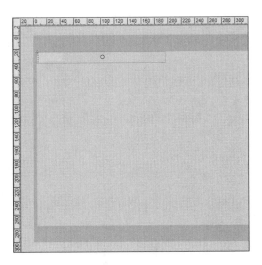

FIGURE 8.20

Position the first button on the Stage.

4. Create a keyframe on frame 29 of the video 1 layer, which should also be in the buttons layer folder, and the actions layer. Drag an instance of the `button_animation` symbol from the Library onto frame 29 of the video 1 layer, position it beneath the movie clip on the home layer, and give it an instance name of **video1Btn_mc**. Add the following ActionScript to frame 29 of the actions layer:

```
video1Btn_mc.label_txt.text = "video 1";
```

5. Repeat step 4 for the video 2 and about layers in the buttons layer folder. The keyframes for the video 2 section should be on frame 31, and the keyframes for the about section should be on frame 33.

Give the video 2 movie clip button an instance name of **video2Btn_mc** and the about movie clip button an instance name of **aboutBtn_mc**, and then add the ActionScript for these two buttons:

```
video2Btn_mc.label_txt.text = "video 2";
aboutBtn_mc.label_txt.text = "about";
```

Position each instance below the previous instance on the Stage, similar to Figure 8.21.

Save your changes to the FLA file before moving on to the next exercise.

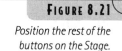

FIGURE 8.21

Position the rest of the buttons on the Stage.

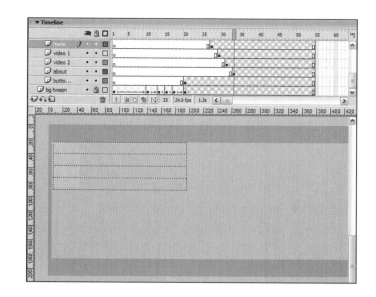

Exercise 6: Adding content and a transition

Buttons are nice, but they're pretty pointless if you don't have anything in your site to go to. In this exercise, you add some content to your site so it has a purpose in life.

1. Press F6 to insert a keyframe on frame 35 for *each* of the layers in the content layer folder, as well as the actions and label layers (Figure 8.22). Select frame 35 of the label layer and add a frame label for this frame using the Property inspector. Type **content** into the Property inspector.

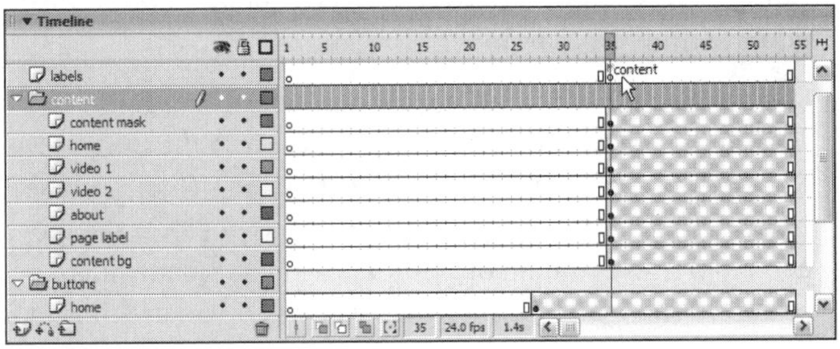

FIGURE 8.22

Add keyframes to each of the layers in the content layer folder and a frame label.

2. Select frame 35 of the actions layer and add the following ActionScript in the Actions panel.

```
stop();
```

You'll add more code in a later step.

3. Create a dynamic text field on frame 35 of the page label layer. Position the text field at the right edge of the light green box (Figure 8.23), and make sure that the text field is approximately 300 pixels wide. Use the Property inspector to check the width, but use the Selection tool to resize the text field.

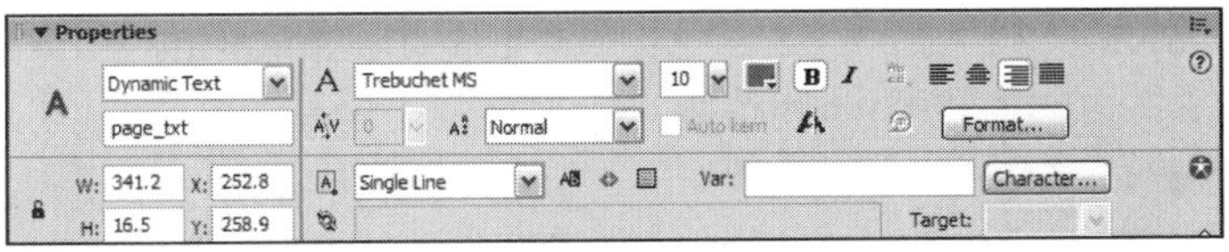

FIGURE 8.23

Position a text field and set its properties.

Use the Property inspector to set the text field's alignment to right align so the text always stays in roughly the same position for each section. Set the font to Trebuchet MS (or any sans-serif font), enable bold, enter a size of 10 points, and set the color to #57733C. Lock the layer when you are finished.

4. Select Insert > New Symbol to create a new symbol. Set the symbol's behavior to Movie clip, and type in a symbol name of **content**. Click OK.

    Click Scene 1 on the Edit Bar to return to the main Timeline. You will put this movie clip on the Stage to load SWF files at runtime, so you don't need to add any shapes, drawings, or graphics to the symbol.

5. Select frame 35 of the home layer in the content folder and drag an instance of the content symbol onto the Stage. Open the Property inspector, and give content an instance name of **home_mc**. Use the Property inspector to position the movie clip at an X coordinate of 230 pixels and a Y coordinate of 24 pixels. In the Timeline, lock the layer when you are finished.

6. Repeat step 5 for the video 1, video 2 and about layers. After you drag a content symbol instance onto each layer, give them instance names of **video1_mc**, **video2_mc**, and **about_mc**, respectively. Each instance should be on the appropriate layer and positioned in the same X and Y coordinates as the home_mc movie clip (see step 5). Lock these three layers when you are finished.

7. Select Insert > New Symbol to create a new movie clip symbol. Set the symbol's behavior to movie clip and give it a symbol name of **transition**. Click OK to enter symbol-editing mode.

    Rename Layer 1 to **animation** and click the Insert Layer button to create a new layer called actions. Create a keyframe on frame 13 of the actions layer and enter the following Action-Script into the Actions panel:

    ```
    stop();
    ```

8. On frame 1 of the animation layer, draw a rectangle that is 10 pixels by 10 pixels. Use the Tools panel to set the rectangle's fill color to white, stroke color to No Color and set the alpha of the fill to 30% using the Color Mixer panel (make sure you

click the paint bucket icon before changing the Alpha slider). Use the Property inspector to position the shape at an X and Y coordinate at 0 pixels.

Then select frame 4 of the animation layer and press F6 to insert a keyframe. Use the Property inspector to resize the shape to 395 pixels wide.

9. Create keyframes on the animation layer on frames 6, 10, and 13. Resize the shape on frame 6 to 190 pixels (height). Resize the shape on frame 10 and 13 to 250 pixels high. Deselect the shape on frame 6, move your cursor along the bottom-right corner of the shape, and wait until the mouse cursor changes into a little L shape. Press the mouse button and drag the right corner up slightly; then release the mouse button (Figure 8.24).

Move the cursor near the bottom edge of the rectangle until the cursor changes to a curved line and drag the bottom edge up slightly to give it a curved look (Figure 8.24).

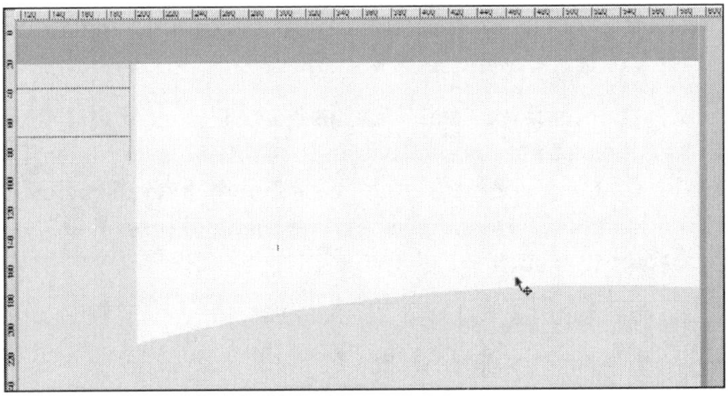

FIGURE 8.24

Add a transition animation to the site.

10. Select the shape on frame 10 of the animation layer and then deselect the shape, Move the cursor the bottom-left corner of the shape, and wait for the corner shape to appear next to the cursor. Drag the lower-left corner up slightly so it is above the bottom-right edge and then release the mouse. Move your cursor along the bottom edge of the shape and wait for the curved shape to appear. Click and drag the bottom edge up slightly and release the mouse so the bottom edge looks slightly curved.

11. Create motion tweens between keyframes in the animation layer. Select a frame between frame 1 and 3, and create a motion tween. Create a motion tween between frames 4 and 5, frames 6 and 9, and frames 10 and 13.

    Scrub the playhead to preview the animation. Return to the main Timeline and save your Flash document.

12. Drag the instance of the transition symbol onto frame 35 of the content bg layer and give the movie clip an instance name of **transition_mc**. Position the movie clip at an X coordinate of 200 pixels and a Y coordinate of 24 pixels.

13. Select Edit > Copy to copy transition_mc on the *content bg* layer, and then select frame 35 of the content mask layer. Select Edit > Paste in Place to paste the instance on the new layer, but in the same position as transition_mc. Change the movie clip's instance name to **mask_mc**.

14. Right-click the content mask layer and select Mask from the context menu. This turns the layer into a mask, which affects the way you display the nested layers beneath the mask. At this point, only the home layer is masked.

    So each layer is masked; drag the video 1, video 2 and about layers beneath the home layer in the content layer folder. Then select frame 45 on each of the layers on the main Timeline (hold the Shift key and click each frame) and press F5 to extend their timelines all at once.

15. The only part left to build for this Flash document is to add the ActionScript. Select frame 35 of the actions layer. Add the following snippet of code beneath the stop action you added previously.

```
_global.previous_mc;
var mclListener_obj:Object = new Object();
mclListener_obj.onLoadInit =
function(target_mc:MovieClip) {
  switch (_global.previous_mc._name) {
  case 'video1_mc' :
  case 'video2_mc' :
   _global.previous_mc.stream_ns.close();
   break;
  }
  mask_mc.gotoAndPlay(1);
```

```
    transition_mc.gotoAndPlay(1);
    _global.previous_mc._visible = false;
    target_mc._visible = true;
    _global.previous_mc = target_mc;
};
```

The first line of code defines a new global variable called previous_mc. You use this variable throughout the remaining ActionScript to keep track of what section previously displayed on the Stage. The second line of code creates a new object that you use as a listener for a movie clip loader instance (created in the next step). The mclListener_obj object defines a single listener, onLoadInit, which you call when the target movie clip finishes loading and you're ready to display it on the Stage.

The first block of code within the onLoadInit listener calls the switch() statement and triggers a block of code based on the previously displayed movie clip (see the following sidebar). If the previous movie clip was one of the video pages, the code closes the video stream that stops the video from playing back or playing audio in the background. Next, both the mask_mc and transition_mc movie clips begin to play back from their first frame, which displays a quick transition between the different sections of the SWF file.

The next line of code (_global.previous_mc._visible = false;) sets the _visible property of the previously displayed movie clip to false so it is no longer displayed on the Stage, and the new section is displayed using the following code (target_mc._visible = true;). Finally the value of _global.previous_mc updates with the currently displayed movie clip.

▶ ▶ USING THE switch STATEMENT

A switch statement tests a condition, and executes a block of code if the condition returns true. You test the first case statement to see if it's true, and then "fall through" to the next case if it doesn't. You should always include a default case as the last case in a switch statement. The default case executes if none of the case statements evaluate true. If nothing evaluates to true and there is no default statement, nothing happens. The break statement prevents the statement from going to the next case.

16. Select frame 35 of the actions layer, and add the following Action-Script to the bottom of the Script pane in the Actions panel:

```
var my_mcl:MovieClipLoader = new MovieClipLoader();
my_mcl.addListener(mclListener_obj);
my_mcl.loadClip("home.swf", home_mc);
```

The previous snippet of code creates a new MovieClipLoader instance named my_mcl and assigns the listener object that you defined in the previous step. The final line of code in the snippet loads the home.swf file, which you find within the same directory as the site.fla file. This code loads home.swf into the home_mc movie clip instance.

17. Add the following ActionScript below the code added in step 16:

```
homeBtn_mc.onRelease = function() {
  my_mcl.loadClip("home.swf", home_mc);
  page_txt.text = "V I D E O S";
};
video1Btn_mc.onRelease = function() {
  my_mcl.loadClip("video1.swf", video1_mc);
  page_txt.text = "V I D E O S - p a g e o n e";
};
video2Btn_mc.onRelease = function() {
  my_mcl.loadClip("video2.swf", video2_mc);
  page_txt.text = "V I D E O S - p a g e t w o";
};
aboutBtn_mc.onRelease = function() {
  my_mcl.loadClip("about.swf", about_mc);
  page_txt.text = "A B O U T U S";
};
```

The previous block of code defines four event handlers (one for each movie clip button on the Stage). Each function performs the same task: when the visitor clicks and releases a specific button, use the movie clip loader instance to load an external SWF file into its target movie clip instance on the Stage (such as "video2.swf"). Next, each event handler updates the page_txt text field on the Stage with the current section name so the user knows exactly where they are within the site.

18. Save the Flash document. At this point, you can test the SWF file (Figure 8.29); however, you haven't created the external SWF files yet, so you will see some errors display in the Output panel when you test the file. Despite this, test the Flash document and see whether the transitions all work and look nice. It might be necessary to return to the FLA file and tweak animations slightly if they don't tween smoothly. Roll over each of the movie clip buttons, and make sure that they fade in and out and turn slightly darker when you hold the mouse button down over them.

FIGURE 8.25

Test the layout and animations that you just created during the exercise.

LOADING VIDEOS INTO FLASH

There are several ways to integrate videos into a Flash document. An easy way to display video in a SWF is to simply import the video (MPEG, AVI, MOV, FLV, and so on) directly onto the Stage or Library. Flash launches an import wizard in which you can control how the video imports. However, you can also load Flash video (FLV) at runtime, which you'll learn how to do in the following exercise.

Exporting FLV video

FLV is a Flash Video file. FLV files can contain both video and encoded audio if your video has some audio. FLV video can both export from Flash and be imported into an FLA filed or loaded into a SWF file at runtime. No compression takes place when you load or import FLV into FLA and SWF files. FLV is economical on file size and can also be streamed if you have the Flash Communication server.

◆ To export video in the Library as FLV, right-click (Windows) or Control-click (Macintosh) the embedded video in the Library. Select Properties from the context menu to open the Embedded Video Properties dialog box. Click the Export button in this dialog box to open a window in which you can name and browse to a place to a location on your hard drive to save the FLV file. Click Save to export the video as FLV. The resulting FLV file is typically rather poor in quality (more so than using the Flash Video Exporter).

◆ To export video from QuickTime Pro as FLV. Open the video in QuickTime Pro. Select File > Export from the menu. Select Movie to Macromedia Flash Video (FLV) from the Export pop-up menu. Click Options to open the Flash Video Exporter (Figure 8.26). Make settings in the exporter for the video. Many are the same as those you make when you import video into an FLA (detailed near the beginning of this chapter). The video output from the Flash Video Exporter is good quality.

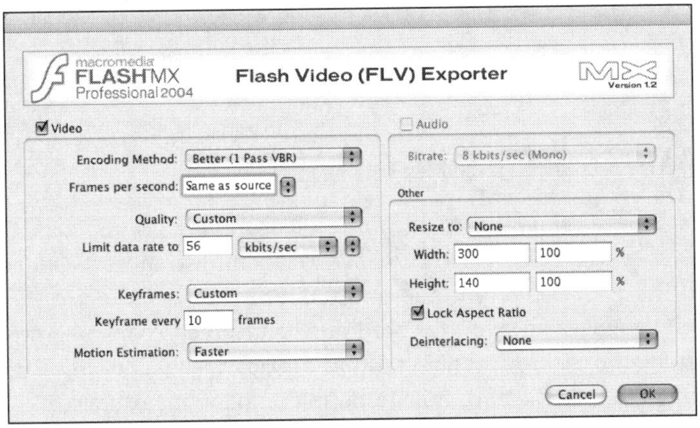

FIGURE 8.26

The Flash Video Exporter is available with Flash MX Professional 2004.

◆ To export video from other editing programs. Other video editing programs that can export FLV video using the FLV Exporter are all slightly different. Typically, you need to figure out how to export or render video from the program, and find either QuickTime or FLV video as one of the options. Then, after you select FLV, find a button or option to open "Settings" (or similar), which typically opens this Options dialog box.

You can dynamically load FLV files much like you load JPEG or SWF files at runtime, except that it requires substantially different code to do so. You also must load the FLV into a video object, which you create from the Options menu in the Library. You learn how to do this in the following exercise.

Exercise 7: Loading FLV files

In the following exercise, you set up the FLA document to load video at runtime. You need to add a video object and some Action-Script to your file in order to do so. It's a very easy process and not much code to dynamically load video content. Additionally, FLV is a superior format to use for video, as outlined near the beginning of this chapter.

1. Create a new Flash document and save it as **video1.fla** in the same folder as site.fla. Select Modify > Document and resize the Stage dimensions to 320 (width) by 240 (height). Save video1.flv and video2.flv from the 08/start folder on the CD-ROM into the same directory as video1.fla.

   You will import this FLV file into video1.swf at runtime, and in turn load video1.swf into the main FLA file (site.swf). You create and load this external file to be consistent with the way you load other content into site.fla.

2. To display a Flash Video file (FLV) on the Stage, you first need to place an instance of a video symbol on the Stage. To create a video instance, open the Library and click the Options menu in the upper right corner of the Library. Select New Video from the context menu, and a new symbol called `Embedded Video 1` appears in the Library.

3. Drag an instance of the embedded video symbol onto the Stage and give it an instance name of **my_video**.

4. Rename Layer 1 to **video**, and insert a second layer and rename it to **actions**.

5. Select frame 1 of the actions layer, and type the following ActionScript into the Actions panel.

   ```
   var connection_nc:NetConnection = new NetConnection();
   connection_nc.connect(null);
   var stream_ns:NetStream = new NetStream(connection_nc);
   my_video.attachVideo(stream_ns);
   stream_ns.play("video1.flv");
   ```

   The first three lines of code use both the NetConnection and NetStream classes so the FLV can play back dynamically. Don't worry too much about the code, it is almost the same any time you want to use Flash to progressively load your video files.

The fourth line of code (starting with my_video) is where you need to do some customization. When you dropped the Embedded Video symbol on the Stage from the Library (in step 3), you gave the instance an instance name of **my_video**. Therefore, this code is saying "Take the embedded video instance my_video on the Stage and attach the NetStream object to it." If you use a different instance name, you need to change the instance that you call the attachVideo() method for. The final line of code tells Flash to play a specific FLV file (in this case, video1.flv), which is in the same directory as the current Flash document. Notice that you don't call the play() method on the embedded video instance; but rather on the NetStream object called stream_ns.

6. Save your changes to the current Flash document and then test the file in either the test environment (Control > Test Movie) or within your default browser (File > Publish Preview > Default HTML).

You will create video2.fla (using File > Save As) in a later tutorial, after making further modifications to video1.fla.

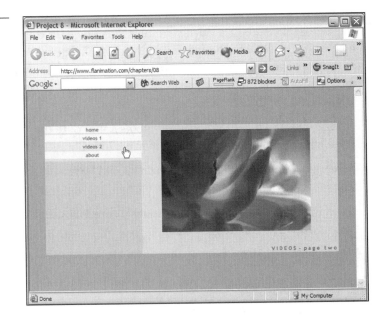

FIGURE 8.27

The SWF file dynamically loads FLV video when you test it.

Exercise 8: Adding playback controls for FLV

Whenever working with video in Flash, it is always best to give the end user some control over the playback. At the very minimum, you should allow the user to pause and resume playback. You could even give them volume controls and a playhead that they can drag to fast forward or rewind the video in case they want to watch a specific portion of video without having to sit through the same material.

This exercise walks you through adding three buttons (play, pause, and stop) that allow the user to control the video.

1. Open video1.fla. Create a play, pause, and stop button on the Stage using the drawing tools (Figure 8.28). Select the drawing you make for each button and press F8 to convert it into a button symbol. Select the Button behavior and click OK.

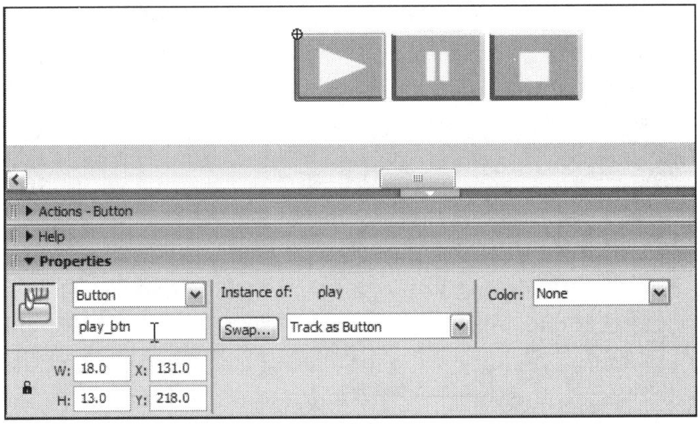

FIGURE 8.28

Create three buttons and give each one an instance name.

Optionally, you can open each button in symbol-editing mode and change the graphics that you use for the over, down, and hit states. If you do not have a solid background area for the button, make sure that you modify the hit state of your button (draw a solid shape around the button's graphic so the user has an area to click).

After you finish creating the buttons, give each button one of the following instance names: **play_btn**, **pause_btn**, and **stop_btn**. Then position the buttons below the video object.

If you don't want to build buttons from scratch, you can use premade buttons from Flash's common libraries, which can be found by selecting Window > Other Panels > Common Libraries > Buttons from the main menu.

If your buttons don't appear to be controlling the video, double-check that each of the buttons and embedded video instances has the appropriate instance names.

2. Select frame 1 of the actions layer and add the following ActionScript to the bottom of the Script pane.

```
play_btn.onRelease = function() {
  stream_ns.pause(false);
};
pause_btn.onRelease = function() {
  stream_ns.pause();
};
stop_btn.onRelease = function() {
  stream_ns.seek(0);
  stream_ns.pause(true);
};
```

This ActionScript creates an event handler function for each of the button instances. The first button instance, play_btn, resumes playback of the video by calling the NetStream class' pause() method and passing a value of false. The second button instance, pause_btn, also calls the pause() method, but doesn't pass any arguments. If the video is playing, the video pauses at its current frame when the visitor presses the pause button. If the video is paused, pressing the pause button resumes video playback.

When you click the stop() button, it calls two of the NetStream class's methods: seek() and pause(). The seek() method moves the video's playhead to the frame closest to the desired number of seconds. For example, passing a value of 0 to the seek() method tells Flash to go to the very beginning of the video, whereas passing a value of 3 tells Flash to go to the frame closest to the three-second mark of the video. Next, you call the pause() method and pass a value of true, which causes the video to pause playback—regardless of whether the video is currently playing or not. If you don't call the pause() method after seeking, the video resumes playback after it moves the playhead to the beginning of the video.

3. Test the SWF file in the test environment (Control > Test Movie) or within your default browser (File > Publish Preview > Default HTML). Now you can click each of the buttons and both pause and resume video playback, based on what button was you click.

4. Repeat steps 1 through 3 for video2.fla.

Exercise 9: Pausing the video

There are several times when you might not want to begin playing back the video until a user clicks a button instance. The primary reason for pausing the video is to conserve bandwidth. Having the user view the video not only costs you bandwidth, but might also cost you money. A visitor might casually click through a site and look at content without any interest in the actual video. Stopping the video and making the user click to view it could spare you some unnecessary bandwidth.

1. In video1.fla, click Insert Layer to create a new layer. Rename the new layer **labels** and drag it beneath the actions layer.

2. Enter the frame label **video** into the Property inspector for frame 1 of the labels layer.

3. Select frame 1 on each of the three layers on the Timeline, drag the frames to frame 10, and release the mouse button (Figure 8.29). Each layer should now have nine blank frames and your previous content on the last frame.

4. It might be necessary to extend each layer on the Timeline to easily read the frame label. Select frame 19 on all three layers (press Shift while selecting each layer) and press F5 to extend their Timelines.

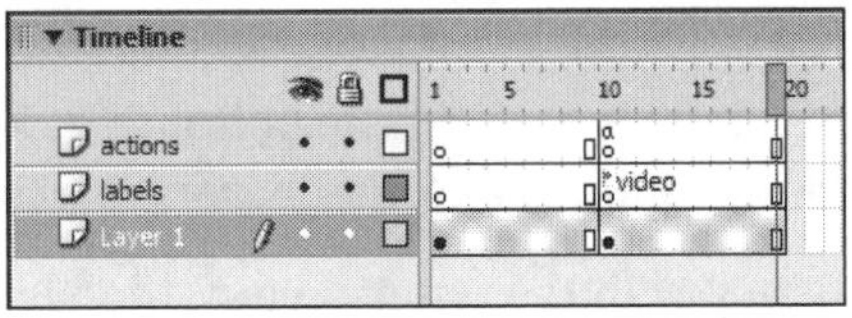

Instead of using a typical text button, you could also take a screen shot from the video itself and use that as a button to start video playback. You might even add a brief description of the video to this page.

If you create a text field and convert it to a button symbol, don't forget to use the Rectangle tool to draw a shape for a hit area. If you don't explicitly create the hit area, Flash makes only the text itself clickable, which is frustrating for users.

FIGURE 8.29

Drag three frames to frame 10 to insert more frames.

5. Create a button instance on frame 1 of the video layer and give it an instance name of **start_btn**. When the visitor clicks the button, the video will play. In the example FLA, the button says "Click to play video," as shown in Figure 8.30.

6. Add the following code to frame 1 of the actions layer:

```
stop();
start_btn.onRelease = function() {
  gotoAndStop("video");
};
```

FIGURE 8.30

Create a button for the user to click to download and see your video.

7. Select Control > Test Movie to test the SWF file in the test environment. The video isn't visible at first, nor does it begin to download until the user clicks the button. The SWF file redirects to the video frame label, and begins to play your footage.

8. If you are happy with the results, return to the authoring environment. With video1.fla open, select File > Save As. Name the new document **video2.fla**. Go to frame 1 of the actions layer and modify the final line of ActionScript in the Script pane to the following:

```
stream_ns.play("video2.flv");
```

Save your changes and then choose File > Publish to export a SWF file.

Before moving on, make sure that you have video1.swf and video2.swf published in the directory.

Working with Text Fields

Many Flash sites, whether they're animation-based, advertisements, or commercial applications, often rely on text to convey messages to the end user. It is imperative that developers not only understand how to create and populate a text field properly, but also how to customize a text field and control its scrolling abilities.

There are two main methods of scrolling content in a Flash text field. The first method consists of making custom scroll buttons that scroll each line of text within the text field (one line at a time). This method enables you to easily scroll text and even customize the look of the scroll buttons to match your site a bit better. With a bit of intermediate ActionScript, you could build a scroll track and scroll thumb (the draggable bar between the two buttons), functionality that exists in all modern operating systems. Another way of creating scrollable content is to use the new UIScrollBar component included in the free Flash 7.2 updater. A sidebar following Example 11 demonstrates how to use the UIScrollBar component.

Example 10: Loading text into a field

If you're using lots of text and text fields within your Flash documents (or perhaps your content changes frequently in your site), you might want to consider loading text in from external files instead of entering it directly into instances on the Stage. One of the simplest ways to load external documents is to use the LoadVars class' onData or onLoad event handlers. The following exercise looks at loading in an HTML-formatted document using the LoadVars class. The following exercise demonstrates how to load in a larger block of HTML text using the LoadVars class' onData event handler.

1. Create a new FLA file, and name the file **home.fla**. Select Modify > Document and resize the Stage dimensions 320 (width) by 240 (height).

2. Use the Text tool in the Tools panel draw a dynamic text field that's approximately 160 pixels wide by 120 pixels high on the Stage. Give the text field an instance name of **news_txt**. Select the text field and enable both the Selectable and Render text as HTML buttons in the Property inspector.

Be careful when you resize text fields. If you resize fields using the width and height text fields in the Property inspector, you skew the text within the field. Always resize your text fields using the handles around the field on the Stage or ActionScript (the width and height properties of the TextField class).

If you enable the border around the text field, you'll find that not only do you get a slight online of the text field but you'll find that the text field has a white background. This white background can make your text fields look as if they don't integrate very well with the rest of your site. If you're using colored backgrounds or an image background for your Flash documents you might want to disable the Show border around text option.

Instead of creating the news_txt text field manually, you can also create the text field dynamically using the createTextField() method.

Set the Line type pop-up menu to Multiline in the Property inspector.

Select the news_txt text field on the Stage, and then click the Character button in the Property inspector. Flash displays the Character Options dialog box, which allows you to choose which characters to embed in the text field. Click the Specify Ranges radio button and select the Uppercase, Lowercase, Numerals, and Punctuation items from the list and click OK to embed the selected font outlines.

3. Click the Insert Layer button to create a new layer at the very top of the Timeline and rename the layer to **actions**.

Add the following code to the first frame of the actions layer:

```
var news_lv:LoadVars = new LoadVars();
news_lv.onData = function(src:String) {
  if (src != undefined) {
    news_txt.htmlText = src;
  } else {
    news_txt.htmlText = "<font color=\"#FF0000\">Error:
Unable to load external text file.</font>";
  }
};
news_lv.load("news.txt");
```

The previous code starts by creating a new instance of the LoadVars object named news_lv. Next an onData event handler is added to the news_lv instance, which accepts one parameter (src) that is a string. This string represents the text that loads into the SWF file. If an error occurs while downloading the contents of the file, the src parameter is undefined; therefore, you need to check the contents of the variable before you display them in the news_txt text field. If the src parameter is undefined, an HTML-formatted error message appears in the news_txt text field. Otherwise, the contents of the file display if everything goes well.

The last line of code in the previous snippet calls the load method of the news_lv instance. After the data loads from the

It's always best to define your event handlers before you attempt to load external data. Problems might arise if your content loads too quickly, and the load() method loads the contents of the external file before Flash has a chance to define the various event handler functions.

external document (in this case, news.txt in the same directory as the SWF file), the onData event handler triggers and displays the file contents (or a friendly error message).

4. Before you can test this exercise, you'll need to create a text file called news.txt that contains some HTML-formatted text that displays in the news_txt text field on the Stage. Create a new document named **news.txt** and save it in the same directory as the current Flash document. Open the news.txt document in a text editor and enter some formatted text:

```
<p><b>Lorem ipsum dolor sit amet</b>, consectetuer
adipiscing elit, sed diam nonummy nibh euismod tincidunt
ut laoreet dolore magna aliquam erat volutpat. Ut wisi
enim ad minim veniam, quis nostrud exerci tation
ullamcorper suscipit lobortis nisl ut aliquip ex ea
commodo consequat.</p>

<p>Duis autem vel eum iriure dolor in hendrerit in
vulputate velit esse molestie consequat, vel illum
dolore eu feugiat nulla facilisis at vero eros et
accumsan et iusto odio dignissim qui blandit praesent
luptatum zzril delenit augue duis dolore te feugait
nulla facilisi.</p>
```

5. Save the modified news.txt document and return to Flash. Test the Flash document in either the test environment (Control > Test Movie). You'll see the contents of the HTML file display within the text field, and the text should scroll if you click and drag your mouse vertically within the text field (Figure 8.31). You add custom buttons to scroll the text fields in the following exercise.

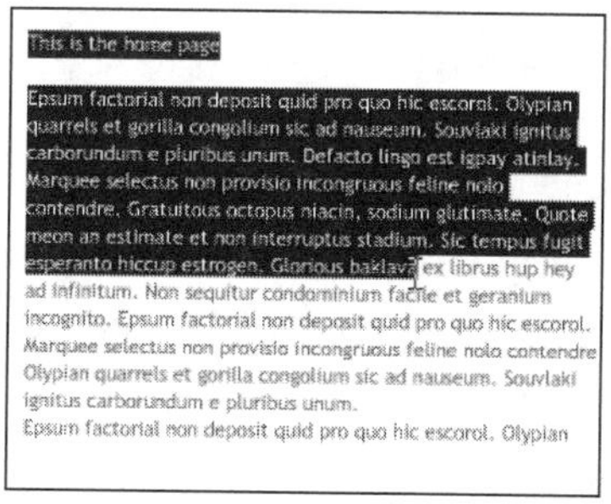

You can copy this text from the finished files on the CD-ROM. It's called home.txt.

There are other formatting options for HTML text, such as embedding JPEG images within HTML text. For a full list, see the section called "Supported HTML tags" in the Flash documentation. Select Help > Help (F1) and use the search feature to search "supported HTML".

FIGURE 8.31

Adding text to your SWF files.

Even if you used onData to load and display an external text file, you also use the LoadVars class to load name/value pairs (similar to passing variables along your browser's query string (for example, my_swf.swf?name= craig&food=jello) from external files. If you're loading documents containing name/value pairs, you'll want to use the onLoad event handler rather than the onData event handler. The difference between onData and onLoad is that onData is called after the contents of the external file have been loaded, but before Flash tries to parse the contents into name/value pairs.

If you use a premade button from the common library, the instance is already a button. You won't need to press F8 to convert it into a button symbol.

6. If you're happy with the results of home.fla, open the FLA file and select File > Save As. Name the new FLA file **about.fla**. Select frame 1 of the actions layer and modify the bold line of ActionScript to match the following code:

```
var news_lv:LoadVars = new LoadVars();
news_lv.onData = function(src:String) {
  if (src != undefined) {
    news_txt.htmlText = src;
  } else {
    news_txt.htmlText = "<font color=\"#FF0000\">Error:
Unable to load external text file.</font>";
  }
};
news_lv.load("about.txt");
```

When you're finished, save your changes, test, and then publish the file (File > Publish).

7. Create a new text file and save it as **about.txt**. Save it in the same directory as about.txt. Copy and paste the text from news.txt into about.txt, or add your own text content in the file.

Example 11: Scrolling text with custom scroll buttons

Unless you're dealing with very small blocks of text, or if your text never changes, you'll possibly never have to worry about whether all your text properly fits into a text field on the Stage. In all other cases, you'll need buttons to scroll the text. Adding basic scrolling abilities to a text field is very simple to do. With a bit of sweat and tears, you can even create your own custom scroll track and scroll thumb, which allow users to scroll through content even more easily. This exercise demonstrates how you can quickly add a couple of buttons so that users can scroll the text in your text fields without having to use their mouse's scroll wheel or drag their mouse within a text field.

1. Open **home.fla** again. Create one button on the Stage with an arrow for the up and down scroll buttons, the same way you made the buttons to control the FLV file (Figure 8.32).

   If you want to use one of Flash's included graphics instead, you can browse various buttons by selecting Window > Other

Panels > Common Libraries > Buttons. This library of assets includes dozens of button symbols organized into nine different folders.

FIGURE 8.21

Up and down arrow buttons that scroll the text.

2. Select the arrow button, which you'll use to scroll text upward. Open the Property inspector and give the new button the instance name **scrollUp_btn**.

3. Now that you have the scrollUp_btn instance ready, you can easily create a second button by duplicating the scrollUp_btn instance on the main Timeline. Select the scrollUp_btn instance, and then select Edit > Duplicate from the main menu to add a copy of the instance to the Stage. Select the new instance and type **scrollDown_btn** into the <Instance Name> text field.

4. Because you don't want the up and down arrows to point the same direction, you need to rotate or flip the scrollDown_btn instance on the Timeline. Select the scrollDown_btn instance on the Stage, and then select Modify > Transform > Flip Vertical. Doing this flips the symbol along its axis so the arrow points downward. Or if you want to rotate the symbol 180 degrees, you could select Modify > Transform > Rotate 90 degrees CCW from the main menu twice, or use the Free Transform tool and rotate the instance into the desired position.

5. Position both the scrollUp_btn and scrollDown_btn buttons next to the right side of the news_txt text field on the Stage.

6. Select frame 1 of the actions layer and add the following code.

```
scrollUp_btn.onRelease = function() {
  if (news_txt.scroll>1) {
    news_txt.scroll—;
  }
};
```

If you use a premade button and the arrow points toward the right of the Stage, you'll need to use the Free Transform tool to rotate the instance on the Stage. Or select the scrollUp_btn instance on the Stage and select Modify > Transform > Rotate 90° CCW from the main menu. This rotates the selected symbol counterclockwise by 90 degrees.

Selecting Edit > Duplicate does not make a duplicate of the scrollup symbol in the Library. If you want to change the graphics of the down button (such as change the color or face), you need to duplicate the scrollUp symbol. Right-click (Windows) or Control-click (Macintosh) the symbol in the Library, and select Duplicate from the context menu. Make edits to the new symbol in the Library.

When you scroll vertically, you use the scroll property in the TextField class. If you need to control horizontal scrolling, use the hscroll property instead.

When you use the scroll property, units are measured in lines. For example, the topmost visible line of text is line 3. When you use the hscroll property, the units of measurement are pixels instead of line numbers.

This code defines a function for the onRelease event handler for the scrollUp_btn instance. When the visitor clicks scrollUp_btn, the code checks to see if the scroll property is greater than 1; if so, it decreases the value of the scroll property by 1. You use the TextField.scroll property to tell you what lines of text are visible within the text field. For example, imagine that you have 10 lines of text in a text field, but only 4 are visible at any point. When the text first loads, the topmost visible line of text is line 1. If you scroll down one line of text, line 1 is no longer visible, and lines 2 through 5 display. The scroll property always lets you know the line number of the topmost line of text that's visible in the text field.

7. Add the following code in the Actions panel, below the code added in step 6:

```
scrollDown_btn.onRelease = function() {
  if (news_txt.scroll<news_txt.maxscroll) {
    news_txt.scroll++;
  }
};
```

The previous snippet of code is similar to the code you added in step 6, although it is responsible for scrolling the text field down instead of up. Notice that the if statement (in the onRelease event handler) uses a new property: TextField.maxscroll. The maxscroll property contains the maximum value that you return by TextField.scroll. This allows you to check whether the text has been scrolled to the bottom or not. If the current value of news_txt.scroll is less than the value of news_txt.maxscroll, then increment the value of news_txt.scroll.

8. Test your Flash document in the test environment. You should be able to scroll the text in the text field by pressing the scrollUp_btn or scrollDown_btn instances. If the text doesn't scroll, return to Flash and check the instance names on the text field as well as the two buttons.

9. If your FLA works correctly in step 8, repeat this exercise for the about.fla document. Publish about.fla when you finish making these modifications.

▶ ▶ USING THE SCROLLBAR COMPONENT

Although absent in versions 7.0 and 7.0.1 of Flash MX 2004, Flash's 7.2 ("Ellipsis") updater reintroduced the ScrollBar component, updated from Flash MX (6.0). You can attach UIScrollBar to a text field on the Stage when you author a Flash document, or you can attach one dynamically at runtime using ActionScript. The UIScrollBar component consists of three main features: arrow buttons, a scroll track, and scroll thumb (box) which lets you quickly scroll through the content in the text field.

There are two ways to integrate the UIScrollBar component. The first way is to drag an instance of the UIScrollBar component onto the Stage and modify the properties directly by using the Property inspector or Component Inspector panel. This method is perhaps the most straight-forward and requires the least amount of code, but it isn't always the most versatile method. The second way involves adding the UIScrollBar component into the Library, and then attaching and configuring the com-ponent using the methods and properties of the UIScrollBar class directly. This second option is more versatile because you can use the component in conjunction with dynamically created text fields. However, it also requires the most amount of code.

To try using the ScrollBar, make sure that you have the Flash 7.2 updater installed (Help > About Flash (Windows) or Flash > About Flash (Macin-tosh)). Create a new Flash document and save it as **scrollbar.fla**. Use the Text tool to add a dynamic text field on the Stage. Resize the text field so it's approximately 160 pixels wide by 120 pixels high. Give the text field an instance name of my_txt. Set the text field to Multiline.

Drag an instance of the UIScrollBar component from the Components panel (within the UI Components folder) onto the Stage. With the UIScrollBar component still selected, enter a value of **my_txt** into the _targetInstanceName property in the Property inspector. This value specifies what text field to attach the ScrollBar instance to. Then add the following code to frame 1 of the FLA document:

```
var my_lv:LoadVars = new LoadVars();
my_lv.onData = function(src:String) {
  if (src != undefined) {
    my_txt.htmlText = src;
  } else {
    my_txt.htmlText = "<font color=\"#FF0000\">Error:
```

continues

```
Unable to load external text file.</font>";
    }
};
my_lv.load("headlines.txt");
```

The previous snippet creates an instance of the LoadVars class named my_lv which you use to load in the contents of an external text file.

Before you can test this example, you need to make sure that there is a file named headlines.txt in the same folder as the FLA. This text file loads in at runtime and displays in the my_txt text field. Select Control > Test Movie to test the document in the test environment.

The scrollbar is the same height as the text field and you can scroll through the text using the scroll buttons or the scroll thumb. You can find this example FLA, called scrollbar.fla, in the 08/bonus folder.

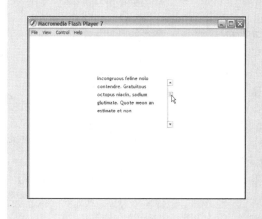

Scrolling text using the ScrollBar component.

PUTTING THE SITE ONLINE

You have created the entire interface and all the parts of the site you need to put online. This site works best in a browser window when it's centered and has a plain background that's the same color as the FLA file background (due to the introductory animation you created).

To center the SWF file, you need to modify the HTML that Flash generates. Follow this simple exercise to put your work online.

Example 12: Editing the HTML

First, you need to publish the project and tweak Flash's autogenerated HTML. For this particular project, you will center the content both horizontally and vertically within the web browser, so that the site appears in the middle of the page (almost) regardless of resolution.

1. Open site.fla. In Flash, select File > Publish Settings to view the publish settings dialog box. On the Formats tab, make sure that you select both the Flash and HTML check boxes, which means that a SWF and HTML file export when you publish site.fla.

2. Click the Flash tab and make sure that both the Protect from import and Omit trace actions are enabled. Omitting trace actions provides an ever-so-slight performance improvement in some cases and Flash Players. Regardless, it doesn't hurt to select it before you publish a SWF for the web. Now click the HTML tab and disable the Display menu in the Playback section.

3. Click the Publish button at the bottom of the Publish Settings dialog box to republish the SWF and HTML documents to the same directory as site.fla. Click OK to close the dialog box.

4. Locate site.html on your hard drive, and open it in your favorite HTML editor (such as Dreamweaver or HomeSite). If you don't have any HTML editors installed you can also use Notepad (PC) or TextEdit (Macintosh).

5. Open the HTML file that Flash generates, and take a look at the code. You need to modify the existing code to match the following listing. The HTML you need to modify appears in bold face font. Also remember to remove HTML from the document. Any code you do not see in the following listing needs to be removed from the HTML file Flash generates.

The site.html file is in the same directory as your site.fla file (unless you specify otherwise in Publish Settings). Use Windows Explorer or Finder if you have difficulty locating the document.

```
<html>
<head>
<meta http-equiv="Content-Type" content="text/html;
charset=iso-8859-1" />
<title>site_4</title>
</head>
```

```
<body bgcolor="#9cbc7c">

<!—url's used in the movie—>
<!—text used in the movie—>
<table width="100%" height="100%">
<tr>
<td align="center"><object classid="clsid:d27cdb6e-ae6d-
11cf-96b8-444553540000"
codebase="http://fpdownload.macromedia.com/pub/shockwave/ca
bs/flash/swflash.cab#version=7,0,0,0" width="600"
height="300" id="site" align="middle">
<param name="allowScriptAccess" value="sameDomain" />
<param name="movie" value="site.swf" />
<param name="quality" value="high" />
<param name="bgcolor" value="#9cbc7c" />
<embed src="site.swf" quality="high" bgcolor="#9cbc7c"
width="600" height="300" name="site" align="middle"
allowScriptAccess="sameDomain" type="application/x-
shockwave-flash"
pluginspage="http://www.macromedia.com/go/getflashplayer"
/>
</object></td>
</tr>
</table>

</body>
```

You can see from the previous two blocks of HTML code that you needed to remove the DOCTYPE as well as modify the attributes within the <html> tag. If you didn't modify these two tags, your web browser wouldn't vertically align the content because the height attribute within the table tag isn't valid XHTML.

The remainder of the modified code is simply defining the table with a single row and cell to force the content to display in the middle of the web browser.

Now you're ready to upload your files to the web. Remember that you do not need to upload the FLA source file. If you do upload the FLA, it's easy for someone to download all your source code. Many other Flash developers try downloading FLA files based on the file locations of your SWF file (sometimes easily found when developers inadvertently—and sometimes advertently—upload the FLA with their SWF and HTML files).

You can find this HTML file in the 08/complete folder on the CD-ROM.

If you republish your Flash document, you need to make sure that you return to the Publish Settings dialog box and uncheck the HTML check box within the Formats tab. If you don't uncheck this document type, Flash will regenerate the HTML file each time you publish, which will overwrite any changes you made to the HTML document in your HTML editor.

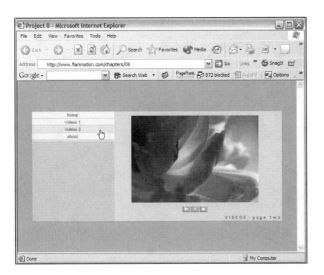

FIGURE 8.33

The finished project in
a web browser.

Moving On

There are many improvements that you can make to this (rather
lengthy) project. First, you can easily add a lot more content to the
file very easily. Add additional buttons and "pages" for the website
by copying button instances and adding text for those buttons. For
example, you can load in more SWF files or JPEG images into the
container movie clips.

Changing the graphics and colors can also make a marked improvement to this document. You can add a variety of backgrounds to the
file, as well as interesting masked transitions or animations that
appear when the SWF file first loads. You might even add a progress
bar (detailed in following chapters), particularly if you add a lot of
content to the document.

You can also make the movie clip buttons more interesting by building upon the animation or perhaps even adding sound to the buttons. Sound is easy to add and sometimes dramatically improves the
interest level in the website. Make sure that you don't go overboard
with sounds. They can easily become irritating, particularly if they all
sound the same (it can quickly seem *too* repetitive).

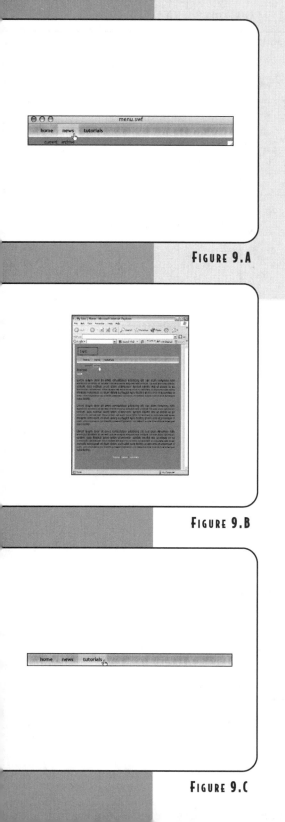

FIGURE 9.A

FIGURE 9.B

FIGURE 9.C

What you learn

- ▶ How to plan websites
- ▶ About flowcharts and flowcharting software
- ▶ How to use the Drawing API
- ▶ About scripted menus
- ▶ About the Debugger panel
- ▶ How to create and attach dynamic menu buttons
- ▶ How to construct and organize the website's HTML files

Lesson Files

Start:

09/start/menu_start.fla   09/start/lorem.txt

09/start/bg.png

Finish:

09/complete/menu.fla   09/complete/menu.html

09/complete/menu.swf   09/complete/site

9

CREATING MENU EFFECTS

WHEN YOU CREATE a menu in Macromedia Flash, it involves adding ActionScript and usually some form of animation. You can add the animation several different ways: by using motion tweens as in Chapter 3, "Using ActionScript," or by using prewritten ActionScript that's built into Flash. It's usually easiest to animate menus primarily using ActionScript because the animation that's involved is usually repetitive and needs to look exactly the same. If you use code, you can guarantee that the animation looks the same much more easily than if you tried to animate on the Timeline.

This chapter constructs a hybrid website that uses a Flash menu to help users navigate between pages. The buttons you add are dynamic and are almost entirely created and controlled by using code. It's much easier than it sounds, and it means you can ensure that the buttons are uniform and evenly spaced and consistently animated in the menu. The finished product is a menu that's both attractive and intuitive for your users. The best part is that the menu is incredibly easy to update as well! You don't need to try and manually create a button while trying to remember how you did so originally. All you have to do is update the ActionScript, and the menu has additional buttons or subnavigation sections for your website. This is particularly useful if you have clients who haven't yet made up their mind about what to call the parts of their website, or if you decide to add a new section to a website later on.

Website: www.FLAnimation.com/chapters/09

Planning Menus and Site Structure

In this chapter, you build a website that contains a Flash menu. You can choose to present the bulk of the website (the part that contains the content) using HTML or Flash. This tutorial uses HTML, but explains how you could use Flash instead using techniques covered in earlier chapters.

Before you build a complete website, you can benefit from planning the site's structure. This might be simple, but drawing a diagram or flow chart of the structure on paper or using software can still help you by clarifying the pieces necessary to complete the site and foresee any problems that you might encounter. A clear plan can save you time and money in the long run because of this, much like making thumbnails before animating a scene (as discussed in Chapter 4). In this section, you look at the structure of the website that you create for this chapter's project.

▶ ▶ Creating flow charts

You can create flow charts on paper, or you can use software to create the diagram. There are several tools available to build flow charts that range greatly in price and features. If you need to plan a website or even just a menu, you should consider creating a flow chart; often doing this on the computer is faster than a pen and napkin. You might want to check out some of these programs, which make building diagrams, flow charts, or organization charts quick and easy. They also contain pre-created graphics and let you install customized or downloaded graphics so you can create attractive and professional diagrams and charts.

- ◆ Microsoft Visio
- ◆ SmartDraw
- ◆ OmniGraffle
- ◆ iGrafx FlowCharter (Corel)

There are many inexpensive programs available to try or purchase if you search www.download.com.

You first need to consider all the main areas for the website. These areas probably contain related areas within them. Each area requires a navigational element, such as a button, that users typically click to navigate to that area. For example, you might have a main area called Products that contains several different topics inside it (subareas). These particular subareas might contain information on each product or type of product. For example, you might plan for the Products area to link to three types of products you sell: Coffee Beans, Mugs, and Accessories. Or, your Products button in the menu might display the three products after the user clicks or rolls the cursor over the button.

So, for this chapter's extremely simple website, there are two main areas that each have subareas within them. The main subjects are News and Tutorials. And each area of the site contains a few topics on each subject. You can see how this is organized in the following diagram.

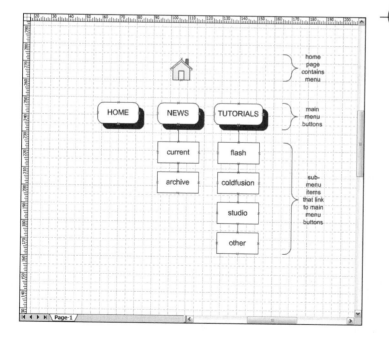

FIGURE 9.1

You might plan a website using a chart or diagram.

This diagram, created using Microsoft Visio, contains the basic site structure. The main areas of the website span across the top of the diagram. Branching out from each of these areas are the topics inside the website. We need to make this into a menu. The main menu items are the topics across the top of the diagram, and the subnavigation elements are the topics that branch out from the main areas. You are probably familiar with drop-down menus on a website. The subnavigation contains the options that are available in the drop-down menu. In this chapter's site, the subnavigation appears when a user rolls over one of the main menu buttons.

After you finish and confirm which areas the site needs to contain, you are ready to create a menu layout and navigation system for your website. You can make a rough draft in Flash, Illustrator, Photoshop, or with a pencil and paper—keep it simple and nonfunctioning at this point. Just draft out in pictures and notes how the overall layout looks and figure out how the navigation *should* work when a user interacts with it.

The key is to create a system that users find intuitive and easy to understand. Some designers even follow the "rule" to make most parts of the site accessible within three user "clicks." Remember that if users cannot find your site's content, the site isn't very useful or successful. After you determine the graphics, layout, and functionality of your navigation system, you are ready to build it.

CREATING SCRIPTED MENUS

One of the most common uses for Flash, besides animations, is the capability to make highly dynamic and interactive navigation systems to present content (such as for websites or CD-ROMs). Although you can easily build a navigation system using some JavaScript and dynamic HTML, you can run into various different browser incompatibility problems, or your menu may not work at all if a person doesn't have JavaScript enabled. Additionally, Flash lets you build presentations that are more creatively designed than those built with other technologies. There are animation and effect possibilities with Flash that you cannot replicate using JavaScript or DHTML.

In this chapter, you build a menu using ActionScript and look at how to embed fonts in a dynamic text field, how to use global variables, and how to use Flash's drawing application programming interface (API). Most of the effects in the menu are created by using ActionScript, instead of motion tweens. Even if that sounds complicated, it is actually much easier than adding the effects manually using motion tweens on the Timeline. It also lets you customize the effects later on to suit your own menus. These advantages might become more obvious during the tutorial.

Project 9: Creating a Menu

In this chapter, you create a menu that triggers submenus when the user rolls over each main button. The submenus are text-based and animate in from the left side of the Stage. When the user rolls over menu items, a rectangle appears as well. Additionally, you design the menu using a PNG graphic that you import into the FLA file.

Users click buttons in the submenus to navigate to different parts of a website. You can use this menu with an all-Flash website or with HTML-formatted content to form a hybrid website.

▶ ▶ What is a hybrid site?

A "hybrid" website contains both HTML formatted and Flash content. Essentially, SWF files are embedded in a page layout alongside HTML content. A hybrid website might include a Flash menu and Flash "widgets" in a column, but use HTML or CSS formatted text to display the main textual content of the website. Or, it might use Flash to create particular areas of the site to avoid page-refreshes. For example, a website might use Flash to display a photo gallery and a Flash menu for navigation, but use a PHP-based content management system to manage and update the site's text content. Therefore, the content is easily to optimize for search engines, and quick to build (using existing prebuilt CMS software), but Flash is used for eye-catching effects and so the HTML page doesn't have to refresh each time a new image loads.

continues

▶ ▶ **WHAT IS A HYBRID SITE?** *continued*

A distinct advantage of hybrid websites is that you can optimize the website for search engines. Although Flash-only websites can rank highly on the search engines like Google, and research is being performed into improving and expanding SWF file searchability, hybrid websites can easily achieve top-ranked results contrary to the opinion of some. For example, at the time of writing (and true for years now), you can search Google for "Flash MX" and "Flash MX 2004" and find two hybrid sites with Flash menus (Macromedia and Flash-MX.com) in the top two or three sites in the results. Therefore, Flash menus do not necessarily mean that you'll end up low in the search engine rankings.

When you build a hybrid website that has Flash elements on each page (such as the same menu on each web page), remember to keep the SWF file small so it appears quickly when the user clicks between each page.

For examples of hybrid websites, see www.macromedia.com, www.ejepo.com, and www.trainingfromthesource.com. The book's website is also a hybrid site.

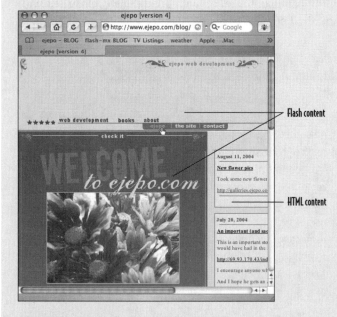

A hybrid site contains Flash and HTML content. This chapter's project is also a hybrid website.

Using the Drawing API

You use the Drawing API (also called *drawing methods*) to draw lines and fills to create shapes, such as rectangles, ovals, stars or lines without any fill. You create these lines and fills using ActionScript, and even specify the transparency, size, and color of the graphics. You use the `moveTo()` method to specify where the line or shape is drawn, and other methods to fill in between lines to create shapes. Your lines or shapes then display when the SWF file plays in Flash Player.

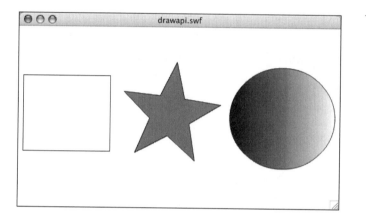

FIGURE 9.2

Draw shapes using Action-Script instead of drawing tools.

You might think this is crazy—why not just draw the shapes using the drawing tools? It can actually be easier for some purposes to draw shapes using code, as you'll find out in this project. If you have to repeat a shape and only change the color, you can use the Drawing API and special functions. Not only does this save you having to draw the same shape, but it can reduce the file size of the SWF file, too.

The Drawing API includes a methods of the MovieClip class: `begin-Fill()`, `beginGradientFill()`, `clear()`, `curveTo()`, `endFill()`, `lineTo()`, `lineStyle()`, and `moveTo()`. You can apply the methods to a movie clip instance, or to a level. You learn how to use this ActionScript in the following exercise.

One of the particularly interesting things you can do with the Drawing API is let your users draw lines and shapes when the SWF file plays. An example FLA of this exists in the Flash MX 2004 install folder. On your hard drive, open the Flash MX 2004 folder in the Applications (Macintosh) or Program Files (Windows) directory. Then navigate to the Samples/HelpExamples/drawingAPI folder.

Exercise 1: Drawing rectangles for the menu

This exercise introduces you to the Drawing API by drawing rectangles on the Stage of varying dimensions and fill colors. The exercise then shows you how to extend the code and turn it into a custom function so it is highly reusable for other purposes, such as later in this project.

1. Select File > New to create a new Flash document, and click Flash Document in the General tab. Click OK to generate the FLA. Select File > Save As to save the new document as **menu.fla**.

2. Rename *Layer 1* to **actions**. Open the Property inspector (Window > Properties) and make the following settings:

   Background color of the Stage set to **#919191**.

   Frame rate set to **24** fps

   Width set to **515** px

   Height set to **400** px

3. Select frame 1 of the actions layer. Add the following code in the Actions panel:

```
this.createEmptyMovieClip("box_mc", 1);
box_mc.beginFill(0x000000, 100);
box_mc.moveTo(0, 0);
box_mc.lineTo(100, 0);
box_mc.lineTo(100, 50);
box_mc.lineTo(0, 50);
box_mc.lineTo(0, 0);
box_mc.endFill();
```

First, you create a new movie clip called box_mc, which you use to apply the drawing methods to. This code introduces several new methods of the MovieClip class, which you apply to box_mc to draw the shape. The first new method you use is beginFill(), which sets a fill color and alpha level for the shape. This example uses a fill color of black (0x000000) and an alpha of 100.

The second new method is the moveTo() method, which defines the current X and Y coordinates where the shape should be drawn relative to the movie clip's registration

Complex shapes require complex code, because you have to tell the SWF file where to render (draw out) the lines at runtime. If your shape has many different points and lines to create, this means you have to add all of those points and lines using code. This requires a fair bit of Math knowledge, but it can be a fun challenge at times.

The optional start file, menu_start.fla, is in the Chapter 09 folder. This FLA document has these settings, has layers already created, and also includes a PNG file you use later on.

point. The registration point is the upper-left corner of the clip when you create a clip using code. This method does not actually draw lines, it just sets the point from which you want to start "drawing."

The next method, `lineTo()`, moves the current drawing position to a new X and Y coordinate. This method actually draws the line, based on the coordinate you set with `moveTo()`. This previous snippet makes four calls to the `lineTo` method to draw each segment of the rectangle. The final method, `endFill()`, applies the fill color and alpha level to the lines drawn by the `lineTo()` or `curveTo()` methods.

4. Select Control > Test Movie to test the Flash document in the test environment. You'll notice a black rectangle that's 100 pixels wide by 50 pixels tall in the upper-left corner of the Stage, as shown in the following figure.

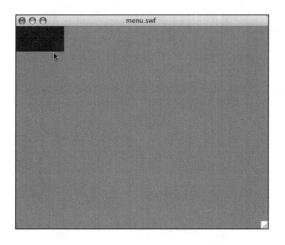

FIGURE 9.3

A black rectangle appears in the corner of the Stage. You "draw" this shape using ActionScript.

5. Now that you understand how to draw a simple rectangle using the drawing API, you can convert the previous snippet into a function, so you can easily reuse the ActionScript. Delete all of the code on the actions layer from step 3, and then type the following snippet:

```
function drawRectangle(target_mc:MovieClip,
fillColor:Number, alpha:Number, width:Number,
height:Number):Void {
  with (target_mc) {
```

"Hard coding" is when you set a value in your Action-Script when it would be better (or easier) to set a variable. Hard-coding values can be quick and easy to do, except it causes problems sometimes because you might forget where you set the hard-coded values or parameters when you need to change them. By setting them as variables, you can centralize where you set values and change them easily and in one spot, no matter how many times you use them throughout the ActionScript.

```
      beginFill(fillColor, alpha);
      moveTo(0, 0);
      lineTo(width, 0);
      lineTo(width, height);
      lineTo(0, height);
      lineTo(0, 0);
      endFill();
  }
}
```

As you can see, this ActionScript is similar to the code that you deleted from step 3 of this exercise. The main difference between the two snippets is that you pass the new ActionScript values when you call the function, instead of hard-coding values.

The second difference is that the ActionScript snippet uses the `with` keyword instead of retyping the path to the movie clip. See the following sidebar for more information on what this means.

▶ ▶ THE with KEYWORD

The `with` keyword lets you specify an object or movie clip to evaluate expressions or actions to. You specify the movie clip, and then apply the actions, set properties, and the like to that particular movie clip. For example, the following two blocks of code behave exactly the same way:

```
//uses with, applied to line1_mc
this.createEmptyMovieClip("line1_mc", 1);
with (line1_mc) {
  lineStyle(1, 0x000000, 100);
  moveTo(0, 0);
  lineTo(100, 0);
}
//is the same as doing this...
this.createEmptyMovieClip("line2_mc", 2);
line2_mc.lineStyle(1, 0x000000, 100);
line2_mc.moveTo(0, 0);
line2_mc.lineTo(100, 0);
```

By using the `with` keyword, you don't have to retype the full path to the specified movie clip, which helps reduce the amount of ActionScript you have to write and clarifies your ActionScript (which is a benefit). In many other situations, it is better to write the full path in your ActionScript and avoid the `with` keyword.

6. Now you can draw a rectangle on the Stage using the following ActionScript. Type this code into the Actions panel.

```
this.createEmptyMovieClip("rectangle_mc", 100);
drawRectangle(rectangle_mc, 0xFFFFFF, 40, 320, 240);
```

This ActionScript creates a new movie clip on the Stage at a depth of 100, and then calls the drawRectangle() function. This function draws a semitransparent white rectangle with an alpha of 40%; that is, 320 pixels wide and 240 pixels high. By default, the rectangle always appears in the upper-left corner of the Stage. If you want to move the shape, you could set the rectangle_mc's _x and _y properties to a specific location.

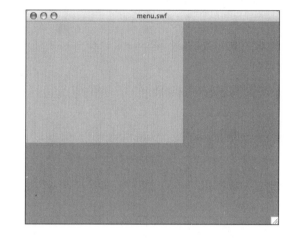

The drawing API also has a curveTo() method, which lets you draw circles or even rounded rectangles. See www.FLAnimation.com for a bonus tutorial that uses this method.

FIGURE 9.4

A transparent white rectangle appears in the corner of the Stage, this time with differing dimensions and color.

You will use the drawRectangle() function later on to add a highlight color when your mouse moves over a button within the navigation.

Understanding Global Variables in Flash

ActionScript allows you to create global variables, which are variables that are accessible on every Timeline and scope within a Flash document. You'll use some in this project's menu.

By putting variables in the global scope, you don't have to worry about providing a fully qualified path to a function in a specific scope. Global variables also allow you to modify values directly rather than having to pass them to a function as an argument and

For more information on variables and scope, see Chapter 6 on ActionScript fundamentals.

Using global variables in small files helps you create this menu quickly and easily. Using global or private variables could be a security issue in larger applications, and can also make application maintenance difficult. If you end up building such applications, consider adopting an application architecture that allows you to avoid global variables.

You cannot strict type global variables. _global is technically an object that already exists when you create your SWF file. If you attempt to declare a new property in the _global scope at runtime using var _global. navXPos:Number = 20; it results in a syntax error when you try to publish or test the Flash document.

return the modified values. To create a global variable, you use the identifier _global before you type the variable name. You do not use the var syntax when you create a global variable; therefore, to create a global variable, you could type the following:

```
_global.myVariable = 10;
```

Exercise 2: Setting global variables

The dynamic menu system uses certain global variables to track the current X coordinate where the next button should be placed. After you add each navigation button to the Stage and position it, the variable containing the X coordinate increments (increases) by the width of the button. This helps ensure that no buttons overlap.

1. Select frame 1 of the actions layer; then add the following code to the first line of the Actions panel:

```
_global.navXPos = 20;
```

This line of ActionScript declares a variable named navXPos in the _global scope and assigns a value of 20.

2. You can see the variables defined in the _global scope in a few different ways. The easiest way to view global variables is to test the current Flash document in the authoring environment and then select Debug > List Variables. Flash launches the Output panel and displays the following text:

```
Global Variables:
 Variable _global.navXPos = 20
Level #0:
Variable _level0.$version = "WIN 7,0,19,0"
Movie Clip: Target="_level0.my_mc"
```

This code tells you that there is one global variable defined, _global.navXPos, with a value of 20. You use this variable, later in this project to keep track of how far the buttons are on the X axis. Every time you dynamically create a new button, the value of _global.navXPos increments to prevent the buttons from overlapping. You initially set the number to 20, so the first button indents 20 pixels instead of being directly on the left edge of the Flash document. If you want the navigation buttons to appear closer to the left edge of the document, you decrease the value of _global.navXPos here; or if you want to shift the navigation further to the right, you increase the value instead.

> ►► THE DEBUGGER PANEL

You can also view global variables using Flash's Debugger panel. To launch the debugger, select Control > Debug Movie. This is the same as using Control > Test Movie, except that Flash displays the Debugger panel. This panel lets you view and change variables within your SWF file. Before you can view global variables, you first need to start the debugger by pressing the Continue button in the Debugger panel. By default, the debugger is paused so you can set breakpoints in your code. When the debugger starts, Flash stops on any line of code that has a breakpoint set. A breakpoint allows you to pause the playback of a SWF file to view which variables are set, as well as their current value in the SWF. This helps make debugging in your Flash document much easier if you're experiencing unexpected results in your documents.

Because the _global scope is technically an object, you can also loop over the structure using a for..in loop to display all the global values, as shown in the following code example:

```
for (var item in _global) {
  trace(item+": "+_global[item]);
}
```

CREATING AND ATTACHING CLIPS

The createEmptyMovieClip() method is great for creating movie clips while the SWF file plays. It not only means that you can avoid creating each movie clip manually, you can even control what kind of movie clip that you create in the SWF file depending on user interaction. In the case of this project, though, it means that you can create a series of movie clips automatically that are exactly the same as each other, differing only in what text appears on the face of the button. You can also make sure that each button executes in a specific way when the user clicks it.

After you create the movie clip at runtime, you will attach it to the Stage at a specific location. You also specify an instance name so you can control the movie clip any way you want by using code (such as giving it the button functionality). In Exercise 4, you attach the buttons to the Stage. First, you create the text fields that will create menu buttons in Exercise 3; then you attach and position them on the Stage.

Exercise 3: Creating dynamic menu buttons

Before you can write the code that creates the navigation system, you need to create a movie clip in the Library. This movie clip later attaches to the Stage using the navButton() function, outlined on the following pages.

1. Select Insert > New Symbol to create a new movie clip symbol. Give it a symbol name of **navBtn**, select the Movie Clip behavior, and click OK to open navBtn in symbol editing mode.

2. Select the Text tool, and click the Stage to create a new text field. With the text field still selected, open the Property inspector. Select dynamic from the Text type pop-up menu, and give it an instance name of **label_txt**. Position the text field at the X coordinate of 10 and Y coordinate of 7, ensure that the Line type pop-up menu is set to single line, Show border around text button is toggled off, and that the Selectable button is toggled off (Figure 9.5).

FIGURE 9.5

Set these text properties in the Property inspector.

3. Select the **label_txt** text field and set the font color to black (#000000), font size to 12 points. Make sure that the text field is set to bold and select a font to use (this example uses Trebuchet MS), as shown in Figure 9.5.

4. Click the Character button in the Property inspector to launch the Character Options dialog box. This dialog box lets you select which font outlines embed into the SWF file when you publish it.

Click the Specify Ranges radio button and select Uppercase, Lowercase and Numerals from the list (as shown in Figure 9.6). Click OK to close the Character Options menu.

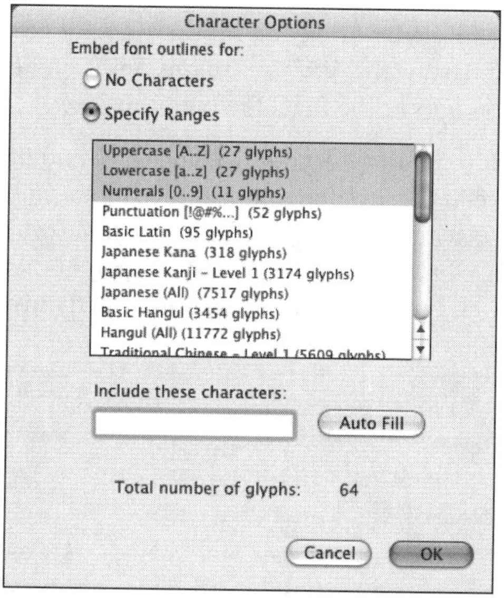

Character Options

Embed font outlines for:

○ No Characters

◉ Specify Ranges

Uppercase [A..Z] (27 glyphs)
Lowercase [a..z] (27 glyphs)
Numerals [0..9] (11 glyphs)
Punctuation [!@#%...] (52 glyphs)
Basic Latin (95 glyphs)
Japanese Kana (318 glyphs)
Japanese Kanji – Level 1 (3174 glyphs)
Japanese (All) (7517 glyphs)
Basic Hangul (3454 glyphs)
Hangul (All) (11772 glyphs)
Traditional Chinese – Level 1 (5609 glyphs)

Include these characters:

[   ]   (Auto Fill)

Total number of glyphs: 64

(Cancel)   (OK)

FIGURE 9.6

Embed text using the Character Options dialog box. Specify a range of characters to embed.

When you select a range of characters instead of embedding the entire set of characters, you reduce the file size of the published SWF file. The fewer outlines you embed, the less data you add to the SWF file.

5. Right-click (Windows) or Control-click (Macintosh) the navBtn symbol in the Library and select Linkage from the context menu. Click the Export for ActionScript check box and type **navBtn** in the Identifier text input field. You use linkage identifiers in Flash to enable you to dynamically attach or reference symbols in the document's Library. Linkage identifiers are similar to instance names, except that they have one important difference. Although you use linkage identifiers to refer to a symbol in the Library panel, you use an instance name to refer to an instance on the Stage.

Click OK after you finish setting the linkage.

6. Click the Scene 1 button in the Edit Bar to return to the main Timeline.

7. Find bg.png on the CD-ROM in the `09/start` folder and save this image onto your hard drive. This helps reduce problems you might encounter importing a file directly into Flash MX 2004 from a CD-ROM.

8. Click the Insert Layer button on the Timeline to create a new layer, and rename the new layer **menu**. Select frame 1 of this layer before you import the PNG file onto this layer.

9. Select File > Import > Import to Stage and find bg.png on your hard drive in the location you just saved it to. Click Import to Library (Macintosh) or Open (Windows). Make sure that the file is placed at the X and Y coordinates of 0,0. If not, select the PNG and place it there using the Property inspector.

FIGURE 9.7

Import bg.png onto the menu layer, and place it at 0,0.

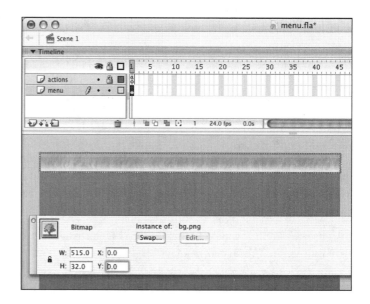

This image serves as the background of the menu. You can use any image that you create, however, as long as it is approximately the same height as this image. You can modify the width of the menu background image and have it work fine with the text and background rollover by changing the size of the text and the background rectangle (what you created in the first two exercises of this chapter).

Exercise 4: Attaching the navigation movie clip

Now that the navBtn symbol is in the current Library and has been assigned the proper linkage identifier, you can attach the movie clip to the Stage dynamically by using the attachMovie() method, as demonstrated in the following steps.

1. Select frame 1 of the actions layer and open the Actions panel. Delete these two lines of ActionScript.

```
this.createEmptyMovieClip("rectangle_mc", 100);
drawRectangle(rectangle_mc, 0xFFFFFF, 40, 320, 240);
```

After you delete the two lines of code, type the following code at the bottom of the existing ActionScript in the Script pane:

```
var root_mc:MovieClip = this;
function navButton(instanceName_str:String,
label_str:String, target_str:String,
subMenu_array:Array):Void {
  var target_mc:MovieClip =
root_mc.createEmptyMovieClip(instanceName_str,
root_mc.getNextHighestDepth());
  var box_mc:MovieClip =
target_mc.createEmptyMovieClip("box_mc",
target_mc.getNextHighestDepth());
  var label_mc:MovieClip =
target_mc.attachMovie("navBtn", "label_mc",
target_mc.getNextHighestDepth(), {_x:_global.navXPos,
_y:0});
}
```

This code first defines a new movie clip, named root_mc, which points to the current Timeline. You use this value throughout the script to let you easily access the main Timeline without having to use long paths or resort to using _root.

The next line of code defines the navButton() function, which takes four arguments (instanceName_str, label_str, target_str, and subMenu_array) and doesn't return a value. These arguments let you define the instance name for the new button, the text that appears in the navigation button, the URL that the SWF file redirects to if a user clicks the button, and which subnavigation items are visible when the user rolls the mouse cursor over a button in the main menu.

►► About _root

You should avoid using `_root` whenever possible. The `_root` identifier refers to the main Timeline of the SWF file whether the code is in a movie clip or on the main Timeline. It's called absolute addressing, much like putting the entire address of a web page starting with `http://` in your HTML code. However, if you have other content loading into a SWF file, using `_root` can cause problems. If those clips or components use `_root`, it targets the main Timeline of the SWF file they load into. This could cause your ActionScript to break because `_root` in the code targets the wrong Timeline. Instead of targeting the main Timeline of the SWF it is in, it targets the main Timeline of the SWF file it's loading into.

Therefore, instead of using `_root`, you should try to use the `this` keyword or `_parent` addressing (known as relative addressing). This addressing is used throughout the code in this book.

The `navButton()` function creates the main navigation buttons, positions them on the Stage, and creates the subnavigation for each button. You base the subnavigation on the value of the `subMenu_array` parameter. For example, the `subMenu_array` is an array of objects and each object in the array represents a single subnavigation item. So the news button you create later has two subnavigation links (*current news* and *archived news*) that point to different HTML pages.

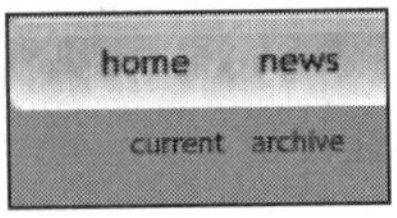

Figure 9.8

Creating and positioning buttons and subnavigation buttons on the Stage.

The first line of code inside the `navButton()` function (the line starting with `var target_mc:MovieClip`) creates a new empty movie clip using the instance name you pass to the `navButton()` function clip. You create a reference to the new movie clip and store it in the `target_mc` variable.

The next line of code (starting with var box_mc:MovieClip) creates an empty movie clip nested inside the target_mc clip you created earlier. This new movie clip has an instance name of box_mc that you will use to draw a semi-transparent white rectangle that is visible when the user moves the mouse cursor over a button in the main menu.

The last line of code in the previous snippet (starting with var label_mc:MovieClip) attaches the navBtn symbol from the Library to the target_mc movie clip you created earlier. When attaching the movie clip, an instance name of label_mc is assigned as well as setting the _x property to the current value of _global.navXPos.

2. Add the following bold face code to the navButton() function (the rest of which you added in step 1):

```
function navButton(instanceName_str:String,
label_str:String, target_str:String,
subMenu_array:Array):Void {
  var target_mc:MovieClip =
root_mc.createEmptyMovieClip(instanceName_str,
root_mc.getNextHighestDepth());
  var box_mc:MovieClip =
target_mc.createEmptyMovieClip("box_mc",
target_mc.getNextHighestDepth());
  var label_mc:MovieClip =
target_mc.attachMovie("navBtn", "label_mc",
target_mc.getNextHighestDepth(), {_x:_global.navXPos,
_y:0});
label_mc.label_txt.text = label_str;
label_mc.label_txt.autoSize = true;
box_mc._x = label_mc._x;
}
```

The bold face code sets the value in the label_txt text field to the value of the navButton() function argument label_str. Next, you set the autoSize method of the label_txt text field to true so that the text field automatically resizes to fit the text. Now, whether you set the value of label_str to something short (such as "home") or something long (such as "frequently asked questions"), the text field shrinks or grows to properly fit the content. The last line of code sets the _x position of the box_mc movie clip to the same position as the label_mc movie clip. By default, movie clips created using the createEmpty-MovieClip() method position content at 0, 0.

3. Add the following code directly after the code you added in step 2 (still inside the navButton() function):

```
var txtWidth:Number = label_mc.label_txt._width+20;
var txtHeight:Number = label_mc.label_txt._height+10;
drawRectangle(box_mc, 0xFFFFFF, 40, txtWidth,
txtHeight);
box_mc._alpha = 0;
_global.navXPos += txtWidth;
```

The previous snippet sets two variables, txtWidth and txtHeight, which represent the width and height of the label_txt text field while adding some padding.

FIGURE 9.9

When you click a Color control in the Tools panel, a color pop-up menu opens where you can select a swatch.

You use these values in the next line of code in the call to the drawRectangle() function you wrote near the beginning of this project. As you may recall, the drawRectangle() function took five arguments (target_mc, fillColor, alpha, width, height), so this causes Flash to draw a white (0xFFFFFF) rectangle within the box_mc movie clip that is 40% transparent with a width equal to txtWidth and a height equal to txtHeight. The _alpha property for the box_mc movie clip is set to 0, and the value of the global variable navXPos is incremented (increased) by the value of txtWidth.

4. Next, you need to create three event handler functions for the box_mc movie clip: onRollOver, onRollOut, and onRelease. When the user rolls over the box_mc rectangle, Flash sets the _alpha on the box_mc movie clip to 100%, which gives the button a semitransparent white background (the rectangle drawn in the previous step was set to only 40% alpha) and the sub-navigation for that particular menu item becomes visible. If

you roll off the Tutorials button, the subnavigation remains active until the user clicks an item or rolls over a different button in the main menu.

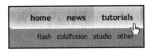

FIGURE 9.10

When you roll over a button, the subnavigation appears under the main menu, and a rectangle appears behind the main menu button because the _alpha *of the* box_mc *clip sets to 100%.*

If the user rolls off of the box_mc movie clip, the box_mc's _alpha property resets to 0, but the subnavigation is still visible. Finally, when the user clicks a menu item (or submenu item), Flash calls the getURL() function, which causes the current page to reload. If you build an all-Flash site, you can replace getURL() with the gotoAndStop() method to go to a different frame number or label instead.

Paste the following code directly below the code you added in step 3, still inside the navButton() function:

```
box_mc.onRollOver = function() {
  // code to be added in upcoming exercise…
};
box_mc.onRollOut = function() {
  new mx.transitions.Tween(this, "_alpha",
mx.transitions.easing.None.easeNone, 100, 0, 7, false);
};
box_mc.onRelease = function() {
  getURL(target_str);
};
```

This code creates the three event handler functions mentioned in step 4. The code for the onRollOut and onRelease events is complete, but the code for onRollOver is a bit long and will be added in a future step. When you roll your mouse off of the box_mc movie clip, the box_mc movie clip fades out using ActionScript's Tween class. You use the Tween class to fade box_mc's _alpha property from 100% to 0% across seven frames.

You added a lot of ActionScript in this exercise, so remember to save your changes before you move on to the next exercise. To see the finished ActionScript, look in frame 1 of the actions layer in the completed menu.fla on the CD-ROM inside the 09/complete folder. In the following section, you add the buttons that this code works with to create an animated menu.

▶ ▶ CODE READABILITY

When you write ActionScript, it is important that you find it easy to read your code. This means that you can scan through your code easily, looking for errors, places to add more ActionScript, or have other people who read your code (or yourself) understand what's occurring in the script.

There are several ways to help make your code readable. One of those ways is to use descriptive variable names: name your variables in a way that they describe what content they contain. Another way is to add comments within your code to tell you and others what various sections of the code accomplish. A third way is to add white space within your ActionScript. This means that you separate sections of code by a few empty lines (press the Enter/Return keys a few times). This helps separate the ActionScript into "paragraphs"—each paragraph contains a separate function or purpose within your FLA file or application.

For more information on code readability, read the Best Practices guide for Flash in Flash documentation (F1). Search for "best practices" within the Help, or look for the "Using Best Practices" chapter within the *Using ActionScript in Flash* book.

▶ ▶ USING THE TWEEN CLASS

This example assumes that you are using the Flash navigation on an HTML site. If you have a complete Flash site, you need to change the code within the `onRelease` event handler to use either the `gotoAndStop()` or `gotoAndPlay()` functions rather than `getURL()`.

The Tween class (introduced in Flash MX 2004) gives developers and designers the ability to easily animate objects on the Stage without having to write lots of code or to manually create motion tweens. For example, in Exercise 4, you used the Tween class to fade out a movie clip on the Stage from 100% alpha to 0% alpha over seven frames, and you do this without touching the Timeline and writing a single line of code! By using the Tween class, you can also modify the `_x` and `_y` properties to animate instances on the Stage, or you can stretch instances on the Stage by modifying the `_xscale` or `_yscale` properties.

For more information on the Tween class, go to the book's website at www.FLAnimation.com.

Exercise 5: Creating dynamic sub menu buttons

Creating a submenu button movie clip is similar to the process of the menu buttons created earlier in this chapter. You need to create a new movie clip in the Library, add a text field, and define a few properties.

1. Click the Create new symbol button in the Library to launch the Create New Symbol dialog box. Enter a symbol name of **subNavBtn** and set the behavior to Movie clip.

2. Before you click the OK button, click Advanced in the Create New Symbol dialog box. The advanced mode of the Create New Symbol window lets you set linkage information without having to set the linkage information later using the Linkage Properties dialog box. In the Linkage section of the Create New Symbol dialog box, click the Export for ActionScript check box and enter an Identifier name of **subNavBtn**. Click OK.

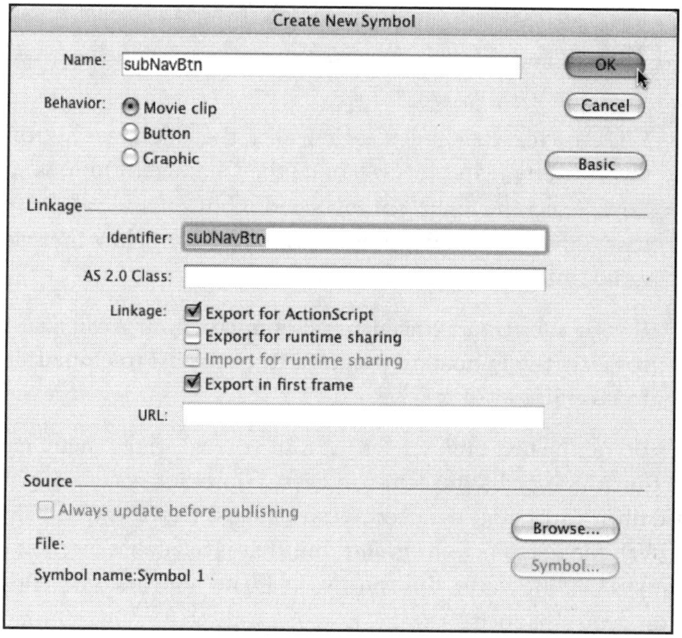

FIGURE 9.11

Setting Linkage in the Create New Symbol dialog box.

3. Double-click the new `subNavBtn` movie clip symbol to enter symbol-editing mode. Click the Text tool and create a dynamic text field on the Stage.

Select the text field and open the Property inspector. Give the text field an instance name of **label_txt**. It is OK that the instance name for the text field is the same as within the navBtn symbol because both text fields are within different movie clips, so they have different target paths.

4. In the Property inspector, position the text field at the X and Y coordinates of 0, 0 and set the font size to 10 points. Make sure that bold isn't selected, set the Line type to Single Line, and confirm that both the Selectable and Show border around text options are both disabled. Set the text color to black (0x000000). Select the same font as you did in Exercise 3.

FIGURE 9.12

Create a text field and set its properties.

5. With the text field still selected, click the Character button in the Property inspector to launch the Character Options window. Select the Specify Ranges radio button and select Uppercase, Lowercase and Numerals from the list below the selected radio button (refer to Figure 9.6).

If your submenu items also used punctuation, you'd also need to select the Punctuation option from the list to embed those font outlines. Click OK.

Embedding the text outlines for the font you use in the menu ensures that the font appears the same on every computer system. If you do not embed fonts, and the user doesn't have the font you specify, then the SWF file defaults to a similar font that is available on their computer system. However, this means the menu appears differently than the one you designed.

FINISHING THE NAVIGATION SYSTEM

The only ActionScript that's left to write for this project is the onRollOver event handler for the box_mc movie clip inside the navButton() function. In Exercise 4, you added the following code:

```
box_mc.onRollOver = function() {
  // code to be added in upcoming exercise…
};
```

This function has three main responsibilities:

◆ Set the appropriate alpha level for the navigation button so you highlight the current movie clip.

◆ Create the subnavigation links (ones that open specified pages on your website) based on the contents of the array you pass to the navButton() function.

◆ Define event handler functions for the onRollOver and onRoll- Out functions for each subnavigation link.

You used arrays in Chapter 7, and you use them again in this project to pass a set of subnavigation items to the navButton() function. In the following exercise, you see how to loop over the array and create a subnavigation button for each array entry. An array is a lot like a structure that holds information you can use in your projects. The values that the array organizes do not have to be the same kind of data (for instance, the array can organize both numerical and string data). You can change the length of an array by adding or subtracting items, or even reorganizing them. For example, if you have an array that is a bunch of words, you can arrange the words alphabetically or change the order of number values so they increase in value.

Exercise 6: Adding tweened subnavigation menus

In this exercise, you use the ActionScript Tween class to fade in the box_mc movie clip instance when the user rolls their mouse over the box_mc instance. You'll also learn how to loop over the subMenu_array array and create a subnavigation link for each item in that array. Finally, you write ActionScript that redirects the user's browser when they click a subnavigation link.

1. Within the box_mc.onRollOver event handler function (where it says code to be added in upcoming exercise), add the following ActionScript:

```
var fade_tween:Object = new mx.transitions.Tween(box_mc,
"_alpha", mx.transitions.easing.None.easeNone, 0, 100,
6, false);
```

This code uses the Tween class to fade the box_mc movie clip in from 0% alpha to 100% alpha across six frames. When you run the SWF file later on (after you add code that adds text to each button), this ActionScript causes a rectangle to fade in. When you roll the cursor off the button, the rectangle fades out.

Now you need to create the subnavigation for each menu item automatically.

2. Add the following snippet to the box_mc.onRollOver event handler function below the existing code. Select frame 1 of the actions layer, and add this snippet directly below the Action-Script you added in step 1.

```
var sub_mc:MovieClip =
root_mc.createEmptyMovieClip("subNav_mc", 999);
sub_mc._y = 36;
_global.subNavXPos = 40;
```

This code creates a new movie clip in the main Timeline with the instance name subNav_mc at depth 999. You hard-code the depth so when you roll over a different button, the subnavigation that was previously visible disappears and replaces the subnavigation area with new links.

The next line of code moves the sub_mc movie clip (a reference to the root_mc.subNav_mc movie clip) to a Y coordinate of 36 pixels. The last line of code in the snippet sets a global variable called subNavXPos to a value of 40 pixels. You use this variable to specify where the SWF positions each of the subnavigation links below the main navigation buttons.

3. At this point, you are ready to create each of the subnavigation links based on the array that you pass to the `navButton()` function. Add the following code to the bottom of the code in the `box_mc.onRollOver` function (it directly follows the code you added in step 2):

```
var numSubMenuItems:Number = subMenu_array.length;
for (var i = 0; i<numSubMenuItems; i++) {
 var thisSubMenuItem:Object = subMenu_array[i];
}
new mx.transitions.Tween(sub_mc, "_xscale",
mx.transitions.easing.Elastic.easeOut, 0, 100, 1, true);
```

The first line of code creates a numeric variable called `numSub-MenuItems` that you use to hold the length of the `subMenu_array`. Next, the code loops one time for each item in the array, and creates a temporary variable called `thisSubMenu-Item`. The temporary variable contains a shortcut to the current object in the `subMenu_array` array. The `subMenu_array` contains an array of objects, representing the various subnavigation links. Each object in `subMenu_array` contains three properties:

◆ **instance**: Assigns an instance name to the subnavigation link because you attach it to the Stage.

◆ **txt**: Contains the text that appears within the navigation link.

◆ **href**: Contains the link where the button redirects to when clicked.

For example, if you use this menu system with an HTML-based site, you might want to redirect the home button to the index page of the site. For example, you could specify the `href` as `/index.html` to link to an index page online.

4. The subnavigation links are built similar to the way the main navigation links. The `subNavBtn` symbol in the Library attaches to the `sub_mc` movie clip, and you give it a specific name that you specify in the `thisSubMenuItem` object. Select frame 1 of the actions layer. Type the following boldface ActionScript inside the `for` loop that you added in step 3.

```
var numSubMenuItems:Number = subMenu_array.length;
for (var i = 0; i<numSubMenuItems; i++) {
 var thisSubMenuItem:Object = subMenu_array[i];
```

```
var subNavBtn_mc:MovieClip =
sub_mc.attachMovie("subNavBtn",
thisSubMenuItem.instance, sub_mc.getNextHighestDepth(),
{_x:_global.subNavXPos});
  subNavBtn_mc.href = thisSubMenuItem.href;
  subNavBtn_mc.label_txt.text = thisSubMenuItem.txt;
  subNavBtn_mc.label_txt.autoSize = true;
}
new mx.transitions.Tween(sub_mc, "_xscale",
mx.transitions.easing.Elastic.easeOut, 0, 100, 1, true);
```

The ActionScript you just added attaches the subNavBtn symbol
to the sub_mc movie clip at the next highest depth available.
You set the _x property to the current value of the global variable subNavXPos, and because the _y property wasn't specified,
it sets to its default value of 0.

The third line of new code copies the target URL for the current
submenu object into the current value of the subNavBtn_mc movie
clip. You use this value later when you redirect the browser
when a user clicks on a subnavigation menu item. The final
two lines of code assign the text to a text field within the sub-
NavBtn_mc movie clip and you resize the text field when you set
the autoSize property to true.

5. The next snippet of code shows two related event handler functions: subNavBtn_mc.onRollOver and subNavBtn_mc.onRollOut.
   You use the two functions to draw and clear a rectangle behind
   the subnavigation movie clips. Enter the following snippet
   below the existing code, within the for loop:

```
subNavBtn_mc.onRollOver = function() {
  var btnWidth:Number = this._width;
  var btnHeight:Number = this._height;
  drawRectangle(this, 0xDFDFDF, 40, btnWidth,
btnHeight);
};
subNavBtn_mc.onRollOut = function() {
  this.clear();
};
```

The subNavBtn_mc.onRollOver event handler sets two temporary variables: (btnWidth and btnHeight). These two variables hold the current width and height of the subNavBtn_mc movie clip, and you pass them to the drawRectangle() function. This causes Flash to draw a rectangle with a background color of 0xDFDFDF (light gray), an alpha of 40%, and a width and height equal to the current movie clip.

FIGURE 9.13

Drawing a light gray rectangle in the subnavigation using code.

The subNavBtn_mc.onRollOut event handler clears the shape that you created in the previous snippet using the drawRectangle() function.

6. Type the following two lines of code directly below the code you added in the previous step (which is still inside the for loop):

```
subNavBtn_mc.onRelease = function() {
  getURL(this.href);
};
_global.subNavXPos += subNavBtn_mc._width+5;
```

The onRelease event handler uses the getURL function to redirect the user's browser to the appropriate page.

The final line of ActionScript increments the value of the global variable subNavXPos by the width of the current subnavigation movie clip, subNavBtn_mc, and also adds a five-pixel padding. Adding the five-pixel padding prevents the buttons from appearing too close together, which would make the text too difficult to read.

In the following exercise, you finally add the text and functionality to the buttons, so you can test the SWF file and see the results. Remember to save your changes before moving on to the next exercise.

✓ If you build an all-Flash site instead of an HTML-based site, you could replace the getURL() functions with either a gotoAndPlay() or gotoAndStop() method to redirect to a different frame on the Timeline instead of an entirely different web page.

Exercise 7: Adding buttons and testing results

Now that you have all the code that you need for the menu system to appear and animate properly, the only code that remains is the ActionScript that you need to link the main and subnavigation to actual content in your website.

1. Add the following snippet of code to the very bottom of the Actions panel outside of both the navButton() and drawRectangle() functions. Therefore, you can add this ActionScript at the very bottom of the Actions panel, following the last curly brace (}).

```
navButton("home_mc", "home", "../home/index.html");

var newsSubNav_array:Array = new Array();
newsSubNav_array.push({instance:'current_mc',
txt:'current', href:'../news/current.html'});
newsSubNav_array.push({instance:'archive_mc',
txt:'archive', href:'../news/archive.html'});
navButton("news_mc", "news", "../news/index.html",
newsSubNav_array);

var tutorialsSubNav_array:Array = new Array();
tutorialsSubNav_array.push({instance:'flash_mc',
txt:'flash', href:'../tutorials/flash.html'});
tutorialsSubNav_array.push({instance:'coldfusion_mc',
txt:'coldfusion', href:'../tutorials/coldfusion.html'});
tutorialsSubNav_array.push({instance:'studio_mc',
txt:'studio', href:'../tutorials/studio.html'});
tutorialsSubNav_array.push({instance:'other_mc',
txt:'other', href:'../tutorials/other.html'});
navButton("tutorials_mc", "tutorials",
"../tutorials/index.html", tutorialsSubNav_array);
```

You can change the navigation to fit the framework of your existing site. The previous code creates three main links, and the last two have different subnavigation.

The first line of code creates a home button, which assigns an instance name of home_mc, a label of home, and redirects the user's browser to the home folder within the site's root.

You can add or remove buttons and subnavigation at this point by modifying this portion of the ActionScript.

The next block of code defines an array named newsSubNav_array, which contains an array of objects representing the subnavigation for the current menu item. There are two subnavigation links: current and archive, which pass as a parameter to the navButton() function.

An *argument* is a variable (value) that you pass into a function. The value is then used within the function.

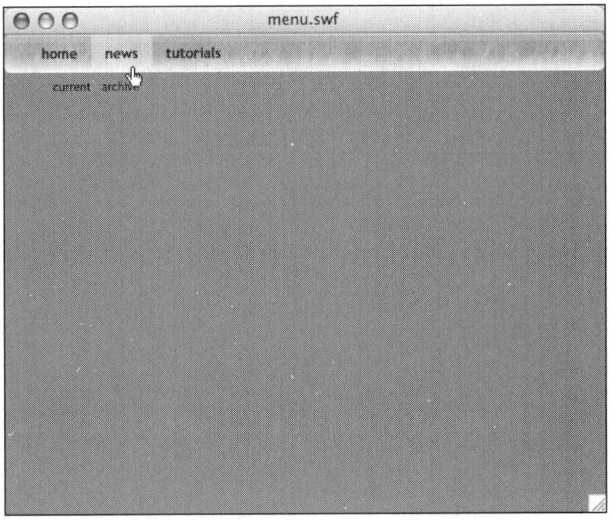

The final block of code defines another array of subnavigation for the tutorials movie clip button. This time there are four subnavigation links: *flash, coldfusion, studio,* and *other.* Each subnavigation link has its own instance name, text label, and target URL, and you pass the array to the to the navButton() function as an argument.

2. Now that you have added some navigation links to the Flash document, it is time to test the code. Select Control > Test Movie to view the file in the test environment and see if you require any modifications.

For information about modifications, see the "Moving On" section at the end of this chapter. If you are happy with the results, move on to the final two exercises in this chapter.

FIGURE 9.14

The menu is complete, and almost ready to add to a website.

Uploading and Constructing the Site

This menu currently targets a hybrid website, so in this final section you create HTML pages to embed the SWF menu in, and each of the pages that the menu targets. You can test this website on your hard drive, or you can upload everything to a server to test it online. There are a few changes you need to make to the SWF file before you place it in an HTML page, though. And then you need to publish the SWF file and create the HTML pages to place it on. The following two exercises step you through this process.

Exercise 8: Modifying and publishing the SWF file

The SWF file is not ready to embed in an HTML page. First, you need to resize the SWF file and publish the file.

1. Open the Property inspector, and change the height of the document. Change the height from 400 px to 55 px to match the height of the menu (with the subnavigation) so it fits nicely on an HTML page. Otherwise, there would be way too much room between the bottom of the menu and the beginning of the HTML content.

   After you finish, select File > Publish Preview > HTML to check the SWF file in a browser to make sure that the height of the SWF file does not cut off the subnavigation.

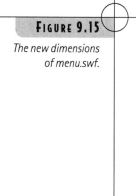

FIGURE 9.15

The new dimensions of menu.swf.

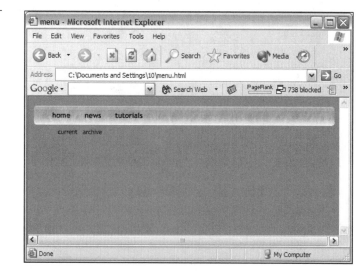

2. Select File > Publish settings to open the Publish Settings window. On the Formats tab, make sure that Flash (.swf) and HTML (.html) are both selected from the list file types that you can publish. You need the HTML file so you can copy and paste the code that you use to embed the SWF file in a web page.

3. Click Publish to publish the SWF and HTML document to the same folder where you saved the FLA file. Remember this location because you will need these files in the following exercise.

4. Save the changes you made to the FLA file, and close Flash. You're now finished building Flash content, and will only continue on with the HTML page in the next exercise.

If you have problems linking to pages on your website, you need to modify some ActionScript in menu.fla. The code that links the SWF file to HTML pages is in Exercise 7. You need to change the target URL arguments to match the URLs on your website.

Exercise 9: Building and organizing the site

Now the SWF file is resized and ready for a website. In this exercise you will see how to build a simple HTML template that you can use to quickly build a website and easily add new HTML pages as the site grows.

1. Create a new HTML document using an HTML editor (such as Dreamweaver or HomeSite) or text editor (such as Notepad or TextEdit). Erase any code that generates by the HTML editor and type the following text:

```
<!DOCTYPE HTML PUBLIC "-//W3C//DTD HTML 4.01
Transitional//EN">

<html>
<head>
  <title>My Site ¦ Home</title>
  <link rel="STYLESHEET" type="text/css"
href="../site.css">
</head>

<body>

<div id="content">
<div id="logo">[My Site]</div>

<h1>Home</h1>
<div id="breadcrumbs"><a
href="../home/index.html">home</a></div>

<p>[content]</p>
```

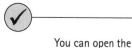

You can open the index.html file inside 09/complete/site/home on the CD-ROM to find this code to copy and paste.

```
<div id="footer"><a href="../home/index.html">home</a> |
<a href="../news/index.html">news</a> | <a
href="../tutorials/index.html">tutorials</a></div>
</div>

</body>
</html>
```

The previous code is a basic layout that you can use for the hybrid website. Instead of relying on tables to position the elements, the code uses a linked style sheet that controls how much borders and padding to use in order to position the content that you add.

2. Navigate to the folder where you saved the menu.fla in the first exercise. Create a new subfolder inside this director named site, to store your HTML files to be uploaded to your web server. Create four more subfolders inside the site folder. Name these new folders **home**, **news**, **tutorials**, and **images**.

   Save the HTML document you created in step 1 inside the home folder with the filename **index.html**.

3. The site.css file for this website is a Cascading Style Sheet (CSS) file that defines the fonts, colors, and image that you use for the HTML background. Rather than define these styles directly within your HTML files, you can define them in an external style sheet so that you can change colors or font sizes in a single place and have the changes updated immediately throughout the entire site.

   Copy the finished site.css file from the 09/complete/site folder on the CD-ROM to the site folder on your hard drive.

Change the color values, font sizes, and so forth inside this file to customize your website. Remember that the background color should still match the background color of your SWF file.

4. Save the bg.gif image from the 09/complete/site/images folder from the CD-ROM onto your hard drive into the images folder (which is inside the site folder on your hard drive). You use this image as a page background along with a solid background color.

5. Open the menu.html file you created in step 3 of Exercise 8. Copy all the text between the opening <body> and closing </body> tags. Switch to your index.html document and paste

the HTML code above the <h1> tag. The HTML code should now look similar to the following snippet:

```
<!DOCTYPE HTML PUBLIC "-//W3C//DTD HTML 4.01
Transitional//EN">

<html>
<head>
  <title>My Site ¦ Home</title>
  <link rel="STYLESHEET" type="text/css"
href="../site.css">
</head>

<body>

<div id="content">
<div id="logo">[My Site]</div>

<!-url's used in the movie->
<!-text used in the movie-->
<object classid="clsid:d27cdb6e-ae6d-11cf-96b8-
444553540000"
codebase="http://fpdownload.macromedia.com/pub/shockwave
/cabs/flash/swflash.cab#version=7,0,0,0" width="515"
height="55" id="menu" align="middle">
<param name="allowScriptAccess" value="sameDomain" />
<param name="movie" value="menu.swf" />
<param name="quality" value="high" />
<param name="bgcolor" value="#919191" />
<embed src="menu.swf" quality="high" bgcolor="#919191"
width="515" height="55" name="menu" align="middle"
allowScriptAccess="sameDomain" type="application/x-
shockwave-flash"
pluginspage="http://www.macromedia.com/go/getflashplayer
" />
</object>

<h1>Home</h1>
<div id="breadcrumbs"><a
href="../home/index.html">home</a></div>
```

Notice that the code you just copied from the menu.html document seems to duplicate a lot of code. You define the width, height, Stage background colors, quality, and movie src twice because of browser differences that exist between Microsoft's Internet Explorer (IE) and Netscape/Mozilla's rendering of HTML tags. Therefore, if you change a value, it is important that that you change it in for both browsers so the site renders the same in IE and Netscape/Mozilla browsers. Because the hybrid site organizes content into different folders, you need to modify the HTML code that Flash generates so the HTML files will look for the Flash menu SWF file in the root folder of the site instead of inside every folder in the site.

Locate both the `param` tag and `embed` tag in the previous snippet of code, and change the filename from menu.swf to the following:

```
../menu.swf
```

6. Copy menu.swf (created in the previous exercise) and paste it into the site folder on your hard drive (where you saved the site.css file you created in step 2).

7. At this point, you can save the changes you made to index.html, and view the site; however, before you do this you should add a bit of content to the HTML page. Locate the lorum.txt text file in the 09/complete/site folder on the CD-ROM, and copy the contents to the clipboard. Locate the following code in the index.html document on your hard drive:

```
<p>[content]</p>
```

Replace `[content]` with the text you copied from the lorum.txt text file on the CD-ROM.

8. Save the current HTML document and view the HTML page "in a web browser. At this point, you should be able to view the main and subnavigation in the Flash document embedded in the HTML page, although clicking any of the buttons will cause your web browser to display an error message because the remaining HTML pages aren't built yet.

9. You can quickly build the remaining pages in the HTML site by saving a copy of index.html file in both the news and tutorials folders. When you change the value of the `<title>` tag, you modify the `<h1>` tag and breadcrumbs, and you can complete the site in minutes.

You can also refer to the finished site on the CD-ROM or copy the HTML files from the CD-ROM to your hard drive. Because the HTML files all share a similar directory structure, you can use the same menu.swf file and CSS file without doing too much coding. If your site uses lots of folders and subfolders, you need to plan your site carefully to make sure that each page knows how to find the menu and style sheet. The easiest way to build sites with complex nested directory structures is to change from relative to absolute addressing. Instead of referring to the home page as `../home/index.html`, you could use `/home/index.html`. Although this works fine for the Internet if your home folder is in the root of your website, it doesn't always work very well if you view the HTML files locally on your computer (instead of on a web server). See the following sidebar for more information.

10. After you build each of the HTML pages, upload the files and folders to your web server. Launch your FTP program and upload each of the files and folders located within the site folder on your local computer. Then test the files again in your web browser.

Make sure that each of the links in the menu works properly with the website.

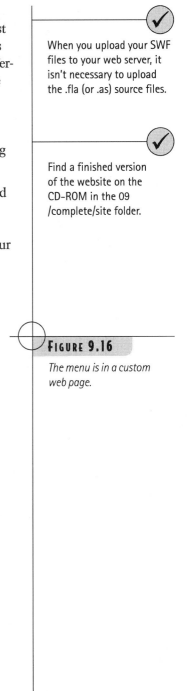

When you upload your SWF files to your web server, it isn't necessary to upload the .fla (or .as) source files.

Find a finished version of the website on the CD-ROM in the 09 /complete/site folder.

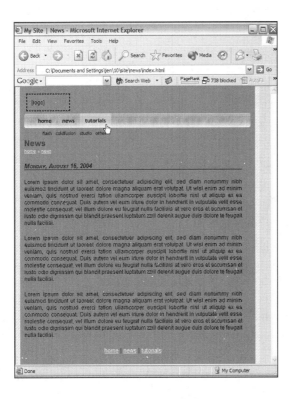

FIGURE 9.16

The menu is in a custom web page.

►► ABSOLUTE AND RELATIVE ADDRESSING

Relative addressing always refers to other files relative from the location of the current file. For example, if you are on a page called index.html and want to refer to a file in the same directory, you could refer to the file as filename.html. If the file is in a subdirectory of the current folder, then you could set the path to foldername/filename.html. Or, if the target file is in a parent directory (one level up) of the current file, you need to use two periods (..) to refer to the parent directory. Then your file path would be ../index.html.

You could also use a preceding backslash (/) to denote the root of your website. For example, if the URL to a webpage is http://www.yoursite.com/foldername/filename.html, you could refer to the filename.html file as /foldername/filename.html throughout your site and not have to worry about having to use syntax such as ../../foldername/filename.html. The primary drawback of using backslash notation is that you might be unable to test files in the Flash authoring environment because it interprets the backslash as the root folder of your hard drive (such as C:\).

If you use absolute addressing, all of your URLs would look like http://www.yoursite.com/foldername/filename.html which can be tedious to type every time. However, absolute referencing enables you to always know exactly how to refer to files regardless of how deeply they are nested within the website. The other benefit of using this method is that you can test the files directly within the Flash authoring environment without any problems.

MOVING ON

In about 74 lines of code, you built a dynamic menu system that allows you to easily add and remove navigation links. With minimal work, you could make this code more portable by putting the functions into an external file and including the file using the #include compiler directive. Using this method allows you to easily copy and paste the external ActionScript file and reuse the menu in a different Flash project.

To make this modification, you need to cut both the navButton() and drawRectangle() functions from the Flash document and create a new ActionScript (.as) file using either Flash MX Professional 2004 or a text editor. Paste the ActionScript code you just cut from the menu.fla document into the .as file, and save the ActionScript file as **menu.as** in the same folder as the menu.fla file. Open the menu.fla file and add the following line of code to the very beginning of the Actions panel:

```
#include "menu.as"
```

When you republish the menu.fla document, the contents of the menu.as file automatically include (insert) into the menu.swf file.

If your movie uses a dark background color, it might be necessary to modify the background colors that you pass to the drawBackground() function. Go back to Exercises 4 and 6 and change the hex value in these lines of ActionScript:

```
drawRectangle(box_mc, 0xFFFFFF, 40, txtWidth, txtHeight);
```
and
```
drawRectangle(this, 0xDFDFDF, 40, btnWidth, btnHeight);
```

Make sure that there is sufficient contrast between the color you select and the background color of your SWF file.

If all your text links don't fit on the Stage, you might need to select a smaller font for the label_txt text fields in the main or subnavigation movie clips in the Library. All you need to do is select the text field in question and change the text size in the Property inspector.

You could also improve the menu system by placing a custom image instead of the bg.png image you imported. Because both the rectangles drawn using the drawRectangle() function set their alpha level to 40%, any image placed behind the menu is still visible when the cursor is over a menu button.

The #include compiler directive in Flash isn't terminated by a semicolon (;).

FIGURE 9.17

Place a different image behind the menu bar in the SWF file. You might need to change the background color of your SWF file and website as well.

Another design modification you can make to the menu system is to modify the drawRectangle() function and incorporate rounded corners. Using the curveTo() method, you can specify a corner radius, along with the width and height of the rectangle to give the layout a bit more polished look. You can see a brief tutorial on the companion website (www.FLAnimation.com) on how to create rounded rectangles using the Flash drawing API. This small change could make an impact on the overall look of your project.

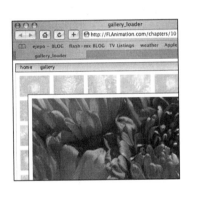

What you learn

- ► How to navigate photographs
- ► About loading content into a SWF
- ► About the MovieClipLoader class
- ► About loading thumbnails and full-sized images
- ► How to create a progress bar
- ► How to put the gallery online

Lesson Files

Start:

None

Finish:

10/complete/gallery.fla

10/complete/gallery.swf

10/complete/gallery_loader.fla

10/complete/gallery_loader.swf

10/complete/gallery_loader.html

10/complete/images

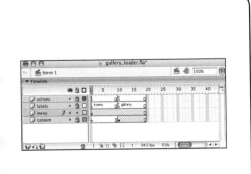

10

CREATING A GALLERY

AN IMAGE GALLERY IS a way to display a series of images, pictures, drawings or other graphics (such as an art portfolio) on your web site. Most galleries consist of a number of thumbnails, which are small photos, that provide a miniature preview for each image in the gallery. When the user clicks one of the thumbnails, a large version of that photo appears. Galleries are typically interactive applications, and when you create one it requires some forethought on how you want to navigate through series of photos, and display small and large versions of an image.

Galleries are common on the web, particularly with the growth of the digital camera industry and proliferation of people logging onto the web and wanting to share their photos. For example, you might want to display personal pictures of your wedding, a new baby, or your cats. Image galleries are important for some businesses too, such as photographers, artists, and models. You might even have a business owner with a shopping cart application on their web site, who wants to display a gallery of their products in conjunction with the cart application. Image galleries can be informal, personal applications (such as 50 images of your cat playing with a toy mouse), or dynamic, professional application displaying art from your latest modern exhibition.

There are many different ways to display digital photos: in an HTML page, by way of email, in a Word document, and of course—Flash. You can use many kinds of animation, sound, and effects to display the images. There are examples of Flash galleries online, and you can find links to some of these examples at the end of this chapter.

Creating and maintaining a photo gallery does not have to be difficult, which is shown in this chapter's project. As long as you plan the project before you start, and organize your application logically, putting together the gallery and updating it with new photographs is easy.

Website: www.FLAnimation.com/chapters/10

Navigating Content

In earlier chapters, you created websites with simple navigation systems that let you move between pages on a site. In Project 8, you create a simple site that had a few buttons to navigate between each page. You used transitions to create interest and fluidity between different areas of the website. Even more important than visual interest is whether or not your website is intuitive. If users cannot find your content, the message or advertisement isn't successful. You must communicate the purpose of your site to the user to create a successful website.

There are several reasons you might choose to use Macromedia Flash for your gallery instead of HTML. If you want to add multimedia elements to your gallery to make it into more of an "experience," Flash makes it easy. For example, you can easily add sound and video to the gallery—more so than with HTML. Additionally, you don't need to worry about your users having the correct plug-ins installed to play back these elements (such as requiring QuickTime or Windows Media Player) because most visitors have Flash Player installed. Not requiring the use of several different plug-ins makes the user experience ideal.

Flash also lets you customize the way you handle multimedia—from user control to the media control buttons. If you use Flash, you can completely control the look of your site. You can add special effects (such as fades, transitions, and brightness levels) to the content of your gallery. For example, you wouldn't be able to add a mask, a brightness tween, or a progress bar to your photos in an HTML gallery. Therefore, Flash lets you have a greater amount of creative control over the effects, navigation, and look of the gallery. What's even more impressive is how easy it is to create a dynamic gallery that loads each photo in when the user requests it, as opposed to loading the entire page of photos at the same time.

In the final two projects (Project 9 and this chapter's project), you create more-involved navigational systems while adding effects and animation to improve usability. In this chapter, you need to organize, control, and navigate content as opposed to menu options—a series of photos—into a system that users can easily navigate.

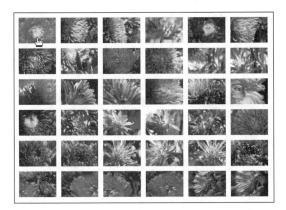

Users intuitively know to click a thumbnail to enlarge a photo. This is knowledge you can assume users have; for example, clicking a menu option to reveal a submenu (as in Chapter 9).

When you plan a gallery, you should make considerations about how you structure it. You might need to consider how many thumbnails you show on a single page, and how to organize those thumbnails. Will users need to scroll through them, or will you arrange them in a grid format? For example, experienced Flash users might randomly scatter photos over the Stage and let users move them around, or they might create a custom scrollbar on the Stage where users can move the scroll bar horizontally to reveal photos from left to right.

FIGURE 10.2

A horizontal scroller reveals thumbnails that dynamically load in at runtime.

You should plan any complex content systems before you start to develop your gallery, much like the Visio flow chart planning demonstrated in Chapter 9. Refer to that chapter if necessary to read more about planning and flow charts. If you have a complex navigational system, this is particularly important.

Loading and progress bars

In this chapter, you create progress bars for your website. You used progress bars in earlier chapters, but in this chapter you create one that loads the full-sized JPEG image, and then a second progress bar that loads the entire gallery. The progress bars use the MovieClip-Loader class to handle loading content into a SWF file. This provides you with better control over the content that you load, and the class helps you display accurate progress of the loading process.

▶ ▶ THE ProgressBar COMPONENT

The ProgressBar component, part of the V2 components that install with Macromedia Flash MX 2004, allows you to display what percentage of the dynamically loaded content has already been loaded into Flash. This lets you show users how far along they are in the loading process and gives them a rough estimate of how long they might need to wait for the content to load. The ProgressBar component consists of two main sections: a bar that grows to display how much of the content has loaded so far and a label that shows the user exactly what percentage of the content has loaded. You can customize each of these sections so they use different colors and bar styles, or display the number of bytes loaded and total bytes of the content being loaded.

To use the ProgressBar component, you can drag it from the Component panel onto the Stage, and set the required parameters using the Property inspector or the Component inspector. For example, drag a copy of the ProgressBar and Loader components onto the Stage. Give the ProgressBar component an instance name of **image_pb** and the Loader component an instance name of **image_ldr**. Click the image_ldr instance and use the Property inspector to set the contentPath property to an image either on your local computer or your web server. Select the image_pb instance, and use the Property inspector to set the mode property to **polled** and the source property to the instance name of your Loader component (image_ldr). Select Control > Test Movie to test the SWF file in the test environment. Your image loads into the Loader component and the ProgressBar component displays the image's loading progress.

Project 10: Building a Dynamic Photo Gallery

This project walks you through the process of building a dynamic photo gallery that allows you to load both thumbnails and full images at runtime without having to add a lot of images to your Library. This means that your visitors can load the gallery quickly, on any number of different connections, and navigate through the gallery without waiting a long time for it to load.

Before you start, copy all the finished files and images from the CD-ROM (10/complete/) to your hard drive, and open gallery.fla in the authoring environment. Glance over the finished code for the document (frame 1 of the actions layer), and try testing the file in a browser window (F12). After you are familiar with the intended result, start with Exercise 1.

Exercise 1: Using the MovieClipLoader class

You set up a new Flash document for the image gallery project in this exercise. You add ActionScript that positions thumbnail images in the image gallery, and you use MovieClipLoader to handle loading images into the SWF file. You will also use the Drawing API to draw a rectangle around the images.

1. Create a new Flash document, and rename Layer 1 to **actions**. Lock the layer to prevent accidentally adding any assets to this layer. Save this file to your hard drive as **gallery.fla**.

2. Select frame 1 of the actions layer and open the Actions panel. Add the following ActionScript code to the Script pane:

    ```
    var padding:Number = 10;
    var maxThumbWidth:Number = 75;
    var maxThumbHeight:Number = 50;
    _global.xPos = padding;
    _global.yPos = padding;
    _global.numImages = 0;
    ```

    You use this code to position each of the thumbnail images added later in Exercise 2. The first variable, `padding`, dictates how far you indent the thumbnails from the top and left edges of the Stage, and how many pixels you add between images.

Leave the FLA file at the default dimensions of 550 px (width) by 400 px (height), with a white background. If you change the default settings, change your FLA file to match these dimensions and background color.

To "invoke" simply means that the code will be called when an event happens. You see this term used in discussions about events, listeners, or functions.

The next two variables, `maxThumbWidth` and `maxThumbHeight`, tell the SWF file the dimensions of the thumbnails that you dynamically load. This helps you determine how high each row of images needs to be so that images won't overlap. The next two variables are global variables that will be referred to throughout the ActionScript to position the various thumbnail images on the Stage. The final variable listed in the previous snippet, `_global.numImages`, is used as a counter that tracks how many thumbnail images you place on the Stage.

3. Select frame 1 of the actions layer. Type the following code below the existing ActionScript in the Actions panel:

```
var thumbListener:Object = new Object();
thumbListener.onLoadInit = function(target_mc:MovieClip) {

};
var thumb_mcl:MovieClipLoader = new MovieClipLoader();
thumb_mcl.addListener(thumbListener);
```

This code begins by defining a new object, which you use to intercept events that generate by the `MovieClipLoader` event handlers. The `thumbListener` object listens for a single event listener: `onLoadInit`. Because this event triggers after the target movie clip finishes loading, and already been initialized, you can access the target movie clip's methods and properties (such as `_width`, `_height` and `_yscale`).

4. Modify the code in the `onLoadInit` listener function (from step 3), and add the following code that's in bold face.

```
thumbListener.onLoadInit = function(target_mc:MovieClip) {
  var boxWidth:Number = target_mc._width;
  var boxHeight:Number = target_mc._height;
  new mx.transitions.Tween(target_mc, "_yscale",
mx.transitions.easing.Elastic.easeOut, 0, 100, 1, true);
};
```

Because the `onLoadInit` listener invokes *after* the image completely loads and initializes, you can access the movie clip's methods and properties and position the movie clip on the Stage. The code begins by creating two local variables, `boxWidth` and `boxHeight`, which you use in the next step to draw a rectangle the same size as the loaded image. Then you use the Tween class to animate the target movie clip on the Stage. The tween stretches the target movie clip's `_yscale` property from 0% to 100%, which causes the thumbnails to look like they stretch downward into place.

5. In frame 1 of the actions layer, add the following code after the snippet from the previous step:

```
target_mc.createEmptyMovieClip("box_mc",
target_mc.getNextHighestDepth());
target_mc.box_mc._visible = false;
with (target_mc.box_mc) {
  beginFill(0xFFFFFF, 30);
  moveTo(0, 0);
  lineTo(boxWidth, 0);
  lineTo(boxWidth, boxHeight);
  lineTo(0, boxHeight);
  lineTo(0, 0);
  endFill();
}
target_mc.onRollOver = function() {
  target_mc.box_mc._visible = true;
};
target_mc.onRollOut = function() {
  target_mc.box_mc._visible = false;
};
target_mc.onRelease = function() {
  full_mc1.loadClip(this._parent.fullImg_str,
full_mc.image_mc);
};
```

For more information on using the Tween class, see Project 9 in Chapter 9. Several sections of Project 9 explain how to use the class in more detail.

The previous code begins by creating an empty movie clip *within* the target thumbnail movie clip. You use Flash's drawing methods inside this new movie clip to draw a semitransparent rectangle over the thumbnail. The rectangle is transparent by default and appears only when the mouse hovers over the thumbnail. This makes the thumbnail appear to have a cover overlay, as shown in the following figure (you can change the color value in the previous ActionScript).

FIGURE 10.3

This ActionScript adds an overlay that appears when users roll over an image.

▶ ▶ USING MovieClipLoader

The MovieClipLoader class allows you to dynamically load SWF or JPEG images into your Flash documents, and also lets you execute blocks of code when you encounter certain events. For example, in this exercise, you create a listener object for the thumbnail movie clip Loader instance. The MovieClipLoader class has the following events:

onLoadStart: Invokes when the specified image begins to load.

onLoadProgress: Continually invokes while the image downloads until the onLoadComplete event triggers.

onLoadComplete: Invokes after the image completely downloads to the users local computer, but before the image initializes. Because the image hasn't initialized yet, you are unable to access the target movie clip's methods or properties at this point.

onLoadInit: Invokes after the specified image has downloaded and been initialized. After this event invokes, you can determine the target movie clip's width and height or go to a different frame using the gotoAndPlay or gotoAndStop methods.

onLoadError: Invokes when the specified image cannot load. If the MovieClipLoader instance does not load the specified image, this is the only event that triggers.

For more information on using the with keyword, see Project 9 in Chapter 9.

After you create the new movie clip using the createEmptyMovieClip() method, you set the new movie clip's _visible property to false so the box is initially invisible. Next, you dynamically draw the rectangle using the MovieClip class' beginFill(), moveTo(), and lineTo() methods. You set the rectangle's fill color to white (0xFFFFFF) and its alpha level is set to 30% transparent.

You then create three event handler functions for the following events: onRollOver, onRollOut and onRelease. The onRollOver and onRollOut event handlers are responsible for toggling the visibility of the box_mc movie clip, which is the 30% visible white rectangle. This means that when the user hovers her mouse cursor over a thumbnail image, the semitransparent white box becomes visible. When a cursor moves off of the thumbnail, the code hides the semi-transparent fill.

The final event handler, `onRelease`, is a bit more complex. When you click the thumbnail image, it causes the full image to display on the Stage using a separate movie clip loader. You create the `full_mcl` movie clip loader instance and the `full_mc` movie clip in Exercise 5 in this chapter.

LOADING AND DISPLAYING IMAGES

The following exercises create the thumbnails for the gallery. This is where you space and arrange the movie clips that will contain each thumbnail, define which images you want to load, and load the images into the thumbnail containers. This is typically where designers like to exhibit the most creativity in the way the photo gallery appears and functions. The arrangement of thumbnails can vary greatly, and the way users can manipulate them to view the pictures that are available to view is determined by the way you build your application at this stage.

After you figure out how to display thumbnails on the Stage, you need to create a function to display the full-size image. The full-size image needs to appear in a new movie clip container, which you use to load the full-sized image from the server. Handling the way images load is important in the application because you need an efficient way to handle loading so users don't have to sit through a lengthy loading process before seeing the gallery. Loading JPEG thumbnails and full-sized images from the server after the SWF file initially loads mean that users never have to wait long to see content.

Exercise 2: Loading thumbnail images

In this exercise, you add a custom function that creates each thumb-nail movie clip and loads each thumbnail image using the `thumb_mcl` movie clip loader instance. The ActionScript in this exercise also posi-tions each of the thumbnail images on the Stage, based on several of the global variables you define in Exercise 1. In this exercise, you hard code the images that appear within the gallery. However, you can also modify the exercise so you get the images from an external source, such as an XML file or text file that loads into the SWF.

1. Select frame 1 of the actions layer. Enter the following Action-Script below all of the existing code that's currently in the Actions panel.

```
function image(thumbSrc_str:String,
fullSrc_str:String):Void {
  var holder_mc:MovieClip =
this.createEmptyMovieClip("thumb"+_global.numImages+"_mc
", this.getNextHighestDepth());
}
```

This previous code defines a function named `image()` that takes two parameters: the URL to a thumbnail and the full image. The function starts by creating a blank movie clip on the Stage for each thumbnail image.

Notice that you assign the new movie clip a dynamic instance name, which is based on the current value of the `_global.numImages` variable. You define this variable in the first exercise of this chapter, and you gave it an initial value of `0`. Doing so causes the first movie clip to be named `thumb0_mc`. The global variable increments later in the image function, and you end up naming future movie clips `thumb1_mc`, `thumb2_mc`, and so on.

2. Add the following code to the `image()` function you added in step 1. Place this ActionScript inside the final closing curly brace.

```
if ((_global.xPos+maxThumbWidth)>Stage.width) {
  _global.xPos = padding;
  _global.yPos += maxThumbHeight+padding;
}
holder_mc._x = _global.xPos;
holder_mc._y = _global.yPos;
holder_mc.fullImg_str = fullSrc_str;
holder_mc.createEmptyMovieClip("image_mc",
holder_mc_mc.getNextHighestDepth());
thumb_mcl.loadClip(thumbSrc_str, holder_mc.image_mc);
_global.numImages++;
_global.xPos += maxThumbWidth+padding;
```

The previous snippet checks whether the current thumbnail image fits in the existing row of images, or if the image exceeds the Stage's width. If the current value of _global.xPos plus the maximum thumbnail width is greater than the Stage width, the _global.xPos variable resets to its initial value, and the value of _global.yPos increments by the maximum thumbnail height plus the amount you specify in the padding variable. This ensures that each photo fits properly on the Stage and overlaps the right edge of the Stage.

The next couple lines of code (starting with holder_mc._x) set the _x and _y properties for the holder_mc movie clip. Next, you create a new variable named fullImg_str in the holder_mc movie clip that contains the value of the fullSrc_str variable, which was passed as a parameter to the image function. This variable contains the URL to the full-sized image for the current thumbnail.

You then create a nested movie clip named image_mc within the holder_mc movie clip (the line starting with holder_mc. createEmptyMovieClip). You use this movie clip to display the thumbnail image. If you didn't use a nested movie clip and load the thumbnail image directly into the holder_mc movie clip, the fullImg_str variable disappears as soon as the image finishes loading in. The next line of code uses the thumb_mcl movie clip loader instance to load the specified thumbnail image into the nested movie clip, holder_mc.image_mc. After the thumbnail image completely loads and initializes, the onLoadInit event listener (created in Exercise 1) triggers.

The last two lines in the previous snippet are responsible for incrementing the _global.numImages variable and adjusting the value of _global.xPos by incrementing the variable's current value by the maximum thumb width and amount of padding.

3. Now that the image function is complete, you can call the function to specify which images load into the dynamic gallery. Add the following snippet of code at the very end

of the ActionScript on frame 1 of the actions layer to specify a few images to load.

```
image("images/t_1.jpg", "images/f_1.jpg");
image("images/t_2.jpg", "images/f_2.jpg");
image("images/t_3.jpg", "images/f_3.jpg");
image("images/t_4.jpg", "images/f_4.jpg");
image("images/t_5.jpg", "images/f_5.jpg");
image("images/t_6.jpg", "images/f_6.jpg");
image("images/t_7.jpg", "images/f_7.jpg");
image("images/t_8.jpg", "images/f_8.jpg");
image("images/t_9.jpg", "images/f_9.jpg");
image("images/t_10.jpg", "images/f_10.jpg");
```

The previous snippet calls the image function 10 times, and defines thumbnail and full images for each call to the function.

4. Before you can test this application, you need to make sure that you copy the images for this example from the CD-ROM onto your hard drive. Create a new folder named **images** in the *same* folder as the current FLA file (gallery.fla). Copy the 10 thumbnail and 10 full images from the CD and paste them into the new images folder on your hard drive.

FIGURE 10.4

File structure for the images and project files.

▶ ▶ LOADING SEQUENTIALLY NAMED IMAGES

Because you name the filenames sequentially, you can easily modify the previous code snippet to use a `for` loop to import the images, instead of defining each one manually. For example, you can swap the code in step 3 with the following code instead.

```
for (var i = 1; i<=10; i++) {
  image("images/t_"+i+".jpg", "images/f_"+i+".jpg");
}
```

You will find this code in the FLA file (except for 36 images instead of 10). For more information on loops and looping, refer to Chapter 7.

5. At this point, you can test your dynamic image gallery. Remember that the code isn't complete yet, and you cannot view the full-sized images. Select File > Publish Preview > Default HTML (or press F12) to launch your default web browser and view the gallery project.

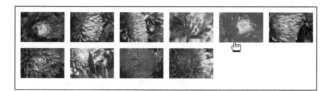

FIGURE 10.5

Testing the thumbnail part of the gallery project.

Each image should display after a small delay. The images should tween downward with a slight elastic effect (the Tween class effect) when they appear. When you move your mouse over a thumbnail image, it should also display the semitransparent white rectangle, which disappears when you move the mouse cursor off of the image.

6. Return to the Flash authoring environment, and save the changes you made to your file.

Exercise 3: Displaying full images

With the hardest part of the gallery already written, the only modules left for you to build are for displaying the full-sized image and adding a preloader (progress bar) effect to display the loading progress for full-sized images.

1. Select frame 1 of the actions layer. Add the following code to the Actions panel below the existing code.

```
this.createEmptyMovieClip("full_mc",
this.getNextHighestDepth());
full_mc._visible = false;
```

The code begins by creating a new movie clip on the Stage named full_mc. You use the full_mc movie clip to hold a custom progress bar that you create in the next exercise. The movie clip also holds a nested movie clip where you eventually load the full-sized image. The next line of code sets the new movie clip's _visible property to false, so it isn't initially visible within your Flash movie.

See Chapter 9 for more information about with.

2. Add the following code below the ActionScript added in the previous step.

```
with (full_mc) {
  beginFill(0xFFFFFF, 80);
  moveTo(0, 0);
  lineTo(Stage.width, 0);
  lineTo(Stage.width, Stage.height);
  lineTo(0, Stage.height);
  lineTo(0, 0);
  endFill();
}
```

This code again uses Flash's drawing methods to draw a rectangle on the Stage that will be 80 percent visible and cover the entire width and height of the Stage. This movie clip will become visible when the full-sized image is displayed so that the thumbnails become faded out and the full image stands out a bit better.

Exercise 4: Creating a progress bar

Because the full-sized images are more than a few kilobytes (KB) in size, they can take a bit longer to load; therefore, it is a good idea to add a progress bar so users know that something is happening. In this exercise, you create a progress bar using a rectangle that you scale according to the percentage of the image that has loaded into the SWF file.

1. Click Insert Layer to create a new layer. Rename the layer **content** and drag it beneath the actions layer. Using the Rectangle tool, select any stroke (outline) and fill color, set the stroke height to 4 pixels, and draw a rectangle approximately 300 pixels wide by 10 pixels high on the Stage.

2. Select the entire shape. Use the width and height text fields in the Property inspector to adjust the size of the rectangle on the Stage to the dimensions in step 1, if necessary. Select a stroke height of 1 pixel.

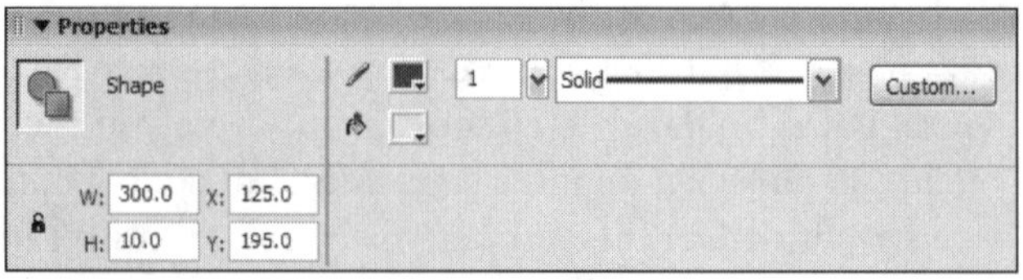

FIGURE 10.6

Adjust the size and stroke height of the rectangle.

3. Double-click the rectangle's stroke and press F8 to convert the stroke into a symbol. Select the Graphic behavior from the Convert to Symbol dialog box, and enter a symbol name of **stroke**. Click OK.

4. Click the rectangle's fill and press F8 to convert the fill shape into a symbol. In the Convert to Symbol dialog box, enter a symbol name of **bar** and choose the Movie Clip behavior. Click OK.

5. Using the Property inspector, select the bar movie clip on the Stage and type in an instance name of **bar_mc**.

6. Next you need to put the bar_mc movie clip behind the stroke graphic created earlier. With the bar_mc instance still selected on the Stage, choose Modify > Arrange > Send to Back. This command positions bar_mc below the stroke graphic.

7. Select both the stroke and fill and press the F8 key to convert the shape into a movie clip symbol. Give the movie clip a symbol name of **progressBar** and click the Advanced button if you aren't already in advanced mode. In the Linkage section of the dialog box, enable the Export for ActionScript check box and set the linkage identifier to **progressBar_mc**. Click OK.

8. Select the progressBar movie clip, and delete the rectangle from the Stage. The movie clip is added from the Library at runtime using ActionScript.

9. Select frame 1 of the actions layer, and add the following code in the Script pane.

```
full_mc.attachMovie("progressBar_mc", "pBar_mc",
full_mc.getNextHighestDepth());
full_mc.pBar_mc._x = Math.round((Stage.width-
full_mc.pBar_mc._width)/2);
full_mc.pBar_mc._y = Math.round((Stage.height-
full_mc.pBar_mc._height)/2);
full_mc.pBar_mc.bar_mc._xscale = 0;
full_mc.createEmptyMovieClip("image_mc",
full_mc.getNextHighestDepth());
```

This code attaches the progressBar movie clip from the Library in the full_mc movie clip instance and assigns an instance name of pBar_mc. The progress bar isn't visible by default because you set the full_mc movie clip's _visible property to false in an earlier exercise.

The next step is to center the progressBar instance horizontally on the Stage by subtracting the width of progressBar from the Stage's width and dividing by 2. By default, the Stage width for a Flash document is 550 pixels wide (which is what your FLA should be set to). If a progress bar movie clip is 300 pixels wide, you subtract 300 from 550, and divide the result by two (giving you 250/2, or 125 pixels from the left edge of the Stage) to center the progress bar.

Then the nested bar_mc movie clip's _xscale property is set to 0. The _xscale property controls the horizontal scaling of a movie clip or button. Because the _xscale property is 0, it will be zero percent of its original width. When you click on a thumbnail in the finished file, the full image loads and the bar_mc's _xscale property increases to 100% to display how much of the image loads.

The final line of code in the previous snippet creates a new movie clip in full_mc called image_mc, which you use to load the full-sized image.

Exercise 5: Using MovieClipListener for large images

In this exercise, you use a MovieClipLoader object to load the full-sized images into the full_mc.image_mc movie clip. This exercise also uses several listeners that are in the MovieClipLoader class to update the custom progress bar that you made in the previous exercise. Ultimately, the full image centers on the Stage and fades in using the Flash's Tween class. You are still working with gallery.fla in this exercise.

1. The first step to load the full-sized images is to write a listener object that handles the various events that throw when using the MovieClipLoader class. This step shows the code that's necessary for handling the onLoadStart listener.

   Select frame 1 of the actions layer and add the following code to the Actions panel below any existing ActionScript.

   ```
   var fullListener:Object = new Object();
   fullListener.onLoadStart = function(target_mc:MovieClip) {
     target_mc._parent._visible = true;
     target_mc._parent.pBar_mc.bar_mc._xscale = 0;
   };
   ```

The first line of code in this snippet creates the actual listener object, named fullListener. The remaining lines of code define an inline function that executes when the onLoadStart listener invokes. This listener has one optional parameter, which is the target movie clip for the MovieClipLoader instance.

The code in the onLoadStart event triggers when the image begins to load. This assumes that you can load the image into the SWF file; otherwise, the onLoadError listener triggers instead.

2. The next listener that you add to the fullListener object is the onLoadProgress listener. This listener triggers while the content loads into the target movie clip. Add the following code snippet *after* the ActionScript that you added in step 1:

```
fullListener.onLoadProgress =
function(target_mc:MovieClip, numBytesLoaded:Number,
numBytesTotal:Number) {
  target_mc._parent.pBar_mc.bar_mc._xscale =
Math.round(numBytesLoaded/numBytesTotal*100);
};
```

Like the onLoadStart listener, the onLoadProgress listener has a few optional parameters. The first optional parameter is the target movie clip that the JPEG image or SWF loads into (target_mc:MovieClip). Notice that you add :MovieClip to strict data type the parameter. This helps avoid errors because you can make sure that the target is actually a movie clip. You can make sure that *numerical* values return for the other two parameters, because you strict data type them with :Number.

The remaining two parameters are the number of bytes currently loaded (numBytesLoaded:Number) and total number of bytes (numBytesTotal:Number), respectively. By dividing the number of bytes loaded by the total number of bytes, you can calculate the percentage of the movie clip that has already been loaded into the target movie clip. For example, if you load a JPEG image that is 200 kilobytes (KB) total, and only 140 KB has loaded so far, you can calculate that only 70 percent of the file has loaded so far (140/200 = 0.7).

You call onLoadProgress multiple times during the loading process unless the image or SWF that you're loading has a small file size. Therefore, the progress bar appears to grow while the image loads.

In step 1, the _xscale property of the pBar_mc.bar_mc movie clip was set to 0. The onLoadProgress listener sets the same movie clip's _xscale property to the percentage that has already being loaded in. Therefore, you set the pBar_mc. bar_mc._xscale property to 70 wide (70%) so the user can see the current loading progress of the movie clip.

3. The next section of ActionScript is a bit longer than the previous two snippets. This code handles the onLoadInit listener, which invokes when the target movie clip completely loads and initializes and can then be manipulated on the Stage.

Select frame 1 of the actions layer, and add the following snippet to the bottom of the Actions panel:

```
fullListener.onLoadInit = function(target_mc:MovieClip) {
  var border:Number = 10;
  var fullWidth:Number = target_mc._width+border;
  var fullHeight:Number = target_mc._height+border;
  with (target_mc) {
   lineStyle(0, 0x000000, 100);
   beginFill(0xFFFFFF, 100);
   moveTo(-border, -border);
   lineTo(fullWidth, -border);
   lineTo(fullWidth, fullHeight);
   lineTo(-border, fullHeight);
   lineTo(-border, -border);
   endFill();
  }
  target_mc._x = Math.round((Stage.width-
target_mc._width)/2);
  target_mc._y = Math.round((Stage.height-
target_mc._height)/2);
  new mx.transitions.Tween(target_mc, "_alpha",
mx.transitions.easing.Strong.easeOut, 0, 100, 2, true);
  target_mc.onPress = function() {
   full_mcl.unloadClip(target_mc);
   target_mc._parent._visible = false;
  };
};
```

The previous code snippet is a bit lengthy, but you've seen most of the code before in previous snippets and even in other projects. The first line of code within the onLoadInit listener (var border:Number = 10;) sets a value for the border variable, which you use to control how much padding appears between the image that you load and the rectangle's stroke. You create two more values, `fullWidth` and `fullHeight`, to record how wide and high the image is, and also adds the value of the `border` variable.

Next, you use Flash's Drawing API to draw a rectangle on the Stage with a very thin black stroke and a white background. This decorative rectangle displays behind the loaded image to help it stand out a bit better from the rest of the Flash document.

FIGURE 10.7

A rectangle displays behind the image in the finished SWF file.

After the `with` statement, the `target_mc` movie clip centers horizontally and vertically on the Stage when you subtract the width of the loaded image from the width of the Stage, and divide by 2. This is similar to the code you use to center the progress bar in the previous exercise.

Using the code that starts with `new mx.transitions.Tween`, the target movie clip then fades in from 0% to 100% alpha over 2 seconds using the Tween class. Finally, you create the `onPress` event handler for the `target_mc` movie clip. This event handler unloads the image in `target_mc` using the `MovieClipLoader` class' `unloadClip()` method. Also, you set the target movie clip's parent movie clip's (`full_mc`) `_visible` property to `false`.

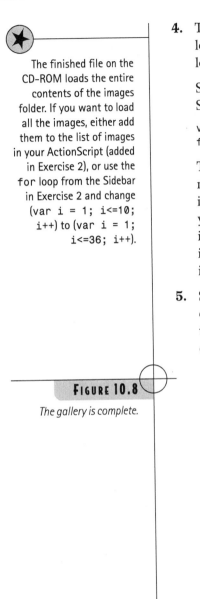

The finished file on the CD-ROM loads the entire contents of the images folder. If you want to load all the images, either add them to the list of images in your ActionScript (added in Exercise 2), or use the `for` loop from the Sidebar in Exercise 2 and change `(var i = 1; i<=10; i++)` to `(var i = 1; i<=36; i++)`.

FIGURE 10.8

The gallery is complete.

4. The only thing that remains is to create the second movie clip loader instance, and assign the listener object to the movie clip loader. This is shown in the following snippet.

   Select frame 1 of the actions layer and add the following Action-Script to the end of the existing code on the actions layer:

   ```
   var full_mcl:MovieClipLoader = new MovieClipLoader();
   full_mcl.addListener(fullListener);
   ```

   The first line of code creates a movie clip loader instance named `full_mcl`. You use `full_mcl` to handle loading full-sized images. The second line of code assigns the listener object that you created earlier, `fullListener`, to the movie clip loader instance `full_mcl`. Loading full-sized images happens earlier in the ActionScript code (when a user clicks a thumbnail image), as demonstrated earlier in this project.

5. Select Control > Test Movie to test the SWF file in the test environment. Click through the images, and make sure that the gallery works correctly and you are happy with the overlay color.

If you are happy with the results, return to the authoring environment. Select File > Publish and close the document.

Incorporating the Gallery into a Flash Site

Now that you have completed the gallery, it's useful to load it into another SWF file. If you have an existing site (for example, a portfolio website), you might want to add this gallery to that site. Or, you might have an established client site in which you want to add a couple of galleries of their products. Loading a gallery into an existing website is useful for many purposes. The gallery for this project is very lightweight because you load most of the content at runtime. However, you might have an elaborate design or more content in a gallery you design yourself (or if you modify this chapter's gallery). Therefore, you might need to add a progress bar so your visitors understand that there is content loading into the SWF file. This section shows you how to load the gallery into another SWF file and display a progress bar.

Exercise 6: Putting the gallery online

Adding your new dynamic photo gallery into a Flash site is quite easy. The first step is to create a new Flash document that serves as the main document that loads the external gallery.swf file. The remainder of this project deals with loading your dynamic image gallery into a separate Flash document.

1. Create a new Flash document in the same folder as gallery.fla. Save the new document as **gallery_loader.fla**.

2. Resize the Stage to 550 px (width) by 420 px (height). The new document is 20 pixels greater in height than the gallery.swf file that you load into it. You need the Stage dimensions to be different because in a Exercise 7 you'll create a couple of buttons to move the playhead at runtime in gallery_loader.swf.

3. Click Insert Layer three times until you have four layers total on the main Timeline. Rename the four layers (from top to bottom): **actions**, **labels**, **menu**, and **content**.

4. To fully test the gallery within a new Flash document you'll need at least two sections. Select frame 1 of the labels layer and type **home** into the Frame Label text field in the Property

inspector. Select frame 10 of the labels layer and press the F6 key to add a new keyframe. With frame 10 still selected, type **gallery** into the Frame Label text field in the Property inspector.

You cannot read the frame label for frame 10 on the Timeline because there isn't enough space on the Timeline's layer. Select frame 19 of the labels panel and press F5 to add some blank frames so you can see the label.

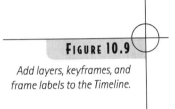

FIGURE 10.9

Add layers, keyframes, and frame labels to the Timeline.

5. On the actions layer of the Timeline, select frame 10 and press F6 to add a keyframe. Then select frame 19 and press F5 to insert a blank frame. In both frames 1 and 10, add the following code to the main timeline using the Actions panel:

```
stop();
```

This simple function stops the playhead on whatever frame you put it on. If you don't add a stop function to the main Timeline in the first frame, the playhead continues to advance along the Timeline, and it might cause your SWF file to loop. You add more code to these frames in later steps.

6. Select frame 19 in the menu layer and press F5 to extend the layer across Timeline. Therefore, you can see the menu on the Stage, no matter where they playhead is.

Exercise 7: Creating navigation buttons

In this exercise, you create two button symbol instances and add the ActionScript that moves the playhead within the SWF file when the user clicks each button.

1. Create a static text field using the Text tool on frame 1 of the menu layer.

   Enter the string **home** in the text field, change the font to Arial and set the font size to 12 pixels. Make sure that your text color is set to black (#000000) and select the bold button.

✓ It is always best to use frame labels instead of using frame numbers. You can target labels using ActionScript, which means that you don't have to target numbered frames that might change while you work on the FLA file.

✓ Depending on your computer system, it might be necessary to type text on the Stage and change the text type to static by using the Property inspector afterward.

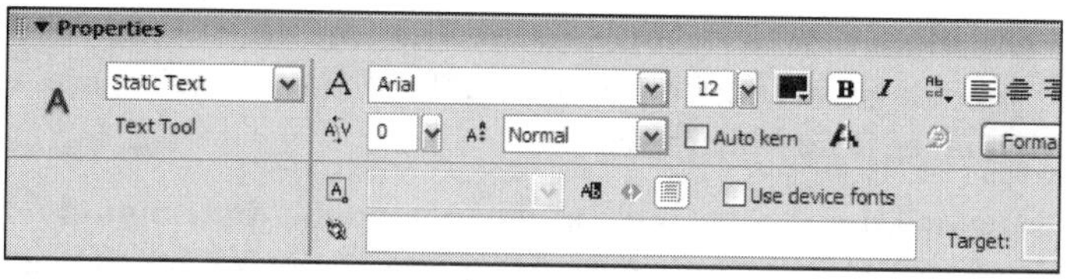

FIGURE 10.10

Create a static text field on the Stage before you convert it into a button.

2. Select the home button on the Stage and press F8 to convert the text field to a symbol. Set the behavior to Button and type in a symbol name of **home_btn**. Click OK.

3. Select the home_btn instance on the Stage and type an instance name of **home_btn** into the Property inspector.

4. If you try testing your Flash document in either the authoring environment or your default browser at this point, you'd notice that only the text itself is clickable and not the bounding box of the instance. Your button needs a hit area.

   Double-click the home_btn instance, and you see the four frames representing the Up, Over, Down, and Hit states for the button.

5. Position your mouse cursor in the Over frame and press F6 to create a new keyframe.

6. Select the Rectangle tool, set the stroke color to No Color and select a fill color of #999999. Draw a rectangle the same size as the text field.

When you move the button between each letter or stem, you cannot click the button. This makes clicking the button extremely difficult. Remember to add a hit area for your buttons.

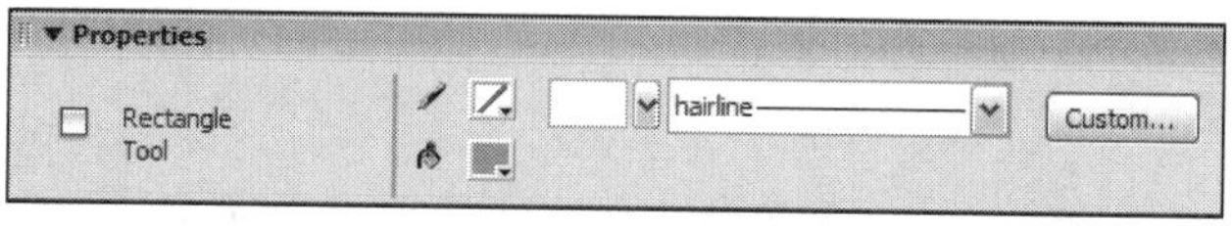

FIGURE 10.11

Draw a background for the text field. Optionally, you could add a gradient fill, as depicted here. The Fill Transform tool was used to rotate and resize a linear gradient.

The easiest way to match the size of the rectangle to the size of the text field is to use the Zoom tool and zoom in on the Stage so that the text field is as large as possible (without going off the Stage). When you select the Rectangle tool, it might be necessary to click the Over frame again so the bounding box becomes visible. Position your cursor in the upper-left corner of the bounding box and drag your mouse to the lower-right corner of the text field. You'll notice that when the rectangle overlaps the bounding box of the text field, the bounding box changes from blue to red.

By drawing the rectangle in the Over frame, your button changes background colors from transparent to gray when the user moves their cursor over the home button. If you do not want rollover colors, create the keyframe from step 5 in the Hit frame instead of the Over or Down frame.

7. Use the Text tool to create a new static text field on the Stage. Type **gallery** using the same settings as the home button you created in step 1.

8. Repeat steps 2–6 with the gallery text field and give it any symbol name, and an instance name of **gallery_btn**.

9. Position the home_btn and gallery_btn instances near the top of the Stage. You use these buttons to navigate between the home and gallery labels that you created in an earlier exercise.

If you want to make the buttons blend into the site a bit better, you can add a background image or a rectangle behind the image that is the same height as the buttons.

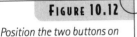

FIGURE 10.12

Position the two buttons on the Stage. You can also add a background for the buttons.

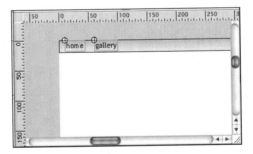

10. Add the following code to the first frame of the actions layer:

```
home_btn.onRelease = function() {
  gotoAndStop("home");
};
gallery_btn.onRelease = function() {
  gotoAndStop("gallery");
};
```

This code creates two event handlers, one for the home_btn button instance and the other for the gallery_btn button. When the user clicks the home_btn, the playhead moves to the *home* frame label. Likewise, when the user clicks gallery_btn, the playhead moves to the *gallery* frame label.

Exercise 8: Adding a progress bar for the gallery

This exercise demonstrates how to create a progress bar that you use to display the loading status of the gallery.swf document as it loads into the current FLA. You create the progress bar the same way you did for the gallery images earlier in this project.

1. Use the Rectangle tool to draw a rectangle on the Stage to use as a preloader.

2. Click the rectangle's fill and press F8. Convert the fill to a movie clip with a symbol name of **bar**. Click OK.

3. Select the bar symbol, and open the Property inspector. Type in an instance name of bar_mc.

4. Select both the fill and the stroke of the rectangle and press F8 to nest them both inside a symbol.

5. In the Convert to Symbol dialog box, enter a symbol name of **progressBar** and switch to advanced mode if you haven't already done so (click the Advanced button).

6. Select the Export for ActionScript check box and set the linkage identifier to **progressBar_mc**. Click OK to close the dialog box. Then, delete the instance of the progressBar symbol on the Stage. Because you attach it to the Stage dynamically, you do not need an instance on the Stage.

Exercise 9: Loading the gallery using MovieClipLoader

Now that you created the progress bar and it exists in the Library, there are only two small steps remaining. You need to create a movie clip symbol to load the external SWF into and add the necessary code to do so.

1. Before you can add any ActionScript, select frame 10 of the content layer and press F6 to insert a keyframe. Also, select

Because you add the progress bar to the Stage dynamically, you don't need to assign an instance name to the progress bar movie clip.

frame 19 of the content layer and press F5 to extend the Time-line to match the other layers.

2. Now you can create a movie clip instance on the Stage that you use to hold the gallery that you load into the SWF file. Click the Create New Symbol button in the Library for the current movie clip. In the Create New Symbol dialog box, set the symbol behavior to Movie Clip and type a symbol name of **gallery**.

3. Switch to Advanced mode (click the Advanced button) and select the Export for ActionScript check box. Type **gallery_mc** into the Identifier text field and then click OK. Click Scene 1 on the Edit Bar to return to the main Timeline.

4. Drag a copy of gallery from the Library onto the Stage and give type the instance name **gallery_mc** into the Property inspector.

5. Position gallery_mc at an X coordinate of 0 pixels and a Y coordinate of 20 pixels.

6. Select frame 10 of the *actions* layer and add the following code:

```
this.attachMovie("progressBar_mc", "pBar_mc",
this.getNextHighestDepth(), {_visible:false, _x:100,
_y:420});
var galleryListener:Object = new Object();
galleryListener.onLoadStart =
function(target_mc:MovieClip) {
  pBar_mc.bar_mc._xscale = 0;
  pBar_mc._visible = true;
};
galleryListener.onLoadProgress =
function(target_mc:MovieClip, numBytesLoaded:Number,
numBytesTotal:Number) {
  pBar_mc.bar_mc._xscale =
Math.round(numBytesLoaded/numBytesTotal*100);
};
```

```
galleryListener.onLoadComplete =
function(target_mc:MovieClip) {
  pBar_mc._visible = false;
};
```

This code begins by attaching the `progressBar_mc` symbol from the Library and giving it an instance name of `pBar_mc`. It then goes on to set the new movie clip's `_visible` property to `false` so it doesn't immediately display on the Stage. The hidden movie clip also moves to an X coordinate of 100 pixels and a Y coordinate of 420 pixels. This places the progress bar near the bottom of the Stage.

You also create an object, which you use to handle the various listeners for the movie clip loader instance that you create later on in the script. The first listener that you add to the `galleryListener` object is `onLoadStart`, which sets the nested `bar_mc` movie clip's `_xscale` property to 0%. Next, the `pBar_mc`'s `_visible` property is set to `true` so the progress bar becomes visible while the content loads in.

You then add the second listener, `onLoadProgress`, which triggers throughout the loading process, unless the content loads too fast. This listener calculates the percentage of the SWF file that's loaded by dividing the number of bytes currently loaded by the total number of bytes for the external file. Then the listener multiplies the result by 100 to return a value between 0 and 100. You use this value to display the percentage of data already loaded by Flash to modify the `bar_mc`'s `_xscale` property.

The third and final listener is `onLoadComplete`. This listener triggers as soon as the external content finishes loading, but it isn't visible on the Stage yet. After this listener is invoked, the content is nearly ready to display, so you can hide the `pBar_mc` movie clip again by setting its `_visible` property to `false`.

7. In frame 10 of the actions layer, add the following code below the snippet you added in the previous step:

```
var gallery_mcl:MovieClipLoader = new MovieClipLoader();
gallery_mcl.addListener(galleryListener);
gallery_mcl.loadClip("gallery.swf", gallery_mc);
```

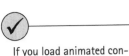

If you load animated content into the SWF file, the loaded animations use the parent SWF file's frame rate. However, if you load Flash Video (FLV files), the FLV frame rate is used, not the SWF frame rate.

FIGURE 10.14

The finished gallery when it loads into another SWF file.

Because gallery.swf is so small, the progress bar might not be visible (display the fill color) if the content loads too quickly from the hard drive. Test it online for a better chance at viewing the progress bar in action.

The last three lines of code in this project create a new `MovieClipLoader` instance, add the listener object that you created in the previous example, and load the external file (gallery.swf) into the `gallery_mc` movie clip. The `gallery_mc` clip is the empty "container" movie clip you created in step 2 of this exercise.

8. Select Modify > Document, and change the frame rate to 24 fps. This means the animations in the gallery will be smoother.

9. Save your Flash document, and test the finished product in Flash's authoring environment (Control > Test Movie) or in your default browser (F12). Now you can click on the home or gallery buttons and navigate to the appropriate section of your website.

MOVING ON

This gallery presents a form of navigation that's different from the other formats you encountered. Instead of navigational buttons, you created interactive rollovers that load new content into movie clips when you click each one. You also created regular buttons that move the playhead to a new frame when you click the button. In the last three chapters, you created interactive effects—which is what Flash is all about.

Some examples of online galleries (at the time of writing) include the following websites:

◆ www.natzke.com

◆ www.thatisthat.com/gallery/

◆ www.airtightinteractive.com/photos/

◆ www.seabiscuitmovie.com

Galleries vary widely in appearance, in organization, but also in the way they function and are built. You might create galleries that are not dynamic, or ones that store the information in XML so the documents are very easily updatable. You might even create a small gallery that contains all the content inside a single SWF file. Whatever way you choose to create a gallery, you can use Flash to make it original using tweens, masks, and creative graphics.

There are a couple of FLA examples of photo galleries in the Flash MX 2004 install directory. Look in C:\Program Files\ Macromedia\Flash MX2004\ Samples\HelpExamples\ gallery (Windows) or HD:Applications:Macro- media Flash MX 2004: Samples:HelpExamples: gallery for the FLA files called gallery_tree.fla and gallery_tween.fla. These two examples show you two different ways of con- structing a gallery. You must have the Flash MX 2004 7.2 updater installed to access these files.

APPENDIX A
PUBLISHING SWF FILES

The way that you publish FLA files is detrimental to your project. The way you publish the file affects how you display and present your work to your audience because the SWF file (or alternative format that you choose to publish) is all the visitor sees. This appendix helps you understand your publish options and how Flash Player works.

Each project throughout this book includes a section for publishing and presenting your work. However, there are a few more situations you might find yourself in when you build projects for clients or create a wide range of different websites. In the following sections, you explore other ways to publish your FLA files and ways to detect Flash Player on your visitor's computer.

UNDERSTANDING FILE SIZE AND LOADING

When you place content on a web page, you need to make considerations about how content loads, how much content you load, when it happens, and unloading content that you no longer need. When you build HTML websites, you have to be conscious about how much information you load onto a single page or whether the visitor has to wait a long time until the entire page loads. It's the same with a SWF file. If you try to load too much data into the SWF at the same time, your visitor has to wait a long time until the file loads.

Therefore, you should try to break up large files into separate files and load them in when necessary, or when the user requests them. For example, when you built the gallery in Chapter 10, you load images in from the server when the SWF file plays. Therefore, you don't need to store all the thumbnails in the SWF file and make the visitor wait while you load them before the gallery appears. Also, you load the full size image when the visitor requests to see it (when they click the thumbnail). Therefore, the visitor doesn't have to download all the full-size images unless they actually want to see the picture. It's a good idea to be considerate to your visitors in this way, particularly those with slow Internet connections who might not want to download a lot of data they're not interested in seeing. Loading content at runtime and upon visitor request also decreases the amount of bandwidth you use on your server.

You can load in text, MP3 files, other SWF files, and JPEG images using the LoadVars class, the Sound class, or `loadMovie` to help avoid putting all of your content in a SWF file. There are other ways to load data into a SWF file at runtime. Check out Appendix D for good resources of information and further tutorials on ActionScript and building SWF files, which elaborate on this subject.

You build several progress bars throughout the projects in this book. Progress bars are useful to display the loading progress of a file. If your file size is particularly small (20K or less), you probably do not need to use a progress bar with or in your SWF file.

Working with Flash Player

Flash Player is the software your visitors use to view the SWF files that you build, so it's helpful to understand the software to some extent. It might be a standalone player if you play the SWF file on their hard drives, such as when you create an executable file for a CD-ROM. There are different versions of Flash Player that have released to the public, and have been installed by the masses over the years. The different versions of Flash Player have different capabilities that coincide with the version of Flash that was current at the time. For example, you could not dynamically load JPEG images until Flash Player 6. Any Flash Player installs released prior to that version do not support that functionality, so your visitors must have Flash Player 6 or greater installed on the system.

When you publish a SWF file, you should test it on as many computers as possible. For example, if you expect many of your visitors to view the content on a Macintosh, you should test the SWF on a Mac. Or, if you expect your audience to have old computers, you should have the SWF tested on old machines. The SWF might play differently on different processors or computers with less RAM, so you should test for potential problems and remedy them before releasing your work to the public.

Memory management is another concern with Flash Player. If you load a lot of intensive content (such as video and sound), you should test the SWF file thoroughly. If you load a lot of video, you might find out that your SWF file crashes or runs very slowly. This might happen if your visitor clicks buttons to load the video in close succession, or if you don't unload your content before loading new content in. Make sure that you load and unload your content appropriately or in succession to avoid potential memory problems.

Publishing alternative files

Just as you can import a variety of formats into the Flash authoring environment, you can export several different file formats from it as well. This can be useful when you want to combine your Flash content in another medium, such as exporting Flash for broadcast media (video), or as a static or animated GIF to display as a banner. To select the formats you want to publish, select File > Publish Settings and then check the formats in the Formats tab. After you select a format to publish, a new tab usually opens, on which you can make settings that specify how you want to export the file.

Formats (other than SWF/HTML) that you can publish to are as follows:

◆ **GIF:** Lets you publish static or animated GIFs, or a GIF image map. If you publish an animated GIF, all or specified frames in your FLA file export as the animation. The GIF tab contains the following options:

Dimensions: Set the height and width of the image.

Playback: Set whether you want the image to be static or animated. If you select animated, you can choose if you want the file to loop.

Appearance settings (Windows), Options (Macintosh): Select how you want to compress the image (affects quality).

Transparency settings: Select whether you want the image to have transparent regions (such as the background area).

Dither options: Select a format for dithering (the way available colors combine to create the appearance of an unavailable color).

Palette type: Select a color palette for the image, or a custom ACT palette from your hard drive.

♦ **JPEG:** Lets you publish a static JPEG image. Exports the first frame of your FLA file as a JPEG unless you specify otherwise.

> **Dimensions:** Set the height and width of the image.
>
> **Quality:** Use the slider to set the quality of the image (a low setting means low quality and a smaller file size).
>
> **Progressive:** Check this option to export a progressive JPEG image. This means the image incrementally displays as it loads into a browser window. Some programs do not support progressive JPEG files. For example, Flash does not support loading progressive images at runtime.

♦ **PNG:** Lets you export a PNG image, which is a bitmap file format that supports transparency. Exports the first frame of your FLA file as a PNG unless you specify otherwise.

> **Dimensions:** Set the height and width of the image.
>
> **Bit depth:** Sets the number of colors to use by number of bits per pixel.
>
> **Appearance settings (Windows), Options (Macintosh):** Select how you want to compress the image (affects quality).
>
> **Dither options:** Select a format for dithering (how available colors combine to create the appearance of an unavailable color).
>
> **Palette type:** Select a color palette for the image, or a custom ACT palette from your hard drive.
>
> **Filter:** Lets you select a filter method that makes the exported PNG file increasingly compressible.

♦ **Windows or Macintosh Projector:** Publishes a standalone projector file (EXE or HQX). This executable includes Flash Player, so your end user does not need to have Flash Player installed on the computer. Useful for kiosks and CD-ROMs.

♦ **QuickTime:** Exports a video in the QuickTime MOV format if you have QuickTime installed on your computer. The Quick-Time player must support the features in your FLA file for them to work. QuickTime usually supports an earlier version of Flash Player (such as Flash Player 5), so you must publish to that version of Flash or you see an error. If you see an error, change your Flash Player publish settings under the Flash tab.

Dimensions: Set the height and width of the image.

Transparency settings: Select whether you want the image to have transparent regions (such as the background area).

Layer options: Let you choose where you want the flash track to layer in the MOV file (in front of or behind other tracks).

Streaming sound: Lets you choose to export streaming sounds as an audio track in the MOV file.

Controller: Specifies the kind of controller you want the MOV file to use.

Playback: Sets whether you want the MOV file to continually loop (or not).

If you publish to GIF, JPEG, PNG, or MOV and select the option to publish an HTML page as well, the HTML contains the code you need to display that format on a web page. This is particularly useful to show visitors who might not have Flash Player installed.

To learn how to detect for Flash Player on your visitor's computer, refer to the following section, "Detecting Flash Player."

You also can publish detection files, which detect whether the visitor has Flash Player on the computer system and takes action based on the results of the detection process. Refer to the following section for more details.

Detecting Flash Player

You can easily add Flash Player detection using the Publish Settings dialog box. For some situations, it's a good idea to use Flash Player detection on your website. Detection is important if you think that some of your visitors might not even have Flash Player installed. If Flash Player is not present, you can direct the visitors to another web page that might be the HTML version of your website or to an HTML page that asks them to download Flash Player. You can detect for Flash Player 4 and greater, which is present on most computers. If Flash Player that's earlier than version 3 is present—or if no Flash Player is present at all—the visitor is redirected to the HTML page.

The easiest way to create a Flash Player detection system is to use the functionality that's built into Flash. Follow these steps to create a Flash Player detection system:

1. Open one of the FLA projects you built for this book or use one of your own.

2. Select File > Publish Settings to open the Publish Setting dialog box. Make sure that HTML is selected on the Formats tab, and then click the HTML tab.

3. Make sure that you select the Detect Flash Version check box.

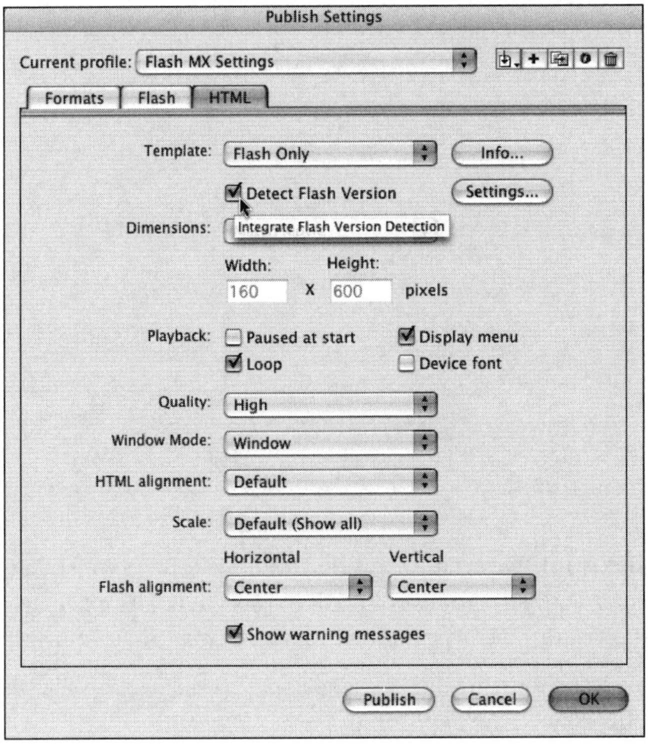

It's not always possible to detect Flash Player. It's impossible to account for every single browser or operating system setup. Just try to account for as many different computer setups as possible.

FIGURE A.1

Select Detect Flash Version to generate Flash Player detection files.

You must have Flash Player 4 or greater selected in the Version pop-up menu on the Flash tab. You can't use this detection process if you have an earlier version selected.

4. Click the Settings button next to the check box. This opens the Version Detection Settings dialog box, in which you can set which minor version of Flash Player you want to detect for. If you use features that were introduced for a certain Flash Player (say Flash Player 6 r42), you can detect for a Flash Player that is this version or greater.

You also see three filenames that you can specify, as shown in Figure A.2. These are the three files that publish as part of the detection system (for a FLA file called site.fla).

FIGURE A.2

Set the minor version of Flash Player to detect for and modify filenames if necessary.

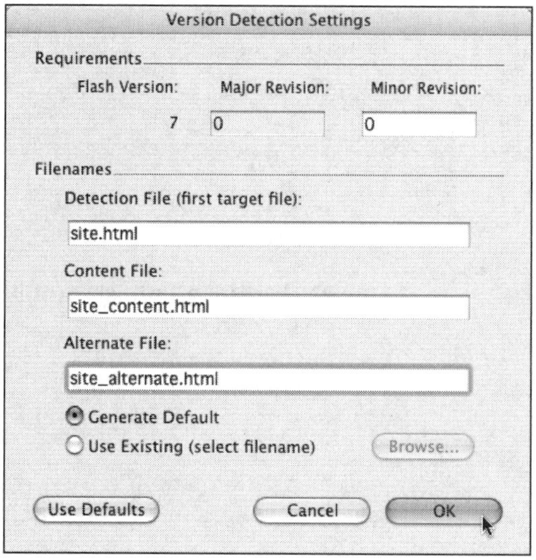

◆ **site.html:** This is the page that your visitors go to when they enter your site. You would link to this page. This page detects if the visitor has the minimum requirements to see your website.

◆ **site_content.html:** This page contains the site.swf file (the FLA file you are exporting).

◆ **site_alternate.html:** If your visitor does not have the proper Flash Player, they redirect to this page. You might want to provide a link to download Flash Player or put an HTML version of your site here. If you have an existing HTML file for this location, click the Use Existing radio button below this text field and browse to that file on your hard drive.

> If you want to choose different filenames for the detection system, you can modify them in this dialog box. Click OK when you're done.

5. Now you can click Publish to export the files. You need to upload all the files that generate from this process (including a special detection SWF file) to your website.

Creating a Publish profile

When you make settings in the Publish Settings dialog box, these settings save with the FLA file. You can also create a *Publish profile* that saves your settings in an external file, export it, and then import the profile into other FLA documents. Using Publish profiles helps you remain consistent in the way you publish certain documents, or streamlines your workflow if you need to routinely publish to different formats. Follow these steps to create a Publish profile:

1. Open one of the FLA projects you built for this book or use one of your own. Select File > Publish Settings to open the Publish Setting dialog box.

2. Click the Create New Profile button, as shown in Figure A.3.

FIGURE A.3

Click the Create New Profile button.

3. Name the Publish profile and then click OK. After you click OK, the profile name appears in the Publish Settings dialog box as the current profile.

4. Select the settings that you want to save as a profile and then click OK. If you want to modify a profile, you need to select that profile in the Publish Settings dialog box. Make the changes to your profile and click OK to save the modifications.

5. To export the Publish profile to use in another document, click the Import/Export Profile button and then select Export (shown in the Figure A.4). Save the profile in the default location or browse to a new location on your hard drive. Click Save.

6. To import a publish profile into a document, click Import/Export Profile and select Import. Browse to the publish profile XML file in the Import Profile dialog box, select a profile, and click Open.

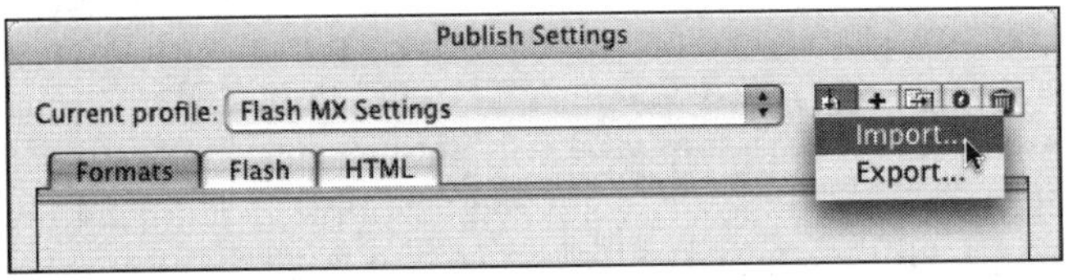

FIGURE A.4

Import or export a profile using this menu.

Publish Settings

Current profile: Flash MX Settings

Formats | Flash | HTML

Import...
Export...

Appendix B

Timeline Effects

Timeline effects make adding animation to a SWF file effortless. Timeline effects are prebuilt effects that you can apply to bitmaps, text, buttons, and graphics (raw graphics, or graphic symbols). They are sometimes useful when you need to add a simple effect, but don't know how to tween such an effect yourself (of course, this isn't applicable to you after reading this book). A couple of effects are useful as time-savers, even if you are experienced with Flash. You will find an overview of the effects that install with Flash in the following section.

When you select an object on the Stage and apply a Timeline effect to it, the effect is then automatically added to the Timeline. However, before the effect is added, you can make selections in a special window that allows you to make settings and selections to control the appearance of the effect and/or the duration of the animation.

For example, you might create a drawing of a badger that you want to add an effect to. You apply a Timeline effect to this badger. Flash creates a new layer, and then takes the badger drawing and puts it on a new layer. The new layer receives the same name as your effect, and each Timeline effect layer you add to the FLA file is sequentially numbered. You'll also find an extra folder in your Library after adding the effect, which contains all of the assets that you need for the effect. Then Flash puts your selection and the animation inside a symbol. Any of the tweens that are added happen inside the symbol.

Despite the benefits of using Timeline effects, there are a few drawbacks to using this feature. These reasons are explained at the end of this Appendix.

Exploring Timeline Effects

There are a variety of effects available in the Flash authoring environment. The following describes and shows the Timeline effects that install with Flash.

Assistants

These effects generally duplicate and arrange the graphics or text that you select on the Stage. The effects can be useful if you need to create static patterns or drawings for an interface, or to animate later on.

◆ **Copy to Grid:** Duplicates your selection by a specified number of columns and rows, at a set distance. A grid generates, similar to Figure B.1.

FIGURE B.1

Use a Timeline Effect to create a grid. This feature is useful for beginners and experienced users alike.

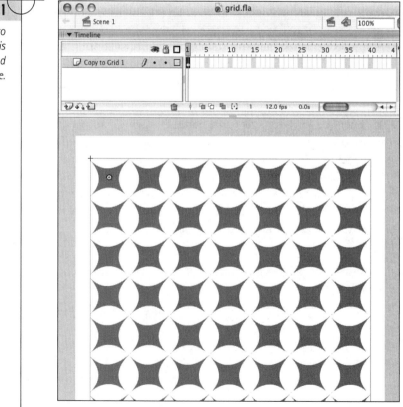

◆ **Distributed Duplicate:** Duplicates and offsets selected graphics. You can choose a color to transition to, number of copies, amount of offset, and set the final _alpha level.

Effects

These static and animated effects manipulate a selection on the Stage in a variety of ways, such as duplicating and offsetting the selection to create the appearance of blurs and shadows, while other effect segments the selection to make it appear to explode. They're useful when you want to create quick prototypes, or are not familiar with creating animation or graphics.

◆ **Blur:** Blurs the selection according to the settings you specify. Alpha, position, and scaling are applied to the object.

◆ **Drop Shadow:** Adds a drop shadow to the selection.

◆ **Expand:** Animates the selections by expanding, contracting, or a combination of both. Essentially, this motion tweens objects in relation to each other with an optional setting that can "squeeze" an object. This effect works best with more than one object.

◆ **Explode:** Animates an instance so it appears to "explode." This effect segments the instance, and tweens it away from the center-point of the instance in an ark, while scaling and fading the segments (Figure B.2).

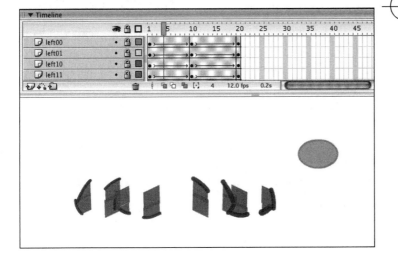

FIGURE B.2

An instance with "Explode" applied to it on the left and a copy of the original instance to the right.

Transform and transition

The transform and transition effects let you create and control effects that animate selections on the Stage. They are handy when you are not familiar with creating animation, or need to create a quick prototype.

◆ **Transform:** Lets you make many adjustments for the scale, rotation, alpha, color and position of a selection (with easing). You can apply a combination of effects to a single instance by making simple settings in a dialog (Figure B.3).

◆ **Transition:** Adds a wipe transition (in or out) by fading, wiping, or adding both effects concurrently.

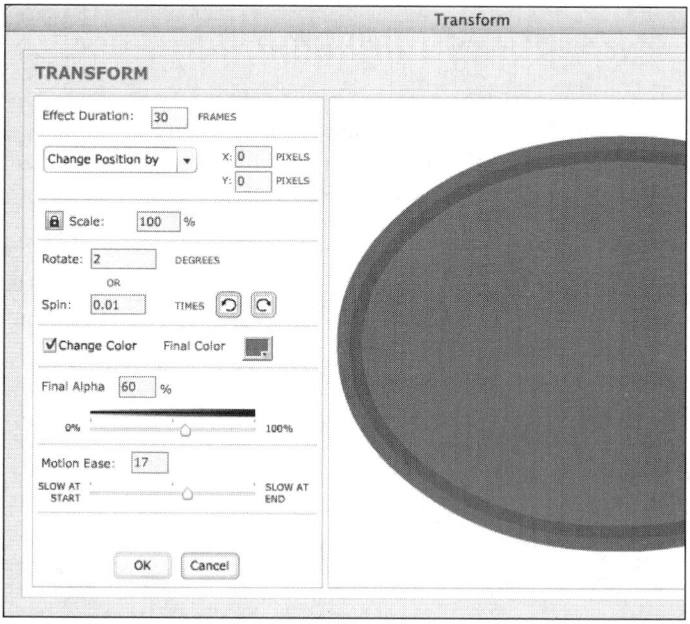

FIGURE B.3

An instance with "Explode" applied to it on the left and a copy of the original instance to the right.

If you don't have the Extension Manager to install components and other extensions, you can download it from www.macromedia.com/exchange/em_download/.

You can find Timeline effects and other extensions for the Flash authoring environment for download on the web (some are free; others are not.) Check out the following links for a place to start:

◆ www.macromedia.com/software/flash/extensions/

◆ www.macromedia.com/cfusion/exchange/

Using Timeline Effects

Timeline effects were engineered to be easy for users to add to or remove from a FLA file. You can add an effect, modify it if necessary, and remove the effect in a single step. There are only a few effects that install with Flash, but you'll find many settings that you can edit for each effect, as demonstrated in the following exercise.

To add a Blur Timeline effect to a FLA document, follow these steps.

1. Create a graphic on the Stage, and select it using the Selection tool. Press F8 and convert the selection to a symbol. Select the movie clip behavior, and name it. Press OK to return to the Stage.

2. Select the object, and then select Insert > Timeline Effects > Effects > Blur.

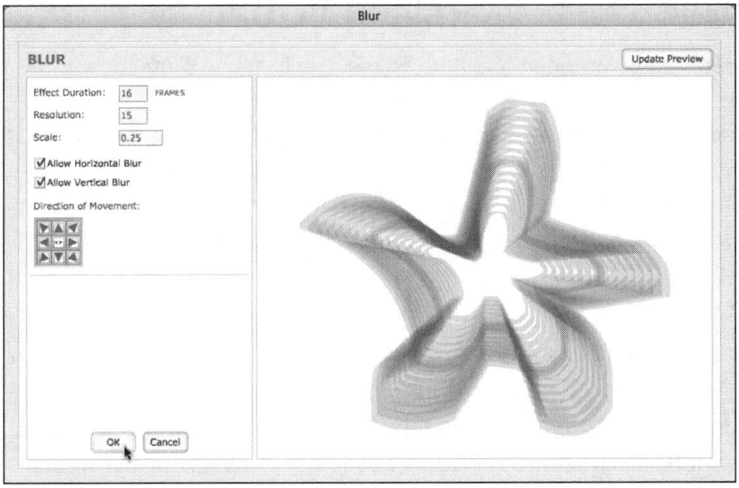

If an effect is dimmed in the window, it means that the object cannot be animated. You might have to change your selection to a symbol before you apply the effect or you might need to select more than one instance.

Figure B.4

Select the Blur Timeline effect from the main menu. This new window opens, in which you can make settings for the effect.

3. In the Blur dialog box, make settings for the animation and then click the Update Preview button. This changes the animation in the pane to the right of the window based on your new settings. For example, you can make changes to the duration, scale, direction, and resolution of the Blur animation and click Update Preview before you apply the changes to the Timeline.

Consult Flash documentation (F1) for outlines of the settings you can make for each Timeline effect.

You can delete a Timeline effect easily. Right-click (Windows) or Control-click (Macintosh) the object that you added the effect to. Then select Timeline Effects > Remove Effect from the context menu.

4. Click OK to apply the animation to the selection. You might need to test the SWF file to view the animation (Control > Test Movie). You can also open the instance that Flash creates in symbol-editing mode to view the animation; however, you will see a warning before you do so about editing Timeline effects.

5. To make edits to the animation, right-click (Windows) or Control-click (Macintosh) the object that you added the effect to. Then select Timeline Effects > Edit Effect from the context menu.

6. The Effects Settings dialog box opens, in which you can modify the settings you made to the selection. Click OK after you finish making changes to the effect.

Benefits and Drawbacks of Timeline Effects

There are several benefits and drawbacks to using Timeline effects. First, test the various Timeline effects in an FLA file and determine whether they are beneficial to you. You might find that the effects are not terribly useful to (or match) your designs. The limited convenience is perhaps the biggest drawback of the Timeline effects that install with Flash. The Blur effect doesn't *really* blur the way many designers might expect, and "Explode" tends to look too chunky for a useful effect.

However, the Copy to Grid and Distributed Duplicate effects might be useful to many designs. These effects simply duplicate symbols instead of creating an animation. There are many designs that need to duplicate the same graphic on the Stage, such as tiled graphics (Figure B.1), so this effect makes that task a lot quicker and easier to accomplish.

Timeline effects are easy to add and remove from a document, so take the time to explore their usefulness to your own designs and presentations. For this book, these effects would not have added any value to the SWF files that you created. However, because Timeline effects are part of the extensibility layer in Flash (what developers use to build extensions—which are essentially plug-ins), you might find a third-party download that is useful for your work.

APPENDIX C
KEYBOARD SHORTCUTS

Visit www.FLAnimation.com/resources/kb.pdf for a printable version of this appendix.

File Menu

Command	Windows Shortcut	Mac Shortcut
New	Ctrl + N	Cmd + N
Open	Ctrl + O	Cmd + O
Close	Ctrl + W	Cmd + W
Save	Ctrl + S	Cmd + S
Save As	Ctrl + Shift + S	Cmd + Shift + S
Publish Settings	Ctrl + Shift + F12	Option + Shift + F12
Publish	Shift + F12	Shift + F12
Print	Ctrl + P	Cmd + P
Exit	Ctrl + Q	Cmd + Q
Import to Stage	Ctrl + R	Cmd + R
Open External Library	Ctrl + Shift + O	Cmd + Shift+ O
Export Movie	Ctrl + Alt + Shift + S	Cmd + Option + Shift + S
Default Publish Preview (HTML)	F12	F12
Open External Library – Mac		Cmd + Shift + O
Publish – Windows	Shift + F12	

Edit Menu

Command	Windows Shortcut	Mac Shortcut
Undo	Ctrl + Z	Cmd + Z
Redo	Ctrl + Y	Cmd + Y
Cut	Ctrl + X	Cmd + X
Copy	Ctrl + C	Cmd + C
Paste in Center	Ctrl + V	Cmd + V
Paste in Place	Ctrl + Shift + V	Cmd + Shift + V
Clear	Backspace, Delete	Delete
Duplicate	Ctrl + D	Cmd + D
Select All	Ctrl + A	Cmd + A
Deselect All	Ctrl + Shift + A	Cmd + Shift + A
Find and Replace	Ctrl + F	Cmd + F
Find Next	F3	F3
Edit Symbols	Ctrl + E	Cmd + E
Cut Frames	Ctrl + Alt + X	Cmd + Option + X
Copy Frames	Ctrl + Alt + C	Cmd + Option + C
Paste Frames	Ctrl + Alt + V	Cmd + Option + V
Clear Frames	Alt + Backspace	Option + Delete
Remove Frames	Shift + F5	Shift + F5
Select All Frames	Ctrl + Alt + A	Cmd + Option + A
Preferences	Ctrl + U	Flash > Preferences
Clear	Backspace, Delete	

View Menu

Command	Windows Shortcut	Mac Shortcut
Go to First	Home	Home
Go to Previous	Page Up	Page Up
Go to Next	Page Down	Page Down
Go to Last	End	End
Zoom In	Ctrl + =	Cmd + =

View Menu (continued)

Command	Windows Shortcut	Mac Shortcut
Zoom Out	Ctrl + -	Cmd + -
Magnification: 100%	Ctrl + 1	Cmd + 1
Magnification: 400%	Ctrl + 4	Cmd + 4
Magnification: 800%	Ctrl + 8	Cmd + 8
Show Frame	Ctrl + 2	Cmd + 2
Show All	Ctrl + 3	Cmd + 3
Outlines	Ctrl + Alt + Shift + O	Cmd + Option + Shift + O
Fast	Ctrl + Alt + Shift + F	Cmd + Option + Shift + F
Antialias	Ctrl + Alt + Shift + A	Cmd + Option + Shift + A
Antialias Text	Ctrl + Alt + Shift + T	Cmd + Option + Shift + T
Work Area	Ctrl + Shift + W	Cmd + Shift + W
Rulers	Ctrl + Alt + Shift + R	Cmd + Option + Shift + R
Show Grid	Ctrl + '	Cmd + '
Edit Grid	Ctrl + Alt + G	Cmd + Option + G
Show Guides	Ctrl + ;	Cmd + ;
Lock Guides	Ctrl + Alt + ;	Cmd + Option + ;
Edit Guides	Ctrl + Alt + Shift + G	Cmd + Option + Shift + G
Snap to Grid	Ctrl + Shift + '	Cmd + Shift + '
Snap to Guides	Ctrl + Shift + ;	Cmd + Shift + ;
Snap to Objects	Ctrl + Shift + /	Cmd + Shift + /
Hide Edges	Ctrl + H	Cmd + Shift + E
Show Shape Hints	Ctrl + Alt + H	Cmd + Option + H

Insert Menu

Command	Windows Shortcut	Mac Shortcut
New Symbol	Ctrl + F8	Cmd + F8
Frame	F5	F5

Modify menu

Command	Windows Shortcut	Mac Shortcut
Document	Ctrl + J	Cmd + J
Convert to Symbol	F8	F8
Break Apart	Ctrl + B	Cmd + B
Optimize	Ctrl + Alt + Shift + C	Cmd + Option + Shift + C
Add Shape Hint	Ctrl + Shift + H	Cmd + Shift + H
Distribute to Layers	Ctrl + Shift + D	Cmd + Shift + D
Convert to Keyframes	F6	F6
Clear Keyframe	Shift + F6	Shift + F6
Convert to Blank Keyframes	F7	F7
Rotate 90 degrees CW	Ctrl + Shift + 9	Cmd + Shift + 9
Rotate 90 degrees CCW	Ctrl + Shift + 7	Cmd + Shift + 7
Remove Transform	Ctrl + Shift + Z	Cmd + Shift + Z
Bring to Front	Ctrl + Shift + Up	Option + Shift + Up
Bring Forward	Ctrl + Up	Cmd + Up
Send Backward	Ctrl + Down	Cmd + Down
Send to Back	Ctrl + Shift + Down	Option + Shift + Down
Lock	Ctrl + Alt + L	Cmd + Option + L
Unlock All	Ctrl + Alt + Shift + L	Cmd + Option + Shift + L
Align Left	Ctrl + Alt + 1	Cmd + Option + 1

Modify menu (continued)

Command	Windows Shortcut	Mac Shortcut
Align Horizontal Center	Ctrl + Alt + 2	Cmd + Option + 2
Align Right	Ctrl + Alt + 3	Cmd + Option + 3
Align Top	Ctrl + Alt + 4	Cmd + Option + 4
Align Vertical Center	Ctrl + Alt + 5	Cmd + Option + 5
Align Bottom	Ctrl + Alt + 6	Cmd + Option + 6
Distribute Widths	Ctrl + Alt + 7	Cmd + Option + 7
Distribute Heights	Ctrl + Alt + 9	Cmd + Option + 9
Make Same Width	Ctrl + Alt + Shift + 7	Cmd + Option + Shift + 7
Make Same Height	Ctrl + Alt + Shift + 9	Cmd + Option + Shift + 9
To Stage	Ctrl + Alt + 8	Cmd + Option + 8
Group	Ctrl + G	Cmd + G
Ungroup	Ctrl + Shift + G	Cmd + Shift + G

Text Menu

Command	Windows Shortcut	Mac Shortcut
Plain	Ctrl + Shift + P	Cmd + Shift + P
Bold	Ctrl + Shift + B	Cmd + Shift + B
Italic	Ctrl + Shift + I	Cmd + Shift + I
Align Left	Ctrl + Shift + L	Cmd + Shift + L
Align Center	Ctrl + Shift + C	Cmd + Shift + C
Align Right	Ctrl + Shift + R	Cmd + Shift + R
Justify	Ctrl + Shift + J	Cmd + Shift + J
Tracking Increase	Ctrl + Alt + Right	Cmd + Option + Right
Tracking Decrease	Ctrl + Alt + Left	Cmd + Option + Left
Tracking Reset	Ctrl + Alt + Up	Cmd + Option + Up

Control Menu

Command	Windows Shortcut	Mac Shortcut
Play	Enter	Enter / Return
Rewind	Ctrl + Alt + R	Cmd + Option + R
Step Forward One Frame	.	.
Step Backward One Frame	,	,
Test Movie	Ctrl + Enter	Cmd + Enter
Debug Movie	Ctrl + Shift + Enter	Cmd + Shift + Enter
Test Scene	Ctrl + Alt + Enter	Cmd + Option + Enter
Test Project	Ctrl + Alt + P	Cmd + Option + P
Enable Simple Buttons	Ctrl + Alt + B	Cmd + Option + B

Window Menu

Command	Windows Shortcut	Mac Shortcut
New Window	Ctrl + Alt + K	Cmd + Option + K
Project	Shift + F8	Shift + F8
Properties	Ctrl + F3	Cmd + F3
Timeline	Ctrl + Alt + T	Cmd + Option + T
Tools	Ctrl + F2	Cmd + F2
Library	Ctrl + L or F11	Cmd + L or F11
Align	Ctrl + K	Cmd + K
Color Mixer	Shift + F9	Shift + F9
Color Swatches	Ctrl + F9	Cmd + F9
Info	Ctrl + I	Cmd + I
Scene	Shift + F2	Shift + F2
Transform	Ctrl + T	Cmd + T
Actions	F9	F9
Behaviors	Shift + F3	Shift + F3
Components	Ctrl + F7	Cmd + F7
Component Inspector	Alt + F7	Option + F7

Window Menu (continued)

Command	Windows Shortcut	Mac Shortcut
Debugger	Shift + F4	Shift + F4
Output	F2	F2
Web Services	Ctrl + Shift + F10	Cmd + Shift + F10
Accessibility	Alt + F2	Option + F2
History	Ctrl + F10	Cmd + F10
Movie Explorer	Alt + F3	Option + F3
Strings	Ctrl + F11	Cmd + F11
Hide Panels	F4	F4

Help Menu

Command	Windows Shortcut	Mac Shortcut
Help	F1	F1

Actions Panel

Command	Windows Shortcut	Mac Shortcut
Pin Script	Ctrl + =	Cmd + =
Close Script	Ctrl + -	Cmd + -
Close All Scripts	Ctrl + Shift + -	Cmd + Shift + -
Go to Line	Ctrl + G	Cmd + ,
Find	Ctrl + F	Cmd + F
Find Again	F3	Cmd + G
Replace	Ctrl + H	Cmd + Shift + H
Auto Format	Ctrl + Shift + F	Cmd + Shift + F
Check Syntax	Ctrl + T	Cmd + T
Show Code Hint	Ctrl + Spacebar	Control + Spacebar
Import Script	Ctrl + Shift + I	Cmd + Shift + I
Export Script	Ctrl + Shift + X	Cmd + Shift + X
View line Numbers	Ctrl + Shift + L	Cmd + Shift + L
Word Wrap	Ctrl + Shift + W	Cmd + Shift + W
Preferences	Ctrl + U	Cmd + U (only in Actions)
Show Code Hint		Ctl - Spacebar

Debugger Panel

Command	Windows Shortcut	Mac Shortcut
Continue	F10	F10
Stop Debugging	F11	F11
Step In	F6	F6
Step Over	F7	F7
Step Out	F8	F8

Output Panel

Command	Windows Shortcut	Mac Shortcut
Copy	Ctrl + C	Cmd + C
Find	Ctrl + F	Cmd + F
Find Again	F3	F3

APPENDIX D
RESOURCES

Online resources are extensive and useful when it comes to answering very specific needs to your Flash-related queries. Forums, email lists, blogs ("weblogs"), and tutorial-based websites are important parts of the Flash community. In recent years, the Flash-related blogs have popped up everywhere. These web pages journal the experiments and learning of many great Flash minds in the community. Searching the Flash blogs is a great way to find out about others who are going down the same path you are and learn a bit more each day. Most of them even allow you to comment on each entry that is made.

Of course, it's always a good idea to visit www.macromedia.com regularly to check the Developer Center (www.macromedia.com/devnet) for new tutorials, software updates (such as the free Flash MX 2004 7.2 updater release), and news. Also make sure to check Flash documentation online (http://livedocs.macromedia.com/flash/mx2004/), or press F1. Documentation is a great place to look when you get stuck, have trouble debugging, or want to find a tutorial. Flash documentation, expanded and improved in the 7.2 updater, includes reference materials (such as the ActionScript dictionary), linear chapters, as well as tutorials and sample applications. For documentation's sample applications, look in the C:\Program Files\Macromedia\Flash MX 2004\Samples\HelpExamples (Windows) directory, or Mac HD:Applications:Macromedia Flash MX 2004: Samples:HelpExamples (Macintosh) directory.

Finally, be sure to check the companion website www.FLAnimation.com, which includes updated information based on reader questions and feedback. Check the website for errata, tutorials, answers to frequently asked questions, and other updates.

The following pages list useful online resources for learning Flash, animation, and effects. Some of the links are Flash-related, but others cover more history and background in traditional animation techniques. These links are just a place to start. After you get a solid grounding in Flash, you'll probably find online resources and forums much more useful than when you're starting out with the program. You can also visit www.FLAnimation.com/resources for an up-to-date list that includes all these links, updates, and more.

General Resources

The following resources are websites that have general information on Flash or a variety of topics. They are great places to start to learn more about Flash, especially when you don't have a specific topic to research. Most forums, blogs, and tutorial sites cover a wide range of topics on Flash. Forums are plentiful out there. Flash forums exist in many languages and many sizes. There are high-traffic forums that contain a huge amount of information, and smaller ones where you can get to know the regulars. Whatever you're looking for, you'll probably find it on a forum somewhere.

If you don't enjoy forums, then there are several email based lists you can subscribe to. These email lists range from high-traffic to moderate and low traffic. There are many out there to join, although sometimes you need to happen across the best ones by chance.

Finally, the Macromedia website should be in your favorites and part of your list of frequently visited sites. It can help you keep up-to-date with Flash and other products that are related to Flash (such as Breeze and Central). You'll find that the site has regular updates and is essential to check for news and downloads (such as Flash point releases).

- ◆ **Home base:** www.macromedia.com

- ◆ **Flash documentation:** http://livedocs.macromedia.com/flash/mx2004/

- ◆ **Macromedia official news aggregator:** www.markme.com/mxna

- ◆ **Book's companion website:** www.FLAnimation.com

The following URLs are valid only at the time of writing, and are subject to change at the whim of the web.

Tutorials and articles

◆ www.macromedia.com/devnet/

◆ www.flash-mx.com

◆ www.kirupa.com

◆ www.informit.com

◆ www.actionscript.org

◆ www.ultrashock.com

◆ www.actionscript-toolbox.com

◆ www.flzone.net

◆ www.actionscript.org/tutorials.shtml

◆ www.lionbichstudios.com/flash_tutorials_01.htm

◆ www.fullasagoog.com

◆ www.flash2004.com/tipoday

◆ www.flashenabled.com

Forums

◆ **Official Flash forums:** http://webforums.macromedia.com/flash/

◆ **Official Flash newsgroups, refer to:** www.macromedia.com/support/forums/news/using.html

◆ **Flash MX 2004 forums:** www.flashmx2004.com

◆ **Were-Here forums:** www.were-here.com

◆ **FlashMove forums:** www.flashmove.com/board/index.php

◆ **FlashKit forums:** www.flashkit.com

Software

◆ **Macromedia software:** www.macromedia.com/software/

◆ **Flash Jester:** www.flashjester.com

◆ **SWF Studio:** www.northcode.com

- **Flash Studio Pro:** www.multidmedia.com
- **Screenweaver:** www.swifftools.com
- **Screentime:** www.screentime.com
- **Swish:** www.swishzone.com
- **Swift Tools:** www.swift-tools.net
- **Viewlets:** www.qarbon.com

Email lists

- **Chattyfig lists:** http://chattyfig.figleaf.com
- **Flasher-L:** www.chinwag.com/flasher
- **DevMX:** www.devmx.com/mailing_list.cfm
- **FlashPro:** www.muinar.org

Macromedia.com

- **Downloads:** www.macromedia.com/downloads/
- **Developer center for Flash:** www.macromedia.com/devnet/mx/flash/
- **Tech Notes (Flash):** www.macromedia.com/support/flash/technotes.html
- **Macromedia Exchange:** www.macromedia.com/cfusion/exchange/index.cfm
- **Third Party Extensions:** www.macromedia.com/software/flash/extensions/
- **Wish List (and bugs):** www.macromedia.com/software/flash/contact/wishlist/
- **User Groups:** www.macromedia.com/cfusion/usergroups/
- **Blog aggregator:** www.markme.com/mxna/

Free web space

◆ **Yahoo GeoCities:** http://geocities.yahoo.com

◆ **Spymac:** www.spymac.com

◆ **Tripod:** www.tripod.lycos.com

◆ **Angelfire:** http://angelfire.lycos.com

◆ **Beigetower:** www.beigetower.org

◆ **Brinkster:** www.brinkster.com/Hosting/Educational.aspx

◆ **Freeservers:** www.freeservers.com

DRAWING, 3D, AND ANIMATION RESOURCES

There are many resources online to help you learn how to draw, create animations—including 3D animations. You might find that some of these third-party tools for animation makes the task much easier. In some cases, it might even be best to use some of these tools for basic or common animations (such as text effects), instead of taking the time to re-create something that a tool can already produce. Certainly avoid these tools if you want a custom look. Other tools will help you create better animations of your own, such as Toon Boom Studio. Toon Boom Studio includes a camera tool to help you achieve a realistic dimension and sophisticated look to your animations.

Tutorials and articles

◆ **Animation timeline:** http://animation.filmtv.ucla.edu/program/anihist.html

◆ **Animation fundamentals:** http://animation.about.com

◆ **Drawing tips:** www.thestoryboardartist.com/tutorial.html

◆ **Drawing/Illustrator:** www.designertoday.com/Desktop Default.aspx?tabindex=31&tabid=40&itemid=1776

◆ **Lip-sync:** www.keithlango.com/lipSync.html

◆ **Lip-sync:** www.comet-cartoons.com/toons/3ddocs/lipsync/lipsync.html

◆ **Lip-sync:** www.garycmartin.com/mouth_shapes.html

◆ **Walk cycle:** www.josh.ch/joshch/tutorials/milkshape, modelling-human-walk-cycle-animation.html

◆ **Walk cycle:** www.idleworm.com/how/anm/02w/walk1.shtml

◆ **Walk cycle:** www.anticz.com/Walks.htm

◆ **Walk cycle:** www.blitzgames.com/gameon/advice_walkcycle.htm

◆ **Animation:** www.video-animation.com

◆ **3D:** www.tutorialized.com/tutorials/Flash/3D/1/

◆ **3D:** www.flash-mx.com/flash/swift1.cfm

◆ **3D:** www.kirupa.com/developer/swift/

◆ **Development with Swift 3D:** www.swiftdev.com

Forums

◆ **Graphics/animation:** www.flashmx2004.com/forums/index.php?showforum=8

◆ **3D:** www.swiftdev.com/forum.php

◆ **Video:** www.flashplayer.com/forum/

◆ **Flash design:** http://forum.deviantart.com/galleries/flash/

◆ **Animation:** http://forums.awn.com

◆ **Art:** http://forums.sijun.com/

Software

◆ **Toon Boom Studio:** www.toonboom.com

◆ **SWiSH:** www.swishzone.com

◆ **Wacom graphics tablets:** www.wacom.com (hardware)

◆ **Crazytalk:** www.reallusion.com/crazytalk/

◆ **Miniml fonts:** www.miniml.com (fonts)

- **FFF fonts:** www.fontsforflash.com (fonts)
- **Swift 3D:** www.swift3d.com or www.erain.com
- **MX3D component:** www.benchun.net/mx3d/

Video Resources

Combining Flash with video can produce some amazing results. There are many resources online to provide inspiration and one-on-one help. Also, there are many tools available from companies to help you work with Flash video and SWF files to manipulate, control, and compress different kinds of video.

Tutorials and articles

- **Developer Center on Flash Video:** www.macromedia.com/devnet/mx/flash/video.html
- **Video Primer:** www.macromedia.com/devnet/mx/flash/articles/video_primer.html
- **Peldi's blog (Flashcom):** www.peldi.com/blog/
- **Flashcom wiki:** www.ultrasaurus.com/cgi-bin/chiq/chiq.cgi?flashcom_wiki
- **Flashcom (Chris Hock):** www.flashcommunicationserver.net
- **Getting started:** www.macromedia.com/devnet/mx/flash/articles/getstart_flv.html
- **StreamingMedia:** www.streamingmedia.com
- **StreamingMediaIQ:** www.streamingmediaiq.com/

Forums

- Flash MX 2004 Video forums: www.flashmx2004.com/forums/index.php?showforum=12
- FlashKit Video forums: www.flashkit.com/board/forumdisplay.php?forumid=66
- Flashcom Guru forums: www.flashcomguru.com/forum

Software and services

- **Sorenson Squeeze:** www.sorenson.com

- **Wildform Flix:** www.wildform.com

- **FLV duration:** www.swfx.org/flv-duration/index.jsp

- **FLV MetaData Injector:** www.buraks.com/flvmdi/

- **FLV Player:** www.martijndevisser.com/archives/000021.php

- **Flash Video Streaming Service:** www.vitalstream.com/macromedia/

ActionScript and Effects Resources

The following resources list resources for sites that will show you how to write ActionScript for script-based animation and effects. Some of these resources also include general information about coding, and tutorials that show you how to build dynamic websites with code (and more). Also check out some of the integration websites for more information on integrating Flash with other technologies to build more complex websites integrating dynamic data with your animations and effects.

Tutorials

- www.macromedia.com/support/flash/action_scripts.html

- www.actionscript.com

- www.actionscript.org

- www.actionscript-toolbox.com

- www.kirupa.com/developer/actionscript/

- www.flash-db.com

Integration and information

- **Flash Remoting:** www.macromedia.com/software/flashremoting/

- **AMFPHP:** www.amfphp.org

- **Flash Communication Server:** www.macromedia.com/software/flashcom/

- **ColdFusion MX:** www.macromedia.com/software/coldfusion/

- **ASP.NET:** www.microsoft.com/net/

- **PHP:** www.php.net

- **Ming:** http://ming.sourceforge.net/

- **Web Service directory:** www.flash-db.com/services/

Forums

- **Flash MX 2004 ActionScript forums:** www.flashmx2004.com/forums/index.php?showforum=4

- **Official Macromedia ActionScript forums:** www.macromedia.com/cfusion/webforums/forum/categories.cfm?catid=288

- **ActionScript forum:** www.actionscripts.org/forums/

- **ActionScript forum:** www.were-over-there.com/board/

- **Flash Application Dev forum:** www.debreuil.com/phpBB/index.php

Software

- **ActionScript Viewer:** www.buraks.com/asv/

- **PrimalScript:** www.sapien.com/primalscript.aspx

- **SciTE|Flash:** www.bomberstudios.com/sciteflash/

INDEX